Making History

Making History

how to remember, record, interpret and share the events of your life
by Kim Pearson

ISBN: 978-1-932279-75-7

SECOND EDITION

Disclaimers

Other than author and historical personages, all names herein have been changed to protect identities. No real names have been used. Details of stories told or read to author have been retold and many details therein deliberately altered for the same reason.

This is not a formal history book, but an invitation to write your own personal history, within the context of historic events. All historic events may be disputed and are subject to interpretation. Although author believes the facts contained herein to be correct, she makes no warranties of any kind, express or implied, regarding the accuracy or reliability of any information in this book.

Primary Sources Books
an imprint of Wyatt-MacKenzie

Issaquah, WA 98027
www.primary-sources.com

Cover design by Dave Caplan, Feedback Graphics
www.feedbackgraphics.com

Imprint information www.WyMacPublishing.com

Making History

How to remember, record,
interpret and share
the events of your life

KIM PEARSON

Primary Sources Books
an imprint of Wyatt-MacKenzie

Acknowledgements
Dedication

I am grateful to the participants in my classes "You Make History" and "Write to Remember," who shared the stories of their lives. Their courage, wisdom, humor, and enthusiasm made these classes arenas of delight. To hear these stories was an great privilege.

This book is dedicated with admiration and love to my parents, Armond and Lois Pearson, both members of that great generation who lived through the Depression and World War II. Their participation and contributions made a positive difference in our world. Their stories made my own possible.

And to my daughters Hannah and Corey, who give my life meaning and whose generation's stories are still to be told.

Contents

"There is no agony like bearing
an untold story inside you."

Zora Neale Hurston

Preface

Why I Wrote This Book

I've always been fascinated by stories. Not surprising, given my upbringing. My mother read me storybooks long before I could talk. She taught me to read for myself by the age of three. She encouraged me to put on little plays and skits dramatizing the stories I read. She was always an enthusiastic audience.

My father is a natural born storyteller with a gift for making the most trivial happening seem dramatic, funny or exciting. One of my favorite pasttimes was to listen to him tell stories of "the old days." So vivid were his stories that I was more familiar with my grandparents, aunts and uncles as young adults and children, rather than the adults I actually knew.

After dinners at our large tribal gatherings on Thanksgiving or the Fourth of July, while my cousins and brothers ran playing and screaming around the house, I was usually hiding under the dinner table listening to the adults talk. Because I was hidden by the long white tablecloth, they didn't know I was there, and freed from the inhibition "not in front of the children!" they would tell the *real* stories of their lives. Beer, wine and scotch would be poured, and sex and death and scandal would ricochet around the table. Long standing jokes would be resurrected and laughed over again. Speculation and opinions about old family mysteries would be offered up and argued over. Politics, religion, history and wars: no topics were taboo. Since my family was filled with loud, passionate people, the stories tended to be juicy.

My eavesdropping habits, which I must confess I never outgrew, have stood me in good stead in my work as a writer. Especially since I not only write my own stories, but help others to write theirs as a personal historian.

I also teach memoir writing, and in 2001, I proposed such a class to a local community college, for their Senior continuing education program. But they turned me down. They already had a writing class. However, they said, we notice you have a degree in history — we could use a history class, so could you teach that?

I did not want to teach History. For one thing, my degree in History was granted in 1971, thirty years before! Not only did I not want to teach it, I didn't think I could. But I did want to teach at this Senior program, because, selfishly, I viewed it as a good way to get my name out there as a personal historian.

So reluctantly I agreed to teach a History class — but a history class with a difference. I proposed I teach people to see their own individual lives *as history*. Most of us tend to see "History" as something that happens *to* us. But the truth is that we ourselves, each of us, contribute to and participate in history. We are actors, not just reactors.

I developed a system, part history lesson, part memoir writing, to help people discover their place in history, and share their discoveries with others. The class, "You Make History," has been a wonderful success. Everyone who takes the class loves it. *I* love it. I hear great stories. It is hiding under the Thanksgiving dinner table all over again.

I also got to tell *my* stories. I asked the participants in my classes to "spill their guts," and I knew I had to be willing to do the same. So I participated in class, sharing my memories from my own personal history. When I taught the decades 1930 through 1959, I thought I wouldn't have much to say. After all, I was born in 1949. I was wrong! I discovered my child's perspective, which is every bit as valuable as an adult's. I remembered old family stories. I reconnected with my parents and saw them in roles other than parental, as the children and young adults they once were.

The class I didn't want to teach turned out to be one of the greatest gifts I have ever been given. It is my hope that this book will be such a gift for you.

connection. When she died she left me, out of all her children, grandchildren and great grandchildren – well over a hundred people – three of her special treasures. She left me her etched drinking glass, her pink handkerchief, and her shell necklace.

I wish so much that I could have known her.

Yes, it would be wonderful to know our ancestors' stories. But what we often forget is that we, too, are someone's ancestor. We are the future historians' primary sources. A primary source is a term historians use to describe the thoughts, opinions and witness of those people who were *really there*. When you record what you saw, what you felt, what you did, you become a primary source. Two hundred years from now, historians could be looking for you. What do you want them to find? Your tombstone with the dates of your birth and death, and perhaps a line of verse? Does that tell your dreams, desires, triumphs, griefs, loves and hates? Does it tell what steps you contributed to this dance of life we're all doing?

A "You Make History" class participant wrote about connection in the vignette she read in class. In September 2001, "Heather's"* daughter had just begun her teaching career. She had been a junior high teacher for less than a week when September 11th happened. On September 12th, she gave her students an in-class assignment. "Write down how you feel about yesterday's events," she told them. "How did you hear about it? What did your parents say? Do you think America will change? What do you think we should do? Why do you think this happened?" The students wrote for ten minutes, then started to hand in their papers. Heather's daughter wouldn't take them. "I don't want them," she told her students. "They are for you to keep. In

---

*Not her real name. All names and many story details in this book have been changed to protect identity.

fifty years, your grandchildren will want to know where you were on September 11, 2001. And now you will be able to tell them. You have just created a primary source."

Telling your stories is affirmation of belonging. You have a rightful place in this world. Without you, the story of the world is incomplete.

Chapter Three
Wisdom

The human species is fortunate to have Elders. In many species, when a female can't reproduce and a male can't hunt or protect, their function ceases and they die. But we have grannies and grandpas who live well beyond the hunting and reproducing stage. These grandparents' function, their natural role, is to pass along their accumulated wisdom to the next generation. The younger generation wants and needs to listen. The elders need to speak.

If you've lived any time at all, you have learned some things. Not only the knowledge you have accumulated, but your wisdom, which is *applied* knowledge. Not only the what, but the where and when and how and why.

The following story teaches appreciation of what we have, and how the past shapes the future.

Every Sunday my father took the family on "The Sunday drive." My father liked to broaden our horizons so our outings nearly always had an educational twist. We visited military installations, old mining towns, power plants, building sites, Indian reservations; anywhere that would give my father a chance to expound on history or science or both. But the Sunday drive I remember best was to a spot neither historic nor scientific. It was just a memory.

We drove to Everett, a city north of Seattle where my father had lived as a teenager. He wanted to pay a visit to his family's old house. We turned off Highway 99 onto a pot-holed side street in a shabby, rundown neighborhood, as close as Everett had to a slum at the time. "This is the street," said Dad. "Looks a lot better than it did then," he commented. "Now it looks pretty good."

Pretty good! The houses wore peeling paint, and the yards were made of patchy grass and littered with broken toys, washing machines, tools and overflowing garbage bags. The smell of yesterday's cooking mingled with the smell of diapers.

Dad pointed to a small shack so lopsided it leaned into the house next to it. "That's it," he said. "That's where we lived when I was thirteen and fourteen."

That was my age at the time. But there was no similarity between my comfortable suburban home and what I saw before me. Our house had three bedrooms and a big daylight basement where there was a pool table and my parents gave parties. Dad's old house looked like it might have two rooms altogether. My father was one of ten children, so it seemed impossible they could have all fit inside that little shack.

"Oh, we didn't all sleep there," he said, in answer to my question. "All the boys slept in the lean-to that my dad built against that wall," pointing to the west wall of the house. "Only Mother and Dad and my three sisters slept inside."

"There wasn't any bathroom," he continued. "Only an outhouse. It was pretty cold in there on winter mornings when the winds came off the Sound. Sometimes my oldest brother used to just pee out the door of the lean-to instead of going all the way to the outhouse. I remember once it was so cold his pee froze in the night and in the morning one of my other brothers slipped on the iced pee and broke his ankle. Mother was pretty angry about that." He was laughing as he spoke, obviously enjoying his little trip down memory lane.

Maybe it was the story about the iced pee that froze this Sunday drive into my memory. But even today I can close my eyes and see that tiny house. If I use my imagination, I can see the scrawny teenage boy shivering in his lean-to bedroom, too young to know how poor he is.

We are all teachers for each other. This is one of our primary roles. Excellent teachers have always used stories in their work. Jesus Christ, one of the greatest teachers who ever lived, was also one of the best storytellers. He used his parables, or story vignettes, to anchor his wisdom into his listeners' minds.

Mothers have known this truth for millennia. Some of the most popular and enduring teaching stories are the stories of pregnancy, birth and childrearing. Every mother has accumulated wisdom and knowledge that she instinctively shares with women who are doing it for the first time. New mothers automatically seek out experienced mothers, to hear, digest and apply their lessons. Even in our technological age, telling and listening to stories is still the primary method of passing along maternal wisdom about birth and babies.

> *"When my wife found a Playboy magazine under our fourteen-year-old son's bed, she told me I had to talk to him about the facts of life," read "Herb" from his in-class writing piece. "I didn't want to, because I didn't know what to say, but she was so upset I promised. So I took him fishing, where I figured we'd have time alone to talk. We drove a couple of hours up to my favorite river, and while we drove I tried to think about how to bring up the subject of sex, but then we got to talking about baseball and so I didn't get around to it. Then at the river we concentrated on fishing, and the only stories I told him were about the ones that got away. Then when we drove home he fell asleep in the car.*
>
> *I never did tell my son the facts of life, but he must have learned them somewhere because he grew up just fine, in spite of my wife's worries."*

When you tell your stories, you are teaching what you yourself have been taught, as well as your own original discoveries. You are passing along your wisdom. What are the lessons you have learned? Who taught you? Who have you taught? Who can you help?

Chapter Four
Inspiration

All of us are desperate for leadership. We read the stories of brave, dedicated, independent, selfless, passionate, daring, compassionate, creative people, and we ourselves are moved to be daring, brave, selfless, creative, passionate. We read the stories of heroes because they give us hope. They prove it is possible. Heroes destroy apathy, despair and cynicism.

Here is a story illustrating that we should never underestimate the power of our heroes.

Ever since I can remember I wanted to be a writer. I wrote plays, poems, stories, and even a newsletter for my family, which I subjected them to every Sunday night at the dinner table during the year that I was nine.

My mother kept some of my early efforts, and it is to her credit that she was able to see anything impressive in them at all. One of the first stories I wrote was a thrilling epistle called "The Cow." It featured a cow who broke out of its pasture and ran amok through a quiet suburban neighborhood, mooing and bellowing in rage while it knocked over cars and trash cans. It even ate pet cats, birds and small dogs. The cow was eventually caught and ground up into hamburger, the moral being that bad behavior is punished.

I wanted to be a writer because I loved books and stories; it seemed a miracle to me that color, excitement and action could bloom out of black lines on white paper. My mother read to me until I was old enough to read on my own. I still remember the Christmas when I was nine or ten and given *Little Women* by Louisa May Alcott. I fell in love with its heroine, Jo March. She too wanted to be a writer, and her "scribbling" meant more to her than anything else. She wasn't one of those namby-pamby, retiring, "good" girls – no, she was exciting, bold, tumultuous, a passionate rebel who had problems with anger and who rebelled against female restrictions. I identified with her strongly.

Jo March was my first author mentor. I read and re-read *Little Women* until the pages came out of the spine and I could recite whole chapters by heart. Jo March was my touchstone. She was how a writer *was*.

I was savagely disappointed when I first read *Little Men*, the sequel to *Little Women*. It told the story of an adult Jo, who had settled down to become a wife and mother, leaving her writing dreams behind. All the focus in the book went to her boys, and Jo was relegated to the sidelines, supporting and comforting. What was even worse was that she seemed happy with her diminished role. How could she? I thought.

I was somewhat relieved when I read the third book about the March family, *Jo's Boys*. Here I learned that Jo had retrieved her writing dreams and become a successful writer in middle age. Better late than never, I thought, although to my eleven year old mind, it seemed like a long time to wait.

As I write this, I am struck with how my life has paralleled that of Jo March. I too, showed early promise and wrote from heart-stopping passions so deep I knew I would always keep writing. But I grew up and married, had children, and left my writing dreams to molder while I made a living and focused on my kids. Just like she did.

But today! Today I too am middle-aged, but my writing dreams are still young and vibrant. I published two books, both in my late forties. I am working on my third. I help others write their books. I make my living scribbling.

Just like Jo.

What we often fail to realize is that all of us have done brave deeds, followed our passions, achieved our goals — at least sometimes, and most of us more often than we think. We pooh-pooh some of our most meaningful acts, as if they didn't matter. They do matter. All of us have moments of heroism. Each of us is a hero to someone.

Most of do not think of ourselves as heroes. But we do not give ourselves enough credit.

When were you at your best? When did you pursue your passion with all that was within you? What was your proudest moment? When did you slog through, day after day, with no hope of reward, only because you knew it was right? When did you have a great burst of creative fire and the guts to carry it through? When did you stand up for yourself, or someone else? When did you speak the truth even though it wasn't easy? When did your kind words comfort another? Find the hero within yourself, and give her voice.

One class participant, "Lisa," was convinced she had no impact on her times, especially the sixties and seventies. She remarked, "I didn't do anything that affected the world – I hardly remember the seventies! I was busy raising my kids and going to the PTA and sports events and making dinner and cleaning the house. My life was pretty narrow."

Oh yeah? During the class on "Science and Technology" we talked about the burgeoning environmental movement of the 1970s. Lisa read her piece on celebrating the first Earth Day in 1970. She was the Leader of ten fifth-grade Girl Scouts, including her own daughter. That year she took her troop to the foothills of the Cascade Mountains to plant trees in honor of Earth Day. Each girl had a tiny fir tree that they carefully planted, digging holes just the right depth and patting in nutritious soil. As they worked, Lisa talked to them about the life-cycle of trees and their benefit to our environment. The girls loved the outing so much that the next year they went back to visit the trees to see how they were doing. Again, they had fun, so they went back the next year. And the next.

Of the ten girls in the troop, four of them are still visiting "their" trees on almost every Earth Day, over thirty years later. Now women in their forties, they have brought their children with them to plant more trees and watch out for the health of "their" forest. Lisa's own daughter and grandchildren are among them.

Did Lisa have an impact? Did she make a difference? Of course she did, and the difference she made is still continuing. Heroism need not be accompanied by blaring bugles and red flags blowing in the wind. Some of the most effective heroism is the quiet kind. It will endure just as long as the kind that wins medals.

Share your stories of bravery, devotion, selflessness, kindness, love, creativity, strength – and you can literally change the course of another person's life. Yes, stories are that powerful.

Chapter Five
Healing

All of us have been wounded by our life experiences. Even the luckiest among us go through pain; it's part of the human package. Some of our wounds are now wrinkled scars or hard lumpy places, and others are still festering sores. Stories are one way we can heal these emotional wounds. When you tell or write your stories, you examine not only what you did, but why you did it, and how, and to whom. You examine the same for other people. You describe circumstances and situations. Through this process you come to understand yourself better, understand others better, and perhaps understand a bigger picture.

Sometimes the understanding brings sadness or regret. Here is a story about a lover's betrayal, seen from the light of maturity.

I remember an old 12 string guitar, its polish scratched by the long fingernails of my lover, a marijuana soaked musician dressed in tattered jeans and a tie-dyed shirt. His hair fell over his eyes and down his back in cascades of disgust for the establishment, while he played the guitar with single minded concentration. His eyes were dark and intense despite the numbing effects of the joint hanging out of his mouth.

I remember what it was to be young and tempestuous, passionate about the truth and furious about the lies we were told by those we had trusted not to betray us. My favorite songs were heavy with E-flat and A-flat, minor chords which echoed the sadness and betrayal of those times, the great late 1960s.

Lovers betray you too. I wish he hadn't. I wish his hair had stayed black and lustrous forever, but I know, even though he is long gone from my life, that now it is gray. I know his face is now lined with his own failures and his own lies.

I wish we could wipe the surface of the guitar clean of scratches and rings where beer cans once stood, and someone would again play songs that no one had ever heard before. I wish we could once more strum the anthems of hope and despair. I wish we did not live to see both the dawn and dusk of the Age of Aquarius.

From understanding comes, inevitably, forgiveness. And forgiveness is a prime component of healing. In fact, there is no true healing without it.

Through revisiting your stories, you learn to forgive the bad stuff. You forgive others, and most importantly, yourself. What's more, other people reading or listening to your story go through the same process. They forgive you, or situations, or themselves. Telling your stories heals the world.

I received a vivid demonstration of this healing power during one of my classes. That week the topic was "Wars and the International Scene," and since the class was made up of seniors, most over 70, World War Two figured prominently in their stories. We made our way around the room, people reading their vignettes. We came to a woman who had a thick German accent. She read an account of her experiences as a member of Hitler Youth in the 1930s, when she was between 9 and 13. She told how the children of her neighborhood believed totally in Hitler, how they bought everything he said, how it never even occurred to them that Germany might lose the war. She did not excuse her conduct or minimize its meaning; she just tried to explain how it felt to be a child in Hitler's Germany. She described her pride in her Hitler Youth uniform, and how much she enjoyed the Youth meetings. All the children did. They sang songs, learned marches, ate cookies, hung out with their friends. All the grownups told them how important they were. What child wouldn't enjoy this?

She told how betrayed she felt when everything she had been told was exposed as a lie. How sad she felt when her country was defeated. How confused she was when everything she had been taught was good was suddenly deemed bad.

The room was quiet as she read. I was dumbstruck at the incredible bravery I was witnessing. It takes a strong and courageous person to admit to a story like this, in front of your neighbors and friends. It takes a great devotion to truth.

There wasn't much feedback to her story. I don't think people knew what to say. I complimented her on her courage, and we moved on.

In the way things often happen, another person in the room spent part of her childhood in Hitler's Germany. And yes, I'm sure you have guessed: she was Jewish. She read her vignette. She read about hearing the boots of the Gestapo coming down the hallway of her apartment building, the night they dragged away her father and eldest brother. She wrote about how she and her mother and sisters barely escaped to South America with their lives.

There was deep silence after she read. Then a sob from across the room, from the ex-Hitler Youth. "I am so sorry," she cried. "I was so young. I didn't know. But I am so sorry!" Her eyes were full of tears. She wasn't the only one: much of the class was close to weeping. I know I was.

The ex-Hitler Youth woman gave the Holocaust survivor a great gift that day. The victims of great evil find it hard to heal, because to heal completely they must be able to forgive the unforgivable. Most cannot. But here in this class, this Holocaust victim was given someone she could forgive. She could forgive a nine-year-old girl.

As an epilogue to this story, a few weeks later I drove into the parking lot on my way to class. Near the door to the school I saw the ex-Hitler Youth and the Holocaust survivor chatting and laughing together. I think they may have been trading recipes.

Chapter Six
The Secretary's Story

Here is a story that illustrates all four reasons to tell your stories: connection, wisdom, inspiration and healing. It goes like this:

"Sue" was born in 1920. Nearing her eightieth birthday, her children urged her to write some of her memories down. "Oh, there's nothing special about me," Sue said. "I was just an ordinary wife and mother at home, and a secretary in an office." But her children kept asking, and finally this story emerged.

After high school, Sue took a secretarial course, although she planned to work only until she got married. She worked as a secretary through World War II, and in 1945 she married her Navy sweetheart. In common with millions of others, they started a family right away. Her husband worked in construction, and Sue stayed home taking care of the children.

In 1949, her husband was killed in an accident, leaving her with two small children, no life insurance, no savings, no job, and no family who could help. She was in deep trouble. But she was a trained secretary, so she soon found an office job, and back to work she went.

Sue worked hard and was valued by her employer as a top-notch secretary. But no matter how hard she worked, how long she worked, or how many management-trainees she trained, she was "just a secretary" and she worked those long hard hours for peanuts and no advancements. That's the way it was for women in the business world of the 1950s.

The lack of recognition or respect for her work irritated Sue, but what really infuriated her were the poor pay and the impossibility of earning more. She did not earn enough to support her children, and they lived on the edge of poverty. Over time, Sue became angrier and angrier at the injustice and imbalance of her pay scale.

Sue took her anger and translated it into action. She joined a chapter of the National Secretary's Association (now the IAAP), an organization formed to professionalize the occupation of secretary. Over the next *thirty-five* years, Sue worked tirelessly for this organization. She attended evening meetings. She lobbied local, state and national politicians. She chaired membership drives. She held elected NSA positions. She worked on the Certified Professional Secretaries Examination, which promoted and standardized excellence in her profession. Sue campaigned ceaselessly for the recognition of the worth of secretaries, and a demand for better pay. It became her passion and her driving force in life.

Through it all, she continued working as a secretary. She raised her children, re-married and had two more children. She did not retire from either her job or the NSA until the mid-1980s.

Sue was not a radical or a feminist, and still isn't. She did not consider herself part of the "Women's Movement." She is not famous.

Sue's children knew their mother was a member of the NSA. In fact they had often complained that she wasn't there for them when they needed her. But they were dumbfounded when she told her story and they learned of the extent of her participation. Much of their hurt over their mother's perceived "neglect" dissipated, and was forgiven. Sue's grandchildren were delighted with her story. "Grandma was a feminist!" they crowed. "Grandma and Gloria Steinem were on the same team!"

Sue's family had always loved her, of course. But they had never known that her work helped to change the course of history. They had never seen her as a hero. But she was.

History, inspiration, wisdom, healing and forgiveness. They are all here in Sue's story. In one way, Sue is correct – there is nothing special about her. We all have stories that need to be told. Please share yours.

Part Two

How to Tell Your Stories

"Life can only be understood backward,
but it must be lived forward."

Niels Bohr

Chapter Seven
Too Much Information, Too Little Time!

Recalling twenty, thirty, fifty or more years of living is a daunting prospect. Putting your memories in a communicable form requires time and energy, and many of us feel overwhelmed just thinking about it. What do you put in? What do you leave out? How do you remember it all?

Good news: you don't have to! There is no need to write a long tome about your life if you don't want to. You don't need to recall exactly what you were doing, thinking and feeling on, say, the 17th of July, 1961.

The vignette, or short-short story, is an excellent form for memoir. Even a few paragraphs may convey a sense of who you are, and what was important to you. A vignette is only a snapshot, but a lot can be learned from a snapshot. Any writing is inevitably revealing about the writer. That's what makes it scary sometimes, but that's what makes it powerful too.

What if you had just one page of a diary from one of your ancestors? You might discover if she had a sense of humor, or an active social conscience, or big dreams, or small timid fears. You might discover who she loved and why she loved them, or who she hated and why. You might uncover petty annoyances or lurid scandals or hints to the proverbial closet skeleton. You might discover how she contributed, participated, and was affected by the events or trends of her time.

Remember: someday you will be someone's ancestor!

But which vignettes, which stories? How do you decide, out of the numerous happenings of your life, which are the important ones to tell?

Again, don't try to tell everything. That will frustrate, exhaust, and eventually defeat you, because telling everything is impossible.

Just tell a piece at a time. Pick one subject and focus on it. Use it as a framework to hang your memories upon. There are many that will work: your working life; your school days; your children; your romances; your military service; your hobbies. And many more.

This book provides you with such a framework: your relationship with "big" history – all that stuff in the newspapers and history books. How did you participate in, and contribute to, the historical events and trends of your time? You don't have to be famous or infamous to affect history. If you were alive, you couldn't help but affect it.

Part three of this book establishes eight different frameworks to explore, working within sixty years of recent American history, from 1930 through 1989. You will have opportunities to create many different vignettes from various angles.

History has been divided into eight categories and two thirty-year time periods. Of course, history doesn't fall into such neat categories, since everything is always related to everything else. I may have categorized an event as "political" when you might think it should be in "arts and entertainment." You might be right. The categories I have established are completely arbitrary.

The eight categories are:

- Economics and Politics
- The Social Fabric: Race, Sex, Religion & Morality
- Wars and the International Scene
- Science and Technology
- Crime and Disaster
- Arts and Entertainment
- Lifestyle Activities
- The Weird and Trivial

I can hear you saying, "But I don't know anything about politics or economics or science or theater or ... whatever! I don't know enough about history to write about it!"

Are you sure? Let's look at these categories.

Economics: Did you make money? Did you have a job? Did you belong to a union? Did you spend money? What on?

Politics: Did you ever vote? Who for? Were you affected by any new laws that were passed?

Social mores: Did your attitudes toward men and women's roles change during your lifetime? Were you or anyone you know discriminated against because of sex, race or religion? Were you or your children bussed to achieve integration in the schools? Did you benefit from affirmative action programs? Did your church change its attitude toward women or sexual morality during your lifetime? Did you and your parents or children have differing ideas of what was "right"?

War: Were you alive during World War II? Korea? Vietnam? Did you or anyone you know serve in the military during those wars? Did you have opinions about those wars? Did you do non-military war work? Did you work against war?

International Affairs: Have you ever traveled outside the United States? Have you ever known people who are not American?

Science: Did you buy or use a "new-fangled" invention, such as a television or computer? Have you ever looked through a telescope or a microscope? Did you learn new skills because of advancements in technology? Did you or anyone you know benefit from advancements in medical technology, such as the polio vaccine, penicillin, or organ transplants?

Crime: Have you or anyone you know, ever been in trouble with the law? Have you been a victim of a crime? Are you afraid to walk the streets at night?

Disaster: Have you had an experience with an earthquake, windstorm, hurricane, avalanche, shipwreck, car crash, airline disaster, explosion, chemical leak, fire, flood, or any of a thousand different disasters?

Arts and Entertainment: Have you seen a movie? Read a book? Gone to a museum or a theater? Listened to music? Sang in the shower?

Lifestyle Activities (this category includes sports, toys and games, food, travel, fashion, advertising and the media, fads and consumer products, among others): Did you have a favorite food? Were you a real man and still eat quiche? Did you go to Disneyland, the State Fair, Mt. Rushmore, or an aquarium? Did you ever wear an Afro? Bobby Sox? Granny glasses? Did you play or watch athletic events? Did you get to see Joe DiMaggio, Bob Cousy, Billie Jean King? Did you have a hula hoop or a pet rock?

The Weird, Trivial and Difficult to Categorize: Did you read about scandals affecting famous people? Did you follow the exploits of Liz and Dick, or John and Yoko, or Charles and Di? Did you have pets during your life, such as a beloved dog or cat? Did you ever ride a horse or go birdwatching? Did you pepper your speech with slang? Did you wonder about UFOs or reincarnation, or other hotly disputed theories? Do you or anyone you know have ESP? Have you ever seen a ghost? Do you think the Loch Ness Monster is real?

Unless you spent your life being dead, you will answer many of the questions above with a "yes."

That's because you *do* make history.

Chapter Eight
Remembering History

Some people hear the word "history" and immediately run away, fearing that a bunch of dry facts and dates will be forced into their unwilling minds. If this is true for you, you can relax. This is *not* a history book! The purpose of the information given is to stimulate memory, not teach you history. I can't teach you your life!

The historical categories in Part Three are organized like this:

1. A brief narrative discussion, covering the major events and trends of each category from 1930 through 1959, and sharing many of the vignettes written by the participants in my classes. (Their names and details of their stories have been changed to protect identity.) The narrative also reflects my subjective opinions, and you are free to disagree! Contrary opinions stimulate memories.

2. A detailed historical timeline from 1930 through 1959. The information in this timeline has been gathered from various historical resources. (See sources listed in the back of this book.) I have attempted to make this information as accurate as possible, but to reiterate, this is not a history book. If you feel there are errors, this means you are remembering the times, which is the goal. And of course, a timeline cannot include every event; if it did, this book would be thousands of pages long! If I have left out something important to your life, I apologize. This timeline also includes a story that I wrote, from my own memories.

3. Another narrative discussion of the events and trends in the category, this time covering 1960 through 1989, with participant vignettes included.

4. Another detailed timeline of events in the category, for the years 1960 through 1989, plus a story that I wrote from my memories of these decades.

5. A host of "Write to Remember" writing topic suggestions. This is covered in more detail below.

Since this book is based on a class, the system was formatted to work in a group setting, but there is no right or wrong way to use this book. Each week at the beginning of class I take the participants on a thirty-minute, thirty-year gallop through history. Here the gallop is replaced by the introductory narratives. You can read them by yourself, or if you have a group, read them aloud and discuss them. Then scan the timelines, and circle the things you remember. Make notes in the margins. Put question marks by things you don't remember. X-out things you think are wrong or misleading. Make a list on a white board. Whatever works for you. The point is to immerse yourself in that time period.

What if you were a child in a particular time period, or not even born yet? You can still participate. Children's memories are just as vivid and real as those of adults, and just as much a part of history. You might be surprised at how much you do remember. And if you are talking about a period before you were born, these timelines will bring to mind your parents' stories — even if you didn't think you were listening. I was born in 1949. Yet the time period between 1930 and 1959, most of which I cannot possibly remember, has provided a rich treasure of memories for me. My fifties childhood comes alive again. My parents' and grandparents' stories from the Depression and the Second World War take on a textured, more personal meaning. Many of the vignettes I have written about this period are scattered throughout this book.

After the narratives and the timelines for each category, there is a list of suggestions of topics to write about. All the suggestions have questions designed to elicit color, detail, actions and emotions.

Before those of you who hate to write slam the book shut at this point, let me hasten to say this is not like a school assignment! Your fifth grade teacher will not show up. No one will grade you. The writing exercises are not difficult, or long, or boring. They are quick, easy and *fun*.

Here are the eight "Write to Remember" un-rules. (They are un-rules because you are free to ignore them. But you will have better results if you follow them.)

1. *Set a time limit or a page-length limit.* I recommend twenty minutes or three notebook-sized pages in longhand. However, fifteen minutes, four pages, or typing on a keyboard will work just as well. You are writing a vignette, a short-short story, so which length is not that important. Having a framework is; which is what the limit provides. If you have more to say, you can go longer, or begin again on another exercise.

2. *Don't stop writing until the limit is up.** This rule is the basis for all the others. It means, once you begin writing, do not stop to think, or scratch your head, or suck your pen, or gaze into the distance. Keep your hand in motion, going back and forth making marks on the paper or the screen.

Before you begin writing, read through the questions, but don't try to arrange your thoughts. Just start writing, and let the story emerge during the process. This kind of writing is called "stream of consciousness" and its purpose is to get all the stuff in your head onto the paper. *Do not edit as you write!* Keeping your hand in motion allows you to get underneath "the editor" and away from its snorts and sniffs and negative judgments. I know you know who I mean. Everyone has an internal editor, usually a combination of the voices of your parents, your teachers, your well-meaning friends, and anyone who has ever criticized you. The editor is the internal voice who tells you that you are poor at spelling, or boring, or stupid, or uneducated, or just plain bad. If you let the editor roam freely through your head, your writing, and your memory, will suffer. The moving-hand technique causes the editor to shut up. You will be amazed by the deep and wonderful memories that will spring freely from your pen.

3. *Use "trigger sentences" if you get stuck.* A trigger sentence is one which starts with an easy noun-verb phrase, such as "I am," "I see," "I hear," "I want," "I went," "I had," and so on. Any phrase in

---

* I am indebted to Natalie Goldberg for her "keep your hand moving" technique discussed in her books, *Writing Down the Bones* and *Wild Mind.*

this format will work. Start with your chosen phrase, and *without stopping*, write the next thought that comes into your head. If you get stuck, repeat your phrase again, and as many times as necessary. This is an excellent way to eliminate the dreaded writer's block, and it also works very well to eliminate "memory block." It gets you started. An especially good phrase for our purposes is "I remember." Here is a piece that I wrote using this technique, with the phrase "I remember:"

I remember hiding on top of the garage roof to escape the interested eyes of my mother. I remember doing my homework in the living room. I remember all the times I hoped I would forget. I remember the color of the hospital curtains the morning my son died, a sickly turquoise. I remember the crows flying through an orange sky the morning of my daughter's birth. I remember dancing in a smoky nightclub with a boy I despised, but boy could he dance. I remember 1968 and the day they bombed the ROTC building on campus. I remember wearing tall leather boots which came up to my knees and were difficult to get off. I remember tie-dying curtains while throwing ripe cherries at my new husband and how the cherry juice dripped onto the curtains and made its own pattern.

Note that none of these sentences is connected to the one before. I let my mind jump around, without trying to exert control. Soon the rhythm of writing will cause the "I remembers" to drop away and I will be writing about one of the topics my mind threw up without me noticing. In the above case I eventually wrote a short article about the fashion of tie-dying in the sixties. I also went back later and wrote a story about walking past the bombed-out ROTC building on my college campus sometime after Robert Kennedy was killed. The point of trigger sentences is to get the memories out into the light of day where you can play with them.

4. *Don't be polite.* In fact, you don't even need to be kind. Write what is not politically correct. Write what you really think, but never

had the courage to say. You don't have to read it aloud if you don't want to. You don't even have to keep it. And you can always edit later. (Despite my harsh words about the editor, editing is not bad; it just needs to know its place.) Courtesy and tact are important virtues, but if you invite them to have free reign while you are writing, they can paralyze you. Here's a vignette I wrote on an impolite subject:

> We were eleven when my best friend Rachel told me she got her period. I hadn't started yet and didn't want to, either. My mother had shown me a sanitary napkin and one of those medieval apparatus made of elastic studded with metal teeth, that you wore around your waist. I stared at her in disbelief, but tried to maintain my cool. I told her in my most superior tone that I already knew all about it. That was a lie. I'm sure she knew it was, but she didn't press it.
>
> Rachel didn't like sanitary napkins either. One day she showed me a tampax that she had swiped from her older sister. She told me what you did with it, and I had to fight hard to keep my mouth from falling open in shock and my eyes from bugging out.
>
> Rachel said you were supposed to wait until you got married to use tampax, but she claimed she wasn't going to wait that long. Rachel liked to be a leader.
>
> I wasn't a leader or a follower either. I just liked to ramble down my own scrubby paths. I decided I wasn't going to have anything to do with belts, napkins or tampax. I determined not to have periods at all, and if it kept me from getting married, so be it.

5. *Be specific and remember that you have at least five senses.* Detail, detail, detail! Einstein said, "God lives in the details," and he was right. Don't write "He gave me flowers," when you could say, "He gave me bluebells." Don't write "We bought a new car," when you could say "We bought a Corvette," or "We bought a VW bug." Be specific with your verbs too. Why write, "She ran across the lawn," when you could say, "She loped across the lawn," or "She scam-

pered across the lawn," or "She skipped across the lawn." Details give your memories authenticity, immediacy, color and life.

Sensory details – what it looked like, felt like, sounded like, smelled like, tasted like – also make your stories come alive, conveying a sense of "you are there." When you are remembering a scene, ask yourself sensory questions, like these examples:

What dress were you wearing the night he proposed? What color was it, and what style? How did the material feel against your skin? Was he nervous? How could you tell? Did his voice boom like thunder? Did he talk so fast you couldn't understand him? Did he whisper as if he was telling an incredible secret? If you were afraid, how did you show it? Did you shake, freeze, become tongue-tied, throw up?

If you tell about a car trip, don't just say, "We drove across the country." What kind of car was it? Did you sit in the back seat? Take turns driving? Was it crowded? Did you play car games? Was it hot? Did your thighs stick to the seat? What states did you go through? Did you sing songs? Which ones?

Our oldest sense, and one of the most powerful for evoking memory, is smell. If you are remembering an event, ask yourself what you smell. Do you remember the sweetness of the lilacs blooming in the front yard, or the hot smell of burning rubber, or the welcoming smell of frying onions? Here is a piece I wrote about the smells of the past:

My mother-in-law once gave me a box of my husband's childhood toys. We found his Davy Crockett coonskin cap that he got at Disneyland when he was ten. It smelled like musty furry sweat, old sweat that had dried and beaded on the hair. I bet the real Davy Crockett had a sweat problem, although he probably didn't care. His sweat would have been rank with squirrel blood and bear grease; his clothes saturated with it. The Disney version of Davy Crockett was sanitized for fifties children: Fess Parker was always clean and polite, saying "yes'm" and "nossir", and joking — clean jokes, of course – with his trusty sidekick Buddy Ebsen. He always saved the day, just like

Mighty Mouse, and just as believable too. Mighty Mouse probably didn't have sweat glands at all. Do mice sweat? Of course they don't wear tight Speedo shorts either.

The smell of sweat is not necessarily a bad thing. Bad smells are largely culturally determined. I once rode a crowded bus in Germany, standing underneath the hairy armpit of a stout German frau who breathed beer over my head and whose sweat smelled like sauerbraten, rich and thick and dark. Maybe her husband thought it was sexy, the smell of woman.

I remember an old smell, one of dark smoky rooms lit by lava lamps, punctuated by the sweet weediness of marijuana and the unwashed armpits of some strung-out hippie whose name no one ever knew; a guy who just turned up at parties. "Party Guy" we called him, and he was. I believe he was a friend of a friend of someone's; he was thought to be "cool" because he once belonged to the SDS, or said he did. I also smelled the ratty carpet thick with long ago spilt beer and blood and cat shit and in the corners the smell of sex against the wall. Surprisingly, this is a good smell, the smell of nostalgia for my youth when I had so much time I could afford to waste it.

6. *You don't have to be right, rational, or logical.* Don't be afraid that you are not remembering the way it really happened. Don't worry if you can't remember if it was 1942 or 1943, or if the setting was New York or Chicago, or if you have forgotten all the details. Tell it as you remember it now. It will be emotionally true.

And here's a really radical thought: if you don't know how it was, imagine how it might have been. Or tell it like you want it to be, or could have been … if. This is especially useful when you are telling about something where all you have is a few tantalizing but incomplete facts. Here is a piece I wrote illustrating this.

These are the facts I know about my mother's grandmother: her name was Amanda Gehlstrom. She was born and raised in Sweden and immigrated to America before she was married. She and her husband came to Washington from Minnesota right after they were married. They had 4 sons and 3 daughters. She died in the flu epidemic of 1918. There is one photograph of her, taken when she was around 40. She is frowning.

Now here is what I think about my mother's grandmother, made up of half-remembered vague family stories plus historical knowledge and yes, a lot of imagination:

Amanda Gehlstrom was a 21-year old spinster in 1890 when she came to the US, bound for a small logging town in Minnesota. The community had advertised in the Stockholm papers for women to come to Minnesota as wives for the lumberjacks.

Amanda hadn't had much luck in the marriage game back in Sweden. Judging from her photograph, this is not surprising. She had a thin, almost gaunt face, with compressed lips and eyes squinted with suspicion. She wore her hair severely scraped back from her high forehead, parted by a rigidly straight line down the middle. Even allowing for poor photography, ugly fashions and a sour, inward look as if she was suffering from repressed diarrhea, she could never have been a pretty woman.

Despite her looks, she wanted to be married, for what else was there for a woman? So she answered the ad and came to America. The town in Minnesota paid for her passage from Stockholm. It turned out to be a bad deal for them, because Amanda did not marry a Minnesota lumberjack.

During the trip from Stockholm, Amanda made friends with a woman traveling to San Francisco, who sold her on the glories of California. Amanda began dreaming of marrying a fisherman or an orange farmer, in a place where it was warm.

She got off the train in Minneapolis, but did not meet her connection for the trip to the small logging town. Instead she took a job as a servant in Minneapolis, saving her money for California and an easier life than a logger's wife.

She didn't make it to California either. In Minneapolis she met a man named Frank Winter, a charming "real American," one of the few people she knew who spoke without a Swedish accent. Frank too wanted to move to the Pacific Coast, but he was interested in Oregon or Washington, not California. He said there was good opportunity there to acquire a horse farm. Amanda, getting close to 25 and afraid of being doomed to spinsterhood, was glad to exchange oranges for horses, and California for the Northwest.

Frank and Amanda were married and moved soon after to Washington State. But Frank failed at starting a horse farm, so he took a job in a small town high in the Cascade Mountains – as a logger. It was a trade he continued the rest of his life.

Amanda gave in and with ill-grace followed her destiny as a logger's wife until set free by the Great Flu Epidemic of 1918.

7. *Forget about the rules of grammar or spelling.* There is a place for these, but it comes after writing, not during it. Do not let your fourth-grade teacher into your head while you are writing! If you share your memories in written form (which I hope you will) you can always edit afterwards, your trusty dictionary by your side.

8. *Trust yourself.* This is the most important rule. Many of us believe that we are too ordinary to have interesting stories. We don't believe we are special. We don't believe we can remember. We don't believe we can write. We don't believe we added much to the world. This is simply not true! Yes you do have interesting stories. Yes you are special. Yes you can remember. Yes you can write. Yes you did contribute and participate in world events. I don't just believe this: I know it. If you are alive and conscious, your memories have worth.

The un-rules make writing your memories fun, not work. When you sit down to write, don't worry about the outcome. Do not judge yourself. Your past lives inside you, and there is no way you can get it wrong.

Just begin. You *do* have stories to tell!

Chapter Nine
Interpreting and Sharing Stories

It can be intimidating, even scary, to think about reading something you wrote out loud to an audience, or letting someone else read it. You are revealing a part of yourself, and may feel vulnerable, even naked.

Even so, I strongly recommend that you do so. Remember the last "un-rule" of the Write to Remember Rules: *Trust yourself.* This rule applies to sharing stories as well as writing them. Trust that your stories have value. Trust that you do have something to say. Trust that someone else does want – may even need – to hear it.

Sharing our stories amplifies their power and strengthens our connections to one another. Sharing your stories allows you to lay claim to your own voice. It allows you to claim your own truth, the reason you are here. You are saying, "This was me. I did this. I made a difference."

Paradoxically, sharing your stories allows you to let them go. They don't need to clutter your psyche with unsaid emotions that may be keeping you stuck. You can let them go into the world without you, to do their work for others. The past does not have to keep you chained. Learn from it and let it go.

There are many ways to share your stories. Take a "Making History" class, in which sharing is an integral part. Form an informal "Making History" group of your own, using this book as a guide. Write your stories down and then read them to your family and friends, and encourage them to do the same with their stories.

Share your stories in written form. Send your vignettes to your family and friends via letters or email. Learn how to make scrapbooks and use your memorabilia to illustrate the vignettes. Create a website and post them. Even submit them for publication in magazines, e-zines, or newsletters. There are many historical, nostalgia or genealogical publications looking for short written pieces. Edit your vignettes and submit them. Why shouldn't you be published?

Edit and organize the vignettes you have written, and combine them into one book. You can do this yourself, or hire a ghostwriter or editor to help you. Submit your book to a publisher, or self-publish it in limited quantities as a living legacy for future generations.

Seek out others and listen to their memories. Witnessing another's story can be as enriching as telling your own. When witnessing another's story, the most important thing you can do is simply pay attention.

Your response is an important part of this experience. Feedback is enormously valuable to the storyteller. We often do not see in our own lives what is obvious to others. Listening to feedback validates our experiences, and reminds us again that we affect the world.

To be valuable, feedback must be encouraging. Criticism often causes people to stop listening, get defensive, or feel guilty, and has no place here. My guidelines for giving feedback on shared stories are these:

1. Do not withhold admiration. Look for something in the storyteller's piece that you find enjoyable, interesting, or moving – and be determined to find it. When you do, say so. Always praise, never condemn.

2. Be honest. Your appreciation cannot be phony. We all know when people are trying to "butter us up" or giving us empty praise. If you are really listening, you will find something that you honestly admire.

3. Ask questions to clarify understanding. When listening to the storyteller, ask yourself if you can see, hear, smell, or touch what is happening in the story. If you can't get a "sense" of the story, ask a question. As tellers of our own stories, we are so close to the action that we often forget to give color and detail. Feedback

Chapter Ten
Economics and Politics

Remember: The discussion and timelines presented here are meant to jog *your* memories. I am not writing history, but presenting you with many facts or my opinions about the facts, in a way that might strike a chord within you. If you don't remember an event the way it's presented here, or if you think it is incorrect – great! How do *you* remember it? You were the one who was there.

We start with Economics and Politics because money and power are the bedrock of all societies. They are the structure upon which everything else is hung.

1930 through 1959

Economics

The one inescapable economic fact of the thirties was the Great Depression. Everyone who lived during the thirties, or whose parents lived through them, was affected by it. Its experiences – Hoovervilles, bank holidays, evictions, breadlines and the like – colored all values and beliefs.

"Susan" shared that the Depression deepened the distrust and suspicion country people like her mother felt for the government. Immediately after her mother heard the first faint rumor of bank failures, she went to town and withdrew her entire savings, $200.00. Then she came home and wrapped the bills individually and carefully in silk, ten silk packets containing twenty dollars each, which she sealed in canning jars and then buried – in twenty different places — in the back yard.

At the breakfast table one morning in 1932, "Sam" watched his mother while she served her children the last food in the house. "There's no more," she said to Sam's father, while tears streaked her face. "And there's no more money either."

His mother's tears so upset Sam that he vowed to get her some money somehow. That night he sneaked out of his bed, and ran miles across town to the wealthy golf and country club. There he climbed the fence and spent the night diving for lost golf balls at the water hazards, even though he was only 9 and could barely swim. When the early morning golfers arrived the next morning, he was waiting outside the gate to sell them his takings. He made $2.50, a huge sum. Then he ran home and walked into the kitchen, just as his parents were wondering where he was. "Here, Mom," he said, and dumped ten quarters on the table. All the way home he had pictured his mother's excitement and joy, so Sam was perplexed when she began sobbing into her apron.

"Patrick" grew up in New York City during the Depression, and remembered the sight of evicted families standing on the street with all their possessions scattered around them. No legal proceedings were necessary to evict anyone. You either paid your rent, or out you went. The pitiful sight so moved the ten-year-old boy that at the age of eleven, and without his mother's knowledge, he became a numbers runner for the neighborhood crime boss. He gave the money he earned to his father so his mother wouldn't have to know her son had turned to a life of crime.

"No one was selfish during the Depression," shared "Grace." "We helped each other. If a family had extra food

or a windfall, they shared it. There was a feeling of 'we're all in this together.' My family was one of the fortunate ones, because my father never lost his job, and we managed to keep our house. Every Tuesday and Friday my mother made dozens of sandwiches and set them on a plate on our back steps, and anyone who wanted one was welcome. We often had lines of out-of-work men at our back door."

The Depression created a host of new economic and political programs, increasing the power of the federal government. This continued far beyond the 1930s. The WPA (Works Progress Administration), Civilian Conservation Corps, NRA, TVA, and others, were born. The Social Security administration came into being, the minimum wage law was enacted, unemployment insurance began, the 40 hour work week was introduced, and income tax withholding began.

In the 1940s, War Production was the economic driving force. Women entered the labor force in record numbers, and Rosie the Riveter was born. Shortages and rationing were facts of life. People grew victory gardens. They found substitutes for butter, sugar, and coffee. They held paper drives, rubber drives, tin foil drives, string drives. They became quite creative in finding substitutes for things they used to feel they could not do without. Many women in the class wrote about painting lines up the backs of their calves, to simulate the seams of silk stockings, or buying tubes of "leg makeup" which when smoothed over the legs made it appear as if they were wearing stockings.

Labor unrest was rife during all three decades. The auto workers went on strike, as did the mine workers, steel workers, meat packers, and more. A new kind of strike was born – the sit-down strike. New unions, such as the AFL/CIO, were formed. In the 1950s, labor unrest and the threat of striking workers, coupled with the fear of communism, caused President Truman to take unheard of actions to prevent strikes.

"Esther" shared about her father's death from "lung rot" at the age of 35. He was a coal miner and had been passionately pro-Union. "At his funeral the Union sent the biggest bunch of flowers I ever saw," she read. "My mother gave each of us kids a rose from the bouquet to keep. I put mine in a vase in my bedroom and kept it there even after all the petals had fallen off."

"Elizabeth" remembered her father and his story about unions too, from the opposite viewpoint. He was the owner of a textile mill, fighting to preserve his mill from becoming unionized. She remembered him ranting about the "Democrats" at the dinner table. He berated them so thoroughly and colorfully that she was an adult before she realized that being a Democrat was actually legal!

Politics

A political trend of these decades was the increasing power and presence of the federal government. Franklin Delano Roosevelt was an overwhelming figure, his personality and presence dominating the political landscape. FDR used the new modern technology of radio to deepen his relationship with the people. Listening to his "fireside chats" made it seem as though he were a guest in your own living room, or that you knew him personally. Many class participants were young adults when FDR died, and could not remember another president. They often wrote about the power of FDR's voice, and how they even now sometimes hear it in their dreams. To them it was the voice of power and of safety.

"Alice" remembered watching her mother cook dinner the day FDR died. Her mother was weeping so heavily and steadily that her tears dropped into the ham-and-bean soup

she was preparing. Although Alice tried to eat the soup at dinner, because wasting food was a great sin in her house, she was unable to. She called it "sad soup" and to this day she cannot eat ham-and-bean soup.

Starting in the latter thirties and reaching a peak in the fifties, the American political landscape was dominated by the fear of communism. This fear was increased after 1945 by the specter of atomic warfare. The House on Un-American Activities was formed. Senator Joseph McCarthy lent his name to the wave of anti-communist hysteria which swept over the country. People lost their jobs and often had their lives ruined by being accused of communist sympathies. Julius and Ethel Rosenberg, convicted of being communist spies, lost their lives. Names such as Alger Hiss and Richard Nixon rose to prominence. The fear of communism and war was real.

"Rose" remembered the first house she and her husband bought in 1951. One of the first things they did was build a bomb shelter in their back yard. She stocked it with canned goods, bottled water, powdered milk, sugar — and bullets for the gun her husband bought her, in case the communists started World War III.

The new technology of television brought the political process even closer. The Senate Army-McCarthy hearings were televised. Senator John F. Kennedy went on "Meet the Press" in 1954, using his good looks and charisma to great effect in the new medium.

Review the following timeline and see what *you* remember ...

1930 - 1959 Events Timeline
Economics & Politics

Year		Event
1930	Mar	Unemployment demonstrations in New York City
1932	Jan	US railway unions accept 10% wage reduction.
1932	Jan	First US state unemployment insurance act — Wisconsin
1932	Mar	Riots at Ford factory in Dearborn, MI
1932	Jun	US Federal gas tax enacted
1932	Jul	President Hoover evicts bonus marchers from encampment
1932	Aug	President Hoover renominated by Republican Convention
1932	Sep	NYC Mayor James "Gentleman Jimmy" Walker resigns due to graft charges
1932	Nov	Franklin D Roosevelt elected President
1933	Jan	FDR pledges to pull the US out of the Depression, saying "We have nothing to fear but fear itself."
1933	Feb	FDR survives assassination attempt
1933	Mar	Bank holidays declared in 6 states, to prevent run on banks
1933	Mar	FDR conducts his first "fireside chat"
1933	Apr	FDR announces the US will leave the gold standard
1933	May	Federal Emergency Relief Administration forms to help farmers & the needy
1933	May	Tennessee Valley Act signed by FDR, to build dams
1933	May	Federal Securities Act signed
1933	Jun	Federal Home Owners Loan Corporation authorized
1933	Jun	National Industrial Recovery Act becomes law
1933	Jun	US Federal Deposit Insurance Corporation (FDIC) created
1933	Jul	Public Works Administration becomes effective
1933	Jul	Civilian Conservation Corps begins
1933	Jul	Congress passes first minimum wage law, mandating .33/hr
1933	Oct	Farmers strike in Midwest against falling farm prices
1933	Nov	FDR creates the Civil Works Administration
1933	Nov	First sit-down strike at Hormel meat packers in Minnesota
1933	Dec	American Newspaper Guild, a union for reporters and editors, founded by columnist Heywood Broun
1934	Apr	4.7 million families report receiving welfare payments
1934	Jun	The Black-McKellar Bill passes, causing Boeing empire to break up into Boeing United Aircraft and United Airlines
1934	Jun	Securities and Exchange Commission (SEC) authorized
1934	Jun	Federal Communications Commission (FCC) created
1934	Jun	Federal Credit Union Act establishes credit unions
1934	Jun	Federal Savings & Loan Association created
1934	Jul	General Strike in San Francisco led by Longshoremen

1935	Jan	WPA employs thousands of artists, photographers, writers, and musicians in the Federal Arts Project
1935	May	Supreme Court declares FDR's National Recovery Act unconstitutional
1935	Jul	FDR signs the National Labor Relations Act
1935	Aug	Social Security Act becomes law
1935	Sep	Sen. Huey P. Long of Louisiana assassinated
1935	Nov	Congress of Industrial Organizations (CIO) union forms
1936		Keynes's *General Theory of Employment, Interest, and Money* published; it says government should increase spending to counter depression
1936	Sep	Radio used for the first time in a presidential campaign
1937	Oct	44-day sit-down strike at General Motors ends
1936	Nov	FDR wins landslide victory over Alfred M. Landon
1936	Dec	United Auto Workers stage first sit-down strike, at the Fisher Body Plant
1937	Jan	Inauguration Day is held for the first time on January 20th
1937	Feb	FDR proposes enlarging the Supreme Court, dubbed "court packing"
1937	Mar	US Steel raises workers' wages to $5 a day
1937	Apr	US Social Security system makes its first benefit payment
1937	May	Memorial Day Massacre: Chicago police fire on union marchers at steel plant
1937	Oct	Pullman Co. formally recognizes Brotherhood of Sleeping Car Porters
1937	Oct	FDR visits Grand Coulee Dam construction site
1938	May	House Committee on Un-American Activities begins
1938	Jun	Federal minimum wage law guarantees workers .40 / hour
1939	Jan	Union leader Tom Mooney freed after 23 years in jail
1939	Feb	US Supreme Court outlaws sit-down strikes
1939	May	Food stamps first issued, to dispose of agricultural surplus
1939	Aug	Hatch Act bars gov't employees from political activity
1939	Nov	Social Security Administration approves first unemployment check
1940		Ten million Americans still unemployed
1940	Jun	The US Fish & Wildlife Service established
1940	Sep	Congress passes the first peace-time conscription bill
1940	Sep	Sam Rayburn of Texas is elected Speaker of the House
1940	Oct	40-hour work week goes into effect
1940	Nov	FDR wins third term, beating Wendell Willkie
1941	Jan	FDR makes his "Four Freedoms" speech
1941	Feb	Strike begins at Bethlehem Steel

Sharing My Stories—My Dad the Hobo

In 1934, when he was 16, my father left his family and went off to "ride the rails". His motives were first, to remove his hungry mouth from his mother's impoverished table; second, to see new places; and lastly, to escape from Mrs. Halvorsen his English teacher, who had informed him that he'd never amount to anything.

Dad doesn't tell many stories of his rail-riding days with the bums and hobos. But all us kids learned, very young, to sing "Hallelujah I'm a bum," a song glorifying the freedom of the open road. Today all my father's grandchildren can sing it too, even the three-year old. It's one of the first things they learn from him.

Dad spent a few years as a bum, until one day he realized that if he didn't change his lifestyle, he would have to admit that Mrs. Halvorsen had been right. But because he was still determined not to be a burden at home, in 1937 he enrolled in the CCCs, the Civilian Conservation Corps, one of FDR's "New Deal" programs. They sent him high in the Cascade Mountains to fight fires, clear underbrush and build trails.

The nearest town to the CCC camp was the tiny logging town of Darrington. Dad enrolled in Darrington High School, even though at 19, almost 20, he was much older than the other students.

His age made him even more attractive to the girls at Darrington High. To the naïve small-town girls, he was a man of the world – he had actually *been* to Los Angeles, California!

But he was not interested in getting serious with anyone. Having seen firsthand what a lack of education will get you, he was dedicated to not only getting his high school diploma, but to graduating from college. That was his first priority, and girls took a definite back seat.

One hometown girl, whose father was the Darrington Fire Chief and mother the Darrington Post Mistress, set her sights on him anyway. She was a very pretty girl and had plenty of boyfriends. But she played it cool with them, making no commitments. Although she and Dad had never even dated in high school, she chose to go to college too, following him to Western Washington College in 1939. She was the very first Darrington girl to go to college.

Persistence pays off. Dad got an education, and Mom got Dad. They were married in 1944.

1941	Feb	United Service Organization (USO) founded
1941	Mar	FDR signs the Lend-Lease Bill, to lend money to Britain
1941	Apr	Price Administration established to handle rationing
1941	Sep	FDR signs tax bill increasing US treasury by 35 billion $$
1941	Oct	US Savings Bonds go on sale
1941	Dec	US Civil Air Patrol (CAP) organizes
1941	Dec	Winston Churchill is first British Prime Minister to address a joint meeting of Congress, warning that the Axis would "stop at nothing"
1941	Dec	Labor leaders swear off strikes for the duration of the war
1941	Dec	US Office ofCensorship created to control war information
1942	Feb	US auto factories switch to war production
1942	May	Food is first rationed in the US
1942	Jul	Gasoline rationing begins
1942	Nov	Minimum draft age is lowered from 21 to 18
1943	Feb	FDR orders minimal 48-hour work week in war industries
1943	Mar	Meat, butter & cheese, sugar, coffee rationed
1943	Jun	FDR signs withholding (W2) tax bill into law
1944		35% of US labor force made up of women
1944	May	Meat rationing ends
1944	May	US Communist Party dissolves
1944	Jun	FDR signs the "GI Bill of Rights"
1944	Nov	FDR wins a fourth term, defeating Thomas E. Dewey
1944	Dec	European Black Markets trade food, clothing and cigarettes
1945	Apr	FDR dies of cerebral hemorrhage; Harry Truman becomes President
1945	Oct	World Federation of Trade Unions is formed
1945	Oct	End of shoe rationing announced
1945	Nov	General Motors workers go on strike
1945	Nov	HUAC begins investigation of 7 radio commentators
1945	Dec	Auto tires rationing ends
1945	Dec	Int'l Monetary Fund & World Bank established
1946	Jan	President Truman sets up the CIA
1946	Apr	400,000 Mine workers strike
1946	May	Truman seizes control of nation's railroads to delay a strike
1946	Aug	Truman establishes the Atomic Energy Commission
1947	Feb	Catholic bishops publish manifesto against "godless communism"
1947	Mar	Truman Doctrine introduced to fight communism; requires all federal employees to pledge allegiance to the US
1947	Mar	Congress proposes a 2-term limitation to the presidency
1947	May	Senate approves Taft-Hartley Act limiting power of unions
1947	Jun	"Marshall Plan" to rebuild Europe introduced

1947	Jul	Air Force, Navy, & War Department form Defense Dept.
1947	Jul	The National Security Act goes into effect
1947	Oct	The first televised presidential address from White House
1947	Oct	HUAC investigates communist influence in Hollywood
1947	Nov	Wage and price controls lifted except for rent and sugar
1947	Nov	HUAC finds the "Hollywood 10" in contempt because o f their refusal to reveal whether they are communists
1947	Dec	United Mine Workers Union withdraws from the AFL
1948	Jan	Trial of 11 US Communist Party members begins in NY
1948	Mar	200,000 coal miners strike for old age pensions
1948	May	GM and United Auto Workers sign the first sliding-scale contract, tying wage increases to cost of living
1948	Jun	National Security Council authorizes covert operations
1948	Jun	Selective Service Act signed, requiring men 18-25 to register for military duty
1948	Jun	Republicans nominate Thomas Dewey for president
1948	Aug	Alger Hiss denies being a Communist agent
1948	Nov	Truman beats Dewey, confounding pollsters & newspapers
1948	Dec	The "Pumpkin Papers" come to light, supposedly from Alger Hiss
1949	Oct	Minimum wage increased to .75 per hour
1949	Jan	Truman labels his administration the "Fair Deal"
1949	Jul	Senate ratifies NATO by a vote of 82-13
1949	Oct	14 US Communist Party leaders convicted of sedition
1949	Oct	Pittsburgh Steel Strike begins
1950	Jan	Alger Hiss found guilty of perjury
1950	Feb	McCarthy says State Dept. infested with 205 communists
1950	May	Diner's Club issues first credit cards
1950	Nov	Puerto Rican nationalists try to kill President Truman at White House
1950	Dec	Truman proclaims a state of emergency against "Communist Imperialism"
1951	Apr	Julius & Ethel Rosenberg sentenced to death for treason
1951	Apr	Truman fires MacArthur
1952	Apr	President Truman seizes steel mills to prevent a strike
1952	Jul	Eisenhower nominated as Republican presidential candidate
1952	Jul	The Commonwealth of Puerto Rico is created
1952	Sep	Richard Nixon makes "Checkers" speech
1952	Nov	Eisenhower elected president over Adlai Stevenson
1953	Jan	John Foster Dulles appointed Secretary of State
1953	Feb	Eisenhower denies clemency to the Rosenbergs
1953	Mar	Department of Health, Education and Welfare created
1953	Jun	Rosenbergs executed at Sing Sing
1953	Oct	Earl Warren becomes Chief Justice of the Supreme Court

1953	Dec	General Electric says all Communist employees will be fired
1953	Dec	First White House Press Conference held; Eisenhower & 161 reporters
1954	Feb	Eisenhower warns against US intervention in Vietnam
1954	Feb	Senator John F. Kennedy appears on "Meet the Press"
1954	Mar	4 Puerto Ricans open fire in the US House of Representatives
1954	Mar	US Army charges Joseph McCarthy with using undue pressure tactics
1954	Apr	The Senate Army-McCarthy hearings begin
1954	May	Amendment to give vote to 18-year olds defeated
1954	Jun	Joseph Welch asks Senator McCarthy, "Have you no sense of decency, sir?" during Senate Army-McCarthy hearings
1954	Jun	The words "under God" added to the Pledge of Allegiance
1954	Aug	Communist Control Act passed
1954	Aug	Census Bureau established
1954	Dec	McCarthy censured by Senate
1955	Jul	Nixon becomes first VP to preside over a cabinet meeting
1955	Aug	Minimum wage raised to $1 an hour
1955	Dec	Trade unions merge into the AFL/CIO, with George Meany as President
1956		W.H. Whyte's *The Organization Man* published
1956	Mar	Union workers end a 156-day strike at Westinghouse
1956	Mar	Dow Jones closes above 500 for the first time
1956	Mar	US government seizes the communist newspaper, "Daily Worker"
1956	May	Eisenhower signs farm bill allowing government to store agricultural surplus
1956	Jun	Federal Interstate Highway System Act signed
1956	Aug	Democrats nominate Adlai Stevenson for President
1956	Nov	Eisenhower re-elected, defeating Stevenson
1957	Apr	Due to lack of funds, Saturday mail delivery is halted. Two days later, Congress gives the Post Office $41M, restoring Saturday delivery
1957	Oct	AFL-CIO votes to expel the Teamsters for corruption
1957	Nov	Eisenhower suffers a mild stroke, impairing his speech
1958	Jan	John Birch Society established
1958	Jul	Alaska becomes the 49th state
1958		Bankamericard issues first credit card
1959	Jul	VP Nixon argues with Khrushchev, known as the "Kitchen Debate"
1959	Aug	Hawaii becomes the 50th US State

1960 through 1989

Economics

In the sixties, a prosperous society declared a "War on Poverty." LBJ introduced a host of economic programs to address social ills, calling it the "Great Society." In 1965 HUD was established, and Medicare passed. Congress passed the Economic Opportunity Act. The Poor People Marched on Washington in 1968. As a result of these new laws and organizations, changes occurred. Between 1959 and 1969, the number of Americans living below the poverty line dropped by almost half.

There was growing public awareness and attention to product safety and the rights of consumers. Consumer spending skyrocketed, in part due to the popularization of credit cards. Millions of Americans voluntarily accepted debt as a way of economic life.

"Fran" vividly remembered the first credit card she received in 1966. She viewed it with a mixture of elation and suspicion, but carried it in her purse always, "just in case." She had it for five years before she dared to actually charge anything on it.

In the seventies, economic troubles began. A recession coupled with soaring inflation scared everyone who remembered the Depression. President Nixon took the drastic step of freezing wages, rents and prices. New York City announced in 1975 that it would go into bankruptcy unless it was saved by the federal government, which it was. President Carter's popularity was jeopardized by the oil crisis; the OPEC oil embargo doubled gas prices, and gas rationing was introduced. Many class participants have written about standing in long gas lines to fill up their tanks.

"Claire" remembered when she forgot to buy gas on her approved day. The next day she begged the service station attendant to let her buy "just a gallon or two" so she could visit her elderly mother. She painted a dramatic word-picture of a lonely old woman, pining for her only daughter to visit her, weeping with fear when her daughter does not show up, and putting her hand on her chest to still the erratic beating of her "tricky heart." The attendant was so moved he allowed Claire to buy her "gallon or two." She then drove to pick up her active 60-year-old mother and they attended the local flower show. Claire felt no guilt because she didn't believe in the shortage—she thought the government had made it up.

In the eighties, Ronald Reagan brought in an economic policy friendly to big business. His stated priorities were to balance the federal budget and reduce the national debt. He also was dedicated to increasing military spending. This led to tax reforms and cuts in social programs. Reagan was not sympathetic to labor, which he proved with his handling of the most famous strike of the decade, the air traffic controllers strike.

Many people followed the ups and downs of the stock market, leading to an atmosphere of excitement not seen since the 1920s — until "Black Monday" of 1987, when the Dow dropped more than it ever had before. Businessmen became famous figures in the eighties; names such as Donald Trump, Lee Iacocca, and Ted Turner were known to everyone. The scandal of Michael Milliken, the "junk bond king" accused of racketeering and insider trading, was reported widely, and not just in the Wall Street Journal.

Another feature of this decade was the phenomenon of mergers and acquisitions, with big companies being swallowed whole by bigger ones. GE bought RCA and NBC. Chrysler bought American Motors. Philip Morris bought Kraft.

"Frank" remembered the confused loyalties brought on by mergers. His employer was bought by their biggest competitor, the one he had been taught to think of as the enemy. "After the merger it was us versus them," he shared. "The atmosphere at work was like high school: a bunch of adolescent egos jockeying for position. Leader-ship was determined by popularity and fueled by gossip, innuendo and backbiting. For a year or two production of quality work was of secondary importance."

Politics

Politically, the sixties was a polarized decade. It was hard for anyone to be neutral on any issue. Conservative versus liberal, rich versus poor, youth versus age, people of color versus white, women versus men, straight versus gay: there were black and white moral stances being taken, and in the middle, a huge gap.

The Kennedys came into the public eye in the sixties. JFK and Jackie brought charm and glamour to the early sixties White House. Bobby Kennedy took on the Mafia as Attorney General, and made a run at the presidency until cut down by assassination. And Ted Kennedy ended the decade with the tragedy of Chappaquidick.

"Sherry" shared her admiration for the new First Lady in the early sixties, motivating her volunteer work for a Washington DC Arts project headed by Mrs. Kennedy. As a thank you, Jackie Kennedy invited the volunteers, all 500 of them, to a White House Tea. Although Sherry was seven months pregnant at the time, she was determined to attend – after all, how many times would Jackie Kennedy ask her to tea? The tea was held in the Red Room, where they were served dainty puff pastry stuffed with tuna pate, made by the French chef Jackie had imported into the White House. Carrying her teacup and plate of pastry, Sherry

gingerly sat down on a delicate antique red-plush sofa. The sofa was not comfortable for a pregnant woman, so she struggled to get up, balancing her teacup, plate, and outsized abdomen. To help herself, she grasped the wooden arm of the sofa and pushed off. Imagine her horror when the arm came off in her hand! She immediately sat down again, hoping no one had seen. But how could she fix the sofa, she wondered desperately. Showing the resourcefulness and creativity that made her such an outstanding volunteer, she stuck the arm back into its socket using tuna pate as glue! As far as she knew, it was never discovered.

Political assassinations colored the temper of the sixties. JFK, RFK, Martin Luther King, even an attempted assassination of George Wallace, Governor of Alabama. Virtually everyone can remember "where they were" when they heard the news bulletins of these assassinations.

Ronald Reagan began his political career in 1966 when he became Governor of California. Richard Nixon started the decade with a loss but returned in triumph in 1968, when the Vietnam mess derailed Lyndon Johnson's career. Vietnam, of course, colored all aspects of American life during the sixties, especially politics. (Vietnam is covered in Chapter Twelve.)

Protest as a political tactic was a feature of the sixties. Civil Rights protests and marches had started during the fifties, led by Dr. Martin Luther King Jr. and others. During the sixties protestors marched not only for civil rights but against poverty, and especially, against the War in Vietnam. Protests and rallies may have begun peacefully, but many turned into riots, infesting numerous American cities. College campuses became hotbeds of radicals and peaceniks, and bombings, sit-ins and shut-downs were everyday occurrences across America. The generation gap widened, and many people were scared. Class participants who were in their teens and twenties in the sixties write of disillusionment, anger, betrayal and fear. Class participants who were parents during this decade also write of the same emotions. But similarity of emotions did not bring them closer together.

Watergate defined the political environment of the early seventies. From a landslide victory over George McGovern in 1972, President Nixon slid rapidly down the political slope until he was forced to resign in 1974 to avoid impeachment. The country was rapt with attention and disgust over what politics was "really like." "What did he know and when did he know it," was the question everyone was asking. The answer, when it came, was another blow to public trust. Disillusionment with the government, already underway in the sixties, was completed by Watergate. President Ford promised "a return to decency" but his pardon of Nixon may have cost him the presidency two years later. President Carter was also seen as a decent man, despite his admission that he had "lusted in his heart," but unfortunately he was also perceived as inefficient. Decency did not do well during the seventies.

Politically, the eighties signaled a return to conservatism under Reagan and then George Bush I. Supreme Court appointees included William Rehnquist, Sandra Day O'Connor, Antonin Scalia, all conservatives. Reagan beefed up the military, the CIA, and developed the Star Wars plan. In 1982 he called the Soviet Union the "Evil Empire."

The seamy underside of politics was still evident in scandals such as Abscam and sex scandals like that which enveloped Gary Hart. One of the biggest scandals of the eighties was the Iran Contra Affair, a secret arms deal which made household names of Oliver North and John Poindexter. Reagan too was implicated, but he emerged from the scandal with his popularity unscathed. Reagan was sometimes called the "Teflon President" because nothing bad seemed to stick on him. When he left office in 1988, his approval ratings were higher than when he was elected in 1980.

Review the following timeline and see what *you* remember ...

1969 - 1989 Event Timeline
Economics and Politics

Year		Event
1960	Jan	John F. Kennedy announces his candidacy for President
1960	Feb	Congress hearings look into the payola scandal
1960	Feb	JFK makes the "missile gap" his campaign issue
1960	Apr	The Senate passes landmark Civil Rights Bill
1960	Jul	Republicans nominate Nixon for President
1960	Sep	Debates between Nixon and Kennedy televised
1960	Nov	JFK wins the Presidency
1961	Jan	Robert Frost recites *The Gift Outright* at JFK's inauguration
1961		23rd Amendment signed, giving DC representation but no vote in Congress
1961	Jan	First live, nationally televised Presidential news conference
1961	Mar	President Kennedy establishes the Peace Corps
1961	Mar	JFK sets up the Alliance for Progress
1961	Dec	Equal access rule goes into effect, on broadcasting time for political parties
1962		Michael Harrington's book *The Other America* published, asserting 25% of Americans live in poverty
1962	Feb	Supreme Court disallows race separation on public transportation
1962	Mar	JFK says US will resume above-ground nuclear testing
1962	Apr	Seven major steel mills cancel a price hike under presidential orders
1962	May	AFL-CIO starts campaign for 35-hour work week
1962	May	US stock market drops $20.8 Billion in one day
1962	Jul	Senate rejects Medicare for the aged
1962	Nov	Edward M. Kennedy first elected to the Senate
1962	Nov	Nixon quits politics and says, "you won't have Nixon to kick around anymore"
1962	Dec	114-day newspaper strike begins in New York City
1963	Jan	George Wallace elected Governor of Alabama; he says: "segregation now, segregation tomorrow, segregation forever."
1963	Feb	CIA Domestic Operations Division created
1963	Jun	JFK says segregation is morally wrong and that it is "time to act."
1963	Nov	JFK assassinated in Dallas, Texas. Lyndon B. Johnson becomes President
1963	Nov	LBJ sets up the Warren Commission to investigate the assassination of JFK

1964	Jan	Teamsters negotiate the first national labor contract
1964	Jan	24th Amendment to the Constitution goes into effect; voting rights cannot be denied due to failure to pay taxes
1964	Jan	Senator Margaret Chase Smith tries for the Republican Presidential bid
1964	May	LBJ declares "War on Poverty" and presents his "Great Society"
1964	May	Economic Opportunity Act signed, creating the Job Corps, Vista, Medicare, Medicaid, food stamps, and HUD
1964	Jun	83-day Southern filibuster ends; Civil Rights act is signed into law by LBJ
1964	Jul	Republicans nominate Barry Goldwater for President
1964	Aug	Teamsters leader Jimmy Hoffa gets prison term for defrauding the union
1964	Sep	Wilderness Act signed into law by LBJ
1964	Sep	Warren Commission finds Lee Harvey Oswald acted alone
1965		United Farm Workers begin 5 year grape boycott to protest conditions of migrant workers
1965	Jan	Martin Luther King begins a drive to register black voters
1965	Feb	Martin Luther King and 700 demonstrators arrested in Selma, Alabama
1965	Jul	LBJ signs Medicare bill, which goes into effect in 1966
1965	Aug	Federal Voting Rights Act guarantees black voting rights
1966	Jan	12-day transit strike shuts down the NY City subway system
1966	Jan	LBJ says US will stay in Vietnam until communist aggression ends
1966	Jan	Robert Weaver is first black person selected for President's cabinet (HUD)
1966	Mar	Selective Service announces college deferments based on grades
1966	Mar	Massive anti-war demonstrations in US, Europe, Australia
1966	Mar	25,000 anti-war demonstrators march in New York City
1966	May	Federal education funding denied to 12 school districts in the South because of violations of 1964 Civil Rights Act
1966	Jul	LBJ signs the Freedom of Information Act
1966	Jul	Governor Rhodes declares state of emergency in Cleveland due to race riots
1966	Nov	Edward Brooke first black person elected to the US Senate
1966	Nov	Ronald Reagan elected Governor of California
1966	Nov	LBJ signs anti-trust immunity to AFL-NFL merger
1967		Race riots in many American cities throughout the year
1967	Jan	Lester Maddox, avowed segregationist, inaugurated as Governor of Georgia

1967	Mar	House of Representatives expels Adam Clayton Powell
1967	Jun	Thurgood Marshall is first black Supreme Court Justice
1967	Jun	Governor Reagan signs liberalized California abortion bill
1967	Oct	Thousands protesting the war storm the Pentagon
1967	Oct	4 people from Baltimore pour blood on selective service records
1968	Feb	Richard Nixon announces candidacy for President
1968	Feb	First US Teachers strike, in Florida
1968	Feb	Tear gas used to stop demonstration at Alcorn A&M
1968	Mar	Martin Luther King announces Poor People's Campaign
1968	Mar	Robert F. Kennedy announces candidacy for President
1968	Mar	Howard Univ. students seize administration building
1968	Mar	Bill removes gold backing from US paper money
1968	Mar	LBJ announces he will not seek re-election
1968	Apr	Martin Luther King assassinated in Memphis
1968	Apr	LBJ signs the 1968 Civil Rights Act
1968	May	The "March of Poor" under Rev. Abernathy reaches Washington DC
1968	May	Truth in Lending Act signed into law
1968	Jun	Robert Kennedy assassinated in Los Angeles, by Sirhan Sirhan
1968	Jun	Supreme Court bans racial discrimination in sale and rental of housing
1968	Jun	50,000 participate in Solidarity Day March of Poor People's campaign
1968	Aug	Democratic Convention opens in Chicago while police and demonstrators meet in a bloody clash on the streets outside
1968	Aug	Hubert Humphrey wins Democratic nomination
1968	Aug	George Wallace announces his bid for the presidency
1968	Nov	Nixon wins presidency
1968	Dec	Nixon names Henry Kissinger as Security Advisor
1969		Race riots in nearly every major American city
1969		Anti war protests held in many American cities
1969	Jan	Congress doubles the presidential salary
1969	Jan	Nixon inaugurated as president
1969	Mar	Chicago 8 indicted in the aftermath of Chicago Democratic Convention
1969	Jun	Warren Burger is confirmed as US Chief Justice
1969	Oct	Vietnam Moratorium Day: millions protest the war
1969	Oct	Ralph Nader sets up a consumer organization known as Nader's Raiders
1969	Nov	VP Spiro Agnew accuses TV news of bias and distortion
1969	Nov	250,000 peacefully demonstrate against Vietnam War in Washington DC

1969	Dec	US government holds first draft lottery since WWII
1969	Dec	Police pull surprise attack on Black Panthers in Los Angeles
1970		Hundreds of thousands across America demonstrate against the war
1970	Jan	UCLA fires Angela Davis for being a communist
1970	Feb	Nixon launches the "Nixon Doctrine"
1970	Mar	The end of US commercial whale hunting
1970	Mar	Supreme Court rules that draft evaders cannot be penalized after 5 years
1970	Mar	Nuclear non-proliferation treaty goes into effect
1970	Mar	San Francisco city employees begin a 4-day strike
1970	May	National Guard kills 4 students at Kent State in Ohio, during anti-war rally
1970	May	Construction workers break up an anti-war rally in NYC's Wall Street
1970	May	Harry Blackmun confirmed as Justice of Supreme Court
1970	Jun	26th Amendment lowers voting age to 18
1970	Sep	Nixon requests 1000 new FBI agents for college campuses
1970	Oct	Angela Davis arrested in NYC
1970	Nov	Trial of Seattle-8 Anti-war protesters begins
1970	Nov	Spiro Agnew calls TV executives "impudent snobs"
1970	Dec	Environmental Protection Agency begins
1970	Dec	Unemployment increases to 5.8%
1970	Dec	OSHA (Occupational Safety & Health Act) enacted
1971		Ralph Nader establishes "Public Citizen," a consumer lobby
1971	Feb	Nixon installs a secret taping system into the White House
1971	Apr	Supreme Court upholds busing to achieve racial desegregation
1971	Apr	Columbia University operations virtually end, because of student strike
1971	May	Government arrests 13,000 anti-war protesters in 3 days
1971	May	Nixon rejects 60 demands of Congressional Black Caucus
1971	Jun	NY Times begins publishing the "Pentagon Papers"
1971	Jun	Daniel Ellsberg indicted for leaking the Pentagon Papers
1971	Jun	Supreme Court overturns draft evasion conviction of Muhammad Ali
1971	Jul	White House Plumbers unit formed to plug news leaks, in response to the Pentagon Papers
1971	Aug	Nixon announces a 90-day freeze on wages, prices and rents
1971	Aug	FBI begins covert investigation of journalist Daniel Schorr
1971	Aug	Nixon announces US will no longer convert dollars abroad into gold, to halt inflation
1971	Sep	Liddy and Hunt break into Ellsberg's psychiatrist's office

1972	Jan	Committee to Re-Elect the President (CREEP) formed
1972	Feb	Columnist Jack Anderson discloses that anti-trust charges against ITT were dropped in exchange for contribution to the Republican Party
1972	Feb	Strom Thurmond suggests John Lennon be deported
1972	Feb	Nixon becomes the first President to visit China
1972	Mar	Congress approves the Equal Rights Amendment
1972	May	NY Times wins Pulitzer for coverage of Pentagon Papers
1972	May	Assassination attempt on Governor George Wallace
1972	May	John Lennon says his phone is tapped by the FBI
1972	May	White House Plumbers break into the Democratic National HQ at the Watergate Apts
1972	Jun	5 arrested for burglarizing the Democratic Headquarters
1972	Jun	Nixon and Haldeman use CIA to cover up Watergate
1972	Jul	Thomas Eagleton withdraws as Democratic VP candidate after admitting he once received psychotherapy
1972	Aug	First Washington Post article by Bernstein-Woodward exposing the Watergate scandal
1972	Aug	Republican Convention re-nominates Nixon and Agnew
1972	Nov	Nixon re-elected over George McGovern
1972	Nov	Dow Jones closes above 1000 for the first time
1973	Jan	LBJ dies
1973	Jan	Roe vs. Wade at the Supreme Court legalizes abortions
1973	Jan	Trial of the Watergate burglars begins
1973	Jan	Watergate defendants Liddy and McCord found guilty
1973	Feb	Nixon signs Endangered Species Act
1973	Feb	Gold goes up $10 overnight to a record $95 an ounce
1973	Feb	American Indian Movement (AIM) occupy Wounded Knee in South Dakota
1973	Mar	John Dean tells Nixon, "There is a cancer growing on the Presidency."
1973	Apr	Nixon announces resignation of Haldeman and Erlichman
1973	May	Indians holding Wounded Knee surrender
1973	May	Daniel Ellsberg acquitted of theft of Pentagon Papers
1973	May	Senate Watergate hearings begin
1973	May	Thomas Bradley elected first black mayor of Los Angeles
1973	Aug	Spiro Agnew calls reports that he took kickbacks from government contracts in Maryland "damned lies" and vows not to resign as Vice President
1973	Sep	Henry Kissinger sworn in as Secretary of State
1973	Oct	Spiro Agnew pleads no contest to tax evasion, and resigns as Vice President
1973	Oct	Nixon nominates Gerald Ford to replace Agnew as VP
1973	Oct	OPEC oil embargo begins

Sharing My Stories—In Camelot the Heroes Die

I remember the Nixon-Kennedy TV debates, because my father forced me to listen to them. He said they were a part of history. I was only ten so most of what they said passed right over my head. During the commercials my father made disparaging comments about Kennedy — although my father had been devoted to FDR, by 1960 he was a devout Republican. So Dad told me that we admired Nixon. I agreed – out loud.

But in my heart I liked Kennedy better. He was so witty, so handsome, so charming, so utterly unlike all those old dreary boring people who were on the news my father also insisted I watch. I fantasized that I was JFK's niece, or something like that. Since I was only ten it never occurred to me to fantasize about being his wife. Besides, I was also enamored of Jackie – so glamorous, so beautiful, and so young. She looked like a movie star, startlingly out of place in the midst of those gray-faced, gray-haired politicians. Jack and Jackie gleamed like polished rubies, deep throbbing red, set amid a gray wasteland of gravel. None of this could I explain to my father, who I knew would scoff at my girlish reasons.

When JFK was killed I was shocked and upset, but I was still too young to feel personally bereaved. JFK had always seemed like a fantasy to me anyway. My father made me watch JFK's funeral on TV, again because it was living history. What I remember best was the sound of the lone bugle playing taps, and the image of John-John saluting. It made me sob, but even as young as I was, I remember being resentful that my emotions were being manipulated by this "show" on TV.

When Martin Luther King was murdered in 1968, my emotions were more my own. I was 19 and my primary emotion was anger. I was furious not so much at the man who they say killed him, but at the society which accepted as normal that a message of brotherhood and tolerance could get you killed. I suspected that the "establishment," as we called it those days, was really to blame in some way.

My anger fueled my politics. I was a supporter of Bobby Kennedy, who I believed was a fierce fighter for justice. When he was murdered, only two months after King, I fell into a kind of cynical despair. Grieving was too painful, and I was tired of being angry. Grief and anger got you nowhere. What was the use?

Bobby Kennedy was the last politician I ever "believed in." It was too dangerous to believe in a hero. Heroes got killed.

Writing Topic Suggestions
Economics & Politics

Pick one of the topics below and write for fifteen to twenty minutes. Remember the un-rules:

- Don't stop writing until the limit is up.
- Use "trigger sentences" if you get stuck.
- Don't be polite.
- Be specific and remember you have at least five senses.
- You don't have to be right, rational or logical.
- Forget about the rules of grammar or spelling.
- Trust yourself.

Remember, you are creating a *primary source*. Write about what you *did*, what you *saw*, what you *thought*, what you *felt*.

1. Scan the timelines. What event sparks a memory? Is there an event listed that makes you think, "Oh, yeah, I remember that!"? If so, write about that event. Were you involved? How did you learn about it? Did you talk about it? With whom? Were you inspired to do something because of this event? Did this event change your life in any way? Did it change your thinking?

2. Did you belong to a union? Did you or any family member or friend participate in a strike? Or were you on the side of management? Did you ever work for a company or organization that had union troubles? Were you a scab or a picketer? Did strikes have an effect on your daily life?

3. What was your first job? What did you do, how old were you, what were you paid? How did you get the job? What did you like

about the job? What didn't you like? Or describe your favorite job; what made that job so great?

4. Do you remember the Depression? How old were you? Were your parents worried or scared? Did they lose money, or were they out of work? Did you stand in bread or dole lines, or did your parents? Did you wear hand-me-downs? Did you have enough to eat? What kind of work did you, or your parents do? Who was to blame for the Depression?

5. Do you remember shortages or rationing during World War Two? How did this affect your life? For instance, did you paint lines down the backs of your legs to look like silk stockings? Did you collect scrap metal or grease, or participate in paper or string drives? Did you learn how to cook without sugar? Did you take the bus instead of drive because gas was rationed? Did you agree with the necessity of rationing? Did saving and rationing make you feel patriotic?

6. Did you participate in any New Deal programs, such as the CCCs or WPA? If so, describe what you did. How did it change your life? For example, if you were in the CCCs, did you fight forest fires, or plant trees, or work in National Forests? Did the New Deal programs help your economic status?

7. How were you affected by the recession and inflation of the 1970s? What did you think about Nixon freezing prices, wages and rents? How did this affect you? Did you lose out on a raise? Were you a landlord who couldn't raise the rent? During the oil crisis, did you stand in long gas lines? Were you concerned about America's dependence on foreign oil? What did you think the answer was?

8. Were you active in the stock market during the 1980s? Did Black Monday of 1987 affect you? How? Or were you affected by a takeover, merger or acquisition? If you company was involved in such, was it a good thing or a bad thing? How did it feel to be "taken over" or "bought out"?

9. Did you ever work for a political party? Which one? Was there a special candidate or issue you campaigned for? Tell about a campaign you remember. What did you do for the campaign? Why did you feel so strongly? Did you win or lose? Tell what election day or night felt like. Were you excited and elated, or downhearted? If your issue or candidate won, how did it change the community, state or country? If your issue or candidate lost, what did the community lose? Did you or anyone you know ever run for political office? If you or anyone you knew held political office, what did you or they accomplish during their term?

10. When did you begin to participate in the American political process? Do you remember the first time you cast your ballot? Who or what was it for? Did you win or lose? Where was your polling place? Did you feel empowered by voting?

11. Do you remember which presidential candidates you voted for? FDR, Truman, Eisenhower, or Wilkie, Dewey or Stevenson? Kennedy or Nixon? Johnson or Goldwater? Nixon or McGovern? Carter or Ford? Reagan? Bush or Dukakis? Why?

12. FDR was a controversial figure during the thirties and forties. Not everyone loved him. What did you think about FDR? Did you think he was increasing the power of the federal government too much? Did his leadership make you feel hopeful, or safe? What was your opinion about Eleanor Roosevelt? Did you think she was too active in political life, for a woman? Were FDR or ER your heroes, or the heroes of your parents or teachers? Did you look up to politicians with admiration and respect? Did you dream about becoming a politician yourself?

13. Were you afraid of communism during the 1950s? What were you told about communism and what it would do to America? What did you think about Joseph McCarthy? Did you watch any TV proceedings? Did you know anyone who was blacklisted? Did you know any communists? Were you a communist?

14. Which "sides" were you on during the polarized sixties? Were you divided by the generation gap from your parents or your children? Or were you divided by race, or the poor vs the rich, or liberal vs conservative? Did you know you were on a side? What names did you call the other side? Did you trust anyone over 30? Were you a member of the "establishment?"

15. Did you participate in protests during the sixties? Did you think protests, rallies and marches were effective political tools? Did you feel "swept up" in the emotions of this decade? Did you march on freeways, get arrested, or know know anyone who was? During the protests, were you afraid, or committed to a cause, or exhilarated by danger? Did you feel you were making a difference by making your voice heard? Or were you a member of the "silent majority" and feel that protests and rallies were just an excuse for lawlessness?

16. How did the assassinations and attempted assassinations of the sixties, seventies and eighties affect you? Do you remember "where you were" when JFK was shot? Or Martin Luther King? Or Bobby Kennedy? Or George Wallace? Or Ronald Reagan? How did you react — with anger, sadness, fear?

17. What did Watergate mean to you? Were you surprised at the revelation of "dirty tricks" from the President and his aides? When were you convinced of Nixon's guilt – or were you ever convinced? Did this issue cause divisiveness in your own family? Did it change the way you viewed the government? Do you think Nixon should have been impeached? What did you feel when Nixon resigned?

18. Did you know what the Iran Contra affair of 1986 was all about? Were you scandalized or had you become inured to scandals? Did you think Oliver North was an upright patriot or an amoral idiot? Did the Iran Contra hearings enhance or tarnish your opinion of Ronald Reagan?

Or anything else you want to write about …

Chapter Eleven
The Social Fabric
Sin & Morality, Sexual Roles, Race & Religion

If politics and economics form the structure of societies, then social and ethical mores are the fabric hung on that structure. In this chapter we explore attitudes: our prejudices and beliefs, our ideas of sin and morality, our notions of right and wrong, proper and improper, good and bad.

There is no question that social attitudes toward race, the sexes, morality and religion changed dramatically from 1930 through 1989. What was often unacceptable or even unspeakable in 1930 had become openly discussed and "no big deal" by 1989.

1930 through 1959

Sin

The concept of "sin" promulgated by the band of European Protestants known as "The Puritans" has colored American attitudes since the 1600s. Often what was considered sinful was mixed up with things pleasurable.

This can be seen in our changeable and often contradictory attitudes toward alcohol. Prohibition was repealed in 1933, changing millions of Americans from "criminals" to law-abiding citizens overnight. Temperance seemed to be dead, yet two years later Alcoholics Anonymous was founded and flourished, and many cities enacted "blue laws" restricting and controlling the sale of liquor. Many comedians from vaudeville to TV made careers out of portraying drunks for laughs. We couldn't seem to make up our minds whether drinking was funny or tragic, classy or dissolute.

"Ben's" father was a doctor during the Depression, thus it was legal for him to have alcohol, which he could prescribe

for medicinal purposes. He kept his bottles of whiskey in a cabinet in his bedroom, to foil those looking to steal it. "We had so many burglaries my father started sleeping with a loaded shotgun by his bed," shared Ben. "Some of his patients were so desperate for booze that Dad was worried he might even be killed for it."

Smoking, today considered a terrible vice, was not only socially acceptable but often the epitome of classiness and sex appeal. Movie stars blew smoke rings into each other's faces while gazing soulfully in each other's eyes. Tough guy soldiers always had their smokes, and indeed cigarettes were issued along with C-rations during World War II, and were a staple on the black market. Women began smoking in increasing numbers.

Gambling underwent a reputation upgrade. While still considered immoral by many, casinos and lotto were no longer run only by criminal elements. Racetrack betting became legal in California in 1933, and over the next six years, betting on horses became legal again in another 21 states, as governments tried to find revenue in the midst of along with quickie divorces, enabling the growth of Las Vegas and Reno. The Flamingo Hotel was built in Las Vegas in 1946, starting an era of glamour, glitz and legalized greed.

Finally, there is a huge gulf between the sexual attitudes of the thirties, forties and fifties and those of today. One of the controversial topics of the day was contraception and birth control. Margaret Sanger opened contraception clinics in the 1930s, the precursor to Planned Parenthood. The clinics disseminated information and sometimes condoms. They were often condemned as immoral, and sometimes even banned by cities. The Vatican finally gave the nod to the rhythm method in the thirties, but condemned all other forms of birth control, a stance they still adhere to today.

Sexuality was not openly discussed, especially in the media. Censorship in movies, radio and television was focused on sex. Married couples in the movies slept in single beds. In bedroom scenes actors had to keep one foot on the floor. When Lucille Ball got pregnant in the early 1950s, the television censors decreed the word "pregnant" could not be used on television. Instead the episode in which she announced the coming event was titled "Lucy is Enciente." (Enciente is French for pregnant; evidently the censors felt that pregnancy was less suggestive in French.) Alfred Kinsey published *Sexual Behavior of the Human Male* in 1948, known popularly as the Kinsey Report, and caused a sensation. *Sexual Behavior in the Human Female* followed a few years later. These books were not considered acceptable reading for unmarried women.

Good girls of the thirties, forties and fifties were expected to be virgins upon marriage, although many of course were not. At the same time it was considered advisable for a young man to obtain sexual experience before he married. (Although not with *your* daughter or sister!) This double standard extended to the fruits of pre-marital sex. Girls got "in trouble" and boys "got girls in trouble." The burden of dealing with the unwanted pregnancy fell upon the woman, if she was unable to convince the man to marry her. Not only teenage girls, but women in their twenties and even thirties, were sent to "unwed mothers' homes" where they could hide their shame and keep family names unstained. Even so, the damage to their reputation was often irrevocable. They were no longer "good girls" and popular wisdom decreed that men would'nt marry them. Several women in my classes, freed by today's more liberal social conventions, have written about the babies they never saw, who were whisked away and never referred to again.

"Mary" shared her private April 14th ritual, the day her first child was born. She was 17 in 1943 when she got pregnant by a soldier on leave, who she never heard from again. Her middle-class parents, horrified and ashamed, sent her to live with a distant relative, where she gave birth to her child, whose sex she was not told, in a town far away. When she came home, her family welcomed her back from her

"trip." No one ever referred to this event again. She took up her normal life and got married a few years later. She had more children. The child she gave up for adoption never sought her out.

And every April 14th, from 1945 to today, she places a single pink tulip in a bud vase by her kitchen window and thinks about the child she never knew.

Gender Roles

Despite sexual strictures, women's "place" changed greatly during the thirties and forties. There were many "firsts." Women moved into public and political life, inspired by the towering figure of Eleanor Roosevelt, a First Lady with enormous power and the courage to use it. She was a hero to millions of American women and girls. Frances Perkins became the first woman in the cabinet as the Secretary of Labor. Hattie Caraway of Arkansas became the first female US Senator in 1932. Amelia Earhardt showed that women too could be daring, brave, and adventurous.

"Christine's" mother was independent and daring long before it was considered proper. Believing that no man would consider a wife who smoked and knew how to ride a motorcycle, she gave up on the idea of marriage rather than give up her independent ways. She became a foreign missionary, one of the few avenues open to women with a taste for adventure. She went to Singapore, where she married a European doctor whose prejudices against independent women were not so strict. "If Mother hadn't been a free spirit," said Christine, "I would not be here."

During the war, women entered the workforce in droves, replacing the men lost to the services, and "Rosie the Riveter" was born. They discovered that they could do a "man's job" and do it well. (Although they were still paid much less.)

"Cora" remembered her short stint as a "Rosie." She was a college girl in Michigan, and during the summer of 1942 she decided to spend her school break doing her bit for the war effort. She went to work in a factory that made army gear. Her job was to sew canvas inserts into backpacks, for which she was paid $1.02 an hour. Her swing shift foreman, a burly working man in his forties, called her "college girl" in a sneering tone, and often held up her work as an example on how to do it wrong. He picked on her relentlessly until he finally made her cry, and then he fired her. She was glad to go back to college, where she knew what she was doing.

"Rachel" shared that when her father went to war and her mother to factory work, the only one left to do house-work and tend to the younger children was her, then twelve. She did badly in school for the next few years, because she had no time to study. She had even less time for play. She was always cooking or cleaning. To this day she hates both.

"Linda" remembered her mother, a Lithuanian immigrant, working as a seamstress in a dark, overheated sweat shop. "My mother loathed her work," shared Linda. "She hated to sew, even though she was very good at it. Her dream for her daughters was for us to marry well so we'd never have to sew. She refused to teach us. I was married and a mother before I ever picked up a needle. Ironically, one of my daughters became an expert seamstress and then a clothing

designer, starting her own successful fashion company in the 1990s. Mom was dead by then, and I don't know if she would have been proud or not."

The WAVES, WACS, and the Women's Marine Corps were started, and women donned military uniforms and served their country. Women trained as pilots. Even in sports, women picked up the proverbial ball and people turned out to see them play baseball in the All American Girls Softball League. Harvard University turned co-ed in 1943, and in 1949 the first twelve women doctors graduated from the Harvard Medical School.

These changes were not always welcomed, and they were not universal, either. There were many people who thought Eleanor Roosevelt was too mouthy for a woman and should stay in the background where she belonged. Women were routinely paid much less than men for the same work, and they were seldom promoted or encouraged into higher education. College preparatory classes in high schools were often open only to the boys. Women teachers and women factory workers often had to quit their jobs when they married, because many school districts and factories would not employ married women.

"Mildred" remembered her job in a box factory. Her husband drank and did not provide enough money to support his family, so she was forced to work. The box factory did not employ married women, so she lied and said she was single. She could not admit to having any children, either, because the box factory only employed "moral" women, and only an "immoral" unmarried woman would have children. Mildred lived this double existence for over two years, until someone who knew her real situation turned her in to the management. However, because of her excellent work record and unfortunate family situation, the factory management

*graciously told her they would make an exception for her,
and she was allowed to keep her job.*

After the war, the gains women had made into public and business life dissipated to an extent. The baby boom was in full swing, and women were encouraged by social pressure to stay at home and go back to being full-time wives and mothers. Many women in my classes have written about how squelched they felt in the fifties. Change cannot be erased so easily, however, and there were signs that things had changed for good, such as the publication of Simone deBeauvoir's landmark book *The Second Sex* in 1949.

Race

Possibly no aspect of American life is as deeply woven into the social fabric as our consciousness of race. And few are as emotionally laden. Americans from the North and the West would like to think that racism was only a Southern problem, but this is not true. It existed everywhere.

*An immigrant from Egypt told of moving with her
husband to a small town in Idaho in the late 1940s. They
became an object of intense curiosity and scrutiny by everyone
in town. Total strangers took photos of them on the street.
People stopped them and asked them absurd questions, such
as, "Is it true that you have a tail?" No one knew how to
treat them because they could not be slotted into a racial
category. They weren't Indian. They weren't black. But they
certainly weren't white. Although no one was actively hostile
to them, no one befriended them either, and so they kept to
themselves. They lasted less than a year until they gave up
and moved to an Arab neighborhood within Los Angeles.*

The Civil Rights movement which hit its zenith in the 1960s was a force in the 1930s too. The NAACP was active and the "racial question" was visible in the media. There were some firsts for African-Americans in the 1930s and 1940s. The socially accepted practice of segregation was being increasingly questioned, especially in public institutions such as the military and the schools. During the war the armed forces were finally desegregated. Jackie Robinson broke the color barrier and was allowed to play major league baseball. None of this came easy. Vicious racist horrors such as lynchings continued to exist in the South. The celebrated blues singer, Bessie Smith, died in 1937 because a segregated hospital refused to treat her. The DAR refused to allow Marian Anderson to sing at the Lincoln Memorial until Eleanor Roosevelt interceded. All through these decades black Americans struggled with institutionalized inequities and well-intentioned white Americans struggled with their guilt.

"Jane" wrote a piece perfectly capturing white guilt over the "racial question." In 1947 she was a 21 year old white office worker in San Francisco. Each day she took the city bus back and forth to work. One evening she boarded the crowded bus and took a bench seat facing the aisle. She sat next to an elderly black woman. At the next stop, a man got on the bus. Jane described this man in detail, even though this incident had happened over fifty years before. He looked like a businessman in his fifties, wearing a well-cut blue suit. He carried an umbrella over his arm. He had pale blue eyes and nicely trimmed hair. The man made his way down the aisle and stopped in front of her and the elderly woman. Suddenly, and with no provocation, he raised his umbrella and brought it down with a zinging swat across the shoulder of the old woman.

The bus became absolutely quiet. No one said anything, not even the old woman who had been struck. She stared straight ahead. As if taking their cue from her, the rest of the passengers, including Jane, stared straight ahead too. No one said or did anything. But inside Jane, a tortured debate was going on. What should she do? What could she do? What he did was wrong, of course, but sometimes that was the way things were. But maybe she should say something. Say what? To whom? What good would it do? What if the man struck her too?

She was still debating internally when the old woman got off the bus at the next stop. An audible sigh of relief from the rest of the passengers could be heard.

After she finished reading her piece, Jane looked around the room. "I should have done or said something," she said. "I know that now. But at the time I didn't know I could." She added, "I've never told that story before. I guess I tried not to think about it, because it made me feel so bad."

In the 1950s, the modern Civil Rights era began. The "Jim Crow" laws came increasingly under attack, and were just as hotly defended. Freedom Riders, young northerners both white and black, came south to help register black voters. Martin Luther King began his ministry and mission. "Separate but equal" was shown to be a fallacy increasingly hard to believe. Drives and marches to integrate lunch counters, busses, water fountains, and especially schools became increasingly common. Rosa Parks made her historic bus ride. James Montgomery fought in the courts to be allowed to attend the University of Mississippi, and won. Brown vs. The Board of Education resulted in black students being allowed to attend previously all-white schools.

"Darlene" was sixteen in 1956, a middle-class white girl living in Georgia. "Today when I look back at how much unrest there was," she shared, "I wonder just where on earth I could have been. I had heard about 'the fuss' as my mother called it, but it seemed like a long way away. I had no idea that schools for black children were inferior to mine. I had never been in a black neighborhood, or had a black friend. My parents preached tolerance and equality, but they weren't activists. I think they just wanted a comfortable life, and they taught me to want the same."

Racism wasn't limited to African-Americans. After Pearl Harbor, Japanese Americans on the west coast were rounded up and put into internment camps, on the theory that they may harbor spies. Millions of loyal Americans lost their freedom, their businesses, their homes and their property, simply because of their race. No one suggested that German Americans should be subject to the same. After all, German Americans were white. There was little or no attempt to check the vicious racial slurs against the Japanese in the media, who portrayed them as grinning yellow apes.

"Bill," of Japanese descent, shared why he was not interned in one of the camps. He was born and raised in Hawaii, where Japanese Americans made up over thirty percent of the population. In fact, they were the largest ethnic/racial group in the state. It was a bitter irony, he wrote, that although the Japanese-Americans in California, Oregon and Washington were interned because they were geographically "close" to Japan, the Japanese-Americans of Hawaii, who were much closer, escaped this fate. Not because they were more trustworthy, but because without them the economic life of Hawaii could not possibly continue. The

whole state economy would crash. So the government made an exception, which they never explained.

"Sandy," a white girl, was eleven in 1941. One of her friends was a girl named Michiko. They played together in the chilly Seattle rain and giggled together in school. One day in early 1942 Michiko did not come to school, and her desk was given to another girl. When Sandy asked why, she was told that President Roosevelt said the Japanese must be sent away, because they were spies. Sandy was surprised to learn that Michiko was a spy, but if President Roosevelt said so, it must be true. Sandy never saw Michiko again. Until taking this class, she had never talked about her. She began to cry as she read the last line of her piece: "I never got to tell her how sorry I was that I had believed that lie."

Religion

Faced with the brutal truth of the Holocaust, Americans were prompted to examine the anti-Semitism that existed in their own country. The movie *Gentlemen's Agreement*, which dealt with this subject, was a controversial and popular film made in 1947. American anti-Semitism existed in subtle and not-so-subtle forms.

"Lucy" remembered moving into a newly developed suburban neighborhood during the early 1950s, a true "Leave it to Beaver" land where all the houses were built to the same design, the neighbors vied for the prettiest lawns, the women traded cookie recipes, and the children rode their bikes freely between each others' houses. One Christmas they instituted a neighborhood competition for the best outdoor display. All the neighbors participated except for one family, whose house remained dark and still amid the gaudy red and

green lights, reindeer, and nativity scenes. This was how the neighborhood discovered that this family was Jewish. They called a neighborhood meeting to discuss how to handle the eyesore of a dark house in the middle of a Christmas street, and how they could force their neighbor to enter into the spirit of the season. Faced with the unpalatable truth that there was nothing they could do, they resorted to an old and cruel technique: they shunned and ignored the Jewish family. From that time onward, that family was no longer invited to barbeques or card parties, or asked to join any neighborhood functions. No one called this anti-Semitism, of course.

Another hotly debated religious topic during these decades was the argument over prayer in the public schools. Generations of children remember starting off their school day with a Christian prayer, even if they were not Christian. In 1948 the U.S. Supreme Court decided that prayer and religious instruction in public schools were unconstitutional.

Many well known religious leaders started their careers during these decades, including the Dalai Lama, who in 1940 at the age of 5 became the religious leader of Tibet; Father Charles Coughlin, the "Radio Priest," whose anti-Semitism and diatribes against FDR in the thirties and forties gathered him millions of listeners; Billy Graham, who began his Crusades in 1950 with his radio show *Hour of Decision*; L. Ron Hubbard, who started the Church of Scientology in 1950; and Sun Myung Moon, who started the Unification Church in Korea in 1954.

Review the following timeline and see what *you* remember …

1930 – 1959 Events Timeline
The Social Fabric

1930	May	Supreme Court rules it's okay to buy liquor
1930	June	NY Times agrees to capitalize the "n" in "Negro"
1930	Dec	Pope releases Encyclical against mixed marriages
1930	Dec	US tobacco industry produced 123 billion cigarettes in 1930
1931	Jan	Pope Pius XI issues encyclical against birth control, approving only the rhythm method
1931	Mar	Scottsboro Boys, accused of raping a white woman, arrested in Alabama
1931	Mar	Nevada legalizes gambling and quick divorces
1932	Jan	Hattie W. Caraway elected first woman senator
1932	May	"We Want Beer!" parade in New York
1932	May	Hoover honors Amelia Earhart with medal, first woman to complete solo transatlantic flight
1933	Mar	Frances Perkins becomes Secretary of Labor, first woman cabinet member
1933	Mar	NAACP begins attack on segregation & discrimination
1933	Mar	Nevada becomes first state to regulate narcotics
1933	May	First female director of US Mint takes office
1933	Jun	French visionary Bernadette of Lourdes is canonized
1933	Nov	Pennsylvania overturns blue law, permit Sunday sports
1933	Nov	First state liquor store in US is authorized in Pennsylvania
1933	Nov	Eleanor Roosevelt opens White House Conference on Women's Problems
1933	Dec	21st Amendment ratified, repealing Prohibition
1933		Racetrack betting becomes legal in California
1934	Jun	W.E.B. DuBois resigns his position at NAACP
1934	Jun	US Indian Reorganization Act becomes law, seeking to return lands to tribal ownership
1934	Nov	Arthur Mitchell is first black Democratic congressman
1935	June	Smith & Wilson form Alcoholics Anonymous
1935	Nov	U of Maryland has to admit black student Donald Murray
1935	Dec	National Council of Negro Women formed by Mary McLeod Bethune
1936	Feb	National Negro Congress organizes in Chicago
1936	May	Poll shows that two-thirds of Americans favor birth control
1936	Dec	NAACP sues for equal pay for black and white teachers
1937	Mar	First state contraceptive clinic in US opens in Raleigh NC
1937	Jun	American Medical Association approves birth control
1937	July	Alabama drops charges against 5 black men accused of rape in Scottsboro

1937	Aug	Marijuana is outlawed
1937	Sep	Blues singer Bessie Smith dies after a car accident when a segregated hospital refuses to treat her
1938	Jan	First woman president of a US National Bank announced
1938	Jan	Benny Goodman refuses to play Carnegie Hall when black members of his band barred from performing
1938	July	NY Yankees suspend Jake Powell, after he said on Chicago radio that he'd "hit every colored person in Chicago over the head with a club."
1938	Nov	First black woman legislator, Crystal Fauset, of Philadelphia
1938	Nov	First documented anti-Semitic remarks by Father Coughlin
1939	Mar	Eugenio Pacelli chosen as Pope Pius XII
1940	Feb	A five year old boy is enthroned as Tibet's new Dalai Lama
1940	May	AVRO-chairman Willem Vogt fires all Jewish employees
1940	May	Richard Wright's *Native Son* published, breakthrough for black writers
1940	Jun	American Negro Theater organizes
1940	Sep	Black leaders protest discrimination in US armed forces
1940	Sep	First merchant ship commanded by black captain launched
1940	Oct	First black general in regular army named
1941	Apr	Supreme Court rules blacks are entitled to all first class services on railroad trains
1941	Jun	At Eleanor's urging, FDR issues Executive Order 8802 forbidding discrimination
1941	Jul	First US Army flying school for black cadets is dedicated
1941	Oct	First woman jockey in North America rides in Mexico
1942	Feb	LA Times urges security measures against Japanese Americans
1942	Feb	Congress tells FDR that Americans of Japanese descent should be locked up so they wouldn't oppose the war effort
1942	Feb	Internment of all west-coast Japanese Americans
1942	Feb	Race riot in Detroit
1942	Mar	2 black players, Jackie Robinson and Nate Moreland, allowed to work out with Chicago White Sox
1942	Mar	Julia Flikke becomes 1ˢᵗ woman colonel in US Army
1942	May	US Women's Army Auxiliary Corps (WAAC) founded
1942	May	US Navy first permits black recruits to serve
1942	Jul	FDR signs bill creating women's Navy Auxiliary agency
1942	Dec	Supreme Court rules Nevada divorces are valid in all states
1943	Jan	William Hastie, aide to Secretary of War, resigns to protest segregation in the armed forces
1943	Feb	Women's Marine Corps created
1943	Feb	Phil Wrigley and Branch Rickey form All-American Girls Softball League

1943	Mar	First woman to receive a medal in the Air Force, Elsie Ott
1943	May	Alabama shipyard riot protest s upgrade of 2 black workers
1943	Jun	Race riot in Beaumont, Texas
1943	Jun	National Congress of Racial Equality organizes
1943	Jun	Federal troops put down race riot in Detroit in which 30 die
1943	Aug	Race riot in Harlem
1943	Sep	Classes at Harvard go co-ed
1943	Dec	Commissioner Landis announces any baseball club may sign Negroes
1943	Dec	W.E.B. DuBois is 1st black member of National Institute of Arts & Letters
1944	Jan	Ralph Bunche appointed 1st black official in US State Dept.
1944	Jan	First Chinese naturalized US citizen since repeal of exclusion acts
1944	Feb	First black reporter accredited to the White House, Harry McAlpin
1944	Apr	Supreme Court finds "white primaries" unconstitutional
1944	Apr	United Negro College Fund incorporates
1944	Aug	Adam Clayton Powell elected first black congressman
1944	Aug	Race riots in Athens, Alabama
1944	Sep	Massachusetts lifts ban on the novel *Strange Fruit* about an interracial love affair
1944	Dec	Japanese Americans released from detention camps
1945	Jan	Youth for Christ organized
1945	Mar	International Women's Day first observed
1945	Mar	New York is first state to prohibit discrimination by race and creed in employment
1945	May	Formation of the Negro Baseball League
1945	Sep	1000 whites walk out of Indiana schools, protesting integration
1945	Oct	Jackie Robinson signs with Montreal Royals
1945	Nov	First issue of *Ebony* magazine published
1946	July	Frances Xavier Cabrini canonized as 1st American saint
1946	Aug	First coin bearing portrait of a Negro is authorized
1946	Nov	Oregon's Indians are granted land payment rights
1946	Dec	President Truman creates Committee on Civil Rights
1946	Dec	Univ. of Tennessee refuses to play Duquesne University, because they may use a black player in their basketball game
1946	Dec	Flamingo Hotel in Las Vegas opens
1947	Apr	Jackie Robinson becomes the first black player in major league baseball
1947	Oct	NAACP petition on racism presented to the UN
1948	Jul	6 female reservists become first women in US Army
1948	Sep	Alfred Kinsey's *Sexual Behavior in the Human Male* published

Sharing My Stories—Singing the Fifties Rag

My mother graduated from high school in 1939, making her better educated than most of the girls from her hometown. Most girls viewed school as simply marking time until they married. Mom was popular and pretty and could have married if she wanted to. But instead she left home and went to college, the very first girl from that town to ever do so. She was written up in the local paper because of her brave, pioneering spirit.

In the 1940s Mom left college to work for the war effort. She was a secretary during the day, and at night worked for the Civil Air Patrol or danced her feet off at the USO. When she saw a newsreel with Eleanor Roosevelt praising women serving in the WACs and WAVEs, Mom was inspired with even more patriotic fervor, and she joined the Marines! (She chose them was she believed their uniform was the best looking.) The Marines sent her to boot camp in South Carolina, a thrill for her because she had never been out of Washington State. After boot camp she served in Philadelphia with the War Department as a secretary.

In the 1960s and 70s, Mom joined, and often ran, volunteer groups. Although terrified of speaking in public, she joined Toastmistress. Then Mom contracted breast cancer and lost her right breast. Two weeks after she came home from the hospital, she put on her prettiest suit, had her hair fixed beautifully, and as a volunteer for Reach for Recovery, set off to visit women who had recently had mastectomies – to give them hope that they too, could recover.

In the 1980s and 90s, Mom traveled, exploring places as diverse and remote as Antarctica, the USSR, South Africa, China, Japan, New Zealand, South America, the Galapagos Islands, – you name it, Mom's been there.

But what of the Fifties? She got married — and changed. She had babies, like millions of other American women, and disappeared into her house. The mother of my childhood was a housewife wearing bouffant skirts, frilly aprons and a lacquered hairstyle. She cooked dinner and cleaned the house and did the laundry. She deferred to her husband. She sat in the passenger seat of the car. She covered her mouth when she laughed. Even though I know she was there, I can't quite remember anything she did or said when I was a child. In my childhood memories she is always in the background, never in the center. It was as though the Fifties pressed a damp gray rag over her face. Thank God they are gone! Thank God she came back.

1948	Sep	Margaret Chase Smith elected Senator, first woman to serve in both houses of Congress
1948	Jan	Executive Order ends segregation in US Armed Forces
1948	Mar	Supreme Court rules that religious instruction in public schools is unconstitutional
1948	May	Glenn Taylor, white Idaho Senator, arrested in Alabama, for trying to enter a door marked "for Negroes"
1948	Oct	Calif. Court voids law banning interracial marriages
1949	Jun	First women graduate from Harvard Medical School
1949	Sep	Simone de Beauvoir's *The Second Sex* is published
1949	Oct	American Contract Bridge League votes to keep blacks out
1950	Feb	L. Ron Hubbard's book *Dianetics* published, leading to the establishment of the Church of Scientology
1950	Apr	Chuck Cooper becomes the 1st black player in the NBA
1950	May	Billy Graham launches weekly radio show, *Hour of Decision*
1950	Jun	1st US Negro delegate to UN appointed, E.S. Sampson
1950	Dec	1st black American awarded Nobel Prize, Ralph Bunche
1951	May	Segregation in Washington DC restaurants is ruled illegal
1951	Nov	*Jet* Magazine founded
1952		Norman Vincent Peale publishes *The Power of Positive Thinking*
1952	Jan	University of Tennessee admits its first black student
1952	Jun	Christine Jorgensen becomes first transsexual to go public
1952	Dec	Tuskegee Institute reports 1952 as first year since 1881 with no lynchings
1952	Dec	First' human birth televised
1952	Dec	First TV acknowledgement of pregnancy, on *I Love Lucy*
1953	Apr	Pope Pius XII approves psychoanalysis for Catholics
1953	Jun	Segregated lunch counters forbidden by Supreme Court
1953	Sep	Kinsey's *Sexual Behavior in the Human Female* published
1954	Feb	Michigan Rep. Ruth Thompson introduces law to ban "obscene, lewd, lascivious or filthy" rock & roll records
1954	May	Supreme Court unanimously rules in Brown v Topeka Board of Education, reversing 1896 "separate but equal" Plessy v Ferguson decision
1954	Jun	Reverend Sun Myung Moon founds the Unification Church
1954	Jul	First White Citizens Council organizes in Indianola, Miss.
1954	Sep	School integration begins in Washington DC public schools
1954	Oct	Defense Dept. announces elimination of all segregated regiments
1955	Jan	Marion Anderson is the first black person to sing at the Metropolitan Opera House in New York City
1955	Apr	All US coins to bear motto "In God We Trust"

1955	May	Supreme Court orders school integration "with all deliberate speed"
1955	Jun	The League of Decency pressures theaters to remove posters of Marilyn Monroe holding down her dress in *The Seven Year Itch*
1955	Dec	Bus boycott begins in Montgomery AL, with Rosa Parks
1955	Dec	Pope Pius XII releases encyclical on popular music
1956	Jan	Presbyterian Church begins accepting women ministers
1956	Jan	Martin Luther King Jr's home is bombed
1956	Feb	Autherine Lucy admitted to University of Alabama, but suspended days later because of a riot
1956	Apr	Singer Nat King Cole attacked on stage of Birmingham theater by whites
1956	May	Bus boycott begins in Tallahassee, Florida
1956	Aug	White mob prevents enrollment of blacks at Texas high school
1956	Sep	First International conference of black writers and artists
1957	Feb	Georgia Senate unanimously approves Senator Leon Butts' bill barring blacks from playing baseball with whites
1957	May	The Prayer Pilgrimage, biggest civil rights demonstration to date, takes place in Washington DC
1957	May	Billy Graham launches his first crusade at Madison Square Garden
1957	Jun	Tuskegee Boycott begins, blacks boycotting city stores
1957	Jul	Althea Gibson becomes first black tennis player to win Wimbledon
1957	Aug	Strom Thurmond ends 24 hour filibuster against civil rights
1957	Aug	Congress passes the Civil Rights Act of 1957
1957	Sep	Eisenhower orders US troops to desegregate Little Rock AR schools
1957	Sep	300 US Army troops guard 9 black kids at Central High School in Little Rock, Arkansas
1957	Sep	Pope Pius XII releases encyclical on movies, radio and TV
1958	Aug	NAACP begins sit-ins at Oklahoma City lunch counters
1958	Oct	Angelo Roncalli elected Pope, takes name of John XXIII
1959	Apr	Vatican edict forbids Catholics for voting for communists
1959	May	Japanese Americans regain their citizenship
1959	Aug	Hiram Fong sworn in as first Chinese-American senator, & Daniel Inouye as first Japanese-American Representative, both from Hawaii
1959	Jun	Postmaster General bans D.H. Lawrence's book, *Lady Chatterley's Lover*

1960 through 1989

Social attitudes beginning in the sixties underwent immense changes in every sphere. These decades were polarized between opposing camps espousing irreconcilable moral differences: conservative vs liberal, rich vs poor, youth vs age, people of color vs white, women vs men, straight vs gay. The most difficult stance of all was middle of the road, and neutrality seemed non-existent.

The vast generation known as the "baby boomers" began to hit adolescence in the sixties and fueled the changes. They were the first generation of youth with real power, by virtue of their sheer numbers. The voting age was lowered to 18 in 1970, so they had some political clout as well. When they came of age, they looked around and didn't like what they saw. "Don't trust anyone over thirty," they warned. The "establishment," consisting of anyone in authority, was distrusted and suspected, beginning a cynicism that continues to this day. College campuses became centers of political and social unrest, and the phrase "generation gap" described a real phenomenon. From sixties hippies to seventies yippies and yuppies to eighties generation X, the attitudes of youth drove social change.

Sin

Marijuana, LSD, cocaine, heroin: drug use was a feature of the counter-culture lifestyle beginning in the sixties and moving into the mainstream in the eighties. Smoking marijuana spread like wild-fire through the youth culture and was ubiquitous at the be-ins, love-ins, and music festivals of the sixties and seventies. The psychedelic drugs such as LSD and mescaline appealed to the hippies trying to sample alternative realities. Popular songs and famous musicians glorified the drug culture. Timothy Leary became famous advising the young to "tune in, turn on, and drop out."

A college student in the late sixties, "Stacy" remembered smoking dope on the way to her English Lit class everyday,

because she thought it made the lectures a lot more
interesting. One day she ran into her professor on his way to
class too, and shared her joint with him. At the time she felt
the joint improved his lecturing ability – although she can't
remember a word of it now.

Harder drugs such as heroin appeared on the streets and consumed the cultures of the inner cities. By the 1980s, the popular
drug of choice had moved to cocaine, infiltrating both the upscale
business community and the inner-city slums. By the end of these
three decades, the drug trade was one of the largest economic forces
on the planet. Drugs touched everyone's life.

Sexual mores changed radically and rapidly. In the early 1960s
the values of the fifties still prevailed – premarital sex was a no-no,
girls who "got in trouble" were sent away if possible, and movies
and TV shows were squeaky clean. But within about a five year
period, everything had changed. Sex became "free" – or at least
that's what was claimed. Freed from the fear of pregnancy by the
birth control pill, girls too were allowed to have sex before marriage without necessarily being judged "bad." Indeed, in some places
girls were expected to "put out" for their boyfriends. Those who
didn't like the new sexual morality were considered to have a "hang
up." By the mid seventies, it became the norm in many areas for
people to live together before they got married. "Living in sin"
became an anachronism. Heated debates erupted over what to call
live-ins, and whether they should be included on insurance policies.

Not everyone easily accepted these radical changes.

"Melissa" remembered her parents' consternation when
she and her boyfriend decided to live together in 1972. Her
mother cried and wondered "where she had gone wrong," and
issued dark warnings about the damage to Melissa's
reputation. Her father asked her how she could demean

herself that way. Both parents lied to their *parents, so they wouldn't know about Melissa's "shame." But her boyfriend's parents were worse. They threatened to call the cops and have them arrested for illegal cohabitation.*

Even within marriage, the lines were being re-drawn in terms of sexual morality. In the seventies, "open marriages" and the "swingers" lifestyle, including such experiments as wife swapping, were openly discussed and sometimes practiced, reflective of the new morality trying to find its bearings and boundaries.

Censorship standards applying to the movies, television and language itself, relaxed. During the early sixties, there were attempts to curb the changes. *Lady Chatterley's Lover* was banned, as was *Fanny Hill, Louie Louie,* and the *Twist.* The excesses of sex, drugs and rock and roll were frightening. But the "free speech" movement begun in Berkeley in 1964 brought "bad" words into the mainstream, and suddenly words like the "f word" and "s word" were heard in mixed company and in the movies. The rating system for the movies came into being in 1968, to protect children from sexual scenes and bad language.

"Wendy" remembered going to see her first X-rated movie, I Am Curious Yellow, *in 1968. "The line to get in stretched more than three blocks," she shared. "And to my surprise, there were a lot of older people in line. I guess they were curious too. The line moved very slowly because everyone — no matter how old they were — had to show their drivers license to prove they were over eighteen."*

In the late seventies and especially the eighties, another change in sexual mores appeared with the open discussion, public recognition, and partial acceptance of homosexuality. The word "gay" went through a radical change in meaning. Millions of gay men and women "came out of the closet" and gay rights became a political crusade, following the tradition of African-Americans and women. *All in the Family* broke ground when it aired an episode about a gay man. It was followed by other openly gay characters on TV and in the movies. As it is today, this was an extremely controversial issue. Many groups, both secular and religious, decried this trend. Anita Bryant mounted a successful anti-gay crusade in Florida. Finally, the gay movement moved center stage in the mid-eighties with the advent of AIDS. Explicit ads for condoms and "safe sex" appeared on television.

By 1989 American attitudes toward sexuality bore little relation to the attitudes of 1959.

Gender Roles

The birth control pill went on the market in the sixties, and was one of the most potent forces changing the status of women. Control over their own reproductive functions liberated millions, allowing them freedom and choice. Also in the area of reproductive rights, Planned Parenthood began, and abortion was legalized in 1973 with the Roe v Wade decision.

The new Women's Movement started in the sixties and took off in the 1970s. NOW, the National Organization of Women, was formed in 1966, to improve the status of women and strive for equal pay for equal work, and other important rights. MS Magazine began in 1972. Names such as Gloria Steinem, Bella Abzug, and Betty Freidan became famous, and now are legendary.

Women's "consciousness raising" groups spread across America, and millions of women started paying attention to the inequities visited upon them. Some burned their bras as a symbol of their commitment to the Cause. Sexual discrimination was named, defined and legislated against. "Sex object" became a popular term, referring to the degradation of women. "Male Chauvinist," or even more descriptive, "male chauvinist pig" were terms applied to men who could not admit that women were equal to them. The Equal Rights Amendment was hotly debated until it was defeated in 1978. Several female class participants wrote about the difficulties breaking the glass ceiling in the business world.

> *"Patricia," who graduated from college in 1967 with a degree in electrical engineering (the only woman in her graduating class), was hired by a prestigious firm — upon the condition that she pass the typing test.*

> *"I had been working as a bank teller for nearly thirty years," remembered Cynthia, "and in all that time all the bank executives had always been men. But then in 1979 my bank hired a woman executive. No one knew how to treat her; not the other executives or the mostly female staff. I was for women's rights in theory, but I was just not prepared for the awkwardness of the reality."*

Women began moving up the corporate ladders in business, became more visible politically, and occupied more powerful positions within institutions such as the military, the churches, and the sports world. There were many firsts for women. Ella Grasso became Governor of Connecticut in 1974, the first female Governor unrelated to an earlier one. Geraldine Ferraro ran for Vice President in 1984. Sandra Day O'Connor was named to the Supreme Court. Dianne Feinstein became Mayor of San Francisco. Elizabeth Dole was appointed to the cabinet. The Episcopal Church allowed the ordination of women in 1976. In the same year, West Point began accepting female cadets. In 1970 the US Army promoted the first women to the rank of General. The FBI admitted women to their ranks in 1972. Billie Jean King beat Bobby Riggs in a much-ballyhooed "battle of the sexes" tennis match, watched by millions on TV. Little Leagues and high schools all over the country developed and promoted sports teams for girls. Sally Ride took her historic space ride in 1983, the first American woman in space. Male bastions such as the Kiwanis, Rotary Clubs and the Jaycees began to admit women, after the Supreme Court said they had to. And in 1987 the New York Stock Exchange put in the first ladies rest room.

Race

The Civil Rights movement that had gained steam during the 1950s continued at an ever escalating pace through the 1960s. The early sixties were marked by freedom marches, demonstrations and drives for voting rights, desegregation of lunch counters, busses, and especially schools. Martin Luther King Jr. continued his political and social ministry. His "I Have a Dream" speech is now widely regarded as one of the best speeches ever given, anywhere. The Civil Rights Act was passed in 1964, and its successor in 1968. Civil Rights was *the* Cause of the early and mid-sixties, until matched by the anti-war movement which took off later.

In the later sixties the Civil Rights movement veered away from the non-violence preached by Martin Luther King Jr., and race riots became a common feature on the American landscape. By the end of the decade there was scarcely a major American city that had escaped a race riot. The Watts section of Los Angeles erupted in riots that lasted 6 days in 1965. After the assassination of Martin Luther King Jr. in 1968, the moderate and peaceful voices of the Civil Rights movement were overshadowed by the angry voices of "black power." Elijah Muhammad of the Nation of Islam, and its spokesman Muhammad X, advocated total separatism, wanting nothing to do with white society. Stokely Carmichael and Eldridge Cleaver, and Huey Newton and Bobby Searle of the Black Panthers advocated violence and revolution. During the playing of the Star Spangled Banner at the 1968 Olympic games in Mexico City, two black athletes raised their closed fists in the "black power salute," powerfully symbolizing for the world the state of tension in race relations in America.

"Sharon," a white woman who attended college during the turbulent sixties, remembered taking a course titled

"Contemporary Black Literature." She was one of three white students, and the only white female, in a class of about thirty. When she walked into the first class, all heads swiveled toward her, and conversation ceased. She sat near the door, next to the two white boys. The professor, who was black, started the class by pointing his finger at the small white group, and saying, "If you need an A here, better transfer out now, because no white people will get an A in this class. You aren't capable of understanding black literature." It was Sharon's first experience of overt prejudice directed at her. She did not drop the class, and earned a B, the only time she ever received less than an A in an English class. But as she remarked, "I learned more in that class where I got a B than I did in most of my classes where I got As."

The sixties also saw substantial gains made by African Americans into powerful and public positions. Bill Russell became the first black coach in the NBA in 1966. Arthur Ashe became the first black man to win the US Open in 1968. Shirley Chisholm became the first black female Congresswoman in 1968. Sidney Poitier was the first black person to win a major Academy Award. Thurgood Marshall became the first black Supreme Court Justice in 1967. And there were many more.

The gains in the mainstream perception of African-Americans continued in the seventies. Black history and black literature were taught in school as separate subjects. Black heritage and black contributions to American culture began to be celebrated. In 1977, 100 million people watched the television mini-series "Roots" which brought the black experience in America into living rooms. The US Post Office put Harriet Tubman on a stamp, the first black female to be so honored.

Also in the seventies, more people of color raised their voices in protest and demands for justice and equality, including Chicanos, Latinos, Filipinos, Native Americans and other ethnic groups. Native Americans staged a protest at Wounded Knee in 1973, facing down government forces. Marlon Brando used his fame to focus public scrutiny on Native American issues when he refused his 1972 Oscar to protest the injustices visited upon them, sending Sasheen Littlefeather to the ceremony in his stead. He was not the only celebrity during these decades to use his fame for political ends.

With the return to more conservative politics in the eighties, the EEOC and Affirmative Action policies were called into question. By this time, people of color occupied many positions of power and authority, especially in middle management or mid-level government positions. Although racism was still a potent facet of American life, and inequities still abounded, no one questioned that people of color were part of the mainstream, and not merely subgroups or adjuncts to it.

Religion

All social attitudes underwent huge changes during these decades, and religion was no exception. Because it was a time of social unrest and upheaval, people felt disconnected and lost. During the sixties among the young, interest in alternative and/or Eastern religions was high. Westerners studied and taught Zen Buddhism and Hinduism. The teachings of Maharishi Mahesh Yogi resonated with many, especially after being popularized by The Beatles. Young people dressed in Hari Krishna garb appeared on city streets.

Islam made many converts in America during the sixties and seventies, especially among African-Americans. Malcolm X became a martyred hero. Muhammad Ali, the former Cassius Clay who publicly converted to Islam in 1964, encouraged millions to follow his example.

Other established religions, notably the Christian churches, were challenged to prove their relevance and meaning to modern devotees. Churches were expected to take stands on social issues such as racism and sexism, and political issues such as the Vietnam War – and follow their stances with action. Otherwise the young viewed the churches as "irrelevant." To avoid losing their followings, many churches made huge changes. The Catholic Church agreed to hold mass in English as well as Latin. Catholics were allowed to eat meat on Friday, except during Lent. Pope John Paul II, more charismatic than his predecessors, ushered in an era of openness when he became Pope in 1978. The Episcopal Church agreed to the ordination of women. There were subtler changes too. Guitars and folk music could be heard during church services in some congregations. Informal dress could be worn to church without reprimand. Some people welcomed these changes, and others felt the standards were being relaxed too far.

In the 1980s, as a reflection of the return to more conservative times, there was an upsurge in Christian fundamentalism. Televangelists, a new word, had huge followings. In 1979 Jerry Falwell formed the Moral Majority, making conservative Christians a political force.

Religion had its dark times during these decades too. Cults such as the People's Temple headed by Jim Jones, made headlines and scared the devil out of millions of parents. A new occupation was born: deprogramming. Various church scandals erupted in the eighties, including the sex scandals enveloping Jimmy Swaggart and Jim Bakker, and the tax evasion charges levied against Unification Church (the "Moonies") founder Sun Myung Moon.

Review the following timeline and see what *you* remember ...

1960-1989 Events Timeline
The Social Fabric

1960	Feb	4 students stage civil rights sit-in at Woolworth's in NC
1960	Feb	1st Playboy Club featuring bunnies opens in Chicago
1960	Apr	Senate passes landmark Civil Rights bill
1960	Apr	Elijah Muhammad of Nation of Islam calls for a black state
1960	May	US is the first country to use the birth control pill legally
1960	Aug	Student "kneel-in" demonstrations in Atlanta churches
1960	Aug	Race riot in Jacksonville, Florida
1960	Oct	Martin Luther King Jr. arrested in Atlanta sit-in
1961	Jan	Supreme Court rules states have right to censor films
1961	May	13 Freedom Riders begin bus trip through South; they are bombed and bus is burned in Alabama by a white mob.
1961	May	27 Freedom Riders arrested in Jackson, Mississippi
1961	Jun	Supreme Court struck down a part of Maryland's constitution requiring state office holders to believe in God
1961	Nov	PGA eliminates the Caucasians Only rule
1961	Nov	Freedom Riders attacked by white mob in Mississippi
1961	Dec	Martin Luther King Jr. arrested in Georgia
1962		Second Vatican Council ushers in major reforms
1962		Helen Gurley Brown publishes *Sex & The Single Girl*
1962	Jan	Catholic Diocese bans Chubby Checker's the Twist
1962	Feb	Bus boycott starts in Macon Georgia
1962	Apr	New Orleans Citizens Council gives free 1-way ride to blacks moving North
1962	Jun	Supreme Court rules school prayer violates 1st amendment
1962	Jul	Martin Luther King Jr. arrested in Georgia
1962	Jul	160 Civil Rights activists jailed in Georgia
1962	Sep	US Circuit Court of Appeals orders James Meredith admitted to Ole Miss
1962	Dec	Edith Sampson sworn in as first US black female judge
1963		Betty Friedan publishes *The Feminine Mystique*
1963		Pope Paul VI invites 5 women to attend Vatican II
1963	Apr	Birmingham police use dogs and cattle prods on peaceful demonstrators
1963	Jun	Pope John XXIII dies, replaced by Pope Paul VI
1963	Jun	Gov. Wallace tries to prevent blacks at U. of Alabama
1963	Aug	200,000 demonstrate for equal rights in Washington DC
1963	Aug	Martin Luther King Jr's "I Have a Dream" speech at Lincoln Memorial
1963	Sep	Alabama Gov. Wallace prevents integration of Tuskegee High School

1963	Sep	4 black girls die in church bombing in Birmingham AL
1963	Oct	225,000 students boycott Chicago schools in Freedom Day
1964	Jan	Surgeon General's Report states that smoking may be hazardous to health
1964	Feb	Black & Puerto Rican students boycott NYC public schools
1964	Feb	Indiana Governor tries to ban "Louie Louie" for obscenity
1964	Feb	Rep. Martha Griffiths' address gets civil rights protection for women added to the 1964 Civil Rights Act
1964	Feb	Cassius Clay becomes a Muslim and Muhammad Ali
1964	Mar	Malcolm X resigns from Nation of Islam
1964	Apr	Sidney Poitier becomes first black man to win Oscar
1964	May	Supreme Court rules that closing schools to avoid desegregation is unconstitutional
1964	Jun	3 Civil rights workers disappear after release from Mississippi jail
1964	Jun	Organization for Afro-American Unity formed in NY by Malcolm X
1964	Jun	Civil Rights Act passed after 83-day filibuster in Senate
1964	Jul	Race riot in Harlem; riots spread to Brooklyn
1964	Aug	Race riot in Jersey City, NJ
1964	Oct	Martin Luther King Jr. wins Nobel Peace Prize
1964	Oct	Free Speech Movement launched at U. Cal. Berkeley
1964	Nov	J. Edgar Hoover calls Martin Luther King Jr. a "most notorious liar"
1964	Nov	US Catholic Church replaces Latin with English
1964	Dec	Police arrest 800 sit-in students at U. of California Berkeley
1965		Harvard professor Timothy Leary begins preaching "Drop out, turn on, tune in" with LSD
1965	Jan	Martin Luther King Jr begins a drive to register black voters
1965	Feb	Martin Luther King Jr. & 700 demonstrators arrested in Selma, Alabama
1965	Feb	Malcolm X assassinated by members of Nation of Islam
1965	Mar	Martin Luther King begins march from Selma
1965	Aug	6 day insurrection starts in Watts section of Los Angeles
1965	Oct	Pope Paul VI proclaims Jews are not guilty for the crucifixion of Jesus
1966	Jan	Julian Bond denied seat in Georgia legislature for opposing Vietnam War
1966	Jan	First black man selected for Presidential cabinet, Robert Weaver for HUD
1966	Apr	Bill Russell becomes first black coach in NBA
1966	May	Stokeley Carmichael named chairman of Student Nonviolent Coordinating Committee

1966	Jun	2400 attend White House Conference on Civil Rights
1966	Jul	Race riots in Omaha, Nebraska; National Guard called
1966	Jul	Race riots in Chicago
1966	Jul	Race riots in Cleveland, state of emergency declared
1966	Aug	Martin Luther King Jr. is stoned during Chicago march
1966	Aug	Race riots in Lansing, Michigan
1966	Sep	Race riots in Atlanta, Georgia
1966	Oct	National Organization of Women (NOW) founded
1966	Oct	Black Panther Party founded by Huey Newton and Bobby Searle, launching "black power" and advocating revolution
1966	Nov	Catholics may eat meat on Fridays except during Lent
1966	Dec	Kwanzaa established as an African-American holiday
1967		Among the many rock stars arrested for drug possession in 1967: all the Grateful Dead, 2 members of Moby Grape, Keith Richards, Brian Jones and Mick Jagger of the Rolling Stones, Jim Morrison, Marianne Faithful, Paul McCartney, John Lennon
1967	Apr	Muhammad Ali refuses induction into army because of religious reasons and is stripped of his boxing title
1967	May	Black students seize building at Northwestern University
1967	May	400 students seize building at Cheyney State College
1967	May	H. Rap Brown replaces Stokely Carmichael as chairman of Student Nonviolent Coordinating Committee
1967	Jun	Race riots in Boston
1967	Jun	Race riots in Tampa, Florida; National Guard mobilized
1967	Jun	Race riots in Cincinnati, Ohio; 300 arrested
1967	Jun	Supreme Court ends laws against interracial marriages
1967	Jun	Thurgood Marshall is first black Supreme Court Justice
1967	Jun	Governor Reagan signs liberalized California abortion bill
1967	Jun	Paul McCartney admits on TV that he used LSD
1967	Jun	Keith Richards sentenced to 1 year in jail on drug charges
1967	June	Cigarette packages required to carry information about health risks
1967	Jul	Race riots in Newark, NJ; 26 killed, 1500 injured
1967	Jul	Race riots in Durham, NC
1967	Jul	Beatles sign a petition to legalize marijuana
1967	Jul	Race riots in Detroit; 43 killed, 2000 injured, over 400 fires
1967	Nov	First black mayor of a major city elected – Cleveland, OH
1967	Dec	First woman to own a seat on NY Stock Exchange
1968		Eldridge Cleaver's *Soul on Ice* is published
1968		Arthur Ashe is first black player to win major US tennis title
1968	Feb	George Harrison, John Lennon go to India to study transcendental meditation with the Maharishi Maresh Yogi
1968	Mar	Howard University students seize administration building

1968	Apr	Martin Luther King Jr. assassinated in Memphis
1968	Apr	LBJ signs 1968 Civil Rights Act
1968	Jul	Race riot in Cleveland, 11 killed, including 3 policemen
1968	Jul	Pope Paul VI reaffirms stand against artificial birth control
1968	Aug	Race riot in Miami, Florida
1968	Oct	Two black athletes give "black power" salute at the opening of the Olympic Games in Mexico City.
1968	Nov	Shirley Chisholm, NY, elected first black Congresswoman
1968	Dec	Apollo 8 astronauts read from the Book of Genesis while orbiting the Moon on Christmas day
1969		Yale University agrees to admit female undergraduates
1969		*Everything You Always Wanted to Know About Sex* by David Reuben is published
1969	Jan	John Lennon's *2 Virgins* album declared pornographic
1969	Mar	Rally for Decency in Miami, Florida
1969	Mar	Jim Morrison arrested for exposing himself in concert
1969	May	Abortion and contraception legalized in Canada
1969	Jun	Race riot in Hartford, CT
1969	Jun	Aretha Franklin arrested in Detroit for creating a disturbance
1969	Jun	Police raid the Stonewall, a gay Bar in Greenwich Village, sparking 3 day riot
1969	Jun	First Jewish worship service at the White House
1969	Jul	Race riots in Baton Rouge; National Guard mobilized
1969	Aug	Racial disturbances in Fort Lauderdale, Florida
1969	Oct	Racial disturbances in Springfield, Massachusetts
1969	Nov	Janis Joplin accused of vulgar & indecent language in Tampa, Florida
1970	Jan	Dollie Mina burns her bra in Amsterdam
1970	Feb	John Lennon pays the fines for people arrested when protesting the South African rugby team playing in Scotland
1970	Feb	Dee Brown publishes *Bury My Heart at Wounded Knee*
1970	May	Race riots in Augusta, Georgia, 6 people killed
1970	May	2 students killed in racial disturbance in Mississippi
1970	May	Elizabeth Hoisington & Anna Mae Mays named first female US Generals
1970	May	Peter Queen quits Fleetwood Mac to join a religious cult
1970	June	Thousands of homosexuals stage protest in NYC
1970	Jul	100 people injured in race riots in Asbury Park, NJ
1970	Jul	6 days of race riots in Hartford, Connecticut
1970	Sep	Jimi Hendrix dies of drug overdose
1970	Oct	Janis Joplin dies of drug overdose
1970	Oct	over 700 Unification Church couples wed in Korea
1970	Nov	Race riots in Daytona Beach, Florida

1970		*The New English Bible* translated into modern language
1971	Jan	Cigarette ads are banned from TV
1971	Feb	Satchel Paige becomes 1ˢᵗ Negro League player elected to Hall of Fame
1971	Feb	1ˢᵗ gay theme episode on TV, on *All in the Family*
1971	Apr	Supreme Court upholds use of busing to achieve racial desegregation
1971	Apr	1ˢᵗ legal off-track betting system begins in New York
1971	May	Race riot in Brooklyn
1971	May	Nixon rejects demands of Congressional Black Caucus
1971	Jun	Vernon Jordan appointed Executive Director of National Urban League
1971	Jun	Racial disturbance in Jacksonville, Florida
1971	Jun	Race riots in Columbus, Georgia
1971	Jun	Supreme Court overturns draft evasion conviction of Muhammad Ali
1971	Oct	Billie Jean King becomes 1ˢᵗ female athlete to win $100,000
1972		Pope Paul VI abolishes the tonsure haircut for seminarians, a requirement since 6 AD
1972	Feb	Alex Comfort publishes *The Joy of Sex*
1972	Mar	Congress approves Equal Rights Amendment
1972	Jun	Nixon signs act barring sex discrimination in college sports
1972	Jul	Ms. Magazine begins publishing
1972	Jul	First women begin training as FBI agents at Quantico
1972	Jul	US health officials admit blacks were used in 40-year syphilis experiment
1972	Oct	40 sailors injured in race riot on aircraft carrier Kitty Hawk
1973		University of Miami is first to offer athletic scholarships to women
1973	Jan	Supreme Court legalizes some abortions, in Roe v Wade
1973	Feb	American Indian Movement occupy Wounded Knee in South Dakota, and hold it for 10 weeks
1973	May	Supreme Court approves equal rights for females in military
1973	May	Thomas Bradley elected 1ˢᵗ black mayor of Los Angeles
1973	Jun	Lawsuit in Detroit challenges Little League's "no girls" rule
1973	Sep	Billie Jean King beats Bobby Riggs in battle-of-the-sexes tennis match
1973	Nov	Abe Beame elected first Jewish mayor of NYC
1973	Dec	American Psychiatric Association declares that homosexuality is not a mental illness
1974		Beverly Johnson is first black woman on cover of Vogue
1974	Oct	National Guard mobilized to restore order in Boston, over court-ordered school busing disagreements
1974	Nov	Ella Grasso of Connecticut elected first woman Governor

		not related to a previous governor
1975	Jan	International Women's Year begins
1975	Jan	Ugandan Bernadette Olowo becomes first female ambassador to Vatican
1975		Junko Tabei of Japan is first woman to ascend Mt. Everest
1975	Mar	First state allows girls to compete with boys in high school sports
1976		Females become eligible for Rhodes scholarships
1976	Mar	First female cadets accepted to West Point
1976	Apr	Barbara Walters becomes first¹ female network news anchor
1976	Sep	Jimmy Carter says he had lusted for women in his heart
1976	Sep	Episcopal Church approves ordination of women as priests
1976	Oct	Governor Wallace grants pardon to Clarence Norris, last known survivor of 9 Scottsboro Boys convicted in 1931
1976		*Your Erroneous Zones* by Dr. Wayne Dyer is published
1977	Jan	First woman formally ordained an Episcopal priest
1977	Jan	*Roots* debuts on TV, watched by 100 million people
1977	May	Janet Guthrie becomes first woman to drive in the Indianapolis 500
1977	Jun	Anita Bryant leads a successful crusade against Miami "gay rights" law
1977	Oct	Supreme Court hears Allan Bakke case, white student denied admission to U of CA, on "reverse discrimination"
1977	Nov	New Orleans elects first black mayor
1978	Feb	Harriet Tubman is 1ˢᵗ black woman honored on a stamp
1978	Apr	Supreme Court rules pension plans cannot require women to pay more
1978	May	Commerce Dept. announces hurricane names will no longer be only female
1978	Jun	The Mormon Church strikes down 150-year policy of excluding black men from membership
1978	Jul	Nearly 100,00 march on Washington DC for ERA
1978	Aug	House of Representatives approves extension for ERA
1978	Sep	Pope John Paul I dies, after only 1 month as Pope
1978	Oct	Polish Cardinal Karol Wojtyla named Pope John Paul II
1978	Dec	Dianne Feinstein named San Francisco's first female mayor
1978	Dec	Susan B Anthony dollar issued, first coin to honor a woman
1979		Jerry Falwell founds The Moral Majority, religious political action group
1979	Jan	President Carter proposes Martin Luther King's birthday be a holiday
1979	Jun	Pope John Paul II visits Poland, first papal visit to a communist country
1979	Aug	Patricia Harris is first black female cabinet member,

		Secretary of HEW
1980	Apr	EEOC begins regulating sexual harassment
1980	Jun	Richard Pryor burnt in free basing cocaine accident
1980	Oct	Reagan promises to name woman to Supreme Court
1981	May	Pope John Paul II shot and wounded in St. Peters Square
1981	May	Billie Jean King admits to lesbian affair
1981	Jul	First woman president of National Bar Association
1981	Sep	Sandra Day O'Connor appointed the 1st woman Supreme Court Justice
1981	Oct	Andrew Young elected mayor of Atlanta, Georgia
1982	Jan	Arkansas judge rules against obligatory teaching of creation
1982	May	Reverend Sun Myung Moon convicted of tax evasion
1982	Jul	Over 2000 Unification couples married in Madison Square Garden
1982	Oct	Over 6000 Unification church couples wed in Korea
1983		Nancy Reagan introduces the "Just Say No" program to combat drug use
1983		Challenger carries first black astronaut, Guion Bluford
1983		National Council of Churches publishes a Bible in which references to God are gender-free
1983	Feb	1st female Secretary of Transportation , Elizabeth Dole
1983	Apr	Harold Washington sworn in as Chicago's 1st black mayor
1983	Jun	Sally Ride is first American woman in space
1983	Jul	Supreme Court rules retirement plans cannot pay women less
1983	Sep	Vanessa Williams becomes first black Miss America
1983	Nov	Reagan signs bill establishing Martin Luther King Day
1983	Nov	Martha Collins elected first female governor of Kentucky
1983	Nov	W. Wilson Goode elected 1st black mayor of Philadelphia
1984	Mar	Supreme Court rules that a city may use public money for Nativity scene
1984	Mar	Senate rejects amendment to permit spoken prayer in public schools
1984	Jul	Supreme Court rules Jaycees can be forced to admit women as members
1984	Jul	Geraldine Ferraro became 1st woman major party VP candidate
1984	Jul	Lynn Rippelmeyer is 1st female to captain a 747 across the Atlantic
1986	Mar	Supreme Court rules Air Force can ban wearing of yaramulkes
1986	Jun	Georgia sodomy law upheld by Supreme Court
1987		Jim Bakker's affair with Jessica Hahn ends his career as a preacher

Sharing My Stories—*Girls Buy Hardware Too*

In 1974, armed with my college degree, I entered the full time workforce. I had worked part time through college as a secretary, and I looked forward to working in a different role. However, the only jobs I was considered for were secretarial jobs. Most, in fact nearly all, of the jobs available for women in business were secretarial jobs.

It was legal to advertise jobs in the want ads as "Men Wanted" and "Women Wanted." I answered the "Women" ads for office help, naively hoping that I could use a secretarial job as a springboard to something better. I was offered quite a few secretarial jobs, but when I asked about paths to advancement, the only thing on offer was as an Office Manager or Head Typist. Although young men with the same education as I were considered for management trainees and entry level sales positions, I was told – in these exact words — that women couldn't manage because their employees wouldn't take them seriously, and that women couldn't be sales people because their customers wouldn't take them seriously.

Eventually I landed a job as a Secretary/Purchasing Agent. That slash was why I agreed to take the job. The company was a furniture manufacturer and it was my job to purchase nails and screws and other small production items. My supervisor bought "bigger" things such as lumber, bedsprings, and mattress ticking. I thought that this was temporary, just until I learned. Then I would be the Buyer for the "bigger" purchases. But when I asked when I would be given that responsibility, I was told — never. I couldn't buy these products because the purchase of lumber and such was really a man's job and the suppliers wouldn't take me seriously.

This was actually true. I learned this the first time my hardware vendor, selling nails and screws, came to see me. He knew my name but had not talked to me. Since Kim is a man's name as well as a woman's, he expected a man. He saw me and his mouth fell open in shock. "*You're a girl!*" he huffed. "I'm not selling nails to a *girl!*" Out he stomped. I never saw him again. I had to find another nail and screw vendor, which should have been easy but wasn't, because I wanted one who wasn't patronizing.

I was in that job five years, and although by the second year I devoted myself to purchasing and performed no secretarial duties, it wasn't until the last year of my employment that my company at last yielded to my pleas to drop the "secretary" from my title and promote me to Purchasing Agent without the slash.

1987		Supreme Court orders Rotary Clubs to admit women
1987		Condom commercials are allowed on TV to combat AIDS epidemic
1987		National Museum of Women in the Arts opens in Washington DC
1987	Feb	NY Stock Exchange finally installs a ladies restroom
1987	Feb	Anti-smoking ad airs for first time on TV, featuring Yul Brynner
1987	Mar	Supreme Court rules women & minorities may get jobs if less qualified
1987	Mar	Vatican registers opposition to in-vitro fertilization and embryo transfer
1987	Apr	FCC imposes a broader definition of indecency over the airwaves
1987	Jul	Kiwanis Clubs end men-only tradition and vote to admit women
1987	Oct	200,000 gays march for civil rights in Washington DC
1987	Nov	Supreme Court nominee Douglas Ginsburg admitted using marijuana
1988	Jan	Jimmy "The Greek" Snyder fired from CBS for racial remarks
1988	Feb	Televangelist Jimmy Swaggart removed from TV show because of sexual scandal
1988	Feb	9th Circuit Court of Appeals in San Francisco strikes down Army's ban on homosexuals (later overturned on appeal)
1988	Aug	Congress votes $20,000 to each Japanese American interned in WWII
1988	Sep	Barbara Harris is elected 1st woman Episcopal Bishop
1988	Oct	2000 anti-abortion protesters arrested for blocking clinics
1989		Spike Lee's *Do The Right Thing* released, a movie about black-white relations
1989	Jan	Salmon Rushdie's *Satanic Verses* is burned by Muslims in England
1989	May	Supreme Court rules employees have to prove non-discriminatory reasons for not hiring or promoting
1989	May	Maxwell House Coffee runs ads during "Roe v Wade" movie despite threat of boycott by right-to-lifers
1989	Aug	Pete Rose is suspended from baseball for life for gambling

Writing Topic Suggestions
The Social Fabric

Pick one of the topics below and write for fifteen to twenty minutes. Remember the un-rules:

- Don't stop writing until the time limit is over.
- Use trigger sentences if you get stuck.
- Don't be polite.
- Be specific and remember you have at least five senses.
- You don't have to be right, rational or logical.
- Forget about the rules of grammar or spelling.
- Trust yourself.

Remember, you are creating a *primary source*. Write about what you *did*, what you *saw*, what you *thought*, what you *felt*.

1. Scan the events timelines. What sparks a memory? Is there an event listed that makes you think, "oh yeah, I remember that"? If so, write about this event. How did you learn about it? Did you talk about it? With whom? Were you inspired to do something because of this event? Did this event change your life in any way? Change your thinking?

2. Did you know anyone who was discriminated against because of race or religion? Were you discriminated against? Did you have friends, co-workers, neighbors, of a different race or religion? How did you interact with them?

3. Write about anti-Semitism. Do you think America was anti-Semitic before World War II? If so, how did you see this anti-Semitism operating? Did the revelation of Nazi atrocities toward the Jews affect anti-Semitism in America after the war?

4. Did you know any Japanese Americans who were interned during World War II? What did you think of this policy? Did it make you angry? Or were you afraid of Japanese Americans? If you are of Asian descent, do you think discrimination toward Asian Americans was worse during World War II than before?

5. If you are white, did your attitudes toward African-Americans change during the 40s through the 70s? What did you think about the Civil Rights movement? If you lived in the South, what was your attitude toward "freedom riders?" Did you believe the schools should be integrated? If you are a person of color, how did your life change during those decades? Were the changes beneficial or painful, or both? Did you go to a segregated or integrated school? Were you, or your children, bussed to different schools? Did you admire Martin Luther King? Did he inspire you to act? Did you support non-white persons into positions of authority or power?

6. Did you admire Eleanor Roosevelt, or did you feel that she was too powerful for a woman? If you are female, did you work in a "male" job during World War II? If so, what did you do? Did you enjoy your job? What did you do for war work? How do you think women contributed to the war effort?

7. If you are a woman, do you feel that you had free choice regarding an occupation during the thirties, forties and fifties? Did you discuss the status of women with your friends or family? What were you taught about women that changed during these decades? Write about what you could or couldn't do do, because of your sex. Or write about what your mother or grandmother could or couldn't do. Did she miss out on opportunities that you had?

8. If you are a man, write about your beliefs during the thirties, forties and fifties about women's roles. Did they change? Did you like women working? Did you want your wife to work outside the home? Did your mother work outside the home? Did you believe that women's work and men's work should be separate?

9. If you are a woman, how did your role change during the women's movement of the 1970s? Were you inspired by women such as Gloria Steinem or Jackie Kennedy? Did you have a female hero? Did you work outside the home? Did you have aspirations for a career that was traditionally "male"? What barriers hampered you in achieving your goals, and how did you overcome those barriers? Did you go to consciousness raising meetings or groups? Did you read MS Magazine? Were you for the ERA? How did you feel when it was not ratified? Did you vote for a female political candidate? What did the men in your life think of the women's movement? Did you identify yourself as a feminist? What effect did the women's movement have on your life?

10. If you are a man, write about your beliefs during the sixties, seventies and eighties about women's roles. Were you ever called a "male chauvinist pig?" Did you support the women's movement, or did you not understand what all the fuss was about? Did you help or mentor your female co-workers? How did the women's movement change your life?

11. Write about drinking. How important was alcohol in your social circle or your family? What was your drink of choice? How did your attitude to drinking change from teenager to adult? Do you remember the first time you got drunk? Do you or your parents remember Prohibition?

12. What were you told by your parents about the rules of dating, or about the opposite sex, or about the "birds and the bees" in the thirties, forties and fifties? Did you hold a double standard of sexual morality for men and women? Did you feel there were "good girls" and "bad girls" and how could you tell the difference? Or write about what was considered risqué or daring in the thirties through the fifties.

13. Sexual attitudes and values changed during the sixties to the eighties. How did this influence you, or your children, and were

these influences positive or negative or both? Was there such a thing as "free sex"? If you were a young adult during the sixties or seventies, were you confused about what was okay to do, and what was not? If you were parents of teenagers during the sixties and seventies, were you concerned that your children's moral standards were degenerating? Did you or your children live together before marriage? Was that a brave step at the time?

14. How did your views about homosexuality change during the 1980s? Did you work for gay rights? Did you or someone you know "come out of the closet" during this decade? How did the new openness about this lifestyle affect your life?

15. How involved were you in your church, temple, or religious life? How did your religious beliefs change during the years of these decades? Did you or your children reject traditional American religious traditions in favor of Eastern traditions such as Zen Buddhism or Hinduism? If you are Christian or Jewish, did you feel that your religion was "out of touch" with contemporary demands during those decades? Did you work for your church, and if so, what did you do?

16. Did you consider yourself part of the "counter culture" during the sixties and seventies? Or were your children or parents part of this counter culture? Were drugs a part of your lifestyle, or your children's lifestyle? Or write about what you thought about the climbing rate of drug use – were you for or against the legalization of marijuana, and what did you do to promote your beliefs? Did you or anyone you knew get caught up in cocaine during the 1980s? If so, what happened? Were you or anyone you knew harmed by the drug culture?

Or anything else you'd like to write about …

Chapter Twelve
Wars and the International Scene

This book has an American focus, concentrating on the events and trends that shaped Americans. But we are not alone on the earth. What happens in other countries affects our lives. What we do here in America affects theirs.

While warm and friendly relations of course exist between nations, conflict is, as they say, what sells newspapers. The horror of War and its aftermath profoundly affects everyone on earth. No one who lives through a war ever forgets the lessons it taught them.

1930 through 1959

When you look at this timeline for 1930 through 1959, you might notice how long it is. You might also notice how few of the entries are happy ones. When I teach this class, I write a list of the wars and conflicts on the board. I seldom have room for them all, even when I have extensive board space. This list – which is abbreviated here — goes like this:

> *1932-33 Stalin engineers a famine in the Ukraine that eventually kills about six million people and stamps out Ukrainian revolt; *1932 Japan bombs Shanghai and invades China the first time; *1933 Hitler becomes Chancellor of Germany and the Nazis take over the German Parliament; *1935 German Jews are deprived of citizenship; *1936 Civil War in Nicaragua; *1936 Civil War in Spain with Franco leading the Fascists; *1937 The first of Stalin's purges which begin the Gulag system of forced labor camps in Russia; *1937 Japan invades China again and puts a puppet governor on the Emperor's throne; * 1938 Germany invades Austria (the Anschluss); *1939-1945 World War II; *1940 Mahatma Gandhi arrested and imprisoned along with 40,000 of his

followers for non-violent protests against British colonial rule; *1942 The "Final Solution" is proposed in Germany, now known as the "Holocaust" and the wholesale murder of more than six million people; *1944 Juan Peron leads a coup in Argentina; *1945 the Atom Bomb is dropped on Hiroshima and Nagasaki; *1945 Chinese Civil War begins, with Mao Zedong vs. Chaing Kai-shek; *1945 The "Cold War" begins and lasts for the next 44 years; *1947 Partition between India and Pakistan leads to bloody uprisings; *1948 Israel is partitioned out of Palestine and war begins; *1949 Republic of Ireland withdraws from Great Britain;*1949 South Africa makes a policy of apartheid, effectively disenfranchising most of its own citizens; *1950-1953 Korean War; *1952-1954 Civil War in Vietnam with Ho Chi Minh leading a revolt against the French;*1952 Batista leads a coup in Cuba; *1952 Mau Mau uprising against the British in Kenya; *1953-1959 Civil War in Cuba ; *1953 US enters Vietnam on the side of the French; *1954 Rebel coup in Guatemala; *1955 British withdraw from Belfast, IRA strikes follow; *1955 Civil War starts in Nicaragua after Somoza assassinated; *1956 Soviets put down revolt in Hungary; *1956 Suez Canal crisis pitting Britain and France against Egypt; *1959 Soviets put down revolt in Afghanistan.

What an ugly list. Words like *Armageddon* and *Apocalypse* come to mind. Looking at that list, it would be forgivable to think that the end of the world *had* come. It is not only the number of events on the list, it is their sheer immensity that awes us. Everything – the events and the actors, good and evil — existed on a grand scale previously unknown. Names that "will live in infamy," to paraphrase FDR, will be recognized forever. Ask anyone who the most evil person who ever existed was, and most will say Adolf Hitler. Others will say Josef Stalin. Both lived during this time. But saints and heroes lived during these decades too; consider Mahatma Gandhi, Mother Theresa, and Nelson Mandela, just to name three. Almost unbelievable horrors such as the Holocaust were visited upon millions of people, featuring cruelty unmatched since the Inquisition, and on a much larger scale. The world was engulfed in cataclysmic convulsions on every continent. Previously "whole" countries were partitioned into different nation camps based on their inability to get along with each other – Israel and Palestine, East and West Berlin, Eastern and Western Europe, India and Pakistan, Northern and Southern Ireland, North and South Korea, North and South Vietnam, plus more. And with the development of the atom bomb, humanity found a way to actually destroy our species itself – if we couldn't learn to get along.

Against this horrendous backdrop, more positive trends such as the establishment of the United Nations, the Marshall Plan which rebuilt war-torn Europe, the Berlin airlift (to name a few), seem puny in contrast. But one of the lessons of these decades is that it was *not* Armageddon or the Apocalypse. Humanity lived through these decades – and not just survived, but progressed. People fell in love, got married, had babies. They went to school, started businesses, built buildings. They invented machines and discovered scientific laws. They wrote stories, painted pictures and sang songs. They cooked and cleaned and went to dances, and they laughed as well as cried. When I look at the people in my classroom who lived during the thirties, forties and fifties, and I reflect upon what their generation went through, I feel hope. As Mahatma Gandhi, who knew about these things, said, "When in despair I remember that all through history the way of truth and love has always won; there have been tyrants and murderers, and for a time they can seem invincible, but in the end they always fall."

Many of the stories that people recall most vividly seem homely and trivial on the surface, but are filled with great meaning underneath.

"Jack" remembered his service in the South Pacific during World War Two, a far cry from his home in Oregon. Every evening as he ate his C-rations from a can, surrounded by ants and other creatures he couldn't name, Jack thought

about the dinners his mother served. She always put a white linen tablecloth on the dinner table, even during the Depression when there wasn't much to eat. It seemed to him, from the depths of the alien jungle, that white linen tablecloths were what was meant by civilization. He longed to eat a civilized dinner with napkins and china and feel the heavy material of the tablecloth resting on his knees. So when Jack went on R&R leave in Australia, while most of the GIs made a beeline for the bars, he sought out and found the most expensive restaurant in Melbourne and convinced three buddies to join him for dinner there. As it turned out, although the restaurant's white linen tablecloths were impeccable, they were not the only thing that made it a memorable dinner. The four uniformed GIs were the only non-Australians in the restaurant and were of great interest to the other diners, although no bothered them until two teenagers, there with their families, came up to their table. "Excuse me," said one teenager, "We were wondering – do you know the words to "Chattanooga Choo Choo?" "Sure, I guess so," said one of the GIs. "Gee, could you sing it for us?" The GIs looked at each other and shrugged – why not, after all? So they stood up and sang "Chattanooga Choo Choo" with gusto. When they were finished, everyone in the restaurant – all the diners, the waiters, even the cooks from the kitchen, stood up and clapped, giving them a standing ovation that lasted at least three minutes. "I think they were clapping for America," said Jack. "It sure couldn't have been our singing."

Review the following timeline and see what *you* remember …

1930 - 1959 Events Timeline
Wars & the International Scene

1931	Dec	Lin-Sen succeeds Chiang Kai-shek as President of China
1932	Jan	Gandhi and Nehru are arrested by the British in India
1932	Jan	4,000 protesters in El Salvador killed by the army
1932	Jan	Japanese bomb Shanghai
1932	Feb	60 countries attend the Geneva Disarmament Conference
1932	Mar	Eamon De Valera becomes President of Ireland
1932	Apr	Haile Selassie abolishes slavery in Ethiopia
1932	Sep	Gandhi begins a "fast unto death" to protest caste system
1933	Jan	Guardia Civil uprising in Spain
1933	Jan	Adolf Hitler becomes Chancellor of Germany
1933	Feb	Hitler dissolves German Parliament
1933	Feb	Germany limits freedom of the press & opinion
1933	Feb	Goering forms the Nazi SS
1933	Feb	Nazis set fire to the German parliament
1933	Feb	The League of Nations tells Japan to leave Manchuria
1933	Mar	Nazi Party wins majority in German parliamentary elections
1933	Mar	Josef Goebbels becomes German Minister of Propaganda
1933	Mar	Dachau, the first concentration camp, is completed
1933	Apr	Nazis place a boycott on Jewish businesses
1933	May	Nazis bans trade unions
1933	May	Nazis stage public book burnings
1933	May	Spanish anarchists call for a general strike
1933	Nov	America establishes diplomatic relations with the USSR
1933		Stalin engineers a famine in the Ukraine that eventually kills between six and seven million people
1934	Mar	Josip Broz (Tito) freed from Yugoslavian jail
1934	Jun	Purge of the Nazi party, called "Night of the Long Knives"
1934	Aug	US ends its occupation of Haiti
1934	Aug	Adolf Hitler becomes President of Germany
1935	Jan	Edward VIII succeeds British King George V
1935	Mar	Hitler violates the Versailles Treaty by ordering rearmament
1935	Sep	Nuremberg Laws enacted, depriving Jews of citizenship and making the swastika the official symbol of Germany
1935	Oct	Italy invades Ethiopia
1936	Jan	Semi-automatic rifles adopted by US Army
1936	Mar	Hitler sends troops to the Rhineland
1936	Jun	General Anastasio Somoza becomes dictator of Nicaragua
1936	Jul	Francisco Franco leads uprising, Spanish Civil War begins
1936	Dec	Armenia, Azerbaijan, Georgia, Kazakhstan, and Kirghis join the USSR

1936	Dec	Edward VIII abdicates the British throne to marry Wallis Simpson, and his brother becomes King George VI
1936	Dec	Chiang Kai-shek of China declares war on Japan
1937	Jan	Stalin's great purge of the Soviet army begins
1937	May	FDR signs Act of Neutrality
1937	Nov	Lord Halifax of Britain visits Germany, beginning a policy of appeasement
1937	Dec	Japanese aircraft sink US gunboat Panay on the Yangtze River in China
1937	Dec	Japanese troops conquer Nanjing
1938	Mar	President Cardena of Mexico nationalizes US and British oil companies
1938	Mar	Germany invades Austria (Anschluss)
1938	Sep	British PM Chamberlain visits Hitler at Berchtesgarden
1938	Sep	Munich Agreement forces Czechoslovakia to give territory to Germany
1938	Oct	Germany annexes Sudentenland from Czechoslovakia
1938	Oct	Germany stamps "J" on all Jewish passports
1938	Nov	Nazi storm troopers attack Jews on "Kristallnacht" (Night of Broken Glass)
1939	Jan	Hitler tells German Parliament his plan to exterminate all European Jews
1939	Feb	German battleship Bismarck is launched
1939	Mar	Germany occupies the rest of Czechoslovakia
1939	Mar	Germany demands Poland cede them Gdansk (Danzig)
1939	Mar	Britain and France agree to support Poland if Germany invades them
1939	Mar	Spanish Civil War ends when Madrid falls to Franco
1939	Apr	US recognizes Franco government in Spain
1939	May	Hitler and Mussolini of Italy sign the "Pact of Steel"
1939	May	Ship carrying 937 Jewish refugees denied US entry
1939	Aug	Germany and USSR sign a 10-year non-aggression pact
1939	Sep	World War II begins. Sep 1st, Germany invades Poland and captures Danzig. Sep 3rd, Britain declares war on Germany, shortly followed by France, Australia, New Zealand, South Africa and Canada
1939	Sep	Polish ghetto of Mir is exterminated by the Germans
1939	Sep	Warsaw surrenders to Germany after 19 days of resistance
1939	Sep	Soviet-German treaty on partition of Poland, giving Lithuania to the USSR
1939	Oct	Winston Churchill gives speech in which he refers to Soviet policy as "a riddle wrapped in a mystery inside an enigma"
1939	Nov	USSR invades Finland
1939	Nov	Jews of Poland are ordered to wear yellow armbands

1939	Nov	Nazis begin the mass murder of Warsaw Jews
1939	Dec	League of Nations drops USSR
1939	Dec	SS Head Himmler begins deportation of Polish Jews
1940	Mar	Construction begins on Auschwitz
1940	Mar	Italy declares war against France and Britain
1940	Apr	Germany invades Norway and Denmark
1940	May	Germany invades the Netherlands, Belgium, & Luxembourg
1940	May	Germany crosses the Meuse River into France
1940	May	Germany bombs Rotterdam, Netherlands surrenders
1940	May	Germany occupies Brussels & begins invasion of France
1940	May	French Army counter attacks under General Charles de Gaulle at Peronne
1940	May	Belgium surrenders to Germany
1940	May	Germans capture Ostend, Ypres, and Lille
1940	May	Winston Churchill succeeds Neville Chamberlain as Britain's Prime Minister
1940	May	German planes bomb ship full of Palestinian Jews
1940	Jun	British evacuate 300,000 trapped troops at Dunkirk
1940	Jun	Germans enter Paris
1940	Jun	Norway surrenders to Germany
1940	Jun	France surrenders to Germany
1940	Jun	US passes Alien Registration Act
1940	Jun	40,000 followers of Gandhi are imprisoned in India
1940	Jul	Battle of Britain begins when Nazis attack by air
1940	Aug	Churchill praises RAF by saying, "Never in the field of human conflict was so much owed by so many to so few."
1940	Sep	Luftwaffe blitzes London for 57 consecutive nights
1940	Nov	Warsaw Jews are forced to live in walled ghetto
1940	Dec	British troops launch first major offence in North Africa
1940	Dec	Germany drops incendiary bombs on London
1941		US Air Raid Volunteers enforce blackout rules
1941		The Jeep makes its combat debut
1941	Jan	British and Australian troops capture Tobruk from Italians
1941	Jan	First mass killing of Jews in Romania
1941	Feb	Nazi SS round up the Jews of Amsterdam
1941	Feb	Japanese attack Singapore
1941	Feb	Rommel and German Africa Corps land in Tripoli, Libya
1941	Feb	First train of Jews to concentration camps leaves Poland
1941	Apr	Germany blitzes Coventry, England
1941	May	First US ship, SS Robin Moore, sunk by German U-boat
1941	May	Martin Bormann succeeds Rudoft Hess as Hitler's deputy
1941	May	Bismarck sinks British ship HMS Hood; 1416 die, 3 survive
1941	May	Britain sinks the Bismarck
1941	Jun	Germany declares war on USSR

1941	Jul	Japanese forces land in Indo-China
1941	Aug	Siege of Leningrad by German troops begins
1941	Sep	Wearing the Yellow star becomes mandatory for all Jews in the German Reich
1941	Sep	Over 3700 Jews are buried alive at Babi Yar ravine near Kiev, Ukraine
1941	Oct	US destroyer, Kearney, torpedoed by Germans off Iceland
1941	Oct	USS Reuben James torpedoed by Germany
1941	Dec	Japanese Emperor Hirohito signs declaration of war
1941	Dec	A day that will live in infamy: Japanese attack Pearl Harbor
1941	Dec	US declares war on Japan and enters WWII
1941	Dec	Japanese troops overrun Guam
1941	Dec	Germany and Italy declare war on the US
1941	Dec	Japanese attack Wake Island
1941	Dec	USS Swordfish is first US submarine to sink a Japanese ship
1941	Dec	British-Canadian garrison at Hong Kong surrenders to Japanese
1941	Dec	Japan bombs Manila although it had been declared an "open city"
1941	Dec	Churchill arrives in Washington CD for wartime conference
1942	Jan	28 nations at war with Axis pledge no separate peace
1942	Jan	Siege of Bataan starts
1942	Jan	Nazis hold Wannsee conference in Berlin, deciding on "Final Solution" of extermination of all European Jews
1942	Jan	German U-boats harassing shipping on US East Coast
1942	Mar	First deportation train leaves Paris for Auschwitz
1942	Mar	Belzec Concentration Camp opens with 30,000 Polish Jews, 2500 immediately massacred
1942	Mar	First "Eichmann transport" to Auschwitz and Birkenau
1942	Mar	Japan camptures Rangoon, Burma
1942	Mar	General MacArthur leaves Corregidor (Bataan) for Australia
1942	Apr	Battle of Bataan: US/Filipino forces overwhelmed by Japan
1942	Apr	"Stars & Stripes" armed forces newspaper begins
1942	Apr	General Jimmy Doolittle bombs Tokyo
1942	May	Luftwaffe bombs Exeter, England
1942	May	Nazis order all Jewish pregnant women of Kovno Ghetto executed
1942	May	Battle of Coral Sea
1942	May	Nazis murder 10,000 Czechoslovakians
1942	May	Corregidor and Philippines surrender to Japan
1942	May	German U-boat sinks American cargo ship at mouth of Mississippi River
1942	May	Luftwaffe bombs Canterbury, England
1942	Jun	Battle of Midway, Japan's first major defeat of war

1942	Jun	USS Yorktown sinks near Midway
1942	Jun	American expeditionary force lands in Africa
1942	Jun	Rommel takes Tobruk in N. Africa
1942	Jun	First American bombing mission over Europe
1942	Jul	Nazis murder over 20,000 Jews in Minsk, Russia
1942	Aug	British arrest Gandhi again
1942	Aug	American offensive at Guadalcanal in Solomon Islands
1942	Sep	German forces attack Stalingrad
1942	Sep	British launch major offensive at El Alamein, Egypt
1942	Oct	Nazis kill over 15,000 Jews in Pinsk, Russia
1942	Dec	US bombers strike Italian mainland for first time
1942		The Pentagon is completed at cost of $83 million
1942	Dec	Japanese women's camp, Ambarawa, commences operation
1943	Jan	Jews in Warsaw Ghetto begin their resistance movement
1943	Feb	Battle of Stalingrad ends with surrender of German army, often cited as the turning point of World War II
1943	Feb	Hans Scholl, German Resistance fighter beheaded
1943	Feb	Epic battle of Guadalcanal ends
1943	Mar	US mistakenly bombs Rotterdam, killing over 300
1943	Mar	SS threatens to kill half of all Jewish children
1943	Mar	Failed assassination attempt on Hitler
1943	May	German troops surrender in Tunisia, North Africa
1943	Jul	US and British troops invade Sicily
1943	Jul	Benito Mussolini is dismissed as Premier of Italy
1943	Aug	US overruns New Georgia in Solomon Islands
1943	Sep	Italy surrenders to Allies
1943	Sep	Chaing Kai-shek becomes President of China
1943	Nov	FDR, Churchill and Chiang Kai-shek meet to discuss the defeat of Japan
1943	Dec	FDR, Churchill & Stalin discuss Operation Overlord (D-Day)
1943	Dec	General Montgomery appointed commandant for D-Day
1943	Dec	Dwight Eisenhower appointed Supreme Commander of Allied forces
1944	Jan	General Clark replaces General Patton as commander of 7th Army
1944	Jan	RAF drops bombs on Berlin
1944	Jan	Battle of Anzio
1944	Jan	Leningrad liberated from German occupation after 880 days and over 600,000 killed
1944	Jan	D-Day postponed until June
1944	Feb	Allied troops first set foot on Japanese territory
1944	Feb	Juan Peron leads coup in Argentina
1944	Mar	US Air Force bombs Berlin during daylight hours

1944	Mar	Cassio, Italy destroyed by Allied bombing
1944	Mar	76 Allied officers escape Stalag Luft 3 (The Great Escape)
1944	May	Generals Rommel, Speidel and von Stupnagel attempt to assassinate Hitler
1944	May	Hundreds of Gypsies transported to Auschwitz from the Netherlands
1944	Jun	Napalm is first used in warfare
1944	Jun	Serviceman's Readjustment Act (GI Bill) is signed
1944	Jun	150,000 Allied forces land in Normandy, France (D-Day)
1944	Jul	US invades Japanese occupied Guam
1944	Aug	The liberation of Paris: American troops march down the Champs Elysees
1944	Aug	70,000 Jews of Lodz, Poland are deported to Auschwitz
1944	Oct	General Rommel commits suicide
1944	Oct	US forces under MacArthur return to the Philippines
1944	Nov	US bombers attack Tokyo
1944	Dec	Battle of the Bulge begins in Belgium
1944	Dec	Hungarian "Death March" of Jews finally ends
1944		Nobel Peace Prize won by International Red Cross
1944		Nearly 3 million people die in the Great Bengal Famine in Bengali, India (now Bangladesh)
1945	Jan	US attacks Okinawa
1945	Jan	Auschwitz concentration camp begins evacuation
1945	Jan	Swede Raoul Wallenberg, who saved tens of thousands of Jews from the Nazis, is arrested by secret police in Hungary
1945	Jan	Gen. "Vinegar Joe" Stillwell reopens Burma Road to China
1945	Feb	Allied planes bomb Dresden, killing over 130,000
1945	Feb	US forces land on Corregidor
1945	Feb	30,000 US Marines land on Iwo Jima
1945	Feb	FDR, Churchill and Stalin meet at Yalta
1945	Mar	US attacks Tokyo with fire bombs, setting Tokyo on fire
1945	Mar	1000 Allied bombers drop bombs on Essen, Germany
1945	Mar	1500 US Navy ships bomb Okinawa
1945	Apr	Allies liberate Buchenwald
1945	Apr	Allies liberate Dachau
1945	May	Heinrich Himmler commits suicide
1945	May	Adolph Hitler commits suicide
1945	May	V-E Day: Germany signs unconditional surrender
1945	May	Gandhi freed from prison
1945	May	Churchill resigns as Prime Minister
1945	May	Admiral Karl Doenitz forms a new German government
1945	Jun	UN Charter is signed by 50 nations in San Francisco
1945	Jul	First atomic bomb detonated at Alamogordo, New Mexico

Sharing My Stories—What Japanese Means

My father fought in the South Pacific during World War II. He was badly wounded in 1943, long before I was born. Nevertheless, his wounds made an impact on my life.

Dad's legs and buttocks were riddled with shrapnel, which often became inflamed by raging infections. He also suffered ongoing debilitating attacks of malaria. Many times the infections or malaria were serious enough to send him to the hospital, where he frequently was during my childhood. Indeed, he was in the hospital the day that I was born, although the story goes that he escaped long enough to take one swift look at me before he had to go back.

My earliest memories of Dad are seeing him shuddering and shivering while huddled underneath a blanket, sweat pouring down his face. I asked my mother why Daddy was so sick, and she told me that he had been shot by the Japanese. At the age of three, I had no idea who or what the Japanese were, but if they had hurt my Daddy, then it was obvious to me that they had to be very, very bad.

So strong was my correlation between "bad" and "Japanese" that I used these words interchangeably. I became an innocent and unknowing racist. When I was angry at one of my friends, I called her "Japanese" – the worst insult I could think of. If I didn't want to eat my vegetables, I would say, "I don't like these Japanese peas."

Once I had a cruel babysitter who I hated and feared. For one thing, she talked funny, making a lot of "zzzz" sounds. I thought she sounded like a snake. She taught me the song *Frere Jacques* by beating time with a thin stick and sharply rapping my hands when I made a mistake. My parents said she was French but I knew they were wrong. It was obvious to me that she was definitely Japanese.

Hatred is so easy to learn.

1945	Aug	Atom bomb dropped on Hiroshima by ship "Enola Gay"
1945	Aug	V-J day: Japan surrenders and World War II ends
1945	Sep	Ho Chi Minh declares Vietnam independent from France
1945	Oct	Chinese civil war begins, between Chiang Kai-Shek and Mao Zedong
1945	Oct	Juan Peron becomes dictator of Argentina
1946	Aug	British transfer illegal Palestinian immigrants to Cyprus
1946	Sep	22 Nazi leaders found guilty of war crimes at Nuremberg
1947	Jan	Gandhi begins "March for Peace" in East Bengali
1947	Feb	Arabs and Jews reject British proposal to split Palestine
1947	Feb	Lord Mountbatten is appointed as the last British Viceroy of India
1947	Aug	India declares independence from Britain; Pakistan declares Islamic state
1947	Nov	Jewish settlements in Palestine attacked by Arabs
1948	Jan	Mahatma Gandhi assassinated
1948	Feb	Communist Party seizes control of Czechoslovakia
1948	Apr	Truman signs Marshall Plan of $5 Billion to aid 16 European countries
1948	May	David Ben-Gurion named first Prime Minister of new State of Israel
1948	May	Israeli Air Force defeats Syrian Army
1948	May	28-year British Mandate over Palestine ends
1948	May	Chaim Weizmann elected first President of Israel
1948	Jun	USSR begins Berlin blockade
1948	Nov	Japanese Premier Tojo sentenced to death by war crimes tribunal
1948	Dec	UN General Assembly adopts the Universal Declaration of Human Rights
1948	Dec	State of Eire declares its independence
1948		Bernard Baruch coins the term "cold war"
1949	Jan	Mao Zedong's Red Army conquers Ten-tsin
1949	Mar	NATO (North Atlantic Treaty Organization) is ratified
1949	Apr	Ireland withdraws from British Commonwealth
1949	May	The Berlin Airlift begins around the Soviet blockade
1949	Jun	South Africa implements apartheid as official state policy
1949	Sep	People's Republic of China proclaimed
1950	Feb	Nuclear physicist Klaus Fuchs arrested on spying charges
1950	Mar	USSR announces they have developed atomic bomb
1950	Jan	Ho Chi Minh begins offensive against French in Indo-China
1950	Feb	Chiang Kai-shek elected President of Nationalist China
1950	May	Ho Chi Minh's troops attack Cambodia
1950	Jun	North Korea invades South Korea; Korean War begins

1950	Jun	UN calls on members for troops to aid South Korea
1950	Jul	Douglas MacArthur named Commander in Chief of UN forces in Korea
1950	Oct	US forces invade Korea by crossing the 38th parallel
1950	Dec	Chinese troops cross 38th parallel into South Korea
1950	Dec	Vietnam, Laos and Cambodia become Independent States in France Union
1951	Jan	UN Headquarters opens in New York City
1951	Jan	China refuses Korean cease-fire
1951	Jan	UN begins counter-offensive in Korea
1951	Feb	UN condemns People's Republic of China as the aggressor in Korea
1951	May	Chinese Communists force Dalai Lama to surrender to Beijing
1951	Jul	Korean War Peace talks at Kaesong begin
1951	Oct	Korean War Peace talks resume at Panmunjom
1951	Feb	Alfred Krupp and 28 other German war criminals freed
1952	Feb	Winston Churchill announces that Britain has atom bomb
1952	Feb	French launch offensive at Hanoi
1952	Mar	Military coup by Batista in Cuba
1952	Mar	Huge demonstrations against apartheid in South Africa
1952	Mar	Failed assassination attempt on German Chancellor Konrad Adenauer
1952	May	Nehru becomes premier of India
1952	Aug	Hussein becomes King of Jordan
1952	Oct	Mau Mau rebellion in Kenya against the British begins
1953	Jan	Yugoslavia elects Marshal Tito as president
1953	Mar	Dag Hammarskjold becomes Secretary General of UN
1953	Sep	Khruschev becomes Secretary of Soviet Communist Party
1953	Jul	Armistice signed ending Korean War
1953	Aug	Operation "Big Switch": Korean War prisoners exchanged at Panmunjom
1954	Sep	SEATO founded to stop communist spread in SE Asia
1954	May	French surrender to Vietminh after siege at Dien Bien Phu
1954	Jun	Rebels overthrow elected government of Guatemala
1955	Jan	US and Panama sign canal treaty
1955	Mar	East Germany granted full sovereignty by USSR
1955	May	Warsaw Pact is signed by USSR, Albania, Bulgaria, Czechoslovakia, East Germany and Hungary
1955	Jun	Pope Pius XII ex-communicates Argentine President Juan Peron
1955	Oct	Ngo Dinh Diem proclaims Vietnam a Republic, and himself President
1955	Feb	Eisenhower sends first US advisors to South Vietnam

1955	Mar	Eisenhower upholds the use of atomic weapons for war
1955	Mar	British Army patrols withdraw from Belfast for first time in 20 years
1955	May	Israel attacks Gaza
1956	Feb	Khrushchev denounces Stalin at Soviet Party Conference
1956	Jul	Egypt seizes Suez Canal
1956	Oct	Hungarian Revolution begins against Stalinist policies
1956	Oct	Britain and France bomb Egypt to reopen Suez Canal
1956	Nov	200,000 Russian troops attack anti-Soviet revolt in Budapest, Hungary
1956	Nov	Holland and Spain withdraw from Olympics in protest of Soviets in Hungary
1956	Nov	Israeli troops reach Suez Canal, and Britain and French forces land in Egypt
1956	Nov	UN demands USSR leave Hungary
1956	Dec	Nelson Mandela arrested for political activities in South Africa
1956	Dec	IRA strikes in Northern Ireland
1957	Mar	Eamon de Valera's Fianna Fail party wins election in Ireland
1957	Mar	Treaty of Rome establishes European Economic Community, or the Common Market
1957	May	South Africa establishes race separation in universities
1957	May	Anti-American riots in Taipei, Taiwan
1957	Jun	John Diefenbacker becomes Prime Minister of Canada
1957	Jan	Eisenhower asks Congress for troops to the Middle East
1957	Mar	Anti-Batista demonstrations in Havana, Cuba
1957	Oct	B-52 bombers flying full-time alert in case of USSR attack
1958	Jan	9000 scientists of 43 nations ask UN for nuclear test ban
1958	Mar	Havana Hilton opens
1958	May	VP Nixon is shoved, stoned, booed and spat upon by protesters in Peru
1958	May	Mao Zedong starts "Great Leap Forward" movement
1958	Jul	King Faisal of Iraq assassinated in Baghdad
1958	Oct	USSR lends money to UAR to build Aswan Dam
1958	Dec	Charles De Gaulle wins term as first President of 5th Republic of France
1958	Jan	Revolutionary forces capture Havana, Batista flees to Dominican Republic, & US recognizes Castro's government
1959	May	Soviet forces invade Afghanistan
1959	Jul	First Americans killed in Vietnam
1959	Sep	Khrushchev visits US
1959	Dec	12 nations sign a treaty for scientific peaceful use of Antarctica

1960 through 1989

The Cold War that began after World War II was in full swing throughout these three decades, finally coming to an end in 1989 with the collapse of the former Soviet Union. This political and philosophical division between East and West colored everything pertinent to international relations, and was responsible for the war that defined the huge baby boomer generation: Vietnam.

The stories that come from the Vietnam War are totally different than those from World War II or Korea. Even the stories of heroism are tinged with sadness, guilt, anger, righteousness, betrayal.

"Peggy" shared about her son who served in Vietnam. She and her husband, patriots of the World War II generation, were proud when their son volunteered for the Army and was sent to Vietnam in 1964. Over the next two years their pride turned to anguish as they read his increasingly disturbed letters home, letters that reeked of despair and anger. In the third year he stopped writing, which was to them the longest year of all. When he was finally discharged, their relief that he had made it home was short-lived, since he spent the next five years spiraling into alcoholism and drug addiction, from which he never recovered. He committed suicide in 1972. "His name isn't on that Wall," said Peggy. "But it should be."

Vietnam was different from previous wars in many ways. It was a televised war, with a war's brutality and horror displayed right in one's living room, often in living color. Images such as the civilian being shot in the head by a police captain, the naked little girl running away from her burning village, the Buddhist monk dousing himself in gasoline and setting himself on fire, are burned into the national consciousness.

Because of the major role journalists played in bringing the war home, the Vietnam War was not seen as heroic. It was an ugly war. There were atrocities on both sides; it wasn't just the other guy who did bad things – so did we. The US sprayed chemical defoliants over the jungles, causing ecological disasters and destroying whole communities. Chemical and germ warfare were experimented with – by America. In 1968 Americans were stunned by the revelations of the My Lai Massacre, in which American servicemen were shown murdering women and children.

All wars contain cruelty on both sides, of course; Vietnam was not unique. But in other wars the cruelty and horror of war was rationalized as being necessary. There was a good reason for those wars — or at least people believed so. It was this belief in war's necessity that eroded during Vietnam, and is another factor defining its difference. Why were we there? What did we gain? Enough to offset the terrible costs? The answer, increasingly, was no. War protests were by the late sixties a raging torrent, necessitating calling out the National Guard in some cases, most unforgettably Kent State University in Ohio. By the early seventies there had been huge war protests in nearly every major American city. Chanting slogans such as "Hey hey LBJ how many kids did you kill today?" and "Hell no we won't go!" some draft-age young men burned their draft cards. Some left for Canada to avoid the draft.

"Doug" remembered the day the first Draft Lottery numbers were announced, in December of 1969 when he was a junior at the University of Washington. He, along with many of his fraternity brothers, didn't go to class that day. Your Lottery number was associated with your birthday. A low Lottery number was bad – it meant you were sure to be drafted. A high lottery number, the best being 366, meant that you wouldn't have to make any difficult decisions, like between exile to Canada or dying in a Vietnamese jungle. They sat on the veranda of the fraternity house, drinking

beer and telling dirty jokes and trying to pretend that they weren't scared while waiting for the numbers to be read over the radio. Doug even remembered the jokes, and the guys who told them. But what he doesn't remember is hearing his number. His memory stops dead at the point the announcer began to read the list. He doesn't remember anything else about that day, or days after. The next day he remembers is the day, weeks later, that he joined the Navy, to avoid being drafted. Doug's number was 10. "It was such a shock," he read. "Everything in my life just went blank."

The Vietnam trauma didn't end after the fall of Saigon. America had lost the war, a blow to national self-esteem. Vietnam veterans were not treated with the same honor and respect as veterans of other wars. They had to cope with their war legacies with little help or understanding. The POW/MIA anguish dragged on for years.

During the sixties through the eighties Americans increasingly saw themselves as part of the world community. The Peace Corps began in 1960, inspiring many young people to try to make the world a better place. Amnesty International was founded in 1961. Travel became more affordable and more Americans than ever before traveled around the globe.

Other important global trends during these decades included the last gasps of colonialism; the rise of virulent and vocal anti-Americanism; the use of terrorism as a deliberate, organized political tactic; and the upsurge in religious fundamentalism (of all kinds) allied with governmental power. Moving around the globe, here are some events and people which may trigger memories.

In Europe: The Irish question still plagued Britain, with events like "Bloody Sunday" in 1972, or the hunger strike of Bobby Sands. Margaret Thatcher became Prime Minister in the late seventies and stayed there for three terms. In 1982 Britain went to war with Argentina over the Falkland islands. Spanish fascists created a hostage crisis in 1981. From 1967 to 1986 the Romanian dictator

Ceausescu was responsible for the killing of millions. In Russia, Nikita Khruschev banged his shoe at the United Nations in 1960, and declared he would bury the US; later Russia put down insurgencies in Afghanistan and Czechosolvakia; dissidents were banished to Siberia in the 1980s; and in 1985 Mikhail Gorbachev came to power. Free elections were held in 1988, and in 1989 the world saw the total collapse of the Soviet Union. With this collapse a number of "new/old" countries appeared, changing the face of Europe.

In the late eighties, "Tom" worked for a company with offices in Germany, and was in Berlin on the day the wall came down. "There aren't any words for how I felt," he wrote. "The Berlin Wall was such a given — I couldn't remember when there wasn't one. It was like a river or a mountain; something huge and natural and always there. When it was torn down I felt this enormous rush of personal power — if we could tear down the Wall, we could accomplish anything."

In Africa: Colonialism ended with a host of independence movements in Somalia, Zaire, Ghana, Nigeria, and others. The turmoil thus unleashed was often very painful, such as the 1967 Biafran war against Nigeria, and the 1971 coup in Uganda that put Idi Amin in power. Muammer Quaddafi of Libya appeared on the world scene and remained a thorn in the US side. There were enormous changes in South Africa, and worldwide protests over the policy of apartheid. Nelson Mandela was jailed in 1964 and finally freed in 1985, when he personally presided over apartheid's overdue last gasp.

In India and Pakistan: Political turmoil abounded. Indira Gandhi dominated the political landscape of India during all three decades until she was assassinated in 1984. In Pakistan, Benazir Bhutto won the first free elections in nearly twenty years in 1988.

*"Delia," a teacher, remembered traveling to an
educational conference in India in 1984. Their group was
granted a personal audience with Indira Gandhi. Delia wrote
how concerned Mrs. Gandhi was with America's perception
of India, often asking the teachers, "What do Americans
think?" Delia also remembers the silent yet looming presence
of Mrs. Gandhi's Sikh bodyguard who attended the meeting.
"He had no expression on his face and he said nothing," she
read. "But I couldn't help wondering what he was
thinking." A few weeks later, reading about the
assassination of Mrs. Gandhi in the newspapers, Delia
wondered if that particular bodyguard was the one who
struck the fatal blow.*

In the Middle East: The names and places may have changed, but the basic fact about this region was the same as it is today: it was torn by the continual war between Israel and one or more of its Arab neighbors. Yassar Arafat formed the Palestine Liberation Organization in 1964, and demonstrated remarkable staying power. Turmoil also defined Iraq and Iran during these decades. The Shah of Iran, with US support, tried to westernize Iran (without granting political freedom) against the opposition of Islamic Fundamentalists, who rose to power in 1979 under the Ayatollah Khomeini. The Shah was exiled and Khomeini's supporters kidnapped and held seventy Americans hostage for 444 days, creating a diplomatic crisis in America that probably cost Jimmy Carter his presidency. The next decade was dominated by the Iran-Iraq war, which saw the rise of Saddam Hussein.

In the Far East: In 1968 North Korean seized a US Navy ship in the Pueblo crisis. In the 1980s during a people's uprising in South Korea over 2000 people were killed by the police. In the 1970s the Khmer Rouge under Pol Pot seized control in Cambodia and conducted a genocidal campaign killed millions. In 1965 China invaded Tibet (again) and over the years suffered in world opinion from numerous human-rights violations. From 1966 to 1976 Mao Zedong's "Cultural Revolution" sought to purify the Chinese Communist party. Richard Nixon made his historic trip to China in 1972, launching a "friendlier" relationship symbolized by zoo trades of Giant Pandas and international ping-pong tournaments. In the 1980s Mao was condemned by the new communist party and his wife was jailed, and in May of 1989 the image of one man facing a tank in Tian'anmen Square was worth thousands of words.

In the Americas: Coups corruption and fighting in countries, including the Contras and the Sandanistas in Nicargua, the Dominican Republic, Guatemala, El Salvador, Allende and Pinochet in Chile, the Perons in Argentina, Marcos in the Phillipines, and Jean Paul Duvalier (Baby Doc) in Haiti, among others. Cuba, due to its geographic proximity, has always been of interest to Americans. Eisenhower was President when Fidel Castro came to power, and nine presidents later, he is still there. Many class participants vividly remember the Cuban Missile Crisis of 1962.

"Kathy" remembered sitting quietly at her desk during her eighth-grade science class in October of 1962, at the height of the Cuban Missile Crisis. For days the teacher hadn't even tried to teach science. Instead she brought in her radio and she and the children listened to the news. The teacher often listened with her head down on her desk, resting on her arms. "The only time she raised her head," shared Kathy, "was to yell at some boy who was acting up. But most of us were as scared as she was, although I don't think any of us really understood what was happening. A lot of us didn't even know where Cuba was."

Review the following timeline and see what *you* remember …

1960-1989 Event Timeline
Wars & the International Scene

1960	Jan	European Free Trade Association forms in Stockholm
1960	Jan	Algeria revolts against France
1960	Mar	President Sukarno disbands Indonesia's parliament
1960	Mar	South African Police kill 72 in the "Sharpville Massacre"
1960	May	Brezhnev becomes President of USSR
1960	Jun	British Somaliland declares independence from Britain
1960	Jun	Belgian Congo gains independence from Belgium and becomes Zaire
1960	Jul	Ghana becomes a republic
1960	Jul	Ivory Coast, Dahomey, Upper Volta, Congo, Chad & Niger declare independence
1960	Aug	Senegal declares independence
1960	Sep	UN admits 13 African countries and Cyprus
1960	Sep	Fidel Castro makes longest speech in UN history
1960	Oct	Nikita Khrushchev gives speech at UN, pounding his shoe and declaring, "We will bury you."
1960	Oct	JFK proposes the Peace Corps
1960	Oct	US imposes embargo on exports to Cuba
1960	Dec	UN condemns apartheid
1960	Dec	King Saudi takes power in Saudi Arabia
1961	Jan	US breaks off diplomatic relations with Cuba
1961	Jan	UN "Genocide Pact" goes into effect
1961	Jan	Portugeuese rebels seize a cruise ship
1961	Jan	Military coup in El Salvador
1961	Jan	Rwanda proclaims itself a State
1961	Jan	David Ben-Gurion resigns as premier of Israel
1961	Jan	Full-scale test of US Minuteman ICBM
1961	Mar	South Africa withdraws from the British Commonwealth
1961	Mar	Nelson Mandela acquitted of treason, after 4 year trial
1961	Apr	Cuban exiles attempt to overthrow Castro in "Bay of Pigs"
1961	Apr	JFK accepts sole responsibility for Bay of Pigs
1961	May	Tanganyika declares independence from Britain
1961	May	Castro offers to exchange Bay of Pigs prisoners
1961	May	Amnesty International is founded
1961	Jun	Iraq claims Kuwait as part of Iraq; Kuwait disagrees
1961	Aug	Construction begins on Berlin Wall
1961	Aug	Former Nazi leader Vorster becomes Minister of Justice in South Africa
1961	Dec	Castro declares Cuba a communist state
1961	Dec	JFK sends military helicopters and crews to South Vietnam

1961	Dec	Marshall plan expires, after sending more than $12 billion
1962	Jan	Mandela leaves South Africa, traveling to Ethiopia, Algeria and England
1962	Jan	US starts spraying foliage in Vietnam to reveal Viet Cong
1962	Jan	British spsy Kim Philby defects to USSR
1962	Feb	JFK bans all trade with Cuba except food and drugs
1962	Feb	First US serviceman in Vietnam killed
1962	Mar	US promises Thailand assistance against communists
1962	Mar	Nasser of Egypt declares Gaza belongs to Palestine
1962	Mar	Algerian War ends after over 7 years of fighting
1962	May	US Marines arrive in Laos
1962	Aug	Nelson Mandela arrested for incitement and illegally leaving South Africa
1962	Aug	Jamaica gains independence from Britain
1962	Sep	US sells anti-aircraft missiles to Israel
1962	Oct	US becomes aware of missiles in Cuba and demands they be removed
1962	Oct	Khrushchev orders withdrawal of missiles from Cuba
1962	Nov	U Thant of Burma elected Secretary General of UN
1963	Feb	Argentina asks for extradition of ex-president Peron
1963	May	Sukarno becomes President of Indonesia
1963	May	Jomo Kenyatta becomes first Prime Minister of Kenya
1963	Jun	US & USSR set up "hot line" – the famous red telephone
1963	Jun	JFK goes to West Berlin and says "Ich bin ein Berliner"
1963	Jun	US, Britain & USSR sign nuclear test-ban treaty
1963	Aug	Martial law declared in South Vietnam
1963	Oct	Trial of Mandela and 8 others for conspiracy begins
1964	Jan	Anti US rioting in Panama Canal Zone
1964	Feb	LBJ reveals secretly developed A-11 jet fighter
1964	May	PLO (Palestine National Congress) formed in Jerusalem
1964	Jun	Nelson Mandela sentenced to life imprisonment
1964	Aug	North Vietnam fires on a US ship in Gulf of Tonkin
1964	Aug	US begins bombing North Vietnam
1964	Aug	US Congress passes Gulf of Tonkin resolution
1964	Oct	Kosygin and Brezhnev replace Nikita Khrushchev
1964	Oct	China becomes a nuclear power
1964	Jan	Winston Churchill dies at the age of 90
1965	Jan	Palestinian organization, al-Fatah, forms
1965	Jan	Military coup in South Vietnam
1965	Feb	US begins regular bombing and strafing of North Vietnam
1965	Mar	First US combat forces arrive in South Vietnam
1965	Mar	US admits to using chemical warfare against the Vietcong
1965	Apr	US Marines sent to Dominican Republic
1965	May	Vietcong offensive against US base in DaNang begins

1965	Sep	Tibet is made an autonomous region of China
1965	Nov	Rhodesia proclaims independence from Britain
1965	Dec	Ferdinand Marcos becomes President of the Philippines
1966	Jan	Indira Gandhi elected Prime Minister of India
1966	Feb	Obote takes power in Uganda
1966	Feb	President Kwame Nkrumah of Ghana ousted by coup
1966	Mar	General Suharto leads military coup in Indonesia
1966	May	Buddhist monk sets himself on fire at US Consulate in South Vietnam
1966	Dec	US first bombs Hanoi
1967	Jan	NY Times reports the Army is conducting secret germ warfare experiments
1967	Jan	Anastasio Somoza elected President of Nicaragua
1967	Mar	Greneda gains partial independence from Britain
1967	Mar	Stalin's daughter asks for political asylum in US
1967	Mar	Univ. of Michigan holds first "Teach-In" after bombing of North Vietnam
1967	Mar	U Thant asks for peace proposals for Vietnam
1967	May	Thousands in US demonstrate against War in Vietnam
1967	Jun	6 day war between Israel and Arab neighbors Syria, Jordan, Iraq & Egypt
1967	Jul	Nigeria invades Biafra
1967	Sep	Ngyuen Van Thieu elected President of South Vietnam
1967	Oct	Che Guevara executed in Bolivia
1967	Oct	Shah of Iran crowns himself
1967	Oct	Thousands opposing Vietnam War storm the Pentagon
1967	Dec	Nicolae Ceausescu becomes President of Romania
1967	Dec	Benjamin Spock and Allen Ginsberg arrested protesting Vietnam War
1968	Jan	Viet Cong Tet Offensive begins in Saigon
1968	Jan	North Korea seizes USS Pueblo and its 83-man crew in Sea of Japan
1968	Feb	Preserved by famous photo, Saigon police chief executes a Viet Cong officer by shooting him in the head
1968	Mar	450 die in the My Lai massacre in Vietnam
1968	Apr	Pierre Trudeau becomes Prime Minister of Canada
1968	Apr	Students take over Columbia University in war protest
1968	Apr	Students seize administration building at Ohio State
1968	May	Vietnam peace talks begin in Paris
1968	May	UN imposes sanctions on white-ruled Rhodesia
1968	Jul	US, Britain, USSR & 58 other nations sign Nuclear Nonproliferation Treaty
1968	Aug	Warsaw Pact troops invade Czechoslovakia to stop political reforms

1968	Oct	LBJ orders halt of bombing of North Vietnam
1968	Dec	82 members of USS Pueblo released by North Korea
1969	Jan	Jan Palach sets himself on fire to protest Soviet invasion of Czechoslovakia
1969	Jan	Expanded Vietnam peace talks begin in Paris
1969	Jan	Syria publicly executes 9 Jews
1969	Feb	Yasser Arafat becomes head of the PLO
1969	Feb	Golda Meir becomes Prime Minister of Israel
1969	May	US troops begin attack on Hamburger Hill
1969	Aug	British troops sent to Northern Ireland
1969	Sep	Ho Chi Minh dies
1969	Sep	Moammer Gadhafi deposes King Idris in Libya
1969	Oct	Vietnam Moratorium Day: millions nationwide protest war
1969	Nov	250,000 demonstrate in Washington DC against the war
1970	Jan	Biafra surrenders to Nigeria, famine sweeps country
1970	Mar	General Lon Nol deposes Prince Sihanuk in Cambodia
1970	Mar	National Guard kills 4 protesters at Kent State in Ohio
1970	Apr	Qatar declares independence from Britain
1970	Apr	US troops invade Cambodia
1970	May	South Africa is excluded from the Olympics
1970	May	Freelance writer Seymour Hersh wins Pulitzer Prize for breaking My Lai story
1970	May	Arab terrorists kills 9 children on a school bus
1970	May	Hundreds of thousands demonstrate against war
1970	Jun	US ends 2-month military offensive into Cambodia
1970	Sep	Anwar Sadat becomes President of Egypt
1970	Oct	Khmer Republic (Cambodia) declares independence
1970	Nov	Salvador Allende becomes President of Chile
1971	Jan	General Idi Amin Dada leads military coup in Uganda
1971	Feb	US, UK, USSR & others sign Seabed Treaty outlawing nuclear weapons
1971	Mar	South Vietnamese troops flee Laos
1971	Mar	Bangladesh, formerly East Pakistan, declares independence
1971	Mar	Allende nationalizes banks and copper mines in Chile
1971	Mar	Radio Hanoi airs Jimi Hendrix's "Star Spangled Banner"
1971	Apr	US table tennis team arrives in China to play on PR mission
1971	Apr	Columbia University shut down by anti-war student strike
1971	Apr	200,000 anti-war protestors, some veterans, demonstrate
1971	Aug	Bahrain proclaims independence from Britain
1971	Aug	British begin a policy of internment without trial in Northern Ireland
1971	Oct	UN admits Mainland China and expels Taiwan
1971	Dec	United Arab Emirates is formed
1971	Dec	Kurt Waldheim becomes Secretary General of UN

Sharing My Stories—Vietnam Lasted Longer Than You Think

I met Matt in 1970. He became one of my best friends, but when I first met him I didn't even like him. He was a severely damaged man.

Matt was a Vietnam vet with a major drug habit. His drug of choice was marijuana, but he used others too. In fact for the first twenty years I knew him I never saw Matt not stoned. He also drank heavily, often drunk enough to pass out on the floor. He couldn't hold down a job very long. He couldn't maintain relationships with women. They would always leave him, usually sooner rather than later. He even tried suicide a few times.

I used to joke that Matt was my first child. We were his surrogate family, and he viewed our home as his. We put up with a lot, because his good qualities were awesome. He was the kindest, gentlest man I ever knew. He was witty, with a quirky sense of humor that could reduce me to helpless laughter. He was bright, with well-reasoned opinions. And he was passionate about protecting the innocent and righting injustice.

Above all else, Matt hated the US government. He believed them to be not only corrupt but incompetent. He had his reasons.

Matt served in Vietnam in the late 1960s, where he picked up his drug habit. He was a corpsman. He rode around in helicopters to battle-fields, picking up dead boys and body parts and stuffing them into body bags. Sometimes the battles were still being fought around him as he stuffed. He was wounded twice, but not seriously enough to be sent home. We only knew some of Matt's war experiences; usually the only stories he told of Vietnam concerned drugs. He could laugh about those.

Matt stayed stoned, alone and unemployed until 1989, the year he turned 40. In that year he moved to Mexico, met and married a girl from a dinky little village a hundred miles from nowhere. He was 41 and she 19 when they married, and her family (the whole town) adopted him. I don't know how, but they saved him. He got clean and sober, he went to college, he began a new career, and became the father of two little girls.

Too bad this story doesn't end here. In 2000, Matt was diagnosed with lymphoma, the kind the US government now admits is caused by exposure to Agent Orange. Thousands of men who served in Vietnam thirty years ago are now dying of it.

Matt died on Christmas day 2001. He was 52. Whenever I think of Vietnam, I think of my friend Matt, and I get angry all over again.

1972	Jan	British soldiers fire on Catholics in Londonderry, killing 13 in what becomes known as "Bloody Sunday"
1972	Feb	Britain joins the European Common Market
1972	Mar	Britian imposes direct rule over Northern Ireland
1972	Mar	North Vietnamese troops enter South Vietnam
1972	Apr	70 nations agree to ban biological weapons
1972	Apr	2 giant pandas arrive in US, a gift from China
1972	May	Vietcong forms revolutionary government in S. Vietnam
1972	May	Nixon and Brezhnev sign SALT accord
1972	Aug	Last American combat ground troops leave Vietnam
1972	Sep	11 Israeli athletes murdered at Olympics in Munich
1972	Sep	Martial law is declared in Philippines
1972	Oct	Henry Kissinger declares "Peace is at hand" in Vietnam
1972	Dec	Imelda Marcos of Philippines, stabbed by assailant
1972	Dec	India and Pakistan agree on new line of control in territory of Kashmir
1973	Jan	Peace talks between US and North Vietnam in Paris
1973	Feb	First US POWs in North Vietnam are released
1973	Feb	US and China establish liaison offices in Beijing and Washington DC
1973	Mar	"Black September" terrorists occupy Saudi Embassy in Khartoum
1973	Mar	Marchers in Ireland carry coffins commemorating Bloody Sunday
1973	Mar	Ellsworth Bunker resigns as US ambassador to S. Vietnam
1973	Sep	Allende of Chile is deposed in a military coup
1973	Sep	Former President Juan Peron returns to power in Argentina
1973	Oct	Yom Kippur War begins as Syria and Egypt attack Israel
1973	Nov	Military coup ousts Greek President George Papadopoulos
1974	Feb	Writer Alexander Solzhenitsyn expelled from USSR
1974	Apr	Yitzhak Rabin becomes PM of Israel
1974	Apr	Last Americans evacuated in the Fall of Saigon
1974	May	Israel and Syria come to agreement on Golan Heights
1974	Dec	Cease fire between IRA and British is signed
1974	Dec	Sandinistas revolt in Nicaragua
1975	Apr	USAF transport carrying Saigon orphans crashes
1975	Apr	Khmer Rouge captures Phnom Penh in Cambodia
1975	Jun	Indira Gandhi declares a state of emergency and imprisons political foes
1975	Oct	Soviet dissident Andrei Sakharov wins Nobel Peace Prize
1975	Oct	Anwar Sadat visits US, first Egyptian president to do so
1975	Nov	Yasser Arafat addresses the UN
1975	Nov	UN votes to seat the PLO
1976	Mar	Isabel Peron deposed as President of Argentina

1976	Mar	Israel rescues Air France crew and passengers held hostage at Entebbe Airport in Uganda by forces of Idi Amin
1976	Dec	Andrew Young named Ambassador to UN
1977	Mar	Anwar Sadat promises to regain Arab territory from Israel
1977	Mar	Carter pleads for support for Palestinian homeland
1977	Mar	Vietnam hands over MIA to US
1977	Mar	Indira Gandhi resigns as Prime Minister of India
1977	May	Menachem Begin becomes Prime Minister of Israel
1977	Sep	Steven Biko, South African leader, dies in police custody
1977	Oct	West German commandos storm hijacked Lufthansa in Mogadishu, Somalia, freeing all 86 hostages
1977	Nov	Egyptian President Sadat addresses the Israeli Knesset
1978	Feb	China lifts ban on Aristotle, Shakespeare, and Dickens
1978	Mar	Aldo Moro of Italy assassinated by Red Brigade terrorists
1978	Apr	US Senate approves transfer of Panama Canal to Panama
1978	Jun	King Hussein of Jordan marries American woman
1978	Sep	Sadat, Begin and Carter hold peace conference at Camp David, Maryland, and sign Camp David Accord
1978	Nov	Shah of Iran puts Iran under military rule
1978	Dec	Anti-Shah protestors roam streets of Tehran chanting "Allah is Great"
1979	Jan	Vietnam captures Phnom Penh from Khmer Rouge
1979	Jan	Shah of Iran flees Iran for Egypt
1979	Feb	Ayatollah Khomeini returns to Iran after a 15 year exile, takes power and proclaims an Islamic Republic
1979	Apr	Idi Amin of Uganda overthrown
1979	May	Margaret Thatcher becomes Prime Minister of Britain
1979	May	US and USSR sign Salt II treaty limiting nuclear weapons
1979	Jul	Sandinistas overthrow Somoza in Nicaragua
1979	Aug	IRA assassinates Earl Mountbatten
1979	Aug	Alexander Godunov, Bolshoi Ballet dancer, defects to US
1979	Oct	Pope John Paul II is first Pope to visit White House
1979	Oct	Mother Theresa of India is awarded the Nobel Peace Prize
1979	Nov	63 Americans taken hostage at US Embassy in Teheran, Iran, beginning the 444-day hostage crisis
1979	Dec	Crowds attack US embassy in Tripoli, Libya
1979	Dec	Zimbabwe (once Rhodesia) gains independence
1980	Jan	Mob storms Russian embassy in Teheran
1980	Jan	Indira Gandhi's Congress Party wins election in India
1980	Feb	Robert Mugabe wins election in Zimbabwe
1980	Mar	US appeals to International Court on Iran hostage issue
1980	Apr	Jimmy Carter breaks all relations with Iran
1980	Apr	US military operation to save hostages in Iran fails, 8 die

1980	May	Quebec voters reject referendum on separatism
1980	May	Iran rejects call from World Court to release US hostages
1980	May	South Korean police end people's uprising, 2000 killed
1980	Jun	UN calls for South Africa to free Nelson Mandela
1980	Jul	Olympics open in Moscow; US and others boycott
1980	Aug	Solidarity Labor Union founded in Poland
1980	Sep	Former Nicaraguan President Somoza assassinated
1980	Sep	Iraq invades part of Iran in border dispute, and war begins
1980	Sep	Cuba closes Mariel Harbor, ending "freedom flotilla"
1980	Sep	Iran rejects truce called for by Iraq's Saddam Hussein
1980	Oct	Soviet Premier Kosygin resigns
1980	Oct	Poland legalizes independent labor union Solidarity
1980	Dec	4 American nuns killed by El Salvadorian death squad
1980	Dec	Iran requests $24 billion in US guarantees to free hostages
1980	Dec	Mexico terminates fishing agreements with US
1980	Dec	Obote restores constitutional government in Uganda
1981	Jan	Philippe President Marcos ends state of siege
1981	Jan	Iran accepts US offer of $7.9 billion in frozen assets
1981	Jan	52 Americans held hostage in Iran for 444 days freed
1981	Jan	Mao's widow Jiang Qing sentenced to death in China
1981	Mar	Bobby Sands of IRA begins 65 day hunger strike in prison
1981	Mar	Pinochet begins second term as President of Chile
1981	Mar	Police and Albanian demonstrators battle in Kosovo
1981	May	US expels Libyan diplomats
1981	May	Francois Mitterrand becomes President of France
1981	May	Barcelona fascists take 200 people hostage in Spain
1981	Jun	Israel destroys alleged Iraqi plutonium production facility
1981	Jun	Chinese Communist Party condemns Mao's policies
1981	Oct	Islamic fundamentalists assassinate Anwar Sadat
1981	Dec	Poland declares martial law and arrests Solidarity activists
1981	Dec	Israel annexes Golan Heights
1981	Dec	Coup d'etat in Ghana
1982	Feb	Syrian army and Moslem fundamentalists battle
1982	Mar	Reagan proclaims economic sanctions against Libya
1982	Mar	Begin and Sadat sign peace treaty in Washington DC
1982	Mar	Nicaragua suspends citizens' rights for 30 days
1982	Mar	4 Dutch TV crewmembers shot dead in El Salvador
1982	Mar	Iran offensive against Iraq
1982	Apr	Argentina seizes Falkland Islands
1982	Apr	UN demands Argentina withdraw from Falklands
1982	Apr	Israel withdraws from Sinai in accordance with Camp David Accord
1982	May	British troops land on Falkland Islands
1982	Jun	Israel attacks South Lebanon to drive out PLO

1982	Jun	Argentina surrenders to Britain, riots in Argentina follow
1982	Jul	Margaret Thatcher begins second term as British PM
1982	Jul	IRA explodes 2 bombs in London parks
1982	Aug	Palestinian terrorists dispersed from Beirut
1982	Sep	Massacre of 1000+ Palestinian refugees in Lebanon
1982	Sep	US, Italian and French troops arrive in Lebanon
1982	Oct	Chancellor Helmut Schmidt ousted by Parliament
1982	Oct	Poland bans Solidarity
1982	Oct	China announces its population is 1 billion plus
1982	Dec	IRA bombs North Ireland disco in Londonderry, killing 17
1983	Jan	US arms embargo against Guatemala ends
1983	Jan	Nigeria expels 2 million illegal aliens, mostly Ghanaians
1983	Jan	Reagan says El Salvador human rights violations makes them ineligible for aid
1983	Feb	Hindus kills 3000 Moslems in Assam, India
1983	May	Israel and Lebanon sign a peace treaty
1983	Sep	Korean jet strays into Siberia, shot down by a Soviet jet
1983	Sep	USSR vetoes UN resolution deploring shooting down of Korean plane
1983	Oct	Lech Walesa, head of Solidarity Labor Union, wins Nobel Peace Prize
1983	Oct	US Marine sharpshooters kill 5 snipers at Beirut Airport
1983	Oct	Suicide terrorist bombs kills 243 US personnel in Beirut
1983	Oct	US invades Grenada
1983	Nov	PLO exchanges 6 Israeli prisoners for 4500 Palestinians and Lebanese
1983	Nov	Syria and Saudi Arabia declare cease-fire in PLO civil war in Tripoli
1983	Dec	Yasser Arafat and 4000 loyalists evacuate Lebanon
1983	Dec	Egyptian President Mubarak meets with Yasser Arafat
1984	Feb	500,000 Iranian soldiers move into Iraq
1984	Feb	Canadian PM Trudeau announces he will step down; Brian Mulroney succeeds
1984	Mar	Iran offensive against Iraq fails
1984	Mar	US accuses Iraq of using poison gas
1984	Apr	US Senate condemns CIA mining of Nicaraguan harbors
1984	May	Duarte becomes president of El Salvador
1984	May	USSR says it will boycott Los Angeles Summer Olympics
1984	May	Indira Gandhi orders attack on Sikh holy site Golden Temple; 1200 die
1984	Sep	Britain agrees to return Hong Kong to China in 1999
1984	Sep	Reagan vetoes sanctions against South Africa
1984	Oct	IRA bombs hotel where Margaret Thatcher is staying
1984	Oct	Desmond Tutu of South Africa wins Nobel Peace Prize

1984	Oct	NBC airs BBC footage of Ethiopian famine
1984	Nov	Indira Gandhi assassinated by 2 of her Sikh bodyguards
1984	Nov	3000 die in a 3-day anti-Sikh riot in India
1984	Nov	Nicaragua holds first free elections in 56 years; Sandinistas win 63%
1984	Dec	Hijackers commandeer Kuwaiti airliner
1984	Dec	Rajiv Gandhi becomes Prime Minister of India, succeeding his mother
1985	Jan	Tancredo Neves, civil rights activist, elected president of Brazil
1985	Jan	President Botha of South Africa offers to release Mandela if he denounces violence; Mandela refuses because only free men can make contracts
1985	Feb	20 countries (not US) sign UN treaty outlawing torture
1985	Feb	Jordan and PLO sign accord
1985	Feb	Polish police arrest 7 Solidarity leaders
1985	Feb	Mickey Mouse welcomed in China
1985	Mar	Mikhail Gorbachev becomes Soviet leader
1985	Mar	Associated Press correspondent taken hostage in Beirut
1985	May	Israel exchanges 1150 Palestinian prisoners for 3 Israeli soldiers
1985	Jun	Lebanese Shiite Moslem gunmen hijack airliner in Athens
1985	Oct	Terrorists seize Italian cruise liner Achille Lauro
1985	Oct	Reagan bans importation of South African Krugerrands
1985	Nov	Reagan and Gorbachev meet for first time
1985	Nov	Egyptian commandos storm hijacked Egypt Air jet
1985	Dec	Terrorists attack El Al at Rome and Vienna airports
1985	Dec	Lebanese Moslem and Christian leaders sign peace accord
1986	Jan	International Peace Year begins
1986	Jan	US places economic sanctions against Libya and freezes Libyan assets in US
1986	Feb	Dalai Lama meets Pope John Paul II in India
1986	Feb	Oscar Sanchez elected president of Costa Rica
1986	Feb	Haiti President Jean-Claude Duvalier (Baby Doc) flees to France
1986	Feb	Marcos wins presidency of Phillappines in rigged election
1986	Feb	Mario Soares is elected Portugal's first civilian president
1986	Feb	Corazon Aquino becomes President of Philippines; Marcos flees
1986	Feb	Thousands of Egyptian military police riot
1986	Mar	4 French TV crewmen kidnapped in West Beirut Lebanon
1986	Mar	US and Libya clash in Gulf of Sidra incident
1986	Apr	Terrorist bombings at Athens Airport and West Berlin disco kill Americans; US responds by raiding Libya

1986	Apr	Worst nuclear disaster in history at Chernobyl, USSR
1986	May	South Africa occupies Botswana, Zimbabwe and Zambia
1986	May	Anti-apartheid activist Helene Pastoors sentenced to 10 years in South Africa
1986	Jun	President Botha declares South African national emergency
1986	Jun	USSR news Pravda declares high-level Chernobyl staff fired for stupidity
1986	Jun	Irish referendum upholds ban on divorce
1986	Jun	World Court rules US aid to Nicaraguan Contras is illegal
1986	Oct	Sikhs attempt to assassinate Indian Prime Minister Rajiv Gandhi
1986	Oct	London Times reports Israel is stocking nuclear arms
1986	Oct	Reagan and Gorbachev meet in Summit at Reykjavik
1986	Oct	South Africa expels International Red Cross
1986	Nov	Lebanese magazine reveals secret US arms sales to Iran
1986	Nov	US violates Iran arms boycott
1986	Dec	South Africa censors the press
1986	Dec	USSR frees dissident Andrei Sakharov
1986	Dec	Terrorists hijack Iraqi jet; it explodes in air
1987	Jan	Fighting along Chinese/Vietnamese border kills 1500
1987	Jan	Reagan signs secret order permitting sale of arms to Iran
1987	Jan	Anglican Church envoy Terry Waite taken hostage in Beirut
1987	Feb	17 civilians murdered by Philippine troops in Lupao
1987	Jun	Margaret Thatcher wins third consecutive term
1987	Jul	First of three massacres by Sikh extremists in India
1987	Oct	US warships destroy 2 Iranian oil platforms in Persian Gulf
1987	Dec	Occupied Palestinians start intefadeh (uprising) against Israel
1987	Dec	Reagan and Gorbachev sign treaty eliminating medium range nuclear weapons
1988	Jan	Reagan and Canadian PM Mulroney sign Canada-US free trade agreement
1988	Jan	US accepts immigration of 30,000 US-Vietnamese children
1988	Jan	Talks break down between Sandinistas and Contras
1988	Feb	Manuel Noriega of Panama, indicted on drug charges
1988	Mar	Northern Ireland Protestant fires on Catholic funeral and kills 3
1988	Mar	US sends soldiers to Honduras
1988	Mar	Iran accuses Iraq of using poison gas
1988	Mar	2 British soldiers lynched in Belfast, Northern Ireland
1988	Mar	US Congress discontinues aid to Nicaraguan Contras
1988	May	Francois Mitterrand elected President of France
1988	Jul	500 scientists boycott Pentagon germ-warfare research

1988	Jul	Winnie Mandela's home in Soweto, South Africa is destroyed by arson
1988	Jul	Gorbachev announces plan for electing president and parliament in 1989
1988	Jul	South Africa bans anti-apartheid film *Cry Freedom*
1988	Aug	Iran-Iraq cease fire begins
1988	Nov	PLO proclaims State of Palestine, and recognizes Israeli existence
1988	Nov	Benazir Bhutto becomes leader of Pakistan
1988	Nov	For first time in nearly 40 years the Soviets stop jamming Radio Liberty
1988	Nov	US is censured by UN for refusing Arafat's visa
1988	Dec	Nelson Mandela is transferred to a prison in Capetown
1988	Dec	Gorbachev is cheered by Wall Street crowds in NYC
1989		The Stealth Bomber is developed
1989	Jan	Russian newspaper Izvestia has first commercial advertisement
1989	Jan	US shoots down 2 Libyan jet fighters over Mediterranean
1989	Jan	International Conference on Limitation of Chemical Weapons in Paris; 140 nations agree to ban them
1989	Mar	First free elections in USSR: Boris Yeltsin elected president
1989	Apr	Zimbabwe gains independence
1989	Apr	Protesting students take over Tiananmen Square in Beijing
1989	May	Noriega loses Panama's presidential election, but nullifies it
1989	May	Kenya places ban on ivory to preserve elephant herds
1989	May	President Bush orders troops to Panama
1989	Jun	Ayatollah Khomeini of Iran dies
1989	Jun	Troops kill hundreds of protesting students in Beijing in Tiananmen Square
1989	Sep	East Germans begin fleeing to the west
1989	Oct	South African President deKlerk frees Sisulu and 4 other political prisoners
1989	Nov	East Berlin opens its borders
1989	Nov	Guerrillas battle with government forces in El Salvador
1989	Nov	Germans begin punching holes in the Berlin Wall
1989	Dec	Elena and Nicolae Ceausescu of Romania are executed
1989	Dec	US troops invade Panama and oust Manuel Noriega
1989	Dec	Alexander Dubcek elected parliament chairman of Czechoslovakia

Writing Topic Suggestions
Wars and the International Scene

Pick one of the topics below and write for fifteen to twenty minutes. Remember the un-rules:

- Don't stop writing until the limit is up.
- Use "trigger sentences" if you get stuck.
- Don't be polite.
- Be specific and remember you have at least five senses.
- You don't have to be right, rational or logical.
- Don't worry about the rules of grammar or spelling.
- Trust yourself.

Remember, you are creating a *primary source*. Write about what you *did*, what you *saw*, what you *thought*, what you *felt*.

1. Scan the timelines of events. What sparks a memory? Is there an event listed that makes you think, "Oh yeah, I remember that"? If so, write about this event. How did you learn about it? Newspaper, radio, TV? Hear others talking? Did you talk about it? With whom? Were you inspired to do something because of this event? Did this event change your life in any way? Did it change your opinions?

2. Did you follow the events in Europe or Asia during the 1930s? Did you have family members living in Europe or Asia? Did you pay attention to newsreels, listen to the radio, read the newspaper? Did you or your parents believe the US should get involved in foreign wars? When (or if) did you or your parents believe the US should get involved in the war? Was it after Pearl Harbor? What do you remember about December 7, 1941? Where were you? What were you doing when you heard? What were your emotions?

3. If you were a non-combatant during World War II, describe how you contributed to the war effort. Did you do "war work"? Collect scrap metal? Dance with the servicemen at USOs? Join the Civil Air Defense? Grow a Victory Garden? If you were in the military in a non-combatant role, what did you do? Describe some of your duties and actions that contributed to victory.

4. Were you or someone you loved in combat during World War Two? Were you or they wounded? What branch of the service were you or your loved one in? Where did you or he serve? What battles were most memorable and why? How did combat change you or your loved one? Was it difficult to adjust to civilian life after the war? If you had to pick one experience that stands out above the rest, what would that be? Describe it in sensory terms – what did you see, smell, taste, hear, touch?

5. How and when did you hear about the Holocaust? Did the revelations of cruelty shock and surprise you, or did you suspect beforehand what was going on? If you are Jewish, how did the Holocaust change your view of the world? If you are not Jewish, did the Holocaust alter your beliefs and opinions about Jews? Did the revelations about the Holocaust cause you to work for or donate to war relief organizations or provide help in another way? Or did it make you angry? How did your anger manifest?

6. Did you work for any relief organizations or charities, such as the Red Cross, that helped people overseas during the thirties, forties and fifties? Did you do volunteer work for organizations that supported the troops? Did you contribute money or goods? Did you work for peace organizations, after or before World War Two?

7. We look at history backward. To later generations, World War Two does not look scary – we know who won. But this is not evident to the people living at the time. Describe the emotional mood of your community during the war – the fears and hopes about the outcome. Were you afraid Germany and Japan would win? What

did you think that would mean to you personally? Were you afraid you, or someone you loved, would be killed? Were you afraid of spies lurking in your midst? Was your community up-beat, positive and patriotic? Did the events of the war seem unreal, a long way away, and that it "could never happen here"?

8. How did you celebrate the end of World War II? Describe what you did, and who you were with. What did you eat or drink? Did you sing or dance? Cry or laugh? What emotions went through you – despair, pain, joy, glee, quiet satisfaction that you were alive?

9. How and when did you learn about Hiroshima, Nagasaki and the atom bomb? Were you exhilarated by the Bomb's power, or aghast at its capacity for destruction? Did the Bomb make you feel safer, or did you feel afraid and vulnerable? Did you have opinions about the ethical implications of the Bomb? Did the images and reports from Japan about the suffering of the populace bother you, or did you feel it was a regrettable but necessary cost of war?

10. Did you or a loved one serve in Korea in the early fifties? Where were you or your loved one stationed? Were you or your loved one a combatant, or in a supportive role? What did you know about Korea before the war and what did you learn? What was your opinion of Korean culture? Did you believe the war was necessary to stop the spread of Communist aggression? How was the Korean War different than World War II?

11. Where were you during the Cuban Missile Crisis? Were you frightened of nuclear war? Did you follow the crisis on radio or TV? If you were a child or a teenager, what did your parents or teachers tell you about the crisis? If you were an adult and a parent, what did you tell your children?

12. Did you or a loved one serve in the military during Vietnam? Were you or your loved one drafted, or did they volunteer? What branch of the service? What were your military experiences? How

were you or your loved one changed by the experiences in Vietnam? Did you or your loved one believe in the importance and necessity of the war? How did the unpopularity of the Vietnam War affect you? Did you know any POWs or MIAs? Did you work to bring them home again, and if so how? Do you know anyone whose name is on the Vietnam Wall Memorial?

13. If you were a non-combatant during the Vietnam War, what was your opinion of the war? Did your opinions change over time, and if so, when and why did they change? Did you watch war news on TV? What scenes impacted you? Did you disagree with others about the war? If so, were the disagreements major or minor? Did Vietnam cause divisiveness in your family?

14. Write about war protest. Did you protest against the Vietnam War? How did you protest – marches, rallies, letters to Congressmen? If you marched, what were the sounds, sights, smells? Did you carry a sign? What did it say? Did you chant "Hey Hey LBJ, how many kids did you kill today?" Did you feel swept in a cause larger than yourself? Do you think your protest activities made a difference? If you did not protest, what did you think of those who did? Did you think draft dodgers were un-American and should be punished? Did you believe that the protests were just excuses for out-of-control bad behavior?

15. Were you or anyone you know in the Peace Corps, or Amnesty International, or other international groups whose aims were understanding, generosity, and peace? Did you or anyone you know adopt war orphans or sponsor refugees? How did you work for peace, or help to mitigate the ravages of war?

16. How did the increase in hijackings and other forms of terrorism in the seventies affect you? Did it make you feel vulnerable? Did it restrict your travel? If you worked in a travel industry, how did terrorism affect your business? Did it change the way you did your job? Did you know anyone who was a victim of terrorist acts?

17. How much did you follow international events? Did your work bring you into contact with people from other countries? Did you hold strong opinions or fears about world crises, such as the Iran Hostage Crisis, the My Lai massacre, CIA sponsored coups in South America, apartheid in South Africa, the USS Pueblo incident, the Iran-Contra hearings, and the ongoing conflicts between Israel and the Arab world? Were you or anyone you know involved in any of these world events? How were you involved? What was your role?

18. If you have traveled, what differences have you seen between America and other countries? What did you notice first? The food? The language? Did the people have different manners, different rules? Did you try to adjust and fit in? Did you appreciate, or learn to appreciate, the culture, habits, terrain, values of a foreign country? Did you learn to appreciate America more? How were foreign opinions on world events different from American opinions? Did you ever run into anti-Americanism, and what was that like?

19. Are you or your parents from another country than the US? Which country? When did you or your parents come to America, and why? What was the assimilation experience like? What was hardest for you or your parents to adjust to? What aspects of your native culture did you retain, and which did you change? How do you think your native culture benefits America? Do you think your close relationship to another country gives you a different viewpoint from most Americans? How did this manifest during wartime?

20. Which foreign leaders or international figures made a difference to your life? Who did you admire – Winston Churchill, Mahatma Gandhi, Nelson Mandela, Mother Theresa, Mikhail Gorbachev? Who did you despise – Adolph Hitler, Josef Stalin, Idi Amin, Ayatollah Khomeini, Ferdinand Marcos? How did their lives, their work, their thought, inspire or change you?

Or anything else you'd like to write about ...

Chapter Thirteen
Technology and Science

From 1930 to 1990, science and technology changed the way we do nearly everything. They changed the way we communicate, the way we travel, the way we go to war, the way we heal ourselves. They even changed our beliefs about who we are. Although some downsides and side effects of these changes were recognized, most technological advancements were perceived as positive.

1930 through 1959

Nuclear Science

One of the most far-reaching, and certainly the most controversial, advancement was the development of "the Bomb" and nuclear technology. From splitting the uranium atom in 1939 to the achievement of thermonuclear fission in 1952, this technology unleashed a truly awesome power that affected humanity's sense of safety. The destructive power seen in Nagasaki and Hiroshima, ending the war with Japan, was viewed by many as a necessary evil, and some as symbolic of the dangers of man playing God. From the beginning of atomic testing done in "remote" locations such as Bikini Atoll, to the establishment of nuclear power plants throughout the country, this technology was rife with high emotion. It still is.

Television

Another invention with enormous ramifications was the development of television, changing the way we communicate, entertain and learn about each other, and making the world seem a much smaller place. Although televisions didn't become a staple of home furnishings until the 1950s, models were being shown to the public in the early 1930s.

"Myra" remembered attending Chicago's 1933 Century of Progress Exposition. In the Hall of Science she and her mother visited a demonstration of the newest wonder, television. Some spectators were invited on stage to be filmed and appear on "the box." Since Myra was a cute seven-year-old, she was one of those chosen. She still remembers what a thrill it was to see herself showing off her tap dancing ability as onlookers oohed and aahed. Today she laughingly refers to it as "my television debut."

Who We Are

In the 1950s some discoveries challenged our long-held concepts of who we are, and where we came from. DNA molecules were first isolated and photographed in 1953, giving us new insights into what made us human. In 1955 Louis Leakey found the then-oldest human skull at Olduvai Gorge in Kenya, showing that humans had been around longer than previously suspected. Radiocarbon dating techniques developed during the 1950s allowed us to know how long the earth had been in existence. The Big Bang theory of creation, first proposed in 1952, gave us a new idea on how the universe itself may have come to be.

Space

The field of astronomy and space exploration boomed. Powerful telescopes such as Edwin Hubble's allowed for new discoveries like the planet Pluto, numerous asteroids, and mysterious black holes. In the fifties the "Space Race" was on, motivated not only by science but international politics. In 1957 the Russians "beat us" when they launched Sputnik, but we launched Explorer 1 soon after, in 1958. Manned space flight was discussed and planned, and millions of children dreamed of becoming astronauts.

"Greta" remembered following the exploits of Flash Gordon, a popular comic strip hero. "My favorite daydream was to be Flash Gordon," she wrote. "It didn't matter that I was a girl and couldn't be a space traveler. Anything was possible in Flash Gordon's universe, so I just changed my sex and became a boy!"

Aviation

Like television, advancements in aviation made the world seem much smaller. Jet engines were invented and the jet stream discovered. Non-stop round the world flights, although arduous at first, became possible. The first Boeing 247 rolled off the assembly line in 1933. World War II saw the first B52 jet plane bomber.

"Jerry," a retired pilot, shared the memory of his first flight. He was two years old in 1922 when his mother took him to a local fair, where short airplane rides were being given for those intrepid enough to try. Jerry's mother, an exuberant, adventurous woman who had been active in the women's suffrage movement, didn't even hesitate. She stuffed two-year old Jerry down the front of her coat and belted him in tight with the coat's sash. Ignoring the pilot's protestations that children weren't allowed, she climbed in the plane and told him to "take off!" The pilot shrugged and did as she asked, and she and Jerry soared off into the blue. "I swear I can remember the wind blowing in my face," he read. "I felt my mother's heart beating really hard and fast, and I heard her laughing. So I laughed too. And that was the start of my career in aviation. I learned to fly on my own at the age of 16, and I worked as a mechanic at an airfield until I joined the Army Air Corps during World War II. I flew bombers during the war, and afterwards I was a commercial pilot until

1982, when I finally retired. But even today, when I think of flying I hear my mother laughing."

Medicine

The medical field blossomed with discoveries and inventions. Among many other firsts, vitamin C was isolated, insulin discovered, X-ray photos invented, and open-heart surgery performed. Vaccines that prevented such deadly diseases such as tuberculosis, yellow fever and polio were developed, and penicillin saved millions from deadly infections. Many class participants wrote of their fathers or brothers or even themselves, wounded during World War II, having their limbs or their lives saved by the timely introduction of penicillin. The elimination of the scourge of polio is also a popular topic. Most people who remember prior to 1960 have vivid recollections of the fear surrounding this dread disease. Mothers warned their children not to go swimming in the summertime. Papers printed "tips" on how to avoid getting polio. It was a rare person who did not know someone who suffered from the disease. The Salk vaccine, introduced to the public in 1954, not only eliminated polio, but lifted the cloud of fear.

Firsts in Daily Life

In the timeline, note how many times the word "first" is stated, especially for inventions that changed people's daily lives. Frozen foods, synthetic rubber, air conditioning, screw-on bottle caps, nylon, water fluoridation, masking tape, weather satellites, microwave ovens, radar, scuba gear, tape recorders, Xerox copiers, the Univac computer, contact lens, electric blankets, transistor radios, burglar alarms, DDT and plastic are just a few of the new-fangled products introduced to Americans during these decades.

"Josie" shared about introducing microwave ovens to the public in the early 1950s. Josie worked as a secretary, not a scientist, but she was an attractive young blond so she was

asked to help demonstrate the easiness and efficiency of the microwave oven at a Home Show. At first she was delighted — it was a welcome break from typing and filing, and seemed quite glamorous to the 22-year-old. "But it became old fast," Josie read. "My job was to boil water in a glass, alternating with cooking a hot dog, over and over again — I must have cooked hundreds of hot dogs and boiled hundreds of glasses of water — all the while smiling and repeating my patter, which was only one line: "The microwave makes cooking so easy anyone can do it!" The only real direction I got was to "look pretty" and I guess I did because they kept me there three days."

Famous People

Scientists who became famous during these decades included such luminaries as Jonas Salk, Linus Pauling, Edwin Hubble, Wernher von Braun, J. Robert Oppenheimer, Robert Shockley, and the most famous scientist of all time: Albert Einstein, whose name is now a synonym for genius.

"Ed," a retired scientist, remembered attending a professional conference where Albert Einstein was speaking. He got to shake hands with the great man after the speech. "He didn't look like a genius — he seemed just like anyone else," he shared. "Except for his hair, of course."

Review the following timeline and see what *you* remember ...

1930-1959 Event Timeline
Technology and Science

1930	Feb	Pluto, the most distant planet in solar system, discovered
1930	Mar	Clarence Birdseye develops method for quick freezing food
1930	Mar	First seaplane glider flown
1930	Apr	Synthetic rubber first produced
1930	May	First US planetarium opens in Chicago
1930	May	Masking tape invented
1930	Jun	First radar detection of planes
1930	Jun	First round-the-world radio broadcast
1930	Sep	Patent awarded on the flashbulb
1930	Mar	First theatre built for rear movie projection
1930		Frank Whittle patents the jet engine
1931	May	First air-conditioned train installed on the B&O Railroad
1931	May	First full-scale wind tunnel for testing airplanes
1931	Jun	Rocket-fueled aircraft design patented
1931	Jun	First photoelectric cell installed commercially
1931	Oct	First infra-red photograph
1931	Oct	Thomas Edison dies
1931	Nov	Commercial teletype service begins
1931	Dec	Coaxial cable patented
1931	Dec	NY Metropolitan Opera broadcasts an opera over radio
1931		Margaret Mead publishes *Growing Up in New Guinea*
1931		Bell Labs develops stereophonic sound system
1931		Vitamin A isolated
1932	Feb	Camera exposure meter patented
1932	Apr	Vitamin C isolated
1932	Apr	Yellow fever vaccine for humans is announced
1932	Nov	Wernher von Braun named head of German liquid-fuel rocket program
1932	Nov	Gas Pump patented that computes quantity and price
1932	Dec	First gyro stabilized vessel to cross Atlantic arrives in NY
1932		Plastic is synthesized at Imperial Chemical Industries
1932		The neutron is discovered
1932		Vitamin D is discovered
1933	Feb	First flight of all-metal Boeing 247
1933	Feb	First genuine aircraft carrier christened, USS Ranger
1933	Jun	First sodium vapor lamps installed in NY
1933	Jul	Wiley Post completes first round-the-world solo flight
1933	Jul	First police radio system operated in Eastchester NY
1933	Sep	First airplane to exceed 300 mph
1933	Oct	First synthetic detergent for home use marketed

1933		First practical contact lens developed
1934	Mar	Congress passes Migratory Bird Conservation Act
1934	May	Dionne quintuplets are born
1934	Jul	First x-ray photo of entire body taken
1934	Jul	Marie Curie dies
1934	Aug	First airplane train: plane towing 3 mail gliders behind it
1934	Sep	First 33 1/3 rpm recording released (Beethoven's 5th)
1934	Dec	Wiley Post discovers the jet stream
1935	Jan	Spectrophotometer patented
1935	Feb	First surgical operation for relief of angina pectoris
1935	Apr	First radio tube made of metal announced
1935	Apr	Radar is patented
1935	Nov	First commercial airplane crossing of Pacific Ocean
1935		Margaret Mead publishes *Sex and Temperament*, theorizing that sexual roles are culturally determined
1936	Jan	First electron tube to enable night vision described
1936	Feb	First radioactive substance produced synthetically
1936	Mar	First flight of airship Hindenberg in Germany
1936	Mar	Boulder Dam completed on the Colorado River, creating Lake Mead, the largest reservoir in the world
1936	May	Screw-on bottle cap patented
1936	Jul	First x-ray photo of arterial circulation
1936	Jul	RCA shows the first real TV program
1936	Oct	First alcohol power plant established in Kansas
1936	Oct	Hoover Dam begins transmitting electricity to LA
1936	Dec	Bell Labs tests coaxial cable for TV use
1936	Dec	First radioactive isotope medicine administered
1937	Feb	Dupont Corp patents nylon
1937	Feb	First automobile/airplane combination tested
1937	Mar	First blood bank is established
1937	Jul	Isolation of pituitary hormone announced
1937	Aug	Bonneville Dam on Columbia River first produces power
1937	Dec	NBC and RCA send first mobile-TV vans onto NY streets
1937		First radio telescope built
1937		Insulin is first used to control diabetes
1938	Jan	GM begins mass production of diesel engines
1938	Feb	First public experimental demonstration of color TV
1938	Feb	DuPont begins production of nylon toothbrush bristles
1938	May	First animal breeding society forms in New Jersey
1938	Oct	First Xerox copy made
1938	Nov	First telecast of an unscheduled event (a fire)
1938	Dec	"Drunkometer," first breath test, introduced
1938		Fiberglass developed
1938		Vitamins E and B are identified

1939	Jan	Uranium atom first split
1939	May	First sports telecast: Columbia vs. Princeton baseball
1939	May	PanAm begins regular transatlantic passenger service
1939	Jun	Test flight of first rocket plane using liquid propellants
1939	Jul	First use of fiberglass sutures
1939	Sep	Physics Review publishes first paper about black holes
1939	Nov	First animal conceived by artificial insemination, a rabbit
1939	Nov	First jet plane demonstrated to German Air Ministry
1939	Nov	First air conditioned automobile (a Packard) exhibited
1939	Nov	WGY-TV in NY, first commercial TV station, begins
1940	Apr	First electron microscope demonstrated
1940	May	First successful helicopter flight in US
1940	Jun	First synthetic rubber tire exhibited in Akron, OH
1940	Jun	Discovery of element 93, neptunium, announced
1940		Rh factor in blood discovered
1940		FDR signs the Bald Eagle Protection Act into law
1941	May	FCC approves regular scheduled commercial TV broadcasts
1941	Jun	Russel Martel discovers how to make synthetic progesterone out of Mexican wild yams, basis for birth control pill
1941	Jul	Penicillin successfully recreated
1941	Dec	Sister Elizabeth Kenny's treatment for polio is approved
1941		Underwater photography pioneered
1942	Jan	First around-the-world flight on Pan Am "Pacific Clipper"
1942	Jan	Henry Ford patents method of making plastic auto bodies
1942	Feb	Radio emissions from the sun discovered
1942	Jun	First nylon parachute jump
1942	Jun	First V-2 rocket launch in Germany
1942	Jun	First bazooka rocket gun produced in US
1942	Dec	First controlled nuclear chain reaction achieved by Fermi
1942		Magnetic recording tape developed
1942		Streptomycin discovered, antibiotic effective against TB
1943	Jul	Jacques Cousteau and Emile Gagnan perfect the aqualung and scuba gear
1943		First kidney machine developed
1944	Nov	First open heart surgery performed
1944		Quinine first used to ward off malaria
1944		First use of Pilots Universal Sighting System; pilots can direct guns, bombs and torpedos automatically
1944		First eye bank opens
1945	Jan	Grand Rapids, MI becomes first US city to fluoridate water
1945	Jul	DDT sprayed on Jones Beach, NY, in first public test
1945	Dec	Microwave oven patented by Raytheon
1945	Dec	Preston Tucker reveals the Torpedo, a new 150 MPH car
1945		Benadryl is developed to treat colds and allergies

1946	Jan	ENIAC, US's first computer is finished
1946	Jan	US Army establishes first radar contact with Moon
1946	Mar	First US rocket to leave the Earth's atmosphere observes Sun's UV spectrum
1946	May	Patent filed in US for H-Bomb
1946	Jun	First transcontinental round-trip flight in 1 day
1946	Jul	US drops atom bomb on Bikini atoll
1946	Sep	First long-distance car-to-car telephone conversation
1946	Oct	First electric blanket manufactured
1946	Nov	First artificial snow produced from a natural cloud
1946		Richard Byrd explores and maps Antarctica
1947	Feb	First instant developing camera shown by E. H. Land
1947	Apr	Atomic Energy Commission formed
1947	May	Radar for commercial and private planes first demonstrated
1947	May	BF Goodrich manufactures first tubeless tire
1947	May	First US ballistic missile fired
1947	Jul	200 million year old dinosaur remains are discovered
1947	Oct	Chuck Yeager makes first supersonic flight
1947	Dec	Transistor invented at Bell Labs
1947		Hewlett Packard incorporates in California
1948	Jan	First tape recorder sold
1948	Mar	Philips begins experimental TV broadcasting
1948	Apr	A flash of light is observed in a crater of the Moon
1948	May	US atmospheric nuclear test at Enewetak
1948	Jun	200" Hale telescope dedicated at Palomar Observatory
1948	Jun	CBS demonstrates "long playing record"
1948	Jun	Bell Labs announces transistor as substitute for radio tubes
1948	Sep	First use of synthetic rubber in concrete
1948	Oct	Facsimile high-speed radio transmission demonstrated
1948	Nov	Zoom lens patented
1948	Dec	New drug prevents tsetse fly from causing sleeping sickness
1948	Nov	First photo of genes taken as USC
1949	Jan	RCA introduces 45 RPM record
1949	Mar	First automatic street light, in Connecticut
1949	May	Second satellite of Neptune discovered
1949	May	US Viking rocket launched, to observe solar x rays
1949	May	First Polaroid camera sold, for $89.95
1949	Jun	Gas turbine-electric locomotive demonstrated
1949	Sep	USSR detonates its first atomic bomb
1949	Dec	Einstein presents his generalized theory of gravitation
1949		Linus Pauling finds the cause of sickle-cell anemia
1949		Holographs, 3-D photographs, are introduced
1950	Mar	Phototransistor invention announced
1950	Apr	First transatlantic jet passenger trip

1950	Jun	First kidney transplant
1950	Sep	First typesetting machine to dispense with metal type
1951	Jan	Thought extinct since 1615, a Cahow is rediscovered
1951	Jan	World's largest gas pipeline opens, from Texas to New York
1951	Jan	First use of a lie detector, in the Netherlands
1951	Jan	US begins over 100 nuclear tests at Nevada Test Site
1951	Feb	First telecast of atomic explosion from Nevada Test Site
1951	Feb	First X-ray moving picture process demonstrated
1951	Apr	Margaret Sanger and Planned Parenthood give grant to Gregory Pincus to work on hormonal contraceptive pill
1951	May	Dacron men's suits introduced
1951	May	Computer Core Memory patented
1951	May	First H Bomb test on Enewetak Atoll
1951	Jun	First self-contained titanium plant opened in Nevada
1951	Jun	First commercial computer, UNIVAC 1, begins service at US Census Bureau
1951	Jun	First color TV broadcast: Arthur Godfrey on CBS
1951	Jul	Junction transistor invented
1951	Sep	First North Pole jet crossing
1951	Oct	Searle Pharmaceutical refuses to give grant to Gregory Pincus for research into hormonal birth control pill
1951	Nov	First underground atomic explosion, in Nevada
1951	Nov	First battery converts radioactive energy to electrical energy
1951		An Wang founds Wang Laboratories in Boston
1952	Mar	First plastic lens for cataract patients is fitted
1952	Apr	Big Bang theory proposed in *Physics Review*
1952	Apr	First B-52 prototype test flight
1952	Jun	Keel is laid for first nuclear powered sub, the Nautilus
1952	Oct	First ultra high frequency (UHF) TV station
1952	Oct	First video recording on magnetic tape, in LA
1952	Oct	First thermonuclear bomb detonated: fusion occurs
1952	Nov	Archaeologists find 2000 year old mosaic of Homer's *Iliad*
1952	Dec	Christine Jorgenson is first to have a sex-change operation
1952	Dec	First transistorized hearing aid offered for sale
1952		World's first nuclear accident occurs near Ottawa, Canada
1952		Willard F. Libby publishes *Radiocarbon Dating* about carbon 14 dating technique
1953	Jan	Premier of first movie in Cinemascope (*The Robe*)
1953	Feb	First 3-D movie, *Bwana Devil*, opens
1953	Feb	Scientists Crick and Watson discover structure of DNA
1953	Mar	Einstein announces revised unified field theory
1953	May	Nuclear explosion in Nevada causes fall-out in Utah
1953	May	Edmund Hillary and Tensing Norgay are first to reach summit of Mt. Everest

1953	Sep	First privately operated atomic reactor
1953	Sep	First successful separation of Siamese twins
1953	Nov	"Piltdown Man" discovered in 1912 is proven to be a hoax
1953	Dec	Chuck Yeager reaches Mach 2.43 in Bell X-1A rocket plane
1953		First kidney transplant performed
1954		Geodesic dome patented by Buckminster Fuller
1954	Jan	First atomic submarine is launched
1954	Feb	First test mass inoculation against polio with Salk vaccine
1954	Feb	First typesetting machine using photo engraving
1954	Mar	US explodes 15 megaton hydrogen bomb at Bikini Atoll
1954	Mar	RCA manufactures first color TV set
1954	Apr	Bell Labs announces first solar battery
1954	May	IBM announces vacuum tube "electronic brain" that can perform 10 million operations an *hour*
1954	Jun	First atomic power station opens (in Russia)
1954	Jun	First human trials of birth control pill begin
1954	Jul	First commercial jet transport lane built by Boeing
1954	Sep	First FORTRAN computer program run
1954	Nov	Linus Pauling wins Nobel Prize in Chemistry
1955	Jan	RCA demonstrates first music synthesizer
1955	Feb	Israel acquires four of seven Dead Sea Scrolls
1955	Mar	First radio facsimile transmission sent across the continent
1955	Mar	USAF unveils self-guided missile
1955	Mar	First seagoing oil drill rig goes into service
1955	Apr	Dr. Jonas Salk's polio vaccine offered to public; he refuses to patent his invention, not wishing to profit personally
1955	Apr	Albert Einstein dies
1955	Jun	First separation of virus into component parts
1955	Jul	First US city lit by nuclear power
1955	Aug	First microgravity research begins
1955	Aug	First solar powered automobile demonstrated
1956	Apr	First commercial videotape recorder demonstrated
1956	May	New mountain range discovered in Antarctica
1956	May	Great Britain performs nuclear test on island near Australia
1956	May	Thermonuclear bomb dropped onto Bikini Atoll
1956	Sep	First prefrontal lobotomy performed
1956	Sep	First transatlantic telephone cable
1957	Feb	1st electric portable typewriter goes on sale
1957	Feb	Borazon, harder than diamonds, is developed
1957	Jun	First commercial coal pipeline begins operations
1957	Jul	First submarine designed to fire guided missiles is launched
1957	Jul	First rocket with nuclear warhead fired, in Nevada
1957		USSR launches Sputnik 1, first artificial satellite
1957	Nov	USSR launches Sputnik 2 with first animal in orbit

Sharing My Stories—The Downside of Progress

My parents moved to Kennewick, Washington in 1947. My father went to work for the Public Utilities Department, and my mother worked on getting pregnant, which she did in 1948. I was born in May of 1949.

The Tri-Cities area, consisting of Kennewick, Pasco and Richland, was undergoing a growth spurt at that time, in common with the rest of the country. This growth was fueled in part because of the nearby newly built Hanford Nuclear Plant, which employed many nuclear scientists, technicians and bureaucrats. The scientists were kept busy testing all sorts of stuff to do with the new, rapidly advancing technology. They weren't overly careful about working with nuclear energy in those days. This was chiefly through ignorance, but exacerbated by arrogance. The arrogance prevented them from knowing how ignorant they were.

The amount of public misinformation about nuclear technology was truly staggering. I once saw an advertisement from the early fifties for men's hats. The ad promoted a particular kind of hat by touting their extended, large brims – which, it was stated in the ad, would shade your face and protect you from radiation burns in case of a nuclear explosion.

This indifference to safety was brought home to me when, sometime around 1995, I got a phone call from an official-sounding person working for, I think, the Department of Health. They were conducting a phone survey of all people born in the Tri-City area between the late forties and mid fifties, making them aware that they were possibly at a higher risk for various kinds of cancers, depending on whether their mothers had used the water or other civic resources during their pregnancies.

Well, duh. Of course my mother drank water while she was pregnant! It would not have occurred to her that tap water could be dangerous. After all, her husband worked for the Public Utilities Department! Of course she washed dishes and clothes and brushed her teeth and cooked with the city-supplied water.

I never had the heart to tell my mother about my call from the state. She is prone to blaming herself for everything anyway, and I saw no reason for her to blame herself for the water she drank nearly fifty years before, which of course was not remotely her fault.

Sometimes scientific progress has such a bad flavor that it lingers for years on your tongue, and perhaps even in your bones.

1957		Eli Lilly begins selling Darvon, powerful painkiller
1957		High speed dental drill becomes available
1958	Jan	Edmund Hillary reaches South Pole
1958	Jan	Gibson patents the Flying V Guitar
1958	Jan	Two light atoms are crashed together to create a heavier atom, resulting in first artificial nuclear fusion
1958	Jan	US launches Explorer 1, their first artifical satellite
1958	Feb	Texas Instruments patents the first integrated circuit
1958	Mar	Explorer III launched, discovers Earth's radiation belt
1958	Mar	CBS Labs announces stereophonic records
1958	Jun	World's longest suspension bridge opens in Michigan
1958	Aug	USS Nautilus' first crossing of Arctic Ocean under icecap
1958	Sep	First welded aluminum girder highway bridge completed
1958	Oct	US manned space-flight project is renamed Project Mercury
1958	Dec	First radio broadcast from space: Eisenhower said, "to all mankind, America's wish for Peace on Earth and Good Will to Men Everywhere"
1959	Jan	Luna 1 launched by USSR, the first lunar flyby, discovering solar wind
1959	Feb	First successful intercontinental ballistic missile (ICBM)
1959	Feb	First weather satellite launched, the Vanguard 2
1959	Mar	Pioneer 4 lunar flyby launched, first US probe to enter solar orbit
1959	Mar	First known radar contact is made with Venus
1959	Mar	NASA names first seven astronauts for Project Mercury
1959	Apr	St. Lawrence Seaway linking Atlantic and Great Lakes opens for shipping
1959	May	First house with built-in bomb shelter exhibited
1959	Jul	Dr. Louis Leakey discovers oldest human skull, over 600,000 years old
1959	Aug	Explorer 6 transmits first TV photo of Earth from space
1959	Sep	Luna 2 launched by USSR, first spacecraft to impact surface of the moon
1959	Oct	USSR Luna 3 returns first image of Moon's hidden side
1959	Dec	First ballistic missile submarine commissioned
1959		Xerox introduces the first plain paper copier
1959		Electrocardiograph and internal pacemaker are developed

1960 through 1989

Space

The Space Race continued, with many firsts achieved by America and other nations, especially the USSR. In 1961 Yuri Gagarin became the first person to orbit the earth, followed by John Glenn in 1962. President Kennedy declared his goal of putting a man on the moon by the end of the decade. In 1962 Telstar, the first communications satellite, was launched, and in 1964 Mariner 4 sent back the first pictures of Mars. Quasars and pulsars were discovered.

Disaster struck in 1967 with the Apollo 1 tragedy when astronauts Chaffee, Grissom and White were killed, but in 1969 their sacrifice seemed redeemed when Armstrong and Aldrin electrified the world by walking on the moon.

"Sarah" shared the personal meaning July 20, 1969 had for her. She had been invited to a party that evening, one that would include "college boys." She was 14 and wild to go, but her parents had heard about the college boys too, and wouldn't let her attend. But teenage-like, she sneaked out and went anyway. When she arrived at the party, everyone was clustered around the TV, watching Walter Cronkite report that "the Eagle had landed." She had known, of course, about the planned moon landing, but it hadn't mattered much to her, immersed in her own teenage concerns — until she saw the awe and pride lighting the faces of the college boys she had come to meet. One boy was even crying, unashamedly. She said later it was his tears that caused her to fall in love with him. They were married exactly ten years later, on July 20, 1979.

The Space program continued into the seventies and eighties, although not at the same pace and with some controversy. Significant achievements such as the first space station Skylab, stunning photos of possible life on Mars and the rings of Saturn, and many more, ensured that humans would continue looking into the skies. Sally Ride became the fist American woman astronaut and a heroine to many American girls and women.

> *"Victoria" had dreamed of being an astronaut in the mid-fifties, when she was a teenager. But girls didn't become astronauts then, and Victoria became a teacher instead. She forgot her adolescent fantasy until one evening in 1983 as she was watching a TV program about Sally Ride with her granddaughter. "I want to go to Space, Grandma," said her granddaughter, giving Victoria a bittersweet thrill as she realized that what had been impossible for her had become possible for her granddaughter.*

Nuclear Science

Nuclear technology continued to develop and to generate controversy. America and other countries continued nuclear testing at Entewak, Bikini Atoll, the New Mexico desert, the Sahara Desert, and other "uninhabited" places. The first atomic reactor was built in Richland, Washington, in 1960. In 1978 the accident at Three Mile Island occurred, in 1983 the first article appeared on a possible "nuclear winter," and in 1986 the Chernobyl nuclear disaster made us all, in the words of Mikhail Gorbachev, "confront the real force of nuclear energy, out of control."

Medicine

Medical science too made outstanding advancements during these decades, although not without some setbacks. In 1961 it was discovered that the new drug thalidomide, prescribed for pregnant women, caused horrifying birth defects, which led to stricter FDA controls on drug testing. Also in the sixties came the realization of the link between smoking and cancer.

Dr. Christian Baarnard of South Africa completed the first human heart transplant in 1967, which was followed in the seventies and eighties by more successful transplants of other organs as well, plus successful implants of artificial organs.

Diseases were eradicated and vaccines developed, such as the measles, mumps & rubella vaccine in 1963, the hepatitis vaccine in 1971, and flu vaccines in 1976. In 1980 the World Health Organization declared that smallpox, once a terrible scourge, had been eliminated from the earth.

Diagnostic tools such as MRI were invented during these decades, as well as safety features such as the childproof safety caps on medicine bottles. Prozac went on the market in 1988 to combat depression. In 1985 AIDS screening tests were developed, and in 1986 AZT was approved by the FDA to combat the plague spreading all over the globe.

"Art," a former urologist, remembered attending a urology convention in 1985 at which the new "miracle cure" for kidney stones was being unveiled. "It was called the 'lithotripter', but we just called it 'the crusher,'" he shared. "It was amazing, like a giant spark plug in a vat of water. It sent shock waves into the patient and blasted the kidney stone into little pieces that could easily be passed. I often treated people with kidney stones, and this invention excited me so much that I could hardly wait for another kidney stone patient to walk into my office. When the next one did, he was puzzled when I told him he had made me very happy."

There were major medical changes affecting women's health and the "population explosion," which was becoming a big concern. By far the most far reaching in terms of cultural change, was the introduction of the birth control pill in the early 1960s, changing the life of nearly every woman in America and giving humankind control over one of our most basic functions.

The women's movement led to changes in medical care for women. The treatment for pregnancy, labor and birth became less clinical and more natural. Breast feeding came "back" and fathers were welcomed into the labor and delivery rooms.

"Ellen" gave birth in 1972 and again in 1977, and shared her impression of the enormous difference in hospital atmosphere in just five years. In 1972, although her husband had dutifully taken the hospital birthing classes, the nurses tried to deny him entry into the delivery room, saying, "Oh, it's way too messy, you don't want to see your wife like that." After the baby was born, Ellen was allowed one peek and then it was whisked away to the nursery and not shown to her until the next morning. By then the nurses had already introduced the baby to the bottle.

But in 1977, in the same hospital, her husband was issued scrubs as a matter of course – he was expected in the delivery room. As soon as the baby was born, she was placed on Ellen's stomach and left there, and the new family was given time to get to know each other. Ellen was given instructions and encouragement on breast feeding. No one suggested a bottle.

Also in the seventies and eighties, the scourge of breast cancer was brought to public attention, aided by women such as Betty Ford and Nancy Reagan who courageously chose to share their experiences with this disease.

In the seventies and eighties fertility research led to break-throughs previously considered the realm of science fiction, such as test tube babies, embryo transplants, and surrogate mothers.

"Carol" shared about giving birth to her daughter the same day in 1978 that Louise Brown, the world's first "test tube" baby, was born in England. "I guess it represented an advancement," she wrote, "and probably helped a lot of people to have children. But I'm glad I did it the old-fashioned way."

Computers & Electronics

Although computers were first developed in the forties, the average American had never seen one. For one thing, they took up a lot of space; *Popular Mechanics* made a prediction in 1949 that "computers in the future may weight no more than 1.5 tons." But the inventions of the sixties, seventies and eighties made the computer an integral part of every American's life. In 1961 Robert Noyce patented the integrated circuit, the same year that Computer Core Memory was invented. In 1964 the programming language BASIC was developed. Intel incorporated in 1968, and in 1970 IBM introduced its 360 family of computers, making it feasible to use the computer in every business, and changing the way many businesses felt about using computer technology. Digital Equipment Corporation introduced the first true minicomputer in 1965, which became used extensively in process control applications such as within telephone systems. In 1971 the microprocessor (a computer on a chip) and the floppy disk were introduced, paving the way for the personal computer. The Altair computer was first — introduced in 1974, it cost $375, had 256 bytes (*not 256K* but simply 256) of memory, no keyboard, no display and no storage. In 1976 Steve Jobs and Steve Wozniak introduced the Apple II that sported a keyboard and a monitor. And in 1981 IBM entered the arena with the IBM PC. In 1983 *Time Magazine* announced their annual "man of the year" — the computer. In 1985 Microsoft shipped the first retail version of Windows software. The computer had transformed our lives.

"Jeff" was a semiconductor salesman during the 1980s. "It's hard to explain the pace and the atmosphere of the electronics industry to someone who wasn't in it," he shared. "So many things changed so fast and so completely, and so much money was involved, that it could make you dizzy. You were almost afraid to take a vacation, because something new could be introduced in the time you were gone, and you could have lost millions for the company and thousands in your own commissions. People were hooked on the adrenalin that the pace and excitement produced, which is why so many suffered burn-out but always came back for more. However, it was worth it because there was a sense that you were on the cutting edge of new technology that was literally changing the world in front of your eyes. It was a wild ride, but boy was it fun."

The Planet

A growing concern over the cost of progress began to make itself felt during these decades, contributing to the growth of environmental science and the ecology movement. Rachel Carson published *Silent Spring* in 1962, exposing the hazards of pesticides and eloquently questioning our blind faith in technological progress. The Wilderness Act was passed in 1964. In 1968 Jacques Cousteau hosted a television special on the dangerous state of our oceans, awakening the world to their peril. Suddenly everyone was talking about pollution, recycling, littering, clean water, clean air, endangered species, global warming, chlorofluorocarbons, car emissions, the hole in the ozone layer. Activism followed talking. Greenpeace was founded in 1971. The Environmental Protection Act (EPA) went into effect in 1970, and in 1973 the Endangered Species Act became law. In 1970 the US put an end to whale hunting. DDT was banned in 1972.

Ecological disasters became big news. The chemical disaster at Love Canal in New York in 1979 horrified and infuriated most people. The oil spill of the Exxon Valdez in 1989 made headlines all over the world.

Exploration and education about the other inhabitants of our planet led to sweeping changes. In 1960 Jane Goodall published her first study showing that chimpanzees made and used tools, contradicting the prevailing scientific wisdom of the time and raising the question of how we define the differences between humans and other animals. Other experimenters taught chimpanzees how to speak, using American Sign Language. It was discovered that chimps and humans share over 98% of their DNA. After the Endangered Species Act of 1973, there was some progress made in halting the widespread extinction of species, some making spectacular comebacks.

"Nancy" remembered watching Jane Goodall's National Geographic television special on the chimps of Gombe. "I had always loved animals," she shared. "At the time (I was 15) my great ambition was to own a ranch full of all kinds of animals — mostly horses, who were my passion, but also goats and jaguars, rabbits and kangaroos. I even wanted a place for mice and rats. I guess what I really wanted was to own Noah's Ark! But I had been told — by my parents, my teachers, even my friends — that my dream was impractical (which of course it was) and I should focus on something attainable like becoming a teacher or a nurse. But when I saw what Jane Goodall had achieved, just an average-looking young woman with a ponytail, a fire was lit under me. She had followed her dream, and so could I. She could work with

animals, so I could too. I don't think I would have become a veterinarian if it hadn't been for Jane Goodall. I even got my ranch in the end — although I did have to give up the jaguars and kangaroos!"

Exploration of the sea floor not only increased our knowledge of the oceans, but had a romantic result that enthralled and intrigued the treasure-hunter in all of us. Advancements in diving apparatus and undersea technology made possible the discovery of sunken ships, some from hundreds of years before. In the eighties the wrecks of the Spanish treasure ship Atocha, the Andrea Doria, and the Titanic, were found and salvaged.

Firsts in daily life

From cassettes tapes to touch tone phones to ATM machines to tampax to watching the weather, everyday life in 1989 was a lot different than it was in 1959. In 1960 the first weather satellite went into orbit, giving us a better idea of what the weather was really going to be. In 1962 the first communications satellite, Telstar, was launched, allowing us to communicate faster all over the globe. In 1975 the early warning system went into effect, saving thousands if not millions of lives from the damages of tornados, hurricanes and other disasters. In the 1980s the cellular phone was introduced for cars, an innovation that made the lives of salespeople much easier, to name just one of its effects. And that's just the proverbial tip of the iceberg.

Review the following timeline and see what *you* remember …

1960-1989 Events Timeline
Technology and Science

1960	Feb	Old handwriting found at Qumran near the Dead Sea
1960	Feb	Nuclear submarine USS Triton sets off on underwater round-world trip
1960	Mar	Pioneer 5 launched into orbit between Earth and Venus
1960	Mar	Key Largo Coral Reef Preserve established as first underwater park
1960	Mar	National Observatory at Kitt Peak, Arizona is dedicated
1960	Mar	First patent for lasers granted
1960	Mar	Explorer 8 fails to reach Earth orbit
1960	Mar	First guided missile launched from nuclear powered sub
1960	Apr	First weather satellite launched
1960	Apr	France explodes A-bomb in Sahara Desert
1960	May	Sputnik 4 launched into Earth orbit
1960	May	First atomic reactor system patented
1960	May	FDA approved "Enovid" as first oral birth control
1960	Jun	Chlorophyll "A" first synthesized
1960	Jul	Echo I, first communications satellite launched
1960	Jul	USSR's Sputnik 5 launched with 2 dogs and 3 mice aboard
1960	Aug	Discoverer 13 launched and returns first object from space
1960	Sep	First nuclear-powered aircraft carrier is launched
1960	Oct	Jane Goodall observes chimpanzees making and using tools, upsetting the scientific contention that humans are the only tool-making species
1960	Nov	First atomic reactor for research and development at Richland, WA
1960	Jan	Ham is first primate in space aboard Mercury Redstone 2
1961	Feb	Niagara Falls hydroelectric project begins producing power
1961	Feb	USSR fires a rocket from Sputnik V to Venus
1961	Feb	First all-solid-propellant rocket put into orbit
1961	Feb	China uses its first nuclear reactor
1961	Feb	US Satellite Explorer 9 is launched
1961	Mar	First animal returned from space, a dog named Blackie aboard Sputnik 9
1961	Mar	Explorer 10 launched into elongated Earth orbit
1961	Apr	Yuri Gagarin becomes first person to orbit Earth
1961	Apr	Robert Noyce of Fairchild Semiconductor patents integrated circuit
1961	Apr	Unmanned Mercury test explodes on launch pad
1961	Apr	NASA launches Explorer 11 to study gamma rays
1961	May	Alan Shepard becomes first American in space

1961	May	First practical seawater conversion plant built in Texas
1961	May	JFK announces US goal of putting a man on Moon before end of the decade
1961	Jun	Thalidomide, a sedative given to pregnant women, revealed to cause birth defects; prompting FDA to enact stricter regulations for human drug tests
1961	Sep	USSR tests nuclear bombs in central Asia
1961	Oct	First Saturn launch vehicle makes an unmanned flight test
1961	Nov	Mercury-Atlas 5 carries a chimp into orbit
1962	Jan	US launches Ranger 3, misses Moon by 22,000 miles
1962	Feb	John Glenn is first American to orbit Earth
1962	Feb	US performs one of many nuclear tests at Nevada Test site
1962	Mar	First atomic power plant in Antarctica goes into operation
1962	Mar	Launch of OSO 1, first satellite studying solar flare data
1962	Mar	Five research groups announce discovery of anti-matter
1962	Apr	Ranger 4, first US satellite to reach Moon launched
1962	Apr	MIT sends TV signal by satellite for first time
1962	May	First nuclear warhead fired from Polaris submarine
1962	May	Laser beam successfully bounced off Moon for first time
1962	May	Scott Carpenter orbits Earth 3 times in US Aurora 7
1962	Jun	Oscar 2, a ham radio satellite, launched into Earth orbit
1962	Jul	Telstar communications satellite launched
1962	Aug	First quasar located by radio
1962	Oct	Wally Schirra in Sigma 7 launched into Earth orbit
1962	Oct	Drs. Watson, Crick and Wilkins win Nobel Prize for Medicine for work in determining structure of DNA
1962		Rachel Carson publishes *Silent Spring*
1963	Feb	Maarten Schmidt discovers enormous red shifts in quasars
1963	Jun	Valentina Tereshkova becomes first woman in space
1963	Sep	Mary Ann Fischer of South Dakota gives birth to America's first surviving quintuplets, 4 girls and a boy
1963	Oct	Archaeological digs begin at Masada, Israel
1963		Jane Goodall publishes first article in National Geographic
1963		Cassette tapes introduced
1963		Touch Tone telephones introduced
1963		Measles vaccine developed
1964	Jan	US Surgeon General connects smoking to lung cancer
1964	Apr	Unmanned Gemini 1 launched
1964	Apr	First BASIC program runs on a computer
1964	Jul	Ranger 7 launched toward Moon, sends back TV pictures
1965	Jan	First ground-to-aircraft radio communication via satellite
1965	Feb	Ranger 8 Lunar Hard Lander arrives on the moon
1965	Mar	Alexei Leonov makes first spacewalk from Voshkod 2

1965	Mar	Gemini 3 launched, first US 2-man space flight
1965	May	Second Chinese atom bomb explodes
1965	Jun	Gemini IV launched with astronauts McDivitt and White
1965	Aug	Gemini V launched with astronauts Cooper and Conrad
1965	Nov	Venera 3 launched, first to land on another planet
1965	Dec	Gemini VI launched with astronauts Schirra and Stafford
1965	Dec	Borman and Lovell end 2 week Gemini VII mission
1966	Feb	First operational weather satellite, ESSA-1, launched
1966	Mar	Gemini VIII launched with astronauts Armstrong and Scott
1966	May	US launches Surveyor 1 to the Moon
1966	Jun	Gemini IX-A launched with astronauts Stafford & Cernan
1966	Jul	Lunar Orbiter 1 launched to Moon
1966	Jul	Gemini X launched with astronauts Young and Collins
1966	Aug	Only known case of meteor entering Earth's atmosphere, daylight meteor seen from Utah to Canada
1966	Sep	Gemini XI launched with astronauts Conrad and Gordon
1966	Nov	Gemini XII launched with astronauts Lovell and Aldrin
1967	Jan	Chafee, Grissom and White die in Apollo 1 fire
1967	Feb	Robert J. Oppenheimer, creator of atomic bomb, dies at 62
1967	Jun	Venera 4 Probe arrives at Venus
1967	Jun	Mariner 5 arrives at Venus and studies magnetic field
1967	Sep	Wildlife Refuge and Sanctuary opens in NY City
1967	Nov	Surveyor 6 lands and takes off again from moon's surface
1967	Dec	First human heart transplant performed by Dr. Christian Barnaard on Louis Washkansky
1967	Dec	DNA created in a test tube
1967		First public boycott of alligator products, leading alligators to be protected until populations recover
1968	Jan	First adult cardiac transplant operation performed in US
1968	Jan	Surveyor 7 lands on the moon
1968	Jan	Jacques Cousteau's first undersea special on TV
1968	Jan	Apollo 5 launched to Moon for lunar module tests
1968	Feb	First pulsar discovered
1968	Mar	USAF displays the biggest plane in the world
1968	Mar	Orbiting Geophysical Observatory 5 launched
1968	Apr	Underground nuclear test of Boxcar, 1 megaton device
1968	Jul	Intel incorporates
1968	Oct	Apollo 7 launched with astronauts Schirra, Eisele, and Cunningham; the first manned Apollo mission
1968	Dec	Apollo 8 launched with Borman, Lovell and Anders & makes first manned moon voyage
1969	Jan	Venera 5 and 6 atmospheric probes arrive at Venus
1969	Mar	Mariner 7 arrives at Mars and returns data and pictures
1969	Mar	Apollo 9 launched with astronauts McDivitt, Scott and

Sharing My Stories—A Political Moonwalk

In 1969, at the wise old age of 20, my opinion of NASA and the entire "Space Race" was uncomplimentary at best. I felt that it was merely a ploy by the government to distract public attention from their disgusting policies responsible for such evils as the War in Vietnam, Racism, and various Capitalist/Fascist establishments that kept the poor, poor and the rich, rich. I was a pinko-liberal hippie and I'm afraid my world view was not only unoriginal but just a little narrow. I was, however, sincere: consumed by anger and lit by passion. I wanted to right all the injustices of the world, and I was young enough to believe this was possible.

I did not see a great scientific achievement in Armstrong's walk on the moon, nor did I see Armstrong himself as a hero. I saw money that could have educated the ignorant or fed the poor instead channeled into a program that exalted the fat cats of the government. All the astronauts were white. All came from the middle classes or upward. All were men. All had short hair. Most were from the military, the real kiss of death for me. To me they weren't heroes; they were establishment tools.

America's race against the Soviets looked like macho posturing to me. Beating our chests and flailing at the windmills in our minds, talking about the "conquest" of Space! What would we do with Space, anyway, if we actually did "conquer" it? Carve it up into more territories that could fight each other? The symbolism of planting the American flag on the moon seemed silly – who were we kidding? Did we think Armstrong was a reincarnation of Columbus? Did we think America could *own* the Moon? Make it the 51st state? It's a good thing the Moon was not inhabited, we might have claimed the natives too, as ours, to exploit or enslave; or at the very least, indoctrinate.

It's hard for me now to remember how angry I was back then, but it was an anger I shared with many of my contemporaries. Now we are older and more tempered in our judgments, less able to view things in such hard-edged black and white.

My political views have not changed much since 1969. But now I realize that by seeing the Space Program in only the light of politics, I shut out the light of intellectual and physical adventure and the intoxicating admiration for accomplishment. Now I am sorry I missed the thrill of excitement and awe that many people felt when we walked on the moon.

		Schweikart; first manned test of Lunar Module
1969	Apr	Dr. Denton Cooley implants first temporary artificial heart
1969	May	Apollo 10 launched with astronauts Stafford, Young and Cernan
1969	Jul	Neil Armstrong and Edwin "Buzz" Aldrin from Apollo 11 become the first people to walk on the moon
1969	Nov	Apollo 12 launched with Conrad, Gordon and Bean, the next to walk on the moon
1969		Rubella vaccine introduced
1970	Jan	First commercial Boeing 747 flight goes from NY to London in 6 ½ hours
1970	Jan	ITOS 1 launched, second generation weather satellite
1970	Mar	500th nuclear explosion by the US since 1945
1970	Apr	Apollo 13 launched with astronauts Lovell, Haise, and Sweigert; narrowly averting tragedy when oxygen tank blew up ("OK Houston we've had a problem here")
1970	Apr	First Earth Day held to conserve natural resources
1970	Aug	Venera 7 arrives on Venus, the first successful landing of a spacecraft on another planet
1970	Sep	IBM announces System 370 computer
1970	Dec	Environmental Protection Agency begins
1970		Congress passes the Clean Water Act
1970		FDA approves lithium as anti-depressant
1970		Medicine bottles adopt childproof safety tops
1971	Jan	Berkeley chemists announce synthetic growth hormones
1971	Jan	Apollo 14 launched with astronauts Shepard, Mitchell and Roosa, who almost get lost on disorienting lunar landscape
1971	Mar	Serum hepatitis vaccine for children announced
1971	May	USSR Mars 3 is first successful landing on Mars
1971	May	Friends of Earth return 1500 non-returnable bottles to Schweppes
1971	Jul	Apollo 15 launched with astronauts Scott, Irwin and Worden; first Apollo space walk
1971		The Cat Scan technology revolutionizes diagnostic medicine
1971		Greenpeace is founded
1971		Cigarette ads are banned from TV
1972	Jan	NASA begins research on manned shuttle
1972	Mar	Pioneer 10 flies by Jupiter and returns images and data of Jupiter and moons
1972	Apr	Apollo 16 launched with astronauts Young, Mattingly and Duke; they stay 3 days exploring on Lunar Rover
1972	Apr	Orbiting Astronomical Observatory 4 launched
1972	Dec	Apollo 17 launched with astronauts Cernan, Evans, and Schmitt become last men on the moon (so far)

1972		EPA bans DDT
1972		Land and Water Management Act becomes law
1972		Oregon passes nation's first returnable bottle law
1972		The first e-mail program is created
1973	Feb	Nixon signs the Endangered Species Act
1973	Apr	Pioneer 11 flies by Jupiter collecting data and images, then flies by Saturn
1973	May	Skylab I, First US manned space station is launched; astronauts take more than 150,000 images of the sun
1973	Nov	Mariner 10 becomes first dual planet mission, flying past Venus and Mercury; first spacecraft with imaging system
1973	Nov	Nixon authorizes construction of the Alaska pipeline
1973		Tool unearthed in Yukon proves humans have been in New World since 27,000 BC
1973		Development begins on TCP/IP protocol, letting computer networks to communicate with each other, a necessary step toward the Internet
1973		Motorola announces prototype of the first cellular phone
1974	Feb	Chimpanzee Nim Chimsky signs his first word
1974	May	Dalkon Shield comes off the market after unsafe reports
1974	Sep	First Lady Betty Ford undergoes radical mastectomy
1974	Dec	Solar probe Helios 1 launched
1974		The Heimlich Maneuver is introduced
1974		Lucy, oldest human skeleton (3 million years+) unearthed
1974		The first ATM machine is introduced
1974		The first use of the term Internet
1975	Jan	Altair 8800 computer appears on the cover of *Popular Electronics*; Paul Allen and Bill Gates develop BASIC language for the Altair
1975	Jan	Landsat 2, Earth Resources Technology Satellite, launched
1975	Jan	Grizzly bear designated as a threatened species
1975	May	Early warnings by REACT lessen damages of tornado
1976	Mar	First Annual World Altair Computer Convention held; opening address given by Bill Gates
1976	Apr	Testing begins on Swine Flu vaccine; later halted following reports of paralysis
1976	Apr	Apple Computer opens, run by Wozniak and Jobs
1976	Aug	Viking 1 orbits Mars and sends back data indicating life
1976	Nov	The trade name "Microsoft" is registered
1976		Scientists at MIT make first synthetic gene
1977	Feb	First killer whale born in captivity
1977	Mar	First CRAY 1 supercomputer shipped to Los Alamos Labs
1977	May	Completion of Trans-Alaska oil pipeline

1977	Jul	FORTRAN-80, Microsoft language product, announced
1977	Aug	Voyager 2 launches to Jupiter, Saturn, Uranus & Neptune
1977	Aug	Dept. of Energy established
1977		Writing found in Mesopotamia dates back to 10,000 BC
1977		Magnetic Resonance Imaging (MRI) introduced
1977		The Jane Goodall Institute for Wildlife Research and Education is established
1977		First Computerland store opens (called Computershack)
1978	Feb	First "micro on a chip" patented by Texas Instruments
1978	Feb	First Computer Bulletin Board System announced
1978	Mar	Major nuclear accident at Three Mile Island in Pennsylvania
1978	Apr	Love Canal crisis begins with discovery that chemical wastes are poisoning NY neighborhood
1978	Jun	Pluto's moon Charon is discovered
1978	Jun	US Seasat 1, first oceanographic satellite, is launched into polar orbit
1978	Jun	Government forced to halt construction of nuclear power plant in New Hampshire because of public opposition
1978	Jul	Louise Brown Oldham of England is the world first "test tube baby"
1978	Aug	NY declares state of emergency at Love Canal
1978		Ultrasound becomes alternative to X-Rays
1978		Congress passes the Manatee Protection Act
1978		Visicalc, first spreadsheet program, is introduced
1979	Jun	The Source, first computer public information service
1979	Oct	Over 1000 "no-nukes" protesters arrested on Wall Street
1979		Audubon Society establishes its Center for Birds of Prey, to increase the population of raptors
1980	Mar	Satellites record gamma rays from remnants of supernova
1980	May	World Health Organization announces smallpox has been eradicated
1980	Oct	Russian astronauts set space endurance record of 184 days
1980	Nov	Voyager 1 space probe discovers 15th moon of Saturn
1980	Dec	A calf lives for 222 days with an artificial heart
1980		Tampons linked to toxic shock syndrome
1980		People for the Ethical Treatment of Animals founded
1980		A French pharmaceutical company invents the abortion pill
1980		Winchester hard drive introduced by Shugart
1981	Mar	Two workers killed in space shuttle Columbia accident
1981	Jul	CERN achieves first proton-antiproton beam collision
1981	Aug	Divers recover a safe found aboard the Andrea Doria
1981	Aug	IBM introduces its Personal Computer, using Microsoft operating system
1981	Sep	Satellites China 10 and 11 launched into Earth orbit

1981	Dec	Spacelab 1 arrives at Kennedy Space Center
1981		First arrest and conviction of animal laboratories on charges of cruelty to animals
1981		Save Our Rivers program is approved
1981		Commodore introduces VIC-20 and sells over 1 million
1982	Jan	10 Arabian oryx, extinct except in zoos, released in Oman
1982	Apr	Sally Ride is announced as first woman astronaut
1982	Jun	Space Shuttle Columbia 4 launched
1982	Jun	750,000 anti-nuclear demonstrators rally in Central Park NY
1982	Jul	Kosmos 1383 is first search & rescue satellite
1982	Sep	First private commercial rocket, Conestoga 1, makes suborbital flight
1982	Oct	English ship Mary Rose, sunk in 1545, raised at Portsmouth
1982	Oct	Mt. Palomar Observatory is first to detect Halley's comet on 13th return
1982	Oct	IBM ROM now capable of EGA graphics
1982	Dec	Retired dentist Barney Clark receives first permanent artificial heart
1982	Dec	Time Magazine's Man of the Year is a computer
1982		Halcyon introduced as a sleeping pill
1982		Plastic surgeons begin performing liposuction
1982		First movie made with computer-generated special effects, Disney's *Tron*
1983	Jan	Infrared telescope satellite is launched into polar orbit
1983	Jan	World's longest sub aqueous tunnel opens in Japan
1983	Jun	Pioneer 10 becomes first man-made object to leave Solar System
1983	Jun	Challenger 2 launched with Sally Ride
1983	Jun	First time a satellite is retrieved from orbit by Space Shuttle
1983	Jul	Baby born alive to a mother brain dead for 84 days
1983	Jul	First non-human primate (baboon) conceived in a lab dish
1983	Dec	*Journal of Science* publishes first report on nuclear winter
1983		Apple Computer introduces the mouse
1984	Feb	First baby conceived by embryo transplant born
1984	Feb	Bruce McCandless makes first untethered space walk
1984	Feb	First heart and liver transplant
1984	Apr	Challenger 5 Space Shuttle is launched, astronauts complete first in-space satellite repair
1984	Apr	Nature Magazine print article on Nemesis, the death star of dinosaurs
1984	Jul	Svetlana Savitskaya is first woman to walk in space
1984	Oct	Kathy Sullivan is first American woman to walk in space
1984	Oct	"Baby Fae" receives baboon heart transplant & lives 21 days
1984	Nov	Anna Fisher becomes the first "mom" astronaut

1984	Dec	Vega 1 launched by USSR for flyby rendezvous with Halley's Comet
1984	Dec	Scientists find a creosote bush determined to be 11,700 years old
1984	Dec	FDA approves shock wave lithotripsy for treating kidney stones
1984		Congress passes the Wetlands Protection Act
1984		Apple announces the birth of the Macintosh
1984		Dell Computer founded
1985	Mar	Pentagon accepts theory that atomic war would cause a nuclear winter
1985	Mar	Screening tests for AIDS are approved
1985	Mar	EPA orders ban on leaded gas
1985	Jul	Christa McAuliffe chosen as first schoolteacher to fly in space
1985	Jul	Divers find wreck of Spanish galleon Atocha
1985	Sep	US-French expedition locates wreckage of The Titanic off Newfoundland
1985	Oct	Space Shuttle Columbia carries Spacelab into orbit
1985	Oct	Intel introduces 32-bit 80386 microcomputer chip
1985	Nov	Microsoft ships first retail version of Windows
1985	Dec	Mary Lund is first woman to receive Jarvik 7 artificial heart
1985		Computer hackers break into the Los Alamos National Laboratory
1986	Jan	Chunnel, railroad tunnel under English Channel, announced
1986	Feb	USSR launches Mir space station into Earth's orbit
1986	Mar	Surrogate baby "Baby M" awarded to her father
1986	Apr	Worst nuclear disaster in history occurs at Chernobyl, Ukraine
1986	Jul	Videotapes released showing remains of Titanic
1986	Sep	Health officials announce AZT will be available to AIDS patients
1986	Dec	First heart, lung and liver transplant
1986		Internet Task Force formed to coordinate an Internet gateway system
1987	Jan	Astronomers at Univ. of California see first sight of the birth of a galaxy
1987	Feb	First naked-eye supernova seen since 1604
1987	Feb	Reagan vetoes Clean Water Act; overridden by Congress
1987	Mar	FDA approves sale of AZT
1987	May	Civil War ship The Monitor discovered by deep sea robot
1987	Aug	Announcement of possible Martian tornadoes

1987	Oct	First military use of trained dolphins
1987	Oct	First Lady Nancy Reagan undergoes modified radical mastectomy
1987		FDA approves high cholesterol drug
1988	Jan	Hewlett-Packard introduces Advanced Scientific Calculator
1988	Mar	NASA reports accelerated breakdown of ozone layer by CFKs
1988	May	Surgeon General Koop reports that nicotine is as addictive as heroin
1988	Jul	Phobos 2 arrives on Mars to probe Martian moons
1988	Jul	500 US scientists pledge to boycott Pentagon germ-warfare experiment
1988	Aug	Deep Rover research submarine unveiled at Crater Lake, Oregon
1988	Aug	IBM introduces artificial intelligence software
1988	Aug	FDA approves a hair loss treatment
1988	Oct	China announces herbal male contraceptive
1988	Nov	Computer virus strikes the Pentagon, SDI research Lab and 6 universities
1988	Nov	Oldest known insect fossils (390 million years) reported in *Science*
1988	Dec	NASA unveils plans for lunar colony and manned missions to Mars
1988		Prozac goes on the market
1989	Jan	Ruins of Mashkan-shapir, occupied from 2050-1720 BC, found in Iraq
1989	Jan	Astronomers discover pulsar in remnants of Supernova
1989	Jan	Five pharaoh sculptures from 1470 BC found at Temple of Luxor
1989	Feb	Worlds first satellite Skyphone opens
1989	Feb	Physicist Stephen Hawking calls Star Wars a "deliberate fraud"
1989	Feb	150-million-year-old fossil egg found, oldest dinosaur embryo
1989	Mar	Two Utah scientists claim they have produced fusion at room temperature
1989	Jul	NASA announces new high-temperature superconductors
1989	Aug	Voyager 2 discovers 2 partial rings of Neptune
1989	Aug	Microsoft announces Microsoft Office
1989	Oct	Galileo, joint US-Europe atmospheric Probe released to study Jupiter
1989	Nov	Conjunction of Venus, Mars, Uranus, Neptune, Saturn and the Moon

Writing Topic Suggestions
Technology and Science

Pick one of the topics below and write for fifteen to twenty minutes. Remember the un-rules:

- Don't stop writing until the limit is up.
- Use "trigger sentences" if you get stuck.
- Don't be polite.
- Be specific and remember you have at least five senses.
- You don't have to be right, rational or logical.
- Forget about the rules of grammar or spelling.
- Trust yourself.

Remember, you are creating a *primary source*. Write about what you *did*, what you *saw*, what you *thought*, what you *felt*.

1. Review the timelines. Do you remember being awed, inspired or surprised by any of the inventions, innovations, discoveries or "firsts?" Did these discoveries or inventions prompt you to do experiments of your own as a child? Were you inspired by scientists like Albert Einstein, Jonas Salk, Christian Baarnard, or Linus Pauling? Did you want to be a scientist? How did you do in science or math at school? Did you make your living as an adult in a science or technology related field?

2. Were you excited, inspired and awed by the possibilities of "Outer Space"? Did you dream of visiting the moon or other planets? Did you think there might be life on other planets or in other galaxies? Did you follow the "space race" and worry about the Russians getting there first? Did you adult work deal with space in any way?

3. When did you get your first TV? Or when did you get your first color TV? How old were you? Did your family watch it together? Did you work in TV or in a related field? If so, what did you do? Did you buy the products advertised on TV? Did having a TV mean you led a less active life? What are the positive and negatives in your life due to TV?

4. How did the knowledge of the atomic bomb affect your life? Do you think you were more fearful after Hiroshima? Did you have a bomb shelter nearby, or in your backyard? How real did you think the atomic threat was? Did you support nuclear testing on "deserted" islands or in the New Mexico desert? Or were you aware of nuclear testing? Or did you protest against it?

5. When did you first ride in an airplane? Describe the experience. What kind of airplane was it? How many passengers? Where did you fly to? Were you excited or fearful? Did you want to be a pilot? If you were a pilot, what led you to this occupation? Were you interested in the discoveries and advances in aviation during the thirties, forties and fifties? Did you work at an aerospace or aviation company? How did you contribute to the advances in aviation?

6. Did you, or anyone you know, have polio? Do you remember getting your first polio shot? Were you afraid, or were you elated that there was a preventative? Do you remember the first time penicillin was prescribed for you or for someone you knew? Did penicillin save your life or the life of someone you know? Did the discoveries of the polio vaccine and penicillin inspire you to go into a medical, research, or science-related field? Did you admire people in the medical field?

7. Many discoveries, such as DNA, carbon dating, archeological discoveries, and the Big Bang theory, gave new answers to the age-old question of "who we are": where do we come from, how did we get here, how long have we been here. What did you think of these theories and discoveries? Did they cause you to question any

of your previous beliefs? Did your work deal with these subjects in any way?

8. In the sixties, seventies and eighties advanced technology made it possible for us to better understand our past. Were you intrigued by deep sea discoveries of shipwrecks such as the Titanic or the Atocha? Or by the ability to understand ancient civilizations? Have you ever visited an archaelogical dig? What do you think the ancient past has to teach us today?

9. Whatever your work, what technological advancements helped you to do it better? Compare your daily life in 1937 with your daily life in 1957, or 1962 with 1982, for instance – what had changed? How were you more efficient? Did you contribute any inventions or ideas to improve your daily work life? Did you ever try to predict what science was going to come up with next? Were you right or wrong? Were the new technologies hard to learn?

10. Were you excited, inspired and awed by the explosion of space exploration during the sixties, seventies and eighties? Did you dream of visiting the moon yourself, or other planets? Do you remember where you were in July 1969 when men first landed on the moon? Do you remember Walter Cronkite being so moved he had to pause and wipe his glasses? Were you as moved as he? Did the photos of Venus, Mars, Jupiter and other planets dazzle you? Were Neil Armstrong, John Glenn, Wally Schirra, Sally Ride or other astronauts your heroes? Or did you think the US spent too much money and time on space exploration, or that our satellites were polluting outer space?

11. Did you have concerns about nuclear testing, or did you feel that it was safe, or worth the risk? Did you or anyone you know work in a nuclear-related field? Did you protest nuclear testing? What were your emotions when you learned about the problems at Three Mile Island or Chernobyl? Surprised – disgusted – alarmed – holier than thou?

12. Were environmental issues a concern of yours? When did you become aware of the ecology movement? What particular issue concerned you most – endangered species, the hole in the ozone layer, pollution? Did you begin to recycle, or stop littering, or become educated about the environment? Do you remember celebrating Earth Day? Did you campaign to change the laws in order to protect the environment and animals? What did you do? Did you spread "the word" to others? Did you volunteer to clean up wilderness or urban areas? Were you inspired by people like Jacques Cousteau or Jane Goodall? Did you give money to their organizations?

13. Did you have opinions on the "population explosion"? Did you think the "pill" was a good thing? If you took the pill, or your wife/girlfriend took the pill, how did that change your lifestyle, or your beliefs about sex? Do you think the pill led to sexual immorality and a decline in moral standards, or do you think it led to more freedom for women? Or both? What did you think about the infertility research that led to "test tube" babies, infertility drugs and multiple births, and lab dish conceptions? Did you or anyone you know participate in infertility research, or did your work involve you with infertility or genetic research?

14. Did you smoke? When and how did you quit? Did the information about the dangers of cigarettes have anything to do with you quitting? Did you think cigarette manufacturers should have been forced to give warnings on packs, and stop advertising on TV? Did anyone you know die or become ill from smoking-related diseases? Did you work for a company that was related to cigarette manufacture?

15. Were you or anyone you know "saved" by new medical techniques such as transplants or artificial organs? Did you or anyone you know deal with breast cancer or AIDS? Did you work in a medical or medical-research field, and if so, what were some of the advances you saw during the sixties, seventies or eighties? How did

you participate in these advances? How did they help you do your work better?

16. When did you first use a computer? What did you use it for? How did you learn the new computer technology? Did your employer send you to computer school? How did the computer change how you worked? Did you work in a computer or engineering related field? When did you first find yourself understanding the new jargon? When did you buy your first personal computer for your home? How did you use it? Did you play computer games or use a word processor? Did you admire people like Steve Jobs, Robert Noyce, Bill Gates? How has the computer changed your life?

Or anything else you'd like to write about ...

Chapter Fourteen
Crime and Disaster

In this chapter we examine the unexpected "bad stuff" that happens in every life. Exposure to crime and experience of disaster both call forth deep and lasting emotional responses. Both may show human nature at its very worst or at its very best. Criminals commit acts which run counter to decency and virtue, but those who fight crime often are motivated by a love of justice. In the midst of disaster people may show courage, selflessness, generosity, kindness and compassion – and they may also show greed, callousness and selfish opportunism. We can be sure that our lives will include some "bad stuff," but the lasting effects are often due to our responses more than the events themselves.

1930 through 1959

Disaster

Disaster comes in three forms: natural, man-made, and a combination of the two. Natural disasters include drought, heat waves, blizzards, hurricanes, typhoons, windstorms, tornados, twisters, floods, earthquakes, tidal waves, lightning strikes, volcanos and pestilence. The heat waves of the early thirties combined with poor farming practices led to one of the greatest American disasters, the Dust Bowl. A windstorm in 1940, plus engineering design errors, caused the Tacoma Narrows Bridge, otherwise known as Galloping Gertie, to collapse. The pandemic of Asian Flu in 1957-1958 killed 70,000 people in the U.S. A devastating 7.2 earthquake hit Yellowstone National Park in 1959. If you lived through these or other natural disasters, you remember them, often in vivid detail.

"Sally" lived in Tacoma, Washington in 1940. "My father was a civil engineer who worked on the design of the

Narrows bridge," she shared. "He was very proud of it. One
windy morning he took the family to the bridge, so we could
watch it sway back and forth — which is what it was
supposed to do. 'This bridge will never collapse,' I remember
him saying. And then a couple hours later it did."

   "Jack" remembered the earthquake which hit
Melbourne, Australia while he was there on leave during
World War II. One minute he was walking down a crowded
city street, and the next minute flying glass and concrete were
falling and people were screaming. But a few minutes after
that he watched as people raced into deserted shops to loot
them. He remembers one man who dashed into the nearest
shop, which happened to sell women's lingerie, and ran out
again with his arms full of brassieres.

   "I remember Hurricane Audrey, which hit Louisiana
and Texas in 1957, when I was about six," shared
"Nadine." "We lived in Seattle, but my mother's sister lived
in Louisiana. After watching news of the hurricane, my
mother spent a long summer night frantically trying to call
Aunt Vickie. She couldn't get through, and it wasn't until
later that news began to trickle in. Over the next few days I
listened to my parents and grandparents talk incessantly
about my aunt, uncle and two cousins and how they had lost
their house and everything they owned. My mother packed
boxes filled with blankets, clothes and canned food and toted
them down to the post office. She asked me to give some of
my toys too, as my cousin Sheila, only a year younger than I,
had no toys. "Where are her toys?" I asked, and my mother
said she had lost them in the hurricane. "Why can't her

*mom help her find them?" I asked, and was told no one
could find them; they were buried underneath the ruins of
her house. "Well why can't her mom buy her new toys?" I
asked, and was horrified to learn that even the stores had
lost their toys. There were none to buy anywhere.*

*When my cousin Sheila lost her toys in Hurricane
Audrey it was my first realization that the world was not
always safe, and that sometimes bad things happened which
no one, not even your parents, could prevent or control."*

Manmade disasters include fires, forest fires, train wrecks, ship
wrecks, airline crashes, car accidents, mine cave-ins, gas explosions,
smog and pollution, among others.

*"George" vividly remembered the London smog of 1952,
which killed over 5000 people. He remembered pressing a
handkerchief over his nose as he walked a few blocks to
school. By the time he arrived the handkerchief had turned
black. George also remembers his father, who was an
electrician, writing a letter to the London Times
recommending and demanding that Londoners switch from
coal to cleaner electricity to heat their homes.*

*He got his wish when England passed the Clean Air
Act of 1956.*

Crime

For most Americans, crime was about "somebody else" during
these decades. The streets seemed safe, and authority was respected.
Crime was an exception.

*"Ruth" remembered her one and only brush with crime.
Her grandfather was a policeman, a tall and bulky man who*

wore his uniform and shiny badges with stern pride.
Whenever they saw each other, his invariable greeting was,
"Well? Have you been a good girl?" Her timid answer was
always a whispered "yes." And she was a good girl, until one
day in 1941, when in a burst of pre-adolescent rebellion she
stole a candy bar from the neighborhood grocery. She was
caught red-handed and turned in to the police. Terrified that
they would notify her grandfather if they knew her real
name, she made up a fake one on the spot. However, she was
so rattled that the name she gave was Betty Boop.

Organized crime was a focus of public interest during the thirties, continuing from the heyday in the twenties. Criminals such as
Al Capone, Legs Diamond, Dutch Schultz, John Dillinger, Bonnie
& Clyde, Pretty Boy Floyd, Babyface Nelson, Bugsy Siegel, and Ma
Barker got plenty of press, many attaining the status of folk legends, like latter-day Billy the Kids. Willie Sutton, the celebrated bank
robber, began his "career" during the 1930s, saying he robbed banks
"because that's where the money is." These criminals thumbed
their noses at the authorities, ringing a sympathetic chord in many
eager to blame these same authorities for the economic woes of
the Depression. However, crime fighters such as Elliot Ness, Thomas Dewey, and J. Edgar Hoover and the FBI, also attained the
status of legends, and the new technological aids such as lie detec-
tors and police radios made it more difficult to be a criminal.

Another crime present in the thirties was lynching. Targeting
African Americans primarily in the Southern states, the number
of lynchings in the U.S. rose to its all time high in 1934, and although an anti-lynching bill was proposed in Congress, it failed to
pass.

The crime celebre of the thirties was undoubtedly the kidnapping and murder of Charles Lindbergh's infant son, riveting the
nation and leading to changes in laws about kidnapping.

In the early 1940s the interest in crime paled in comparison to the war news, so criminals did not get as much press. Illustrative of this was the case of New York City's Mad Bomber, who planted his first bomb in 1940 and another in 1941, events which the newspapers nearly ignored. After his first few bombs, and citing patriotism as his reason, in 1942 the Bomber voluntarily ceased planting bombs for the duration of the war, although he became active again in the late 1940s. He wasn't caught until 1957. After the war, there seemed to be an increase in "sick" killers who murdered for "kicks" and not for gain, including Evelyn Dick, the Honeymoon Killers, the Black Dahlia murderer, and Howard Unruh of New Jersey who killed 13 of his neighbors at random before killing himself.

In the 1950s organized crime was again in the forefront of crime fighters' sights. The Kefauver congressional hearings into the Mafia began in 1950, and were televised live to a national audience.

"Ernie" shared the story of the uncle who his family always suspected of working for the Mob, even though it was never talked about openly. "I didn't know there was anything different about Uncle Sid," he wrote. "I liked him because he always had extra money and when he came to visit us he usually gave my brother and I a dollar. My mother took it away from us as soon as he left because she said she didn't want us spending 'that' kind of money."

The FBI debuted its "10 Most Wanted" list in 1950. Infamous murderers of the 1950s included Ed Gein, the model for *Psycho*'s Norman Bates, and Richard Hickock and Perry Smith whose murder of the Clutter family formed the story for Truman Capote's *In Cold Blood*.

Four celebrated criminal cases during the fifties raised the issues of the nature of guilt, innocence and appropriate punishment. An upscale doctor, Sam Shepherd, was found guilty of the murder of his wife, a case that was hotly debated even after his death, inspiring a hit television show and movie, *The Fugitive*. Julius and Ethel Rosenberg were found guilty of treason and executed, and the appropriateness of their punishment debated for decades. Most people agreed they were guilty, but did their extreme punishment owe more to the political climate of the day than justice? The case of Emmett Till, a black child of 14 from the North murdered in the South for an off-hand remark made about white girls, stoked the Civil Rights Movement when his killers were found innocent by a legally constituted jury, even though it was apparent to all that they were clearly guilty. Charles Starkwether and his 14 year old girlfriend, Carol Ann Fugate, went on a murderous rampage through the Midwest, a crime for which Starkwether, an adult, was executed. But how guilty was Fugate? Could a 14-year-old girl be held accountable for her actions when under the "spell" of her older lover? The jury decided she could.

Review the following timeline and see what *you* remember …

1930-1959 Events Timeline
Crime & Disaster

1930	Jan	James Irvin lynched in Georgia
1930	Apr	Fire at Ohio State Penitentiary kills over 300
1930	Jun	Federal Bureau of Narcotics is established
1930	Nov	Coal mine explosion in Virginia kills 38
1931	Oct	In Arizona, "Trunk Murderess" Winnie Ruth Judd shoots Anne LeRoi & Sammy Samuelson then chops them in pieces and stuffs them in a trunk
1931	Oct	Al Capone convicted of tax evasion and sent to prison
1931	Dec	Gangster John "Legs" Diamond is murdered
1931		Paul Muni's film *I am a Fugitive from a Chain Gang* sparks prison reform
1932	Feb	Gangster Vincent "Mad Dog" Coll killed by Dutch Schultz gang
1932	Feb	"Baby Face" Nelson escapes from prison
1932	Mar	Charles Lindbergh's infant son kidnapped and found dead 2 months later
1932	Aug	Clyde Barrow and Raymond Hamilton kill two policemen
1932	Dec	Bank robber Willie Sutton escapes from Sing Sing
1933	Mar	Major earthquake in Long Beach CA
1933	Apr	US Dirigible crashes off coast of New Jersey, killing 73
1933	Jun	Barker-Karpis gang kidnaps William Hamms of Hamms Brewing Co., and collects ransom
1933	Jun	Bonnie and Clyde rob the Alma Texas State Bank
1933	Jul	First police radio system operated, in New York
1933	Jul	George "Machine Gun" Kelly kidnaps millionaire oilman Charles Urschel
1933	Aug	The Barker Gang holds up a mail truck and kills a highway patrolman
1933	Sep	Fire in Oregon destroys 2 billion board feet of lumber
1933	Nov	"Great Black Blizzard", the first great dust storm in the Great Plains
1934	Jan	"Anti-lynching" bill is proposed in congress, but defeated
1934	Jan	Fenway Park in Boston catches fire
1934	Jan	Willie Sutton carries off his first successful bank robbery
1934	May	$25,000 reward offered for Dillinger "dead or alive" by Dept. of Justice
1934	May	Lindbergh Act approved by Congress makes kidnapping a capital offense
1934	May	Bonnie & Clyde killed in a shoot-out with police in Louisiana

1934	Jul	John Dillinger killed at Biograph Theater in Chicago
1934	Jul	High temperature state records set in New Mexico, Iowa, Ohio, and Idaho
1934	Sep	Ocean Liner Morro Castle burns off New Jersey, killing 134
1934	Oct	Charles "Pretty Boy" Floyd shot dead by FBI agents
1935	Feb	Lie detector first used in court
1935	Feb	Thirty-one prisoners escape from Oklahoma prison after murdering a guard
1935	Feb	Bruno Hauptmann convicted of kidnap and murder of Lindbergh baby
1935	Apr	Bruno Hauptmann executed
1935	May	NY state first to use blood tests as evidence in court
1935	Jul	Rubin Stacy, on his way to Miami jail for a crime he was later proven not to have committed, lynched by mob
1935	Sep	Hurricane in Florida Keys kills 423
1936	Apr	Tornado hits Tupelo Mississippi, almost leveling the town and killing 215
1936	Apr	Tornado hits Gainesville Georgia and kills over 200
1936	May	J Edgar Hoover arrests Alvin Karpis of the Barker-Karpis gang
1936	Jul	High temperature records set in South Dakota, Minnesota, Maryland, N. Dakota, Pennsylvania, Michigan, Wisconsin, Indiana, Nebraska and Kansas
1937	Mar	Gas explosion in school in Texas, nearly 300 die
1937	May	Dirigible Hindenburg explodes in New Jersey
1937	Jul	Amelia Earhart disappears over the Pacific Ocean
1937	Aug	Marijuana is outlawed
1937	Sep	Wyoming forest fire kills 14
1938	Feb	California police uncover plot to harm Seabiscuit by "sponging" him
1938	Mar	Landslides and floods cause over 200 deaths in Los Angeles
1938	May	Terminal Hotel in Atlanta destroyed by fire, killing 38
1938	Jun	"Olympia Flyer" train crashes in Montana, killing 47
1938	Sep	Hurricane in New England kills 700
1938	Dec	School bus and train collision in Salt Lake City
1939	May	Flash floods in Kentucky kill 75
1939	Aug	Sabotage suspected to have caused crash of the "City of San Francisco," which fell into the Humboldt River
1939	Aug	Louis "Lepke" Buchalter, leader of Murder Inc, gives himself up to columnist Walter Winchell, who turns him over to J Edgar Hoover
1939	Nov	Benjamin "Bugsy" Siegal murders Harry "Big Greenie" Greenberg in LA

1940	Mar	Truck full of migrant workers collides with a train in Texas, killing 30
1940	Apr	"Lake Shore Ltd" derails in NY, killing 34
1940	Apr	Dance hall fire in Natchez Mississippi kills 198
1940	Nov	Tacoma Narrows Bridge ("Galloping Gertie") collapses in windstorm in Washington State
1940	Nov	George "Mad Bomber" Matesky leaves his first pipe bomb in Con Edison Building in NY City
1940	Nov	Blizzard in Midwest kills 154
1941	Mar	Blizzard in North Dakota kills 151
1942	Mar	Stone quarry in Pennsylvania destroyed by 20 tons of gelignite, killing 21
1942	Apr	Tornado in Oklahoma kills 100
1942	Jul	3 feet of rain falls in Pennsylvania, causing floods
1942	Jul	Coal waste heap slides in river valley in Virginia kill 8
1942	Oct	Train crashes into bus in Detroit, killing 16
1942	Nov	Nearly 500 die in a fire that destroys Coconut Grove nightclub in Boston
1943	Mar	Al Capone's chief enforcer Frank Nitti commits suicide rather than go to jail
1943	Sep	"Congressional Limited" train derails in Pennsylvania
1943	Sep	Gulf Hotel in Texas destroyed by fire, killing 45
1944	Mar	Bus falls off bridge into Passaic River in New Jersey
1944	Jun	4 tornadoes strike Appalachia, killing over 150
1944	Jul	170 die in fire at Ringling Bros Circus in Connecticut
1944	Jul	2 ammunition ships explode in California, killing 322
1944	Oct	Liquid gas factory explodes in Cleveland OH, burning 30 city blocks
1944	Dec	Train accident in Utah kills 48
1945	Apr	Willie Sutton escapes from prison in Pennsylvania
1945	Jul	B-25 bomber crashes into Empire State Building, killing 14
1945	Nov	Snow storm in Washington causes school bus crash
1946	Apr	Tsunamis generated by quake in Aleutians hit Hilo, Hawaii
1946	Apr	Train crash in Illinois kills 45
1946	May	Alcatraz prison riot leaves 5 dead
1946	May	United flight 521 crashes on takeoff at LaGuardia Airport
1946	Jun	Cocktail lounge in Chicago's LaSalle Hotel burns, killing 61
1946	Jun	Canfield Hotel in Dubuque Iowa burns down, 19 guests die
1946	Jun	Fire at Baker Hotel in Dallas Texas kills 10
1946	Sep	Evelyn Dick charged with murder and dismemberment of husband
1946	Dec	Fire at Winecoff Hotel in Atlanta kills 119
1946	Dec	Ice plant collapses on tenement building, burying 38 people

1947	Feb	Bank robber Willie Sutton escapes from jail in Philadelphia
1947	Feb	Chemical mixing error causes explosion destroying 42 blocks of Los Angeles
1947	Mar	Coal mine explosion in Illinois kills 111
1947	Apr	Tornadoes strike Texas and Oklahoma, killing 169
1947	Apr	Massive explosion kills 500 in Texas City, Texas
1947	May	Mississippi Valley floods kills 16 and cause $850 million in damage
1947	May	Coal dust explosion at Centralia Coal Company Mine
1947	Jun	Bugsy Siegal is shot dead at the Beverly Hills mansion of his girlfriend
1947	Jul	Gas leak explodes in Pennsylvania beauty parlor, killing 10
1947	Oct	Series of forest fires burn $30 million of timber in New England
1947	Dec	27" of snow falls during blizzard in New York
1948	Oct	Smog in Pennsylvania kills 20 and makes 6000 sick
1948	Dec	Janet Fay hammered to death by the "Honeymoon Killers" Raymond Fernandez and Martha Beck, later found to have murdered nearly 20 women
1949	Jan	"Black Dahlia" Beth Short found brutally murdered in LA; crime never solved
1949	Apr	St. Anthony's Hospital in Illinois burns, killing 77
1949	Sep	Howard Unruh kills 13 neighbors in 12 minutes in Camden, New Jersey
1950	Jan	Mercy Hospital in Iowa burns, killing 41
1950	Jan	11 men rob Brink's Boston office of $1.2M cash and $1.5M securities
1950	Mar	Willie Sutton robs NY Manufacturers Bank of $64,000
1950	Mar	FBI's "10 Most Wanted" list debuts
1950	Mar	Mad Bomber leaves bomb in Grand Central Station
1950	Sep	Train crash in Ohio kills 33
1950	Nov	Train crash in NY kills 79
1951	Feb	"Broker Special" train crashes in New Jersey, killing 84
1951	Feb	Fire in San Francisco City Hall Dome
1951	Feb	Senate Kefauver Committee reports on at least 2 major US crime syndicates
1951	Apr	Julius and Ethel Rosenberg sentenced to death for spying
1951	Jun	Most expensive US hailstorm; $1.5M crop damage and $14M property damage
1952	Jan	Snow storm in Sierra Nevada Mountains kills 26
1952	Feb	Willie Sutton recaptured after his 1947 escape from prison
1952	Mar	Tornadoes in Arkansas, Tennessee, Missouri, Mississippi, Alabama and Kentucky cause 343 deaths
1952	Apr	US minesweeper rams aircraft carrier and kills 176

Sharing My Stories—Too Dark to Learn

In the summer of 1959, when I was ten and my brother was three, we drove from Seattle to Yellowstone Park for our yearly vacation.

We were almost there when my father saw a sign advertising the Lewis and Clark Caves – "See the fabulous stalactites and stalagmites!" it said. So we went. We rode a funicular down into the depths of the earth, then small groups were led by a guide with a flashlight into the caves.

We stood in a circle in a round rock room lit by dim electric lights. The stalactites glistened and looked pretty. Our guide was a college kid who pointed out the wierd convoluted shapes and coppery colors of the walls, while the group oohed and aahed. He made a point of telling us about the bottomless pits that yawned beyond the roped-off trails. He told parents to hold onto their kids or they'd never see them again. He threw a penny down a pit so we could hear that it never hit the bottom. My mother clutched my brother's hand so tightly he squealed.

The guide led us down a rock chute to another room. We slid down the chute one by one. My family was near the back, and when about half our group had gone and I was nervously awaiting my turn to slide down the chute, the earth suddenly shook violently and all the lights went out.

Our group was split. The guide, who had the only light, climbed up and down the chute between us, trying to reassure us. We had no way to communicate, so we didn't know what had happened except we'd had an earthquake. All we could do was wait in the dark.

It was totally black. Not even shadows moved. Some men lit matches but that made it spooky. My brother fidgeted, but my father took him in his arms and held him tight. Dad kept telling us what a great adventure we were having. His voice was so steady that I almost believed him.

Not all fathers were like this. There was a family of father, mother and three little girls in back of us. The father had been making a whining noise ever since the lights went out, and suddenly he shouted, "We're all gonna die!" and began to sob, which set off the rest of his family. The littlest girl's hysterical shrieks bounced and echoed off the cave walls.

Many hours later the lights finally came back on. I zipped down that chute as if I had been greased, and the rest of the tour passed in a blur. Everyone was in a great hurry to leave, and no one cared about the stalactities any more.

1952	Dec	4000+ die in the London Smog of 1952, worst smog ever
1953	May	114 die in tornado in Waco, Texas
1953	Jun	6 tornadoes in Flint, Michigan kill 113
1953	Jun	USAF airplane crashes near Tokyo killing 129 servicemen
1954	Aug	Hurricane Carol (first named storm) kills 70
1954	Sep	Hurricane Edna hits NY City; $50 million in damage
1954	Dec	Dr. Sam Sheppard convicted of the murder of his wife
1955	Apr	Record rainfall in Alabama causes flooding
1955	May	Series of 19 twisters destroy towns in Kansas and Okla.
1955	Aug	Hurricane Connie pounds US for 11 days straight
1955	Aug	Hurricane Diane kills 200 and causes $1 Billion in damages
1955	Aug	Black 14-year-old Emmett Till kidnapped and murdered in Mississippi for comments made about a white girl; killers acquitted by all white jury
1955	Nov	Time bomb aboard United airplane kills 44 above Colorado
1956	Jan	Train crash in Los Angeles kills 30
1956	May	Aircraft carrier burns off Rhode Island, killing 103
1956	Jun	51 die in collision of Andrea Doria and Stockholm, off Cape Cod
1956	Jun	United and TWA jets collide over Grand Canyon, 128 die
1957	Jan	Mad Bomber finally arrested, after 30 explosions
1957	Feb	Fire in Warrenton, MO, kills 72
1957	Mar	8.1 earthquake in Alaska
1957	Mar	Earthquake in San Francisco
1957	Jun	Hurricane Audrey kills 500 in Louisiana
1957	Dec	Ed Gein judged insane and committed for life for the torture, murder and butchering of women
1958	Jan	Murderer Charles Starkwether and Carol Ann Fugate captured in Wyoming after a violent crime spree
1958	Apr	Tornado winds of 450 mph in Wichita Falls, Texas
1958	Sep	Commuter train crashes through drawbridge in New Jersey
1958	Dec	Our Lady of Angels School in Chicago burns, killing 92 students and 3 nuns
1959	Feb	American Airlines jet crashes in New York's East River, killing 65
1959	Feb	$3.6 million heroin seizure in NY City
1959	Jun	Charles Starkwether executed
1959	Aug	7.1 quake at Yellowstone National Park
1959	Oct	Pacific hurricane kills 2,000 in Mexico
1959	Nov	Kilauea in Hawaii erupts
1959	Nov	Richard Hickock and Perry Smith kill Clutter family in Kansas; their story later written by Truman Capote in his book "In Cold Blood"

1960 through 1989

Disaster

Natural disasters during these decades included huge snow-storms blanketing New York City three winters in a row in the early sixties, a tsunami which leveled Hilo, Hawaii in 1960, tornados in Bangladesh, famine in Biafra, the eruption of the volcano Mt. St. Helens in Washington State in 1980, and the San Francisco earthquake of 1989.

"Wally" recalled with pride how his daughter, a firefighter working for the Parks Department, fought forest fires in the California Sierras. "I liked to hear about them afterward," he shared, "because I was thrilled by her heroism and fascinated by the techniques of modern fire-fighting. But while the fires were raging I'd spend days with a nauseous sinking feeling in the pit of my stomach, praying that she'd be all right."

Diseases which appeared during this time frame include Legionnaire's Disease, appearing in 1976; the Hong Kong Flu of 1968-1969, which killed over 30,000 people in the U.S., the Mad Cow outbreak in Britain in 1986, and finally, the ultimate horror of AIDS, which surfaced in the early 1980s. There is no way to underestimate the effects of AIDS on society. It has been compared to the Black Plague in its power to panic as well as kill. Misinformation and hysteria abounded. Affected children such as Ryan White had to fight for their rights to attend public school. Rock Hudson, who died in 1985 from AIDS, brought awareness and sympathy to the plight of AIDS victims. AIDS increased homophobia and yet inspired compassion. Explicit condom commercials appeared on television. AIDS killed the myth that there was such a thing as "free sex."

"In 1982 my son came out of the closet," shared "Louise," "although everyone in the family had suspected he was gay long before. I can't say that it didn't bother me — it did. It didn't change my love for him, but I wished he had chosen a lifestyle that wasn't so hated. I worried that some cretin would beat him up, or worse, just because he was gay. And since he was my only child, I had to give up any hope of grandchildren. But those concerns were nothing compared with how much I worried later, once we knew about AIDS. I read about the disease compulsively, but in the early days it seemed like there was just as much misinformation as truth. The only thing I was really sure of was that gay people were dying. My son's friends were dying. I was so afraid it was just a matter of time before it would be him."

The politically charged, crusading spirit of these decades showed up in the arena of disaster prevention. Famous manmade disasters included mining and gas explosions due to unsafe practices; nuclear and chemical disasters such as Three Mile Island, Love Canal, and Chernobyl; oil spills such as the Exxon Valdez; and recalls of unsafe automobiles such as the allegedly unsafe Pinto. Crusaders like Karen Silkwood called our attention to these problems, and Jane Goodall and Dyan Fossey and many others warned us of animal extinction due to erosion of natural habitats.

Crime

Random, brutal, senseless crimes seemed to be on the increase during these decades. Serial killers include Richard Speck and his murder of eight nurses, Charles Whitman shooting random victims from atop a Texas tower, Albert deSalvo the Boston Strangler, Charles Manson and his "family," Juan Corona murdering 25 migrant workers, Ted Bundy murdering young women from Washington to Florida; Son of Sam David Berkowitz, Kenneth Bianci the

Hillside Strangler, John Wayne Gacy killing 33 people in Chicago, the Atlanta child murders, the Green River killings, and the Night Stalker of Los Angeles. Twenty-one people were killed at a McDonalds in 1984, in a random drive-by shooting; in fact, "drive-by" became a new word in the 1980s. Cyanide-laced Tylenol capsules killed seven people in Chicago in 1982, an unsolved crime that led to better tamper-proof packaging laws. In 1980, John Lennon was shot and killed by a deranged fan, right outside his apartnment building in daylight. One of the most frightening aspects of these kinds of crimes was that the victims did nothing to provoke the crime, except be in the wrong place at the wrong time.

"Paul" remembered his first experience observing a courtroom when he was a pre-law student. His strongest impression was of the banality of crime and the pitiable nature of criminals. "It was astonishing how much grief was caused by that one poor, deluded excuse for a human being." he commented.

Crimes due to greed during these decades included two celebrated kidnappings in the sixties, of Frank Sinatra Jr. and Paul Getty III. Teamster leader Jimmy Hoffa was indicted for fraud and conspiracy, although pardoned by President Nixon. (He was later murdered.) Religious leaders Jim Bakker and Jimmy Swaggart were indicted for fraud and conspiracy. The Friday the 13th computer virus cost American businesses millions of dollars. Art thieves stole Picasso and Renoir canvases, in 1963 the Great Train Robbery was committed, in 1964 the Star of India was stolen, in 1983 Lloyds of London paid 10.6 million pounds because of a horse theft, and the greatest robbery of all time was committed in 1983 when 25 million dollars in gold was stolen from Heathrow airport. Finally, organized crime continued to flourish, despite the efforts of law enforcement, such as Attorney General Robert Kennedy's efforts in the early 1960s, to stop it.

Another category of crime which blossomed during these decades was drugs. From marijuana to acid to heroin, drugs were everywhere. So many baby boomers smoked marijuana during the 1960s and 1970s that virtually an entire generation became "criminals" in the eyes of the law, including many of the most famous. Distrust between the hippie generation and the police was so pervasive that police were known as pigs in the vernacular, and many young men were arrested on suspicion simply because they had long hair. In the 1980s, drugs became more sophisticated and cocaine became the drug of choice for the yuppies, while heroin and crack cocaine use soared on the streets and AIDS was transmitted via dirty needles.

Political crimes, or crimes committed for a "moral" or political reason made news. Assassinations included JFK, Robert Kennedy, Martin Luther King, Malcolm X, George Lincoln Rockwell, and San Francisco Mayor Moscone; and attempted assassinations included two attempts on Gerald Ford, three on Pope Paul VI, George Wallace, Ronald Reagan and even Queen Elizabeth II. Racially motivated crimes such as the murder of Emmett Till, Medgar Evers, and church and school bombings in the south lit the fires of the Civil Rights Movement, which although initially dedicated to non-violence, turned ugly in the big city riots throughout the 1960s. Gang warfare, often organized along racial lines, erupted in nearly every major American city.

"Norman" lived in Los Angeles in 1965, and since his hardware store was located on the fringes of Watts, he watched the city burn before his eyes. So traumatized were his wife and children by the riots that in 1966 Norman sold his business and moved his family north to a small town in Washington State, where he hoped they would be safer.

War related crimes were a feature of the sixties and seventies, as war protestors got angrier and angrier and their tactics escalated, from peaceful sit-ins to out of control anti-war demonstrations with hundreds of thousands of people participating. Young men evading the draft escaped to Canada rather than go to war, and could not legally return until Jimmy Carter pardoned them in 1977. Nazi hunters Elia Weisel and Simon Weisenthal brought criminals from World War II to justice, and crimes from the Vietnam War, such as the My Lai Massacre, horrified the nation.

Finally, the phenomenon known as Terrorism began its modern odyssey. A spate of airline hijackings changed the way we traveled. The SLA kidnapped and brainwashed Patty Hearst for some vague political aims. Terrorists murdered Israeli athletes competing in the Olympic Games held in Munich. The PLO hijacked a luxury ocean liner and murdered one of the passengers. The PLO, the Unabomber, the Red Brigade, the Weatherman, and the IRA believed bombs should be used as change agents, and that the slaughter of innocents was justified in the name of greater good.

Three huge debates about crime and punishment raged during these decades, and are still raging today: the legality and morality of capital punishment – should it be outlawed or used; the legality and morality of abortion – is it murder or is it a woman's right; and gun control laws versus the Bill of Rights – what restrictions, if any, should be placed on the right to bear arms.

Review the following timelines and see what *you* remember …

1960-1989 Events Timeline
Crime & Disaster

1960	Mar	Train crash in Bakersfield, CA, killing 14
1960	May	Alan Freed and 8 other DJs accused of taking radio payola
1960	May	Tsunami hits Hilo, Hawaii, wrecking coastal towns
1960	Oct	Eastern Airlines plane crashes in Boston Harbor, killing 61
1960	Dec	United DC-8 and TWA Constellation collide in mid-air
1960	Dec	50 die in fire aboard US Constellation under construction
1960	Dec	Auschwitz commandant Richard Bar arrested
1961	Feb	Entire US figure skating team dies in airline crash
1961	May	First US airplane hijacked to Cuba
1961	Jul	Another airplane hijacked to Cuba
1961	Sep	Hurricane Carla hits Texas with winds of 175 mph
1961	Dec	Eichmann found guilty of war crimes
1962	Jun	Frank Morris, Joseph Angelin and Charles Angelin escape from Alcatraz. No trace of them was ever found.
1962	Aug	US mail truck in Massachusetts robbed of more than $1.5 million by the "White Glove Gang" who were never caught
1962	Aug	Shady Grove Baptist Church burned in Georgia by KKK
1962	Sep	Black church destroyed by arson in Macon, Georgia
1963	Mar	Alcatraz penitentiary in San Francisco Bay is closed
1963	Apr	US atomic powered submarine Thresher sinks
1963	Sep	4 children killed in bombing of black Baptist church in Birmingham Alabama
1963	Sep	Train collides with bus full of migrant workers, killing 32
1963	Oct	Gas explosion at "Holiday on Ice" in Indiana; 64 die
1963	Nov	Two high-speed commuter trains collide with derailed freight car
1963	Nov	John F Kennedy assassinated
1963	Nov	Lee Harvey Oswald shot dead by Jack Ruby on national TV
1963	Dec	Jetliner struck by lightning and explodes near Maryland
1963	Dec	Frank Sinatra Jr. is kidnapped
1963	Dec	Trial of 21 Auschwitz camp guards begins
1964	Mar	Jimmy Hoffa convicted of jury tampering
1964	Mar	Jack Ruby sentenced to death for murder of Oswald
1964	Mar	38 residents of Queens New York fail to respond to the cries of Kitty Genovese as she was being stabbed to death
1964	Mar	9.2 earthquake in Anchorage Alaska, largest earthquake ever
1964	May	Charles Schmid, the "Pied Piper of Tucson" serial killer, kills first victim
1964	Aug	Civil rights workers Michael Schwerner, Andrew Goodman and James Cheney found buried a Mississippi dam

1964	Oct	Star of India and other jewels stolen from NY Museum of Natural History
1965	Feb	Malcolm X assassinated in NY City
1965	Feb	27 copper miners die in avalanche in British Columbia
1965	Feb	Norman Butler is arrested for the murder of Malcolm X
1965	Mar	James Reeb, civil rights activist, murdered
1965	Apr	40 tornadoes strike Midwest, killing 272
1965	Apr	5 die in earthquake in Seattle, Washington
1965	Aug	6-day riots in Watts section of Los Angeles
1965	Sep	Hurricane Betsy kills 75 in Louisiana and Florida
1965	Nov	Massive power failure in New England and Ontario
1965	Dec	2 passenger planes collide above Connecticut, 4 die
1966	Jan	Snow storm in Northeast kills 165
1966	Mar	57 die in twister in Jackson, Mississippi
1966	Jun	Civil Rights Activist James Meredith shot in Mississippi
1966	Jun	Supreme Court makes famous Miranda decision
1966	Jul	Richard Speck rapes and kills 8 nurses in Chicago
1966	Jul	Charles Whitman kills 5 at Univ. of Texas tower
1966	Oct	144 die in coal waste landslide in Wales
1966	Nov	After 9 years in jail, Sam Sheppard acquitted of murder
1966	Nov	400 die of respiratory failure & heart attacks in NYC smog
1967	Jan	Carl Wilson of the Beach Boys is indicted for draft evasion
1967	Jan	Albert DeSalvo, the Boston Strangler, sentenced to life
1967	Mar	Charles Manson released from prison
1967	Jul	Race Riots in New Jersey lead to 26 killed and 1500 injured
1967	Jul	Prison riot kills 37 in Florida
1967	Aug	George Rockwell, American Nazi Party leader, is murdered
1967	Sep	Hurricane Beulah hits Texas and Mexico, killing 38
1967	Oct	Federal jury convicts 7 in murder of 3 civil rights workers
1967	Dec	Benjamin Spock and Allen Ginsberg arrested protesting Vietnam war
1968	Apr	Martin Luther King Jr. is assassinated in Memphis
1968	Jun	Sirhan Sirhan assassinates Bobby Kennedy
1968	Jun	James Earl Ray, alleged murderer of Martin Luther King, is captured
1968	Dec	First murder by the "Zodiac Killer" in San Francisco
1969	Jun	Stonewall Inn riots in NY City between police and gay rights activists
1969	Aug	Charles Manson and "family" murder Tates & LoBiancos
1970	Feb	Jeffrey McDonald's wife and daughters murdered
1970	Mar	SDS Weathermen terrorists bomb 11th Street in NY City
1970	Apr	Apollo 13 announces "Houston we've got a problem" as oxygen tank explodes on the way to Moon
1970	May	National Guard kills 4 at Kent State in Ohio

1970	Aug	Hurricane Celia hits Gulf
1970	Aug	Courthouse shootout in San Rafael CA kills 4 including judge; Angela Davis charged with supplying weapons
1970	Aug	Black Panthers confront police in Philadelphia, 1 cop killed
1970	Aug	Lonnie McLucas, Black Panther activist, convicted
1970	Nov	Trial of Seattle 8 anti-war protesters begin
1971	Jan	Rev. Philip Berrigan and 5 others charged with plotting to kidnap Kissinger
1971	Jan	Charles Manson and 3 women followers convicted of Tate-LaBianca murders
1971	Feb	California earthquake kills 65, causes $1B damage
1971	Feb	Series of tornadoes hits Mississippi and Louisiana, 117 die
1971	Feb	Lt William Calley confesses to My Lai massacre; he is sentenced to life
1971	Jun	Air West flight collides with navy Phantom jet over LA
1971	Jul	Juan Corona indicted for 25 murders
1971	Sep	Alaska airpline crashes into a mountain, killing 109
1971	Sep	1000 convicts seize prison in Attica, NY; 9 hostages and 28 prisoners die
1971	Sep	6 Klansmen arrested for bombing 10 school buses
1971	Nov	John List kills his entire family and disappears; not apprehended for 18 years
1971	Nov	Dan "DB" Cooper parachutes from Northwest airplane with $200,000; he is never found
1971	Nov	Prison riots at Rahway State Prison in New Jersey
1971	Dec	President Nixon commutes Jimmy Hoffa's jail term
1972	Feb	California Supreme Court abolishes the death penalty
1972	Feb	Slag heap dam collapses in West Virginia, killing 125
1972	Mar	Attempted assassination of Ala. Governor George Wallace
1972	Apr	"Crazy" Joe Gallo, mobster, killed at his 43rd birthday party
1972	May	Electrical fire at Sunshine Silver Mine in Idaho; 126 die
1972	May	White House "plumbers" break into Democratic National Headquarters at Watergate complex in Washington DC
1972	Jun	14" of rain in 6 hours bursts dam in South Dakota; 200 die
1972	Jun	Supreme Court abolishes death penalty
1972	Jul	In New York City, 57 murders occur in 24 hours
1972	Sep	11 Israeli athletes killed by terrorists at Munich Olympics
1972	Nov	Hijackers divert a jet to Detroit and demand $10 million
1972	Dec	Gas tank explosion on Staten Island, killing 40
1973	Jan	Watergate burglars go on trial
1973	Mar	FBI agent is shot at Wounded Knee in South Dakota
1973	Jun	J Paul Getty III is kidnapped, his ear is cut off and mailed
1973	Aug	Dean Corll, Houston's "Candy Man" who raped and killed 26 boys, shot

1973	Oct	65-car collision on New Jersey Turnpike, caused by fog
1973	Dec	After 6 months, J. Paul Getty III released for $750K ransom
1974	Feb	First victim of Ted Bundy is murdered in Seattle; more women victims follow over next 4 years and 4 states
1974	Feb	Patricia Hearst kidnapped by Symbionese Liberation Army
1974	Apr	148 tornadoes reported over 12 states
1974	May	Shootout destroys Symbionese Liberation Army
1974	Jun	Mother of Martin Luther King murdered in church
1974	Aug	Explosion and fire destroy Great Northern Railroad yard in Wenatchee, WA
1974	Sep	President Ford pardons former President Nixon
1974	Nov	Karen Silkwood killed in a suspicious car crash
1974	Dec	Los Angeles Skid Row Slasher kills first of 8 victims
1975	Jan	Haldeman, Erlichman, Mitchell and Mardian convicted
1975	Feb	Theft of Cezanne, Gauguin, Renoir and Van Gogh from Milan museum
1975	May	Hail stones as large as tennis balls hit Tennessee
1975	Jun	113 killed in Eastern Airlines crash at JFK Airport
1975	Jul	Teamsters President Jimmy Hoffa disappears
1975	Sep	Lynette "Squeaky" Fromme attempts to kill Gerald Ford
1975	Sep	Patricia Hearst captured by FBI in San Francisco
1975	Sep	Sara Jane Moore attempts to assassinate President Ford
1975	Nov	Ore ship Edmund Fitzgerald and crew of 29 lost in storm on Lake Superior
1975	Nov	Kilauea Volcano erupts in Hawaii
1975	Dec	Terrorist bomb at LaGuardia Airport kills 11
1976	Feb	Actor Sal Mineo stabbed to death
1976	Mar	Rubin "Hurricane" Carter is retried
1976	Mar	Patricia Hearst convicted of armed robbery
1976	Mar	8 Ohio National Guardsmen indicted for shooting 4 Kent State students
1976	Jun	Teton Dam in Idaho bursts; $1 billion damage & 14 die
1976	Jul	26 schoolchildren and bus driver kidnapped in California
1976	Jul	First outbreak of "Legionnaires Disease" in Philadelphia
1977	Jan	Gary Gilmore executed in Utah, 1st execution since 1967
1977	Jan	President Carter pardons Vietnam War draft evaders
1977	Feb	"El" in Chicago jumps track, killing 11
1977	Mar	Hanafi Moslems invade 3 buildings in Washington DC, starting 3 day siege
1977	May	Nightclub fire in Cincinnati kills 164
1977	May	165 killed in Kentucky supper club fire
1977	Jun	Supreme Court rules out death penalty for rapists of adults
1977	Jul	25 hour blackout in NY City unleashes crime spree
1977	Aug	David Berkowitz arrested in NY for "Son of Sam" killings

1977	Dec	Ted Bundy escapes from jail in Colorado; he flees to Florida and murders more women
1978	Feb	Ted Bundy recaptured in Florida
1978	Feb	Director Roman Polanski flees to France after pleading guilty to charges of having sex with a minor
1978	Mar	Hustler publisher Larry Flynt shot and crippled by a sniper
1978	Jun	Actor Bob Crane is murdered
1978	Dec	6 masked men bind 10 employees at NY Kennedy Airport and make off with money and jewels
1979	Jan	Sex Pistols' Sid Vicious on trial for murder of girlfriend
1979	Jan	Hillside Strangler Kenneth Bianchi arrested
1979	Jan	President Carter commutes Patricia Hearst's sentence
1979	Feb	Metropolitan Museum suffers first theft in 100 year history
1979	Mar	Major nuclear accident at 3 Mile Island in Pennsylvania
1979	May	Dan White convicted of deaths of San Francisco mayor Moscone and Harvey Milk
1979	May	American Airlines plane crashes in Chicago, killing 275
1979	Jun	Oil rig in Gulf of Mexico blows up & spills oil
1979	Jul	2 supertankers collide and spill 260,000 tons of oil
1979	Sep	Hurricane David kills over 1000
1979	Nov	Tanker in Galveston Bay, Texas, spills 10.7 million gallons of oil; worst oil spill in US history to date
1979	Nov	5 killed in anti-KKK demonstration in North Carolina
1979	Dec	11 trampled to death at Who concert in Cincinnati
1979	Dec	Arthur McDuffie, a black insurance executive, fatally beaten by Miami police and causes flare up of racial tension, when four white policemen acquitted of any charges
1980	Jan	Studio 54 owners Steve Rubell and Ian Schrager sent to prison for tax evasion
1980	Mar	Herman Tarnower of Scarsdale Diet, killed by Jean Harris
1980	Mar	John Wayne Gacy found guilty of 33 murders in Chicago
1980	Mar	Ford Motor Co found innocent in death of 3 women burned in a Pinto
1980	May	Mount St. Helens in Washington State erupts, 57 die
1980	May	710 families in Love Canal area evacuated
1980	Nov	MGM Grand Hotel in Las Vegas burns, killing 84
1980	Nov	Oil tanker spills 1.3 million gallons of oil into the Gulf
1980	Dec	John Lennon murdered by Mark David Chapman
1981	Jan	British police arrest Peter Sutcliffe, the "Yorkshire Ripper"
1981	Jan	Oil tanker in Galveston Bay spills 1 million gallons of oil
1981	Feb	Jean Harris is convicted of murder Scarsdale diet doc
1981	Mar	John Hinkley Jr attempts to assassinate President Reagan
1981	Jun	Center of Disease Control issues report of a pneumonia affecting homosexuals, later called AIDS

Sharing My Stories—It Could Have Been Me

I well remember the big flap about the disappearance of young women from Lake Sammamish State Park in the summer of 1974. We lived near Lake Sammamish at the time, and I often took my small daughter to the park to chase the ducks and play on the playground. Sometimes on Sundays my husband would go with us. He would take our daughter and spend "quality time" with her while I lay on a blanket and relished my moments alone, free from the demands of an active toddler.

When we started hearing about the disappearances and about the man known only as "Ted," I tried hard to recall any person with his arm in a sling who asked for help with his VW Beetle, for it's quite likely that I was on the park grounds at the same time he was. But I could remember nothing. I was certainly never approached by any strange man.

I feel lucky about this because Ted Bundy's "type," as we learned later, was pretty, twenty-ish women who wore their dark hair long and parted in the middle – and that description fit me perfectly. What would I have done if Ted had approached me as I lay alone on my blanket while my husband and daughter frolicked on the beach?

I would like to think I would have noticed something "off" or "weird" about him, but the truth is I probably wouldn't have. I think I would have helped him.

Such is the nature of random chance. It could have easily been me instead of those other girls. Perhaps it was this realization that caused me to follow Ted Bundy's "career" with such morbid fascination. It was like visiting the reptile house at the zoo. I don't like snakes, but somehow I have to go in.

Ted Bundy polluted Lake Sammamish State Park for me. I never again felt safe there, and even today, thirty years later, it holds more menace than beauty.

1981	Jun	Supreme Court upholds male-only draft registration
1981	Jul	Laurel Canyon murders occur
1981	Jul	Wayne Williams indicted for murder of 28 young men
1981	Sep	Joseph Paul Franklin, avowed racist, sentenced to life for killing 2 black joggers in Salt Lake City
1981	Oct	Members of Weathermen underground arrested for armored truck robbery
1982	Jan	7 miners killed in a mine explosion in Kentucky
1982	Feb	Oil-drilling platform lost off Newfoundland, 84 die
1982	Mar	Actress Theresa Saladana stabbed by obsessed fan
1982	Mar	Comedian John Belushi dies of drug overdose
1982	Mar	National Guard jet tanker crashes, killing 27
1982	Mar	Tanker in Louisiana spills 1.47 million gallons of oil
1982	Apr	3 CBS employees shot to death in NY City parking lot
1982	Jul	Pan Am flight crashes in Louisiana, killing 153
1982	Jul	FEMA promises survivors of nuclear war will get their mail
1982	Jul	First Green River victim found near Seattle
1982	Sep	Pennsylvania prison guard George Banks kills 13, 5 were his own children
1982	Sep	First reports appear of deaths from cyanide-laced Tylenol capsules
1982	Dec	Norman Mayer threatens to blow up the Washington Monument, demanding an end to nuclear weapons; he is killed by sharpshooters
1983	Jan	Klaus Barbie, SS chief of Lyon in Nazi France, arrested in Bolivia
1983	Feb	Champion thoroughbred Shergar kidnapped in Ireland; he is never found
1983	Mar	Massachusetts woman brings charges of gang-rape atop tavern pool table; four men later convicted
1983	May	First National Missing Children's Day proclaimed
1983	Aug	Hurricane Alicia damages Houston and Galveston, Texas
1983	Nov	Bomb explosion in US Capitol causes damage
1983	Dec	Propane gas fire destroys 16 square blocks of Buffalo NY
1983		Crack cocaine becomes a "drug of choice"
1983		First Lady Nancy Reagan unveils the "Just Say No" anti-drugs campaign
1984	Jan	Supreme Court reinstates $10M award to family of Karen Silkwood
1984	Mar	Mobil tanker spills 200,000 gallons of oil into Columbia River
1984	Apr	Marvin Gaye shot to death by his father, Marvin Gaye Sr.
1984	Jul	James Huberty kills 21 McDonalds patrons in California
1984	Oct	11 members of the Colombo crime family arrested

1984	Dec	Bernhard Goetz shoots 4 black men on NY subway, saying they were trying to mug him; he is later acquitted of attempted murder and assault
1985	May	41 tornados in Pennsylvania, Ohio, New York and Canada
1985	Jun	Claus von Bulow acquitted on charges of attempted murder of his wife
1985	Aug	Night Stalker suspect who terrorized Southern California is captured
1985	Sep	PLO hijackers of Achille Lauro cruise liner throw Leon Klinghoffer off boat
1985	Oct	9 paintings, including 5 Monets and 2 Renoirs, are stolen
1985	Oct	Rock Hudson dies of AIDS
1985	Dec	Dian Fossey, zoologist, murdered in Africa
1985	Dec	Reputed organized crime boss Paul Castellano killed outside NYC restaurant, allegedly by his successor John Gotti
1986	Jan	25th Space Shuttle Challenger 10 explodes a minute after liftoff, killing Christa McAuliffe and 6 other astronauts
1986	Feb	AIDS patient Ryan White returns to school
1986	Apr	Worst nuclear disaster in history at Chernobyl USSR; 31 die
1986	Jul	Attorney General's Pornography Report links hard-core porn to sex crimes
1986	Nov	UN's WHO announces first global effort to combat AIDS
1987	Jan	7 NY Mafia bosses sentenced to 100 years in prison each
1987	Feb	Bomb blamed on Unabomber explodes in Salt Lake City
1987	May	Supreme Court rules dangerous defendants may be held without bail
1987	Jun	Nightline presents first Town Meeting; the subject is AIDS
1987	Oct	1 year old Jessica McClure falls down a well in Texas
1987	Oct	Air Force jet crashes into a Ramada Inn near Indianapolis
1987	Oct	An investor who loses heavily in stock market kills Miami brokerage managers and then commits suicide
1987	Dec	3 Missouri teenagers bludgeon friend to death for Satanist "fun"
1987	Dec	Lynette "Squeaky" Fromme escapes and is recaptured 2 days later
1987	Dec	R. Gene Simmons goes on killing rampage in Arkansas
1987		Condom commercials allowed on TV because of AIDS epidemic
1988	Jan	Oil storage tank spills 3.8 million gallons of oil in Pennsylvania
1988	Jan	Barge sinks near Anacortes, WA, spills 70,000 gallons of oil
1988	Mar	NASA reports breakdown of ozone layer by CFKs
1988	Mar	Federal grand jury indicts Marine Lt. Colonel Oliver North and Navy Vice Admiral Poindexter in Iran-Contra affair

1988	Mar	Robert Chambers Jr pleads guilty of manslaughter in the Preppie murder case
1988	May	4200 kg Colombian cocaine seized in Florida
1988	Aug	First case of Rocky Mountain Spotted Fever, in NYC
1988	Aug	Forest fires in Yellowstone National Park burn 160,000 acres in 1 day
1988	Oct	Seattle Space Needle fire causes evacuation and damage
1988	Nov	Computer virus strikes Pentagon, research lab and 6 universities; Cornell grad student proves to be culprit
1988	Dec	PTL founder Jim Bakker indicted on fraud and conspiracy
1988	Dec	Pan Am Flight 103 bound for NYC explodes over Scotland, killing 259 aboard
1988	Dec	Tugboat collides with oil barge, spills 231,000 gallons of oil
1988		Fox TV debuts *America's Most Wanted*
1989	Jan	Bronx kindergartener brings loaded handgun to school
1989	Jan	Riots in Miami after policeman fatally shoots black motorcyclist
1989	Jan	"Friday the 13th" virus strikes hundreds of IBM computers in Britain
1989	Jan	Gunman opens fire in California schoolyard, killing 5
1989	Jan	Joel Steinberg found guilty of killing his daughter
1989	Jan	First reported case of AIDS transmitted by heterosexual oral sex
1989	Feb	Boeing 707 crashes into Santa Maria mountain, killing 145
1989	Feb	Boeing 747 loses parts of its roof over Pacific ocean; 9 die
1989	Feb	US busts Chinese heroin ring and capture record of 820 pounds of heroin
1989	Mar	12 European nations agree to ban chlorofluorocarbon production by 2000
1989	Mar	Exxon Houston runs aground in Hawaii and spills 117,000 gallons of oil
1989	Mar	2 cyanide-laced Chilean grapes found in Philadelphia
1989	Mar	Worst US oil spill: Exxon Valdez spills 11.3 million gallons off Alaska
1989	Jul	Actress Rebecca Schaeffer murdered by obsessed fan
1989	Aug	Lyle and Erik Menendez murder their parents
1989	Aug	Leona Helmsley convicted of tax evasion and fraud
1989	Sep	Hurricane Hugo sweeps through Caribbean
1989	Oct	6.9 earthquake in San Francisco kills 67 and causes cancellation of 3rd game of World Series
1989	Oct	Buck Helm found alive after being buried 4 days under concrete of destroyed Bay Bridge in San Francisco

Writing Topic Suggestions
Crime and Disaster

Pick one of the topics below and write for fifteen to twenty minutes. Remember the un-rules:

- Don't stop writing until the limit is up.
- Use "trigger sentences" if you get stuck.
- Don't be polite.
- Be specific and remember you have at least five senses.
- You don't have to be right, rational or logical.
- Forget about the rules of grammar or spelling.
- Trust yourself.

Remember, you are creating a *primary source*. Write about what you *did*, what you *saw*, what you *thought*, what you *felt*.

1. What is your experience with the criminal justice system? Did you know any criminals personally? Describe them: did he or she "look" like a criminal? Were their crimes the result of bad luck or poor judgment? What drove them to commit a crime? Were you ever a victim of a crime? Were you ever a witness to a crime? Did you testify at a trial? Tell the story.

2. Did your work involve you in the justice system – were you a lawyer, a judge, a bailiff, a cop, a legal secretary, a social worker, child welfare case worker, court reporter? How did your work change, augment or improve the American criminal justice system? Did your opinion of the justice system change over time? Did you become disillusioned, cynical, bitter? Or more determined, more idealistic, more passionate? How do you think the justice system protects the American people?

3. Have you served on a jury in a criminal trial? If so, what kind of crime was it? Was it a "big" crime like kidnapping, rape or murder? Or was it a "white collar" crime, such as fraud or embezzlement? What did you learn about the justice system? How did you feel about the judge or the trial lawyers? What was your experience in the jury room? Was it difficult to decide the guilt or innocence of the accused? Or was it an "open and shut" case? How did the jury get along? Do you feel you served the cause of justice?

4. If you lived in the South in the 1930s and 1940s, what did you know about lynchings or other crimes motivated by race? Were you aware of lynchings? How did you think they should be eradicated? Did you feel helpless in the face of such brutality? If you lived in the North or West, were you aware of lynchings, burnings and bombs motivated by racial hatred? Were you motivated to stop this kind of violence? If so, how did you act?

5. Did you watch the Kefauver hearings on organized crime on television? Were you aware of the Mafia or the mob? Did you live in a city with a Mob presence? Did you know anyone with mob connections? Were you or anyone you knew a victim of mob violence or extortion? Did you secretly admire some of the exploits of the Depression-era gangsters as folk heroes, such as Bonnie & Clyde, Pretty Boy Floyd, Legs Diamond? Or did you admire the crime fighters such as Eliot Ness, Thomas Dewey, J. Edgar Hoover?

6. What were your opinions on the controversial cases of the 1950s, such as Sam Shepard, Julius & Ethel Rosenberg, Charles Starkwether and Carol Ann Fugate, or others? Did you question their guilt or innocence? Did you question their punishment?

7. Did you have opinions on "controversial" or "political" crimes such as the laws against marijuana, or the draft laws, or free-speech/incitement to riot laws? Did you have opinions on "controversial criminals" such as Dr. Benjamin Spock, Allan Ginsberg, Angela Davis, John Lennon, the Chicago 8, Patty Hearst? Did you work to

change any laws that you considered unfair or wrong? Or did you work to change the penalties for crimes – for instance, did you campaign or work for/against the death penalty?

8. Did the increasing notoriety of vicious or serial killers like the Honeymoon Killers, the Mad Bomber, Richard Hickock & Perry Smith, Richard Speck, Charles Manson, Ted Bundy, Son of Sam, the Green River Killer, etc., cause you to feel more vulnerable or afraid? Were you or anyone you know affected by killers such as these? Did you stop going out at night? Did you install a burglar alarm in your house? Did you buy a gun? Did you worry about the safety of your children?

9. Did the increase in "random and impersonal" violence in the seventies and eighties, such as the Tylenol poisonings or drive-by shootings, cause you to change your lifestyle? If you were afraid, how did your fear manifest? Did you work to change conditions or laws, such as the gun laws? Did you move away from a neighborhood you considered dangerous? Who or what did you blame for this increase in violence?

10. Almost everyone has an experience of a disaster – a fire, flood, hurricane, earthquake, shipwreck, train collision, car crash, explosion, etc. And everyone has a story too. Tell the story of your brush with disaster. Write about the heroism you saw — the kindness, courage, generosity, tenacity of people coping with disaster. Or write about the greed and selfishness you saw, if that was your experience. How did your disaster experience change you? How did it change your perception of others? What did you do after the disaster that you hoped would keep you safe from another one? Did you move away? Did you campaign for better safeguards?

11. Review the timelines. Were you or someone you knew a participant in or witness to any of these "headline" disasters? What do you remember about this famous event? How was your experience different than portrayed in the media?

12. Write about yours or others' responses to disaster in terms of prevention or relief. This could be a disaster you experienced yourself, or one that you read or heard about. Did you work for or contribute to relief organizations, such as the Red Cross? Did you contribute money or food or blankets or clothing, or your own personal time? Did you take in refugees or those hurt by disaster? Why did you do this? How do you think you made a difference to others' lives?

13. In the seventies and eighties ecological disasters made big news. Alarm and outrage were engendered by the incidents at Three Mile Island, Love Canal, numerous oil spills all over the world (culminating in the worst of them all, the Exxon Valdez in 1989). What was your reaction to ecological disasters? Did you work for or contribute to reform of the systems or laws that caused or did not prevent these disasters? Did you write articles or Letters to the Editor, or letters to your political representatives? Did you join organizations such as Greenpeace, the Nature Conservancy, the Union of Concerned Scientists, or others? How do you think your efforts helped, or did they?

Or anything else you'd like to write about ...

Chapter Fifteen
Arts & Entertainment

Nothing brings back memories faster and stronger than the arts of a particular era. Hearing a popular song from the year you were sixteen will make you *feel* sixteen again. Perhaps you'll remember what you were wearing the night you first heard it, or the boy or girl you were dancing with, or the smell of perfume and sweat, or playing the air guitar while singing it to your bathroom mirror. The visual, literary, theatre and film arts are equally evocative.

Our dreams and our deepest emotions are mirrored in the arts. There's a line in the 1989 movie *Dead Poet's Society.* "Medicine, law, business, engineering — these are noble pursuits, and necessary to sustain life," says John Keating, played by Robin Williams. "But poetry, beauty, romance, love – these are what we stay alive *for.*"

The timelines in this section are slightly different from the other categories. Each year includes lists of "winners" from various categories: popular hit songs, Oscar winning movies, Tony award-winning plays and musicals, Pulitzer and Nobel prize-winning books, National Book Award winners, Emmy-winning television shows, and others. Even if the winners listed weren't your personal favorites, you will probably remember them.

1930 through 1959

Books

The literary world was rich during these decades. Writers whose work will still be read hundreds or perhaps thousands of years from now, were at their zenith. Novelists such as William Faulkner, Ernest Hemingway, Pearl Buck, James Joyce, JRR Tolkien, John Steinbeck, Ayn Rand, Ralph Ellison, Henry Miller, JD Salinger, and many more, wrote some of their strongest work. Poets included such luminaries as Carl Sandburg, TS Eliot, WH Auden, Wallace Stevens, Robert Frost, ee cummings, William Carlos Williams, Lawrence

Ferlinghetti, and more. Popular fiction such as mysteries were written by Mickey Spillane, Erle Stanley Gardner (*Perry Mason*), Ellery Queen, Dashiell Hammett, and the wildly successful Agatha Christie. Children's literature too, was illuminated by classics still being read today, such as EB White's *Charlotte's Web*, Astrid Lindstrom's *Pippi Longstocking*, and the inimitable Dr. Suess.

"Arlene" remembered reading Little Toot, *a children's book about a courageous little tugboat, to her young son. It became his favorite book, and he demanded that she read it nearly every night for about a year. "I guess it's true that literature has great power," shared Arlene, "because he was fascinated by boats from then on. In fact, he made them his life's work — he's now the captain of a ferry boat!"*

Probably the most popular book published during these decades was Margaret Mitchell's *Gone With the Wind*, a bestseller from its publication in 1936. Another popular book was Grace Metalious' sexy, steamy *Peyton Place*, which scandalized readers but zoomed to the top of the bestseller list.

"Betty" grew up near the small town where Grace Metalious and her family lived. She remembers the brouhaha that engulfed the town when Peyton Place *was published. Gossip was rife, with everyone trying to guess which people in town were the originals for the book. Betty's father was disgusted by the sensationalism, and forbade anyone in his family to buy, read or even discuss the book. "I had to read* Peyton Place *at my girlfriend's house," shared Betty, "in her bedroom with the door locked. Little did we know that downstairs in the living room our mothers were doing the same thing!"*

Visual Arts

The thirties, forties and fifties saw giants of the visual arts emerge. Georgia O'Keefe was painting her luminous, luscious fruits and flowers. Diego Rivera and Frida Kallow from Mexico scandalized America with their left-wing politics but were hailed for their art. The Lascaux Caves in France were discovered in 1940, electrifying the world with its discoveries of ancient cave art. Jackson Pollock burst onto the art scene, as well as Jasper Johns and Andrew Wyeth. The popularity of photographic art grew enormously, fueled by the genius of photographers such as Ansel Adams.

"When I was a teenager we lived in Fresno, California and often went to Yosemite on family vacations or weekend camping trips," shared "Cecile." "In my opinion it was the most beautiful place on earth, and when I saw the photographs of Ansel Adams I was stunned to see that beauty actually captured in a photograph. I started pestering my parents for a camera, so that I could be a great photographer too. Finally, for my sixteenth birthday in 1951 they gave me a Kodak Brownie box camera.

Oh, how I loved my Brownie! I took it everywhere with me, snapping pictures of anything that would hold still. I usually spent my entire allowance on film. I remember once having to choose between buying a new lipstick or buying more film. I bought the film — my lips could stay pale for another month, but I couldn't go without taking pictures that long. Besides, my mouth didn't even show when I was behind the camera."

Music

In music, the new technology of radio contributed to the enormous influence of this art form. Billboard Magazine announced the Hit Parade in 1936. In the thirties, the popular sound was jazz, with names such as Duke Ellington, Benny Goodman, Cab Calloway, Guy Lombardo, Paul Whiteman, Ella Fitzgerald, Billie Holiday, Ethel Waters and many more topping the charts. Rudy Vallee and Bing Crosby started crooning in the thirties and continued for decades. Country music, or "hillbilly" music as it was first called, was popularized by stars such as Woody Guthrie and Hank Williams. Swing and the Big Band sound was popular during the late thirties and early forties, with artists such as Count Basie, Tommy & Jimmy Dorsey, Artie Shaw, Harry James, Kay Kyser, and especially Glenn Miller.

"Jenny" remembered dancing to Glenn Miller's recording of Stardust *with her soldier boyfriend. "That was the night he asked me to marry him as soon as he came home from the war," she read. "But I was only 16 and my parents wouldn't let me, so I had to say no. We broke up soon after, and lost touch with each other, although I'd hear about him from time to time from my mother, who knew his mother. And every time I heard* Stardust *I would think of him, even though we both eventually married other people.*

Forty years later in 1982, while visiting relatives in my old hometown, I ran into him — on the street! We started talking, and found out that we were both single again. We started dating, and in 1983 we got married. At our wedding reception we danced to Stardust *again."*

After the war a more mellow sound became popular, made so by crooners such as Frank Sinatra, Bing Crosby, Perry Como, Nat King Cole, Rosemary Clooney, Peggy Lee, Harry Belafonte, the Andrews Sisters, and Dinah Shore, among others. In the late fifties another sound came along – early rock and roll, popularized by such names such as Bill Haley and the Comets, Buddy Holly,

Little Richard, Jerry Lee Lewis, and of course, the King, Elvis Presley. A fusion of earlier rhythm and blues, jazz, boogie-woogie and country music, with some raw sensuality thrown in, rock, like many innovations, was not well received by the "establishment." "Noise" was the kindest epithet thrown at it, and many pronounced it "decadent."

In the world of classical music, luminaries such as Shostakovich, Prokovief, Benjamin Britten, Bela Bartok, Arturo Toscanini and others contributed their genius. Leonard Bernstein especially was notable for helping to make classical music accessible and popular with more people.

Theatre

In the thirties vaudeville was dying, but the theatre was thriving, and continued to do so throughout the thirties, forties and fifties. Arthur Miller, Lillian Hellman, Tennessee Williams, Eugene O'Neill, Clifford Odets, William Inge, Terrance Rattigan, and Thornton Wilder were some of the greats of the theatre writing during this time. Lighthearted plays came from the pens of Noel Coward, Cole Porter, George and Ira Gershwin, and Irving Berlin. Rogers and Hammerstein, Lerner and Lowe, and others turned out classical musicals such as *My Fair Lady, West Side Story, The Music Man, The King and I, South Pacific, the Sound of Music, Brigadoon* and *Oklahoma.* George Ballanchine American School of Ballet began in 1934, and in 1937 Margot Fonteyn made her debut. Just as in every other pursuit during these explosive decades, the theater was populated by giants.

Movies

More giants inhabited the world of film during the thirties, forties and fifties. One year, 1939, has been called the best year for movies in history, turning out classics such as *Gone With The Wind,* the first true "blockbuster" movie, and *The Wizard of Oz,* among others.

The Hollywood star system and the beginnings of the cult of celebrity came into being. It was the era of the big studios such as RKO and MGM, headed by legends like Louis B. Mayer, Dory Shary, King Vidor and others. Directors included geniuses such as Alfred Hitchcock, John Huston, and Frank Capra.

There are too many great stars and great movies to list; any list will inevitably leave out someone's favorite. All Americans have been affected by this art form.

Along with millions of other children, "Bertha" loved all the Shirley Temple movies. "I wanted my hair to be like hers," she remembered, "even though my mother tried to warn me that it would take a lot of work. I said I didn't care, so one evening my mother poured vinegar over my head (because that's how Shirley kept her hair so shiny) and tied my hair up in rag curls and pin curls all over my head. Then I had to sleep like that all night! The rags were knobby, the bobby pins were sharp, and the vinegar fumes made my eyes water. It was a horrible night, and the next morning I told my mother I preferred my hair straight. I always felt sorry for Shirley Temple after that."

"Larry" remembered his participation in the high school talent show. He sang 'Hooray for Captain Spalding' from the Marx Brothers movie Animal Crackers, *complete with Groucho's gestures and a fake mustache. He won first prize. "I was so puffed up by my success that I decided to become an actor," shared Larry. "We had a community playhouse in our town, and I turned out for the auditions for their next musical, sure that I would get the lead. Then I was going to tell my parents I was quitting school and leaving for New York.*

Well, I didn't get the lead, or any part whatsoever. So I had to finish high school after all."

"Diane" remembered going to see On The Waterfront *when she was a teenager in 1954. "I was pretty excited," she wrote. "Not because I wanted to see the movie but because it was my very first date. I had a crush on this cute boy and I was so happy when he asked me out. He was a Brando fan, and was amazed when I said I had never seen any of his movies. So he said he had to show me what I was missing. It turned out to be a mistake on his part, because I was overwhelmed by how beautiful and powerful Marlon Brando was. I couldn't take my eyes off him, and suddenly my date didn't seem quite as cute. In fact, he seemed downright boring compared with Brando, and my crush died a swift and complete death."*

One innovation in movie making was full length animated features. Many class participants, especially the "baby boomers" have written about the Disney movies they saw. Most of them mention the shooting of Bambi's mother and the multiplying dancing brooms from *Fantasia*, two movies that made deep impressions on this generation.

Television & Radio

Radio, and later television, revolutionized how families spent their leisure time together, and also how children spent their time alone. The radio and then the television set usually held pride of place in the living room. From scanty programming in the beginning, the entertainment industry blossomed into a plethora of entertainment choices available. Variety and musical shows included Arthur Godfrey, Jack Benny, Burns and Allen, Sid Caesar & His Show of Shows, Kate Smith, Ed Sullivan and Milton Berle. Quiz

Shows were highly popular, and the scandal that erupted over Charles Van Doren's admission of cheating mesmerized the nation. Westerns were a big favorite, including *The Lone Ranger, Hopalong Cassidy, Gunsmoke* and *Bonanza*, among many others; as were cop shows, mysteries and superheroes such as *Dragnet, The Green Hornet*, and *The Shadow*. Comedies included shows such as *The Great Gildersleeve, Fibber McGee & Molly*, and on television the great *I Love Lucy*, still shown and enjoyed in reruns today. News and talk shows were born with *Meet the Press, Paul Harvey, Larry King*, and the *Tonight Show* with Steve Allen. In the fifties the heyday of children's programming began, with such shows as *My Friend Flicka, Lassie, Howdy Doody, Ding Dong School*, and of course *The Mickey Mouse Club*. Sports events glued men to their chairs.

"Dave" remembered listening to the Saturday Night Fights on the radio with his father in the late forties. "It was almost as good as the real thing," he shared. "The sound effects were great. It never occurred to me that those thuds weren't real punches landing, or the splats weren't real blood, or the crunch wasn't real bones breaking. And I don't think it occurred to my dad, either. After a particularly loud noise he would turn to me and say, "Wow, that had to hurt!"

Review the following timeline and see what *you* remember …

1930-1959 Events Timeline
Arts and Entertainment

1930		Hit songs from 1930 include:
		Body and Soul by Paul Whiteman
		Bye Bye Blues by Bert Lown
		A Cottage for Sale by Guy Lombardo
		Dancing with Tears in my Eyes by Nat Shilkret
		Happy Days are Here Again by Benny Mereoff
		I Can Dream, Can't I? by Tommy Dorsey
		It Happened in Monterey by Paul Whiteman
		More Than You Know by Ruth Etting
		On The Sunny Side of the Street by Ted Lewis
		The Stein Song by Rudy Vallee
		Sunny Side Up by Earl Burtnett
		Ten Cents a Dance by Ruth Etting
		Three Little Words by Duke Ellington
		What is This Thing Called Love by Leo Reisman
		You're Driving Me Crazy by Guy Lombardo
1930		Oscar winners from 1930 include:
		Best Picture *All Quiet on the Western Front*
		George Arliss in *Disraeli*, Best Actor
		Norma Shearer in *The Divorcee*, Best Actress
		Lewis Milestone, *All Quiet on the Western Front*, Best Director
1930		Sinclair Lewis wins Nobel Prize for Fiction
1930		Pulitzer Prize in Drama to Marc Connelly for *Green Pastures*
1930		Conrad Aiken wins Pulitzer Prize for Poetry
1930		Pulitzer Prize for Fiction to Oliver Lafare for *Laughing Boy*
1930		*As I Lay Dying* published by William Faulker
1930	Feb	Georgia O'Keefe exhibition at American Place
1930	Dec	Bette Davis first arrives in Hollywood
1931		Hit songs from 1931 include:
		Dancing in the Dark by Bing Crosby
		Dream A Little Dream of Me by Wayne King
		Goodnight Sweetheart by Guy Lombardo
		I Found a Million Dollar Baby by Fred Waring
		I Got Rhythm by Red Nichols
		Just One More Chance by Bing Crosby
		Life is Just a Bowl of Cherries by Rudy Vallee
		Love Letters in the Sand by Ted Black
		Out of Nowhere by Bing Crosby
		Shine On Harvest Moon by Ethel Waters
		Star Dust by Isham Jones

		Sweet and Lovely by Gus Arnheim
		Wabash Moon by Wayne King
		Walkin' my Baby Back Home by Ted Weems
		When the Moon Comes Over the Mountain by Kate Smith
1931		Oscar winners for 1931 include:
		Cimarron for Best Picture
		Lionel Barrymore in *Free Soul* for Best Actor
		Marie Dressler in *Min and Bill* for Best Actress
		Norman Taurog, *Skippy*, for Best Director
1931		Erik Axel Karlfeldt wins Nobel Prize for Fiction
1931		Pulitzer Prize for Drama to Susan Glaspell for *Alison's House*
1931		Robert Frost wins Pulitzer Prize for Poetry
1931		Pulitzer Prize for Fiction: Margaret Barnes for *Years of Grace*
1931		Ansel Adams exhibits 60 prints at The Smithsonian
1931		Surrealist artist Salvador Dali paints *The Persistence of Memory*
1931	Jan	Charlie Chaplin's *City Lights* premieres in Los Angeles
1931	Feb	First Dracula movie released
1931	May	Singer Kate Smith begins her radio program on CBS
1931	Dec	The Gershwin's *Of Thee I Sing* premieres on Broadway
1932		Hit songs from 1932 include:
		All of Me by Louis Armstrong
		Brother Can You Spare a Dime by Bing Crosby
		How Deep is the Ocean by Guy Lombardo
		In A Shanty in Old Shanty Town by Ted Lewis
		Just A Little Street Where Old Friends Meet by Isham Jones
		Louisiana Hayride by Leo Reisman
		Night and Day by Leo Reisman with Fred Astaire
		Paradise by Guy Lombardo
		River Stay 'way From My Door by Kate Smith
		Say It Isn't So by George Olsen
		Soft Lights and Sweet Music by Fred Waring's Pennsylvanians
		Someday I'll Find You by Gertrude Lawrence
		Underneath the Harlem Moon by Joe Rines
		We Just Couldn't Say Goodbye by Guy Lombardo
1932		Oscar winners from 1932 include:
		Grand Hotel for Best Picture
		Fredric March in *Dr Jekyll and Mr Hyde* and Wallace Beery in *The Champ*, both for Best Actor
		Helen Hayes in *The Sin of Madelon Claudet* for Best Actress
		Frank Borzage, *Bad Girl*, for Best Director
		Special Oscar to Walt Disney for *Mickey Mouse*
1932		John Galsworthy wins Nobel Prize for Literature
1932		Pulitzer Prize to Pearl Buck for Fiction for *The Good Earth*
1932		Pulitzer Prize to George S. Kaufman for *Of Thee I Sing*

1932		Pulitzer Prize for Poetry awarded to George Dillon
1932		Nordhoff & Hall publish *Mutiny on the Bounty*
1932		*One Man's Family* debuts on radio
1932		Johnny Weismuller stars in *Tarzan the Ape Man*
1932	Feb	*Free Eats* introduces Spanky McFarland to Our Gang
1932	Feb	George Burns & Gracie Allen debut on *Guy Lombardo Show*
1932	Oct	The *Fred Allen Show* makes it's radio premiere
1932	Dec	Fred Astaire and Ginger Rogers make *Flying Down to Rio*
1932	Dec	Radio City Music Hall opens in NY City
1933		Hit songs from 1933 include:

Easter Parade by Leo Reisman
Forty-Second Street by Don Bestor
Gold-Digger's Song (We're in the Money) by Ted Lewis
Heat Wave by Ethel Waters
I Cover the Waterfront by Eddy Duchin
It's Only a Paper Moon by Paul Whiteman
Lazy Bones by Ted Lewis
Let's All Sing like The Birdies Sing by Ben Bernie
Love is the Sweetest Thing by Ray Noble
Night and Day by Eddy Duchin
Shadow Waltz by Bing Crosby
Sophisticated Lady by Duke Ellington
Stormy Weather by Ethel Waters
Try a Little Tenderness by Ted Lewis
Who's Afraid of the Big Bad Wolf? By Ben Bernie

1933		Oscar winners for 1933 include:

Cavalcade for Best Picture
Best Actor: Charles Laughton, *The Private Life of Henry VIII*
Katharine Hepburn in *Morning Glory* for Best Actress
Frank Lloyd, *Cavalcade*, for Best Director

1933		Ivan Bunin wins the Nobel Prize for Literature
1933		Archibald Macleish wins Pulitzer Prize for *Conquistador*
1933		Maxwell Anderson wins Pulitzer Prize ifor *Both Your Houses*
1933		T.S. Stribling wins Pulitzer Prize in Fiction for *The Store*
1933		*Autobiography of Alice B Toklas* by Gertrude Stein published
1933		First drive in movie theater in US opens, in New Jersey
1933		Erle Stanley Gardner's first *Perry Mason* book is published
1933	Jan	*The Lone Ranger* premieres on ABC radio
1933	Mar	*King Kong* premiers at Radio City Music Hall in NY City
1933	May	Walt Disney's *Three Little Pigs* released
1934		Hit songs from 1934 include:

Carioca by Enric Madriguera
Cocktails for Two by Duke Ellington
Continental by Leo Reisman

I Only Have Eyes for You by Ben Selvin
June in January by Bing Crosby
Let's Fall in Love by Eddy Duchin
Love in Between by Bing Crosby
Moon Glow by Benny Goodman
The Object of My Affection by Jimmie Greer
The Old Spinning Wheel by Ray Noble
One Night of Love by Grace Moore
Smoke Gets in Your Eyes by Paul Whiteman
Stars Fell on Alabama by Guy Lombardo
Stay As Sweet as You Are by Jimmie Greer
The Very Thought of You by Ray Noble
Two Cigarettes in the Dark by Johnny Green
Wagon Wheels by Paul Whiteman

1934		Oscar winners from 1934 include:
		It Happened One Night as Best Picture
		Clark Gable in *It Happened One Night* for Best Actor
		Claudette Colbert in *It Happened One Night* for Best Actress
		Frank Capra, *It Happened One Night*, for Best Director
1934		Luigi Pirandello wins the Nobel Prize for Literature
1934		Pulitzer Prize for Fiction for *Lamb in His Bosom*
1934		Pulitzer Prize, Drama to Sidney Kingsley for *Men in White*
1934		Robert Hillyer wins Pulitzer Prize for Poetry
1934		*Tropic of Cancer* published by Henry Miller
1934		*Goodbye Mr. Chips* written by James Hilton
1934		*Mary Poppins* by P.L. Travers is published
1934		George Ballanchine establishes School of American Ballet
1934		16-year old Ella Fitzgerald debuts at Harlem Opera House
1934	Feb	Diego Rivera fresco in RCA bldg. lobby in Rockefeller Center destroyed because of political content (Lenin)
1934	Apr	Shirley Temple, 5, stars in first movie, *Stand Up And Cheer*
1934	May	The Academy Award is first called "Oscar" in print
1935		Hit songs of 1935 include:

Blue Moon by Glen Gray
Chasing Shadows by Dorsey Brothers Orchestra
Cheek to Cheek by Fred Astaire
I'm In the Mood for Love by Little Jack Little
In A Little Gypsy Tea Room by Bob Crosby
Isle of Capri by Ray Noble
It's a Sin to Tell a Lie by Fats Waller
Let's Swing It by Ray Noble
A Little Bit Independent by Fats Waller
Lovely to Look At by Eddy Duchin
Lullaby of Broadway by Dorsey Brothers Orchestra

		Paris in the Spring by Ray Noble

Paris in the Spring by Ray Noble
Red Sails in the Sunset by Bing Crosby
She's A Latin from Manhattan by Victor Young
Truckin' by Fats Waller
When I Grow Too Old to Dream by Glen Gray
You Are my Lucky Star by Eddy Duchin

1935		Oscar winners from 1935 include:

Mutiny on the Bounty for Best Picture
Victor McLaughlen in *The Informer* as Best Actor
Bette Davis in *Dangerous* as Best Actress
John Ford, *The Informer*, for Best Director

1935		Pulitzer Prize in Poetry: Audrey Wurdemann f
1935		Zoe Akins wins Pulitzer Prize in Drama for *The Old Maid*
1935		Josephine Johnson wins Pulitzer Prize in Fiction
1935	Jan	Clifford Odets' *Waiting for Lefty* premieres in NY City
1935	Feb	James Farrell finishes the *Studs Lonigan* trilogy
1935	Feb	*Awake and Sing* by Clifford Odets premieres in NY City
1935	Mar	*Your Hit Parade* makes its radio debut
1935	Apr	First radio broadcast of *Fibber McGee and Molly*
1935	Oct	Gershwin's *Porgy and Bess* opens on Broadway
1936		Hit songs from 1936 include:

All My Life by Fats Waller
Alone by Tommy Dorsey
The Glory of Love by Benny Goodman
Goody Goody by Benny Goodman
Is It True What They Say About Dixie? By Jimmy Dorsey
It's Been So Long by Benny Goodman
Moon Over Miami by Eddy Duchin
The Music Goes Round and Round by Tommy Dorsey
Pennies from Heaven by Bing Crosby
Take My Heart by Eddy Duchin
These Foolish Things by Benny Goodman
Until the Real Thing Comes Along by Andy Kirk
The Way You Look Tonight by Fred Astaire
When I'm With You by Hal Kemp
You by Tommy Dorsey
You Turned the Tables on Me by Benny Goodman

1936		Oscar winners from 1936 include:

The Great Ziegfeld as Best Picture
Paul Muni in *The Story of Louis Pasteur* as Best Actor
Luise Rainer in *The Great Ziegfeld* as Best Actress
Walter Brennan in *Come and Get It* as Best Supporting Actor
Best Supporting Actress: Gale Songergaard, *Anthony Adverse*
Frank Capra, *Mr. Deeds Goes to Town*, as Best Director

1936		Nobel Prize for Literature awarded to Eugene O'Neill
1936		Pulitzer Prize Fiction: Harold Davis for *Honey in the Horn*
1936		Pulitzer Prize for Poetry: Robert Coffin for *Strange Holiness*
1936		Pulitzer Prize for Drama: Robert Sherwood for *Idiot's Delight*
1936		Andrew Wyeth's first exhibition of watercolors at age of 19
1936	Jan	Screen Actors Guild begins with King Vidor as president
1936	Jan	Billboard magazine publishes its first music hit parade
1936	Jan	*Green Hornet* radio show first heard
1936	May	*Peter and the Wolf* premieres in Moscow
1936	Oct	First radio quiz show premieres, *Professor Quiz*
1936	Dec	Edgar Bergen and Charlie McCarthy first appear on TV
1937		Hit songs from 1937 include:

Carelessly by Teddy Wilson featuring Billie Holiday
The Dipsy Doodle by Tommy Dorsey
Goodnight My Love by Benny Goodman
It's De-Lovely by Eddy Duchin
Marie by Tommy Dorsey
The Merry Go Round Broke Down by Russ Morgan
The Moon Got in My Eyes by Bing Crosby
Once In A While by Tommy Dorsey
Satan Takes A Holiday by Tommy Dorsey
September in the Rain by Guy Lombardo
Sweet Leilani by Bing Crosby
Taking a Chance on Love by Benny Goodman
They Can't Take That Away From Me by Fred Astaire
Too Marvelous for Words by Bing Crosby with Jimmy Dorsey
Vieni Vieni by Rudy Vallee
Where or When by Hal Kemp

1937	Oscar winners from 1937 include:

The Life of Emile Zola as Best Picture
Spencer Tracy in *Captains Courageous* for Best Actor
Luise Rainer in *The Good Earth* for Best Actress
Best Supporting Actor: Joseph Schildkraut in *The Life of Emile Zola*
Alice Brady in *In Old Chicago* for Best Supporting Actress
Leo McCarey, *The Awful Truth*, for Best Director

1937	Nobel Prize for Literature: Roger Martin du Gard
1937	Pulitzer Prize Fiction: Margaret Mitchell, *Gone with the Wind*
1937	Pulitzer Prize in Poetry : Robert Frost for *A Further Range*
1937	Moss Hart and George S. Kaufman awarded Pulitzer Prize in Drama for *You Can't Take it With You*
1937	Dr. Suess' first book, *And To Think That I Saw It On Mulberry Street*, published
1937	Ballerina Margot Fonteyn makes debut at age 18, in *Giselle*

1937		Pablo Picasso paints *Guernica*, inspired by Spanish Civil War
1937	Jan	Soap Opera *Guiding Light* premieres on NBC radio
1937	Feb	First Charlie Chaplin talkie, *Modern Times* is released
1937	Jun	*A Day at the Races* with the Marx Brothers opens in LA
1937	Sep	*The Hobbit* by J.R.R. Tolkien is published
1937	Oct	Ernest Hemingway publishes *To Have and Have Not*
1937	Dec	First feature-length cartoon premieres, Disney's *Snow White*
1937	Dec	Mae West's "Adam and Eve" skit banned from NBC radio
1938		Hit songs from 1938 include:

A-Tisket, A-Tasket by Ella Fitzgerald
Alexander's Ragtime Band by Bing Crosby
Bei Mir Bist Du Schon by the Andrews Sisters
Cathedral in the Pines by Shep Fields
Change Partners by Fred Astaire
Cry, Baby, Cry by Larry Clinton
Don't Be that Way by Benny Goodman
Heart and Soul by Larry Clinton
I Let A Song Go Out Of My Heart by Duke Ellington
I've Got A Pocketful of Dreams by Bing Crosby
Love Walked In by Sammy Kaye
My Reverie by Larry Clinton
Nice Work If You Can Get It by Fred Astaire
Rosalie by Sammy Kaye
Thanks for the Memory by Shep Fields
Two Sleepy People by Fats Waller
You Must Have Been A Beautiful Baby by Bing Crosby

| 1938 | | Oscar Winners from 1938 include: |

You Can't Take It With You for Best Picture
Spencer Tracy in *Boy's Town* for Best Actor
Bette Davis in *Jezebel* for Best Actress
Walter Brennan in *Kentucky* for Best Supporting Actor
Fay Bainter in *Jezebel* for Best Supporting Actress
Frank Capra, *You Can't Take It With You*, for Best Director

1938		Pearl S. Buck wins Nobel Prize for Literature
1938		Thornton Wilder wins Pulitzer Prize in Drama for *Our Town*
1938		Pulitzer Prize in Poetry: Marya Zaturenska *Cold Morning Sky*
1938		Completion of artist Joan Miro's painting *Painting-Poem*
1938		The Cloisters, in NY Metropolitan Museum of Art, is built
1938	Jun	Dorothy Lathrop wins the Caldecott Medal
1938	Oct	Orson Wells broadcasts *War of the Worlds*
1938	Dec	Margaret Hamilton's costume catches fire during filming of *The Wizard of Oz*
1938	Dec	George Cukor announces Vivien Leigh will play Scarlett O'Hara in the film *Gone With The Wind*

1939		Hit songs from 1939 include:
		Address Unknown by The Ink Spots
		And the Angels Sing by Benny Goodman
		Beer Barrel Polka by Will Glahe
		Blue Orchids by Glenn Miller
		Deep Purple by Larry Clinton
		Heart and Soul by Larry Clinton
		Jeepers Creepers by Al Donohue
		Moon Love by Glenn Miller
		Our Love by Tommy Dorsey
		Over the Rainbow by Glenn Miller
		Penny Serenade by Guy Lombardo
		South of the Border by Shep Fields
		Stairway to the Stars by Glenn Miller
		Sunrise Serenade by Glen Gray
		Thanks for Everything by Artie Shaw
		The Umbrella Man by Kay Kyser
		Wishing Will Make It So by Glenn Miller
1939		Oscar winners from 1939 include:
		Gone With The Wind for Best Picture
		Robert Donat in *Goodbye Mr. Chips* for Best Actor
		Vivien Leigh in *Gone With The Wind* for Best Actress
		Thomas Mitchell in *Stage Coach* for Best Supporting Actor
		Hattie McDaniel *in Gone With The Wind* for Best Supporting Actress
		Victor Fleming, *Gone With The Wind*, for best Director
1939		Pulitzer Prize Fiction: Marjorie Kinnan Rawlings *The Yearling*
1939		John Gould Fletcher wins Pulitzer Prize in Poetry
1939		Pulitzer in Drama: Robert Sherwood, *Abe Lincoln in Illinois*
1939	Feb	*Little Foxes* by Lillian Hellman premieres in NY City
1939	Mar	Philip Barry's *The Philadelphia Story* premieres in NY City
1939	Apr	Marian Anderson sings at Lincoln Memorial
1939	Nov	Kate Smith first sings Irving Berlin's *God Bless America*
1939	Dec	World premiere of *Gone with the Wind* in Atlanta, GA
1939	Dec	Premiere of Dmitri Shostakovich's Sixth Symphony
1940		Hit songs from 1940 include:
		All the Things You Are by Tommy Dorsey
		Blueberry Hill by Glenn Miller
		The Breeze and I by Jimmy Dorsey
		Darn That Dream by Benny Goodman
		Ferry Boat Serenade by the Andrews Sisters
		Fools Rush In by Glenn Miller
		I'll Never Smile Again by Tommy Dorsey
		Imagination by Glenn Miller

		In The Mood by Glenn Miller
		Indian Summer by Tommy Dorsey
		Only Forever by Bing Crosby
		Sierra Sue by Bing Crosby
		Trade Winds by Bing Crosby
		When You Wish Upon A Star by Frances Langford
		Where Was I by Charlie Barnet
		The Woodpecker Song by Glenn Miller
1940		Oscar winners from 1940 include:
		Rebecca for Best Picture
		James Stewart in *The Philadelphia Story* for Best Actor
		Ginger Rogers in *Kitty Foyle* for Best Actress
		Walter Brennan in *The Westerner* for Best Supporting Actor
		Best Supporting Actress: Jane Darwell *The Grapes of Wrath*
		John Ford, *The Grapes of Wrath*, for Best Director
1940		Pulitzer PrizeFiction: John Steinbeck, *The Grapes of Wrath*
1940		Mark Van Doren wins Pulitzer Prize in Poetry
1940		Pulitzer PrizeDrama: William Saroyan, *The Time of Your Life*
1940		*For Whom the Bell Tolls* by Ernest Hemingway is published
1940		*Of Mice and Men* by John Steinbeck is published
1940		*Pat the Bunny*, first tactile book, is published
1940	Feb	*Native Son* by Richard Wright is published
1940	Feb	Disney's second feature length movie, *Pinocchio*, premieres
1940	Feb	Woody Guthrie writes *This Land is Your Land*
1940	Feb	Frank Sinatra makes his singing debut
1940	Feb	*The Male Animal* By James Thurber premiers in NY City
1940	Mar	First radio broadcast of *Truth or Consequences* on CBS
1940	Jun	*Quiz Kids* premieres on radio
1940	Jul	Singles record charts first published by Billboard
1940	Sep	The Lascaux Cave in southwestern France is discovered
1940	Nov	Disney's *Fantasia* is released
1941		Hit songs from 1941 include:
		Beat Me Daddy (Eight to the Bar) by Will Bradley
		Blue Champagne by Jimmy Dorsey
		Chatanooga Choo Choo by Glenn Miller
		Daddy by Sammy Kaye
		Dancing in the Dark by Artie Shaw
		Elmer's Tune by Glenn Miller
		Green Eyes by Jimmy Dorsey
		I Don't Want to Set the World on Fire by Horace Heidt
		I Hear a Rhapsody by Jimmy Dorsey
		In the Mood by Glenn Miller
		Intermezzo by Guy Lombardo
		Maria Elena by Jimmy Dorsey

My Sister and I by Jimmy Dorsey
'Till Reveille by Kay Kyser
Tonight We Love by Freddy Martin
We Three (My Echo, My Shadow and Me) by The Ink Spots
You and I by Glenn Miller

1941   Oscar winners from 1941 include:
How Green was my Valley for Best Picture
Gary Cooper in *Sergeant York* for Best Actor
Joan Fontaine in *Suspicion* for Best Actress
Donald Crisp in *How Green Was My Valley* for Best
Supporting Actor
Mary Astor in *The Great Lie* for Best Supporting Actress
John Ford, *How Green Was My Valley*, for Best Director

1941   Pulitzer for Drama to Robert Sherwood
1941   Pulitzer for Poetry: Leonard Bacon for *Sunderland Capture*
1941   Jan   *"Arsenic and Old Lace"* premieres in NY City
1941   Feb   *"Reflections in as Golden Eye"* by Carson McCullers published
1941   Feb   First gold record: Glenn Miller for *Chatanooga Choo Choo*
1941   May   *Citizen Kane* premieres
1941   Aug   *Great Gildersleeve*, spin-off of *Fibber McGee and Molly*, debuts
1941   Oct   Walt Disney releases *Dumbo*
1942   Hit songs from 1942 include:
Blues in the Night by Woody Herman
Deep in the Heart of Texas by Alvino Ray
Don't Sit Under the Apple Tree by Glenn Miller
For Me and My Gal by Judy Garland and Gene Kelly
He Wears a Pair of Silver Wings by Kay Kyser
I've Got A Gal in Kalamazoo by Glenn Miller
Jingle, Jangle, Jingle by Kay Kyser
Manhattan Serenade by Harry James
Moonlight Cocktail by Glenn Miller
One Dozen Roses by Harry James
Skylark by Glenn Miller
Sleep Lagoon by Harry James
Somebody Else is Taking My Place by Benny Goodman
Tangerine by Jimmy Dorsey
There Will Never Be Another You by Woody Herman
White Christmas by Bing Crosby
The White Cliffs of Dover by Kay Kyser

1942   Oscar winners from 1942 include:
Mrs. Miniver as Best Picture
James Cagney in *Yankee Doodle Dandy* for Best Actor
Greer Garson in *Mrs. Miniver* for Best Actress
Van Heflin in *Johnny Eager* for Best Supporting Actor

		Teresa Wright in *Mrs. Miniver* for Best Supporting Actress
		William Wyler, *Mrs. Miniver,* for Best Director
1942		Pulitzer for Fiction to Ellen Glasgow for *In This Our Life*
1942		Pulitzer in Poetry to William Benet, *The Dust Which Is God*
1942		Albert Camus writes *The Stranger*
1942	Jan	Carole Lombard killed in a plane crash
1942	Feb	*Woman of the Year* starring Hepburn and Tracy, opens
1942	Jun	Walt Disney releases *Bambi*
1942	Jun	Capitol Record Company opens
1943		Hit songs from 1943 include
		All or Nothing at All by Frank Sinatra with Harry James
		As Time Goes By by Rudy Vallee
		Comin' In On A Wing and A Prayer by Song Spinners
		I'll Be Home for Christmas by Bing Crosby
		I've Heard That Song Before by Harry James
		In The Blue of the Evening by Tommy Dorsey
		It Can't be Wrong by Dick Haymes
		Mister Five By Five by Harry James
		Moonlight Becomes You by Bing Crosby
		Paper Doll by The Mills Brothers
		Pistol Packin' Mama by Al Dexter
		Praise the Lord and Pass the Ammunition by Kay Kyser
		Taking a Chance on Love by Benny Goodman
		That Old Black Magic by Glenn Miller
		There Are Such Things by Tommy Dorsey
		When the Lights Go On Again by Vaughn Monroe
		You'll Never Know by Dick Haymes with the Song Spinners
1943		Oscar winners from 1943 include:
		Casablanca as Best Picture
		Paul Lukas in *Watch on the Rhine* for Best Actor
		Jennifer Jones in *The Song of Bernadette* for Best Actress
		Best Supporting Actor: Charles Coburn *The More the Merrier*
		Katina Paxinou in *For Whom The Bell Tolls* for Best Supporting Actress
		Michael Curtiz, *Casablanca,* for Best Director
1943		William Schuman Pulitzer for Music for *Secular Cantata 2*
1943		Pulitzer in Fiction to Upton Sinclair for *Dragon's Teeth*
1943		Pulitzer in Poetry to Robert Frost for *A Witness Tree*
1943		Pulitzer in Drama to Thornton Wilder. *The Skin of Our Teeth*
1943		Artist Jackson Pollock's one-man show opens
1943		Betty Smith writes *A Tree Grows in Brooklyn*
1943		*The Fountainhead* by Ayn Rand is published
1943	Jan	Opening of Georgia O'Keefe Retrospective
1943	Feb	*Porgy and Bess* opens on Broadway

1943	Mar	Rodgers and Hammerstein musical *Oklahoma!* opens
1943	Dec	Terence Rattigan's *While the Sun Shines* London premiere
1944		Hit songs from 1944 include:

Amor by Bing Crosby
Besame Mucho by Jimmy Dorsey
Don't Fence Me In by Bing Crosby and the Andrews Sisters
G.I. Jive by Louis Jordan
I Love You by Bing Crosby
I'll Walk Alone by Dinah Shore
I'm Making Believe by Ella Fitzgerald and The Ink Spots
It Had to Be You by Helen Forrest and Dick Haymes
It's Love, Love, Love by Guy Lombardo
Mairzy Doats by Merry Macs
Oh, What A Beautiful Morning by Bing Crosby
Poinciana by Bing Crosby
Shoo Shoo Baby by The Andrews Sisters
Swinging on a Star by Bing Crosby
Too-ra-loo-ra-loo-ral by Bing Crosby
White Christmas by Bing Crosby

1944		Oscar winners of 1944 include:

Going My Way as Best Picture
Bing Crosby in *Going My Way* for Best Actor
Ingrid Bergman in *Gaslight* for Best Actress
Barry Fitzgerald in *Going My Way* for Best Supporting Actor
Ethel Barrymore in *None But the Lonely Heart* for Best Supporting Actress
Leo McCarey, *Going My Way*, for Best Director

1944		Johannes V. Jensen wins Nobel Prize for Literature
1944		Howard Hanson wins Pulitzer for Music for *Symphony No.4*
1944		Pulitzer for Fiction to Martin Flavin for *Journey in the Dark*
1944		Pulitzer in Poetry: Stephen Vincent Benet for *Western Star*
1944		Tennessee Willimas publishes *The Glass Menagerie*
1944		Aaron Copeland's ballet *Appalachian Spring* with choreography by Martha Graham, premieres
1944		30,000 fans mostly teenage girls, hear Frank Sinatra sing at NY City's Paramount Theatre
1944		First hi-fi recordings are released
1944	Mar	Astrid Lindgren writes *Pippi Longstocking*
1944	Oct	*Adventures of Ozzie and Harriet* debuts on CBS radio
1944	Dec	Glenn Miller disappears and believed killed in plane crash
1944	Dec	Bela Bartok's "Concerto" premieres
1944	Dec	Leonard Bernstein's *On The Town* premieres
1944	Dec	Tennessee Williams' play *The Glass Menagerie* premieres
1945		Hit songs from 1945 include:

		Accentuate the Positive by Johnny Mercer

Accentuate the Positive by Johnny Mercer
Along the Navajo Trail by Bing Crosby/Andrews Sisters
Bell Bottom Trousers by Tony Pastor
Candy by Johnny Mercer and Jo Stafford
Dream by Pied Pipers
I Can't Begin to Tell You by Bing Crosby
I Dream Of You by Frank Sinatra
I'm Always Chasing Rainbows by Perry Como
It's Been A Long, Long, Time by Harry James
Laura by Woody Herman
My Dreams Are Getting Better All the Time by Les Brown
On the Atchison, Topeka, and the Santa Fe by Johnny Mercer
Rum and Coca-Cola by The Andrews Sisters
Saturday Night by Frank Sinatra
Sentimental Journey by Les Brown
There, I've Said It Again by Vaughn Monroe
White Christmas by Bing Crosby

1945   Oscar winners from 1945 include:
The Lost Weekend as Best Picture
Ray Milland in *The Lost Weekend* for Best Actor
Joan Crawford in *Mildred Pierce* for Best Actress
Best Supporting Actor: James Dunn, *A Tree Grows in Brooklyn*
Anne Revere in *National Velvet* for Best Supporting Actress
Billy Wilder, *The Lost Weekend*, for Best Director

1945   Gabriela Mistral wins Nobel Prize for Literature
1945   Pulitzer for Music: Aaron Copland for *Appalachian Spring*
1945   John Hersey wins Pulitzer for Fiction for *A Bell for Adano*
1945   Mary Chase wins Pulitzer Prize for Poetry for *V-Letter*
1945   Abbott & Costello unveil their "who's on first" routine
1945   Mar   Billboard Magazine publishes the first album chart
1945   Apr   *Arthur Godfrey Time* begins a 27-year run on CBS radio
1945   Oct   *Meet the Press* premieres on radio
1946   Hit songs from 1946 include:
Come Rain or Come Shine by Margaret Whiting
Doctor, Lawyer, Indian Chief by Betty Hutton
Doin' What Comes Naturally by Dinah Shore
Full Moon and Empty Arms by Frank Sinatra
I Love You for Sentimental Reasons by Nat King Cole
Five Minutes More by Frank Sinatra
The Gypsy by The Ink Spots
Laughing on the Outside, Crying on the Inside by Dinah Shore
The Old Lamplighter by Sammy Kaye
Ole Buttermilk Sky by Kay Kyser

Personality by Johnny Mercer
Prisoner of Love by Perry Como
Rumors Are Flying by Les Paul
Surrender by Perry Como
They Say It's Wonderful by Frank Sinatra
To Each His Own by The Ink Spots

1946   Oscar winners from 1946 include:
The Best Years of Our Lives as Best Picture
Fredric March in *The Best Years of Our Lives* for Best Actor
Olivia de Havilland in *To Each His Own* as Best Actress
Harold Russell in *The Best Years of Our Lives* for Best
Supporting Actor
Anne Baxter in *The Razor's Edge* as Best Supporting Actress
William Wyler, *The Best Years of Our Lives*, as Best Director

1946   Hermann Hesse wins Nobel Prize for Literature
1946   Pulitzer in Music: Leo Sowerby for *The Canticle of the Sun*
1946   Russel Crouse wins Pulitzer for Drama for *State of the Union*
1946   Ansel Adams receives his first Guggenheim Fellowship
1946   Feb   Garson Kanin's *Born Yesterday* premieres in NY City
1946   Nov   Disney's *Song of the South* released
1946   Dec   Premiere of Frank Capra's *It's a Wonderful Life*
1946   Dec   Hank Williams' first recording
1947   Hit songs from 1947 include
The Anniversary Song by Dinah Shore
Chi-Baba Chi-Baba by Perry Como
Feudin' and Fightin' by Dorothy Shay
Heartaches by Ted Weems
How Are Things in Glocca Morra? by Buddy Clark
Huggin' and Chalkin' by Hoagy Carmichael
Mam'selle by Frank Sinatra
Managua, Nicaragua by Guy Lombardo
My Adobe Hacienda by Eddy Howard
Near You by Francis Craig
The Ole Lamplighter by Kay Kyser
Open The Door, Richard by Count Basie
Peg O' My Heart by Harmonicats
Temptation by Red Ingle
That's My Desire by Sammy Kaye
Too Fat Polka by Arthur Godfrey
Zip-A-Dee-Doo-Dah by Johnny Mercer

1947   Oscar winners from 1947 include:
Gentlemen's Agreement as Best Picture
Ronald Colman in *A Double Life* for Best Actor
Loretta Young in *The Farmer's Daughter* for Best Actress

Best Supporting Actor: Edmund Gwenn*Miracle on 34th Street*
Best Supporting Actress: Celeste Holm *Gentlemen's Agreement*
Elia Kazan, *Gentlemen's Agreement*, for Best Director

1947		Andre Gide wins Nobel Prize for Literature
1947		Charles Ives wins Pulitzer for Music for *Symphony No. 3*
1947		Pulitzer in Fiction: Robert Penn Warren , *All the King's Men*
1947		Robert Lowell wins Pulitzer in Poetry for *Lord Weary's Castle*
1947	Mar	*Brigadoon* opens in NY City for 581 performances
1947	Oct	*Kukla, Fran & Ollie* premieres on radio
1947	Oct	*You Bet Your Life* with Groucho Marx premieres on radio
1947	Dec	Tennessee Williams' play *A Streetcar Named Desire* premieres
1947	Dec	First *Howdy Doody Show* telecast on NBC
1948		Hit songs from 1948 include:

Buttons and Bows by Dinah Shore
Cuanto Le Gusta by The Andrews Sisters & Carmen Miranda
How Soon by Bing Crosby
I'm Looking Over A Four Leaf Clover by Art Mooney
It's Magic by Doris Day
Laroo, Laroo, Lilli Bolero by Peggy Lee
Little White Lies by Dick Haymes
Love Somebody by Doris Day and Buddy Clark
Manana by Peggy Lee
My Happiness by Jon and Sandra Steele
Nature Boy by Nat King Cole
On A Slow Boat to China by Kay Kyser
Toolie, Oolie, Doolie by The Andrews Sisters
A Tree In the Meadow by Margaret Whiting
Woody Woodpecker by Kay Kyser
You Call Everybody Darling by Al Trace
You Can't Be True Dear by Ken Griffin

| 1948 | Oscar winners from 1948 include: |

Hamlet as Best Picture
Laurence Olivier in *Hamlet* for Best Actor
Jane Wyman in *Johnny Belinda* for Best Actress
Walter Huston in *Treasure of Sierra Madre* for Best
Supporting Actor
Claire Trevor in *Key Largo* for Best Supporting Actress
John Huston, *Treasure of Sierra Madre*, for Best Director

1948	Tony award winners include *Mister Roberts*
1948	T.S. Eliot wins Nobel Prize for Literature
1948	Walter Piston wins Pulitzer for Music for *Symphony No. 3*
1948	W.H. Auden wins Pulitzer for Poetry for *The Age of Anxiety*
1948	Pulitzer for Drama: Tennessee Williams, *A Streetcar Named Desire*

1948		James Michener wins Pulitzer for *Tales of the South Pacific*
1948		Long playing (LP) records invented
1948		Georges Braque wins first prize at Venice Art Festival
1948	Jan	Jackson Pollock gains prominence in art world
1948	May	Benjamin Britten's *Beggar's Opera* premieres
1948	Jun	*The Milton Berle Show* premieres on NBC TV
1948	Jun	*Toast of the Town* hosted by Ed Sullivan premieres on TV
1948	Aug	Allen Funt's *Candid Camera* debuts on TV
1949		Hit songs from 1949 include:

Again by Doris Day
A You're Adorable by Perry Como
All I Want For Christmas is My Two Front Teeth by Spike Jones
Baby It's Cold Outside by Ella Fitzgerald and Louis Jordan
Bali Hai by Perry Como
Careless Hands by Mel Torme
I Can Dream, Can't I by The Andrews Sisters
I've Got My Love To Keep Me Warm by Les Brown
A Little Bird Told Me by Evelyn Knight
Mule Train by Frankie Laine
My Darling, My Darling by Jo Stafford and Gordon McRae
Riders In The Sky by Vaughn Monroe
Slippin' Around by Margaret Whiting and Jimmy Wakely
Some Enchanted Evening by Perry Como
Someday by Vaughn Monroe
That Lucky Old Sun by Frankie Laine
You're Breaking My Heart by Vic Damone

1949	Oscar winners from 1949 include:
	All The King's Men as Best Picture
	Broderick Crawford in *All The King's Men* for Best Actor
	Olivia de Havilland in *The Heiress* for Best Actress
	Best Supporting Actor: Dean Jagger *Twelve O'Clock High*
	Mercedes McCambridge in *All the Kings Men* for Best Supporting Actress
	Best Director: Joseph L. Mankiewicz, *Letter to Three Wives*
1949	Tony winners include: *Death of a Salesman, Kiss Me Kate*
1949	First Emmy Awards. Winners include *The Necklace* and Shirley Dinsdale
1949	William Faulkner wins Nobel Prize for Literature
1949	Pulitzer for Drama : Arthur Miller, *Death of a Salesman*
1949	Virgil Thomson wins Pulitzer for Music
1949	Pulitzer for Poetry: Peter Viereck for *Terror and Deception*
1949	Pulitzer for Fiction: James Gould Cozzens, *Guard of Honor*
1949	RCA introduces the 45 rpm record
1949	George Orwell publishes *1984*

1949	Feb	First Bollingen Prize for poetry awarded to Ezra Pound
1949	Jun	*Dragnet* first broadcast on radio
1949	Jun	*Hopalong Cassidy* becomes first network western
1949	Sep	*The Lone Ranger* debuts on ABC-TV
1950		Hit songs from 1950 include:

All I Want for Christmas is My Two Front Teeth by Spike Jones

All My Love by Patti Page

Bibbidi Bobbidi Boo by Perry Como

A Bushel and A Peck by Perry Como

Chattanoogie Shoe Shine Boy by Red Foley

Daddy's Little Girl by The Mills Brothers

Goodnight Irene by Gordon Jenkins and The Weavers

Harbor Lights by Sammy Kaye

Hoop Dee Doo by Perry Como

I Wanna Be Loved by The Andrews Sisters

If I Knew You Were Comin Id've Baked a Cake by Eileen Barton

Mona Lisa by Nat King Cole

The Old Master Painter by Richard Hayes

Rag Mop by The Ames Brothers

Sentimental Me by The Ames Brothers

The Tennessee Waltz by Patti Page

The Third Man Theme by Guy Lombardo

| 1950 | | Oscar winners from 1950 include: |

All About Eve as Best Picture

Jose Ferrer in *Cyrano de Bergerac* as Best Actor

Judy Holliday in *Born Yesterday* as Best Actress

George Sanders in *All About Eve* as Best Supporting Actor

Josephine Hull in *Harvey* as Best Supporting Actress

Joseph L. Mankiewicz, *All About Eve*, as Best Director

1950		Tony award winners include *The Cocktail Party, South Pacific*
1950		Emmy winners from 1950 include Milton Berle, Ed Wynn
1950		Nobel Prize for Literature awarded to Bertrand Russell
1950		Pulitzer for Music:Gian-Carlo Menotti for *Music in the Consul*
1950		Pulitzer for Drama: Rodgers & Hammerstein, *South Pacific*
1950		Gwendolyn Brooks wins Pulitzer for poetry for *Annie Allen*
1950		Pulitzer Prize for Fiction: A.B. Guthrie for *The Way West*
1950		National Book Award for Fiction: Nelson Algren, *The Man With the Golden Arm*
1950		Muddy Waters releases *Rollin Stone*, the song for which the rock group and the magazine are later named
1950	Jan	Hank Snow's first appearance on "Grand Ole Opry"
1950	Feb	Dylan Thomas' first US poetry reading tour begins
1950	Feb	Walt Disney's *Cinderella* is released
1950	Feb	*What's My Line* debuts on CBS

1950	Feb	*Your Show of Shows* with Sid Caesar and Imogene Coca premieres writers include Mel Brooks, Neil Simon and Woody Allen
1950	May	Wallace Stevens awarded the Bollingen Prize for poetry
1950	Jul	*Arthur Murray Party* premieres on ABC TV
1950	Dec	Paul Harvey begins his national radio broadcasts
1950	Dec	James Dean begins career by starring in a Pepsi commercial
1950	Dec	The play *Harvey* starring James Stewart, premieres in NY
1951		Hit songs from 1951 include:

Be My Love by Mario Lanza

Beautiful Brown Eyes by Rosemary Clooney

Cold, Cold Heart by Tony Bennett

Come On-a My House by Rosemary Clooney

Cry by Johnny Ray and the Four Lads

How High the Moon by Les Paul and Mary Ford

Kisses Sweeter than Wine by The Weavers

Mockin' Bird Hill by Patti Page

My Heart Cries For You by Guy Mitchell

Sins by Eddy Howard and his Orchestra

Sixty Minute Man by Billy Ward and his Dominoes

There's No Boat Like a Rowboat by Perry Como

Too Young by Nat King Cole

With All My Heart and Soul by Perry Como

The World is Waiting for the Sunrise by Les Paul and Mary Ford

Zing Zing Zoom Zoom by Perry Como

1951		Oscar winners from 1951 include:

An American in Paris as Best Picture

Humphrey Bogart in *The African Queen* for Best Actor

Vivien Leigh in *A Streetcar Named Desire* for Best Actress

Best Supporting Actor: Karl Malden, *A Streetcar Named Desire*

Kim Hunter in *A Streetcar Named Desire* for Best Supporting Actress

George Stevens, *A Place in the Sun*, for Best Director

1951		Tony award winners include *The Rose Tattoo, Guys and Dolls*
1951		Emmy winners from 1951 include: Alan Young, Gertrude Berg, and the *Pulitzer Prize Playhouse*
1951		Par Lagerkvist wins Nobel Prize for Literature
1951		Pulitzer for Music: Douglas Moore, *Giants in the Earth*
1951		Conrad Richter wins the Pulitzer for Fiction for *The Town*
1951		Carl Sandburg wins Pulitzer Prize for Poetry
1951		National Book Award won by William Faulkner
1951	Jan	Bollingen Prize for Poetry is awarded to John Ransom
1951	Mar	*The Caine Mutiny* by Herman Wouk is published

1951	May	*The Ernie Kovacs Show* debuts on NBC-TV
1951	Jul	JD Salinger's novel *The Catcher in the Rye* is published
1951	Jul	Disney's *Alice In Wonderland* is released
1951	Sep	TV soap opera *Search for Tomorrow* debuts
1951	Oct	*I Love Lucy* debuts on CBS-TV
1951	Dec	Opera *Billy Budd* by Benjamin Britten premieres in London
1951	Dec	TV show *Dragnet* premieres

1952   Hit songs from 1952 include:

Blue Tango by Leroy Anderson
Botch-A-Me by Rosemary Clooney
Come What May by Patti Page
Delicado by Percy Faith
The Glow Worm by The Mills Brothers
A Guy Is a Guy by Doris Day
Half As Much by Rosemary Clooney
Heart and Soul by The Four Acres
I Saw Mommy Kissing Santa Claus by Jimmy Boyd
I Went To Your Wedding by Patti Page
Kiss of Fire by Georgia Gibbs
Slow Poke by Pee Wee King
Tenderly by Rosemary Clooney
Wheel of Fortune by Kay Starr
Why Don't You Believe Me by Joni James
Wish You Were Here by Eddie Fisher
You Belong To Me by Jo Stafford

1952   Oscar winners from 1952 include:

The Greatest Show on Earth as Best Picture
Gary Cooper in *High Noon* for Best Actor
Shirley Booth in *Come Back Little Sheba* for Best Actress
Anthony Quinn in *Viva Zapata!* for Best Supporting Actor
Gloria Grahame in *The Bad and the Beautiful* for Best Supporting Actress
John Ford, *The Quiet Man*, for Best Director

1952   Tony award winners include *The Fourposter, The King and I*
1952   Emmy winners from 1952 include: Sid Caesar, Imogene Coca, Red Skelton, Studio One, and *Your Show of Shows*
1952   Nobel Prize for Literature awarded to Francois Mauriac
1952   Joseph Kramm wins Pulitzer Prize for Drama for *The Shrike*
1952   Marianne Moore wins Pulitzer Prize for Poetry
1952   Gail Kubik wins Pulitzer for Music for *Symphony Concertante*
1952   Herman Wouk wins Pulitzer in Fiction for *The Caine Mutiny*
1952   National Book award: James Jones for *From Here to Eternity*
1952   Allen Konigsburg publishes his first joke, under the name of Woody Allen

1952		EB White publishes *Charlotte's Web*
1952	Jan	*Today Show* premieres on NBC-TV with Dave Garroway
1952	Jun	*I've Got A Secret* debuts on CBS-TV with Garry Moore
1952	Nov	*The Mousetrap* by Agatha Christie opens in London
1953		Hit songs from 1953 include:

C'est Si Bon by Eartha Kitt
Changing Partners by Patti Page
The Doggie in the Window by Patti Page
Don't Let the Stars Get In Your Eyes by Perry Como
Hi Lili Hi Lo by Leslie Caron and Mel Ferrer
I'm Gonna Sit Right Down and Write Myself a Letter by Connee Boswell
I'm Walking Behind You by Eddie Fisher
I've Got the World on a String by Frank Sinatra
Oh My Papa by Eddie Fisher
Pretend by Nat King Cole
Rags to Riches by Tony Bennett
The Song from Moulin Rouge by Percy Faith
South of the Border by Frank Sinatra
Stranger in Paradise by Tony Bennett
Till I Waltz Again With You by Teresa Brewer
Vaya Con Dios by Les Paul and Mary Ford
You You You by The Ames Brothers

1953		Oscar winners from 1953 include:

From Here to Eternity as Best Picture
William Holden in *Stalag 17* for Best Actor
Audrey Hepburn in *Roman Holiday* for Best Actress
Best Supporting Actor: Frank Sinatra in *From Here to Eternity*
Best Supporting Actress: Donna Reed *From Here to Eternity*
Fred Zinnemann, *From Here to Eternity*, as Best Director

1953		Tony award winners include *The Crucible*, *Wonderful Town*
1953		Emmy winners from 1953 include: Thomas Mitchell, Helen Hayes, *Dragnet*, and *I Love Lucy*
1953		Winston Churchill wins the Nobel Prize for Literature
1953		Archibald MacLeish wins the Pulitzer Prize for Poetry
1953		Pulitzer Prize for Drama awarded to William Inge for *Picnic*
1953		Pulitzer for Fiction: Ernest Hemingway for *The Old Man &The Sea*
1953		National Book award won by Ralph Ellison for *Invisible Man*
1953		Artist Frida Kahlo's first solo exhibition in Mexico
1953	Feb	*You Are There* with Walter Cronkite premieres on CBS-TV
1953	Apr	The first 3-D movie, *House of Wax* is released in NY City
1953	Oct	Singer Julius LaRosa is fired on live TV by Arthur Godfrey
1954		Hit songs from 1954 include:

Bell Bottom Blues by Teresa Brewer
Count Your Blessings by Eddie Fisher
Good Night Sweetheart Goodnight by The McGuire Sisters
Hernando's Hideaway by Archie Bleyer
Hey There by Rosemary Clooney
If I Give My Heart to You by Doris Day
I Need You Now by Eddie Fisher
Make Love To Me by Jo Stafford
Mambo Italiano by Rosemary Clooney
Mr. Sandman by The Chordettes
Secret Love by Doris Day
Shake Rattle and Roll by Bill Haley and the Comets
Sh-Boom by The Crew Cuts
This Ole House by Rosemary Clooney
Three Coins in the Fountain by the Four Aces

1954		Oscar winners from 1954 include:
		On the Waterfront as Best Picture
		Marlon Brando in *On The Waterfront* for Best Actor
		Grace Kelly in *The Country Girl* for Best Actress
		Edmond O'Brien in *The Barefoot Contessa* for Best Supporting Actor
		Eva Marie Saint in *On The Waterfront* for Best Supporting Actress
		Elia Kazan, *On The Waterfront*, as Best Director
1954		Tony winners include *The Teahouse of the August Moon, Kismet*
1954		Emmy winners from 1954 include: *This Is Your Life, What's My Line, Our Miss Brooks, Make Room for Daddy, I Love Lucy*, Eve Arden, Art Carney, Vivian Vance
1954		Nobel Prize for Literature awarded to Ernest Hemingway
1954		Pulitzer Prize for Music awarded to Quincy Porter
1954		Pulitzer for Poetry to Theodore Roethke for *The Waking*
1954		Pulitzer for Drama :John Patrick for *The Teahouse of the August Moon*
1954		National Book award won by Saul Bellow
1954		William Golding publishes *Lord of the Flies*
1954		*The Fellowship of the Ring* by J.R.R. Tolkien is published
1954		Brigitte Bardot makes her debut in *And God Created Woman*
1954	Jan	Elvis Presley pays $4 to a Memphis studio and records his first two songs
1954	Apr	Elvis Presley records his debut single, *That's All Right*
1954	Sep	*The Tonight Show* with Steve Allen premiers
1954	Oct	*Father Knows Best* premieres on TV
1954	Oct	Walt Disney's first TV show, *Disneyland*, premieres on ABC
1955		Hit songs from 1955 include:

Sharing My Stories—The First One on the Block

My father was a great admirer of scientific progress but he was only mildly tolerant of anything to do with the arts. He especially didn't like what he termed "mindless entertainment" because he felt it numbed the minds and wasted the energy of the young.

He was a businessman, so he was a strong capitalist. However, he was a modest man originally from a poor family, so he disapproved of conspicuous consumption and unbridled materialism. Advertisements for "more! better! faster!" cut no ice with him.

This made it difficult for him to know what to think of television. It was a technological wonder, and a showcase of American ingenuity, but the programs were, in his opinion, stupid. The spectacle of children lined up in front of "the box," mouths open and eyes glazed, was not one that would be welcomed in his home.

In 1955 we lived in a middle class suburb in a modest home that would later be described as "ticky-tacky": a house just like all the others on the block. I was only six, so I loved our neighborhood. It was a great place to be a kid, because there were swarms of us. I had lots of friends. I knew all our neighbors.

One night Dad's appreciation of technology finally won over his suspicion, and he brought home a TV. It was a surprise to my mother. Her eyes grew big and she gasped, "My Goodness!" in an awestruck whisper. While he spent all evening hooking it up, I traveled the length of the block telling the exciting news to everyone I knew. I believe I went into every single house on the block. It was big, glorious news because no one else had a TV! We were the *first*.

Soon Dad had "help" from the other fathers on the block, as the mothers watched the men play with rabbit ears. We kids crowded around, eager to see *Hopalong Cassidy* or *The Lone Ranger*, but mostly what we saw that first night was snow. Eventually we got tired of waiting and went outside, while the grownups continued to ooh and aah. They were the ones with the open mouths that night.

		Ain't That a Shame by Pat Boone
		The Ballad of Davy Crockett by Bill Hayes
		A Blossom Fell by Nat King Cole
		Cry Me A River by Julie London
		Dance with Me Henry by Georgia Gibbs
		Domani by Julius LaRosa
		Hearts of Stone by The Fontaine Sisters
		I Hear You Knocking by Gale Storm
		Learnin' the Blues by Frank Sinatra
		Love Is a Many Splendored Thing by The Four Aces
		Medic by Les Baxter
		Only You by the Platters
		Sincerely by The McGuire Sisters
		Sixteen Tons by Tennessee Ernie Ford
		Unchained Melody by Les Baxter
		Rock Around the Clock by Bill Haley & the Comets
		The Yellow Rose of Texas by Mitch Miller
1955		Oscar Winners from 1955 include:
		Marty as Best Picture
		Ernest Borgnine in *Marty* as Best Actor
		Anna Magnani in *The Rose Tattoo* as Best Actress
		Jack Lemmon in *Mister Roberts* as Best Supporting Actor
		Jo Van Fleet in *East of Eden* as Best Supporting Actress
		Delbert Mann, *Marty*, as Best Director
1955		Tony winners include *The Desperate Hours, Pajama Game*
1955		Emmy award winners from 1955 include: Danny Thomas, Loretta Young, Jackie Gleason, and *Lassie*
1955		Pulitzer for Music awarded to Gian-Carlo Menotti
1955		Pulitzer Prize for Fiction awarded to William Faulkner
1955		Tennessee Williams wins Pulitzer for Drama for *Cat on a Hot Tin Roof*
1955		Wallace Stevens wins Pulitzer Prize for Poetry
1955		National Book award won by William Faulker for *A Fable*
1955	Mar	*Bus Stop* by William Inge premieres on Broadway
1955	Mar	Elvis Presley makes TV appearance, on *Louisiana Hayride*
1955	Jun	*The $64,000 Dollar Question* premieres on CBS-TV
1955	Jul	*The Lawrence Welk Show* premieres on ABC-TV
1955	Sep	*Gunsmoke* premieres on CBS-TV
1955	Oct	*The Honeymooners* premieres
1955	Oct	*Alfred Hitchcock Presents* premieres
1955	Oct	*Captain Kangaroo* premieres
1955	Oct	*Mickey Mouse Club* premieres
1956		Hit songs from 1956 include:
		Allegheny Moon by Patti Page

Be Bop A Lula by Gene Vincent & His Blue Caps
Don't Be Cruel by Elvis Presley
The Great Pretender by The Platters
Heartbreak Hotel by Elvis Presley
Hot Diggity by Perry Como
Hound Dog by Elvis Presley
I Want You, I Need You, I Love You by Elvis Presley
Love Me Tender by Elvis Presley
Memories Are Made of This by Dean Martin
Moonglow by Morris Stoloff and Orchestra
My Prayer by The Platters
The Poor People of Paris by Les Baxter
Rock and Roll Waltz by Kay Starr
Singing the Blues by Guy Mitchell
Tutti Frutti by Little Richard
The Wayward Wind by Gogi Grant

1956		Oscar winners from 1956 include:
		Around the World in 80 Days for Best Picture
		Yul Brynner in *The King and I* as Best Actor
		Ingrid Bergman in *Anastasia* as Best Actress
		Anthony Quinn in *Lust for Life* as Best Supporting Actor
		Dorothy Malone in *Written on the Wind* as Best Supporting Actress
		George Stevens, *Giant*, for Best Director
1956		Tony winners: *The Diary of Anne Frank, Damn Yankees*
1956		Emmy winners from 1956 include: *Davy Crockett, Honeymooners, Phil Silvers Show*, Lucille Ball, Mary Martin in *Peter Pan, The Ed Sullivan Show*
1956		Nobel Prize for Literature awarded to Juan Ramon Jimenez
1956		Elizabeth Bishop wins Pulitzer for Poetry for *North & South*
1956		Albert Hackett and Frances Goodrich win Pulitzer Prize for Drama for *The Diary of Anne Frank*
1956		Pulitzer for Fiction: MacKinlay Kantor for *Andersonville*
1956		Pulitzer for Music to Ernst Toch for *Symphony No. 3*
1956		National Book Award: John O'Hara for *Ten North Frederick*
1956	Jan	Conrad Aiken wins Bollingen Prize for poetry
1956	Apr	Soap operas *As The World Turns* and *Edge of Night* premiere
1956	Jul	Dick Clark first hosts *American Bandstand* in Philadelphia
1956	Sep	Harry Belafonte's album *Calypso* stays #1 for 31 weeks
1956	Sep	Elvis Presley appears on the *Ed Sullivan Show*
1957		Hit songs from 1957 include:

All Shook Up by Elvis Presley
Chances Are by Johnny Mathis
Day-O by Harry Belafonte

Diana by Paul Anka
Don't Forbid Me by Pat Boone
Great Balls of Fire by Jerry Lee Lewis
Honeycomb by Jimmie Rodgers
Jailhouse Rock by Elvis Presley
Love Letters in the Sand by Pat Boone
Party Doll by Buddy Knox
Round and Round by Perry Como
Tammy by Debbie Reynolds
Teddy Bear by Elvis Presley
That'll Be The Day by Buddy Holly and the Crickets
Wake Up Little Susie by The Everly Brothers
You Send Me by Sam Cooke
Young Love by Sonny James

1957		Oscar winners from 1957 include:
		The Bridge on the River Kwai as Best Picture
		Alec Guinness in *The Bridge on the River Kwai* as Best Actor
		Joanne Woodward in *The Three Faces of Eve* as Best Actress
		Red Buttons in *Sayonara* as Best Supporting Actor
		Miyoshi Umeki in *Sayonara* as Best Supporting Actress
		David Lean, *The Bridge on the River Kwai*, as Best Director
1957		Tony award winners include: *A Long Day's Journey into Night*, *My Fair Lady*
1957		Emmy winners from 1957 include: Phil Silvers, Sid Caesar, Robert Young in *Father Knows Best*, Rod Serling for *Requiem for a Heavyweight*
1957		Albert Camus is awarded the Nobel Prize for Literature
1957		Pulitzer Prize for Music awarded to Norman Dello Joio
1957		Pulitzer for Drama to Eugene O'Neill
1957		Pulitzer Prize for Poetry awarded to Richard Wilbur
1957		National Book Award : Wright Morris for *The Field of Vision*
1957		Dr. Suess publishes *The Cat in the Hat*
1957		*Atlas Shrugged* by Ayn Rand is published
1957		*On The Road* by Jack Kerouac is published
1957	Jun	Howard Cosell has his first TV show
1957	Aug	*American Bandstand* premieres on network TV (ABC)
1957	Sep	*West Side Story* opens on Broadway
1957	Sep	*Wagon Train* premieres on TV
1957	Oct	Albert Camus is awarded the Nobel Prize for Literature
1957	Oct	*Leave It to Beaver* premieres on CBS TV
1957	Dec	Sam Cooke and Buddy Holly debut on the *Ed Sullivan Show*
1958		Hit songs from 1958 include:
		All I Have to Do is Dream by The Everly Brothers
		Bird Dog by The Everly Brothers

Christmas Don't Be Late by Alvin and the Chipmunks
Get a Job by The Silhouettes
Hard Headed Woman by Elvis Prelsy
He's Got the Whole World in His Hands by Laurie London
It's All in the Game by Tommy Edwards
Patricia by Perez Prado & His Orchestra
Poor Little Fool by Ricky Nelson
The Purple People Eater by Sheb Wooley
Sugartime by The McGuire Sisters
Tequila by The Champs
To Know Him Is To Love Him by The Teddy Bears
Tom Dooley by The Kingston Trio
Twilight Time by The Platters
The Witch Doctor by David Seville
Yakety Yak by The Coasters

1958		Oscar winners from 1958 include:
		Gigi as Best Picture
		David Niven in *Separate Tables* for Best Actor
		Susan Hayward in *I Want To Live* for Best Actress
		Burl Ives in *The Big Country* for Best Supporting Actor
		Wendy Hiller in *Separate Tables* for Best Supporting Actress
		Vincente Minelli, *Gigi*, for Best Director
1958		Tony winners include: *Sunrise at Campobello*, *The Music Man*
1958		Emmy winners from 1958 include: Dinah Shore, Phil Silvers, Jack Benny, Jane Wyatt, *The Bob Cummings Show*, *See It Now* with Edward R. Murrow
1958		Nobel Prize for Literature awarded to Boris Pasternak
1958		Pulitzer Prize for Music awarded to Samuel Barber
1958		Pulitzer for Fiction: James Agee for *A Death In The Family*
1958		Robert Penn Warren wins Pultizer Prize for Poetry
1958		Pulitzer for Drama: Ketti Frings for *Look Homeward Angel*
1958		National Book Award : John Cheever, *The Wapshot Chronicles*
1958		Jasper Johns introduces Abstract Expressionism
1958	Jan	ee cummings wins the Bollingen Prize for poetry
1958	Mar	First Gold Record : *Catch a Falling Star* by Perry Como
1958	Apr	Van Cliburn, 23, wins Tchaikovsky Piano Competition
1958	Aug	Vladimir Nabokov publishes *Lolita*
1958	Aug	Investigation into TV game shows begins
1958	Sep	Boris Pasternak's novel *Dr. Zhivago* published in the US
1958	Dec	Alan Freed opens his "Christmas Rock & Roll Spectacular"
1959		Hit songs from 1959 include:

The Battle of New Orleans by Johnny Horton
A Big Hunk O'Love by Elvis Presley
Come Softly to Me by The Fleetwoods

Dream Lover by Bobby Darin
Heartaches by the Number by Guy Mitchell
It's Late by Ricky Nelson
Kansas City by Wilbert Harrison
Lipstick on Your Collar by Connie Francis
Lonely Boy by Paul Anka
Lonely Teardrops by Jackie Wilson
Mack the Knife by Bobby Darin
Mr. Blue by The Fleetwoods
Sixteen Candles by The Crests
Sleep Walk by Santo & Johnny
Smoke Gets in Your Eyes by The Platters
Stagger Lee by Lloyd Price
Venus by Frankie Avalon

1959		Oscar winners from 1959 include:
		Ben Hur as Best Picture
		Charlton Heston in *Ben Hur* for Best Actor
		Simone Signoret in *Room At the Top* for Best Actress
		Hugh Griffith in *Ben Hur* for Best Supporting Actor
		Shelley Winters in *The Diary of Anne Frank* for Best Supporting Actress
		William Wyler, *Ben Hur*, as Best Director
1959		Tony award winners include: *J.B.*, *Redhead*
1959		Emmy winners from 1959 include: Raymond Burr in *Perry Mason*, Loretta Young, Jane Wyatt, Perry Como, Dennis Weaver in *Gunsmoke*, *Maverick*, *Playhouse 90*, *Jack Benny Show*
1959		Salvatore Quasimodo wins Nobel Prize for Literature
1959		Pulitzer Prize for Music awarded to John LaMontaine
1959		Pulitzer Prize for Poetry awarded to Stanley Kunitz
1959		Pulitzer for Drama awarded to Archibald MacLeish for *J.B.*
1959		Pulitzer Prize for Fiction awarded to Robert Lewis Taylor for *The Travels of Jaimie McPheeters*
1959		National Book Award : Bernard Malamud, *The Magic Barrell*
1959		The Guggenheim Museum, designed by Frank Lloyd Wright, opens in NY City
1959	Jan	Theodore Roethke wins Bollingen Prize for poetry
1959	Jan	*Rawhide* with Clint Eastwood premieres on CBS-TV
1959	Mar	*Some Like It Hot* with Marilyn Monroe premieres
1959	Mar	*Raisin in the Sun* opens on Broadway
1959	May	First Grammy winners are Perry Como and Ella Fitzgerald
1959	Sep	*Bonanza* premieres
1959	Oct	Rod Serling's *Twilight Zone* premieres
1959	Nov	First episode of *Rocky and Bullwinkle*
1959	Nov	Charles Van Doren confesses that TV quiz show was fixed

1960 through 1989

Books

Books published from 1960 to 1989 often reflected the political and social unrest of the time. In the early sixties some powerfully influential books helped create change as well as reflect it. Like the sixties themselves, their themes questioned authority and the status quo. Some of these classics included Harper Lee's *To Kill a Mockingbird* in 1960, Joseph Heller's *Catch 22* in 1961, Sylvia Plath's *The Bell Jar* in 1962, *One Flew Over the Cuckoo's Nest* by Ken Kesey in 1962, and *The Group* by Mary McCarthy in 1963.

Other important authors writing during these decades include Kurt Vonnegut (*Slaughterhouse 5*, 1969), Wallace Stegner (*Angle of Repose*, 1971), William Styron (*Sophie's Choice*, 1979), Thomas Wolfe (*The Right Stuff*, 1981) Toni Morrison (*Song of Solomon* 1977, *Beloved* 1987), Alice Walker (*The Color Purple*, 1982), and poets Gwendolyn Brooks and Maya Angelou, to name just a few. The position of US Poet Laureate was created in 1982, and the first to hold this honor was Robert Penn Warren.

Some popular books that swept the reading public were Jacqueline Susann's *Valley of the Dolls* in 1966, Colleen McCullough's *The Thorn Birds* in 1977, *Portnoy's Complaint* by Philip Roth in 1979, and the novels of Stephen King, including *Carrie* published in 1974, *Salem's Lot* in 1975, *The Shining* in 1977 and *The Stand* in 1978. Three hugely successful books became even more successful as movies: Peter Benchley's *Jaws*, Mario Puzo's *The Godfather*, and William Peter Blatty's *The Exorcist*.

In children's literature, Shel Silverstein published *Lafcadio* in 1963, *The Giving Tree* in 1964, *Where the Sidewalk Ends* in 1974, and *A Light in the Attic* in 1981, among others. Roald Dahl's works included 1964's *Charlie and the Chocolate Factory*, *Danny the Champion of the World* from 1975, and 1982's *The BFG*. Maurice Sendak created a sensation with *Where the Wild Things Are*, which won the Caldecott Medal in 1964, and remains a classic to this day.

Visual Arts

The visual arts too underwent spectacular changes, following the social and political trends of these decades. In the sixties many artists broke the rules and seemed to be encouraging viewers to take a leap into the unknown with them. New artistic forms such as pop art (Andy Warhol, David Hockney), op art (Victor Vasarely), assemblage art, kinetic abstraction (Marcel Duchamp), and others made their debuts in the sixties.

In the seventies earth art, land art and environmental art were prominent, represented by artists such as Robert Smithson, Alice Aycock and others. Illusionism, photo realism, hyperrealism and performance art were other notable movements. The influence of the women's movement was felt in such artists as Judy Chicago, who created the feminist art exhibition *The Dinner Party* in 1974.

The eighties were a highly successful decade for art museums and artists. Art works brought record prices. Picasso's *Yo* sold for 5.4 million, Van Gogh's *Sunflowers* sold for nearly 40 million and his *Irises* for over 50 million. The Musuem of Modern Art reopened at twice its previous size. Underscoring the immense and growing value of art, in 1989 the Isabella Stewart Gardner Museum in Boston was robbed of twelve artworks by Degas, Rembrandt, Renoir and Vermeer, valued at one hundred million dollars and never yet recovered.

Music

Music in the early sixties was much like the fifties – male crooners such as Perry Como, Frank Sinatra, and Dean Martin, and female singers like Dinah Shore and Rosemary Clooney, remained popular with adults. Teenagers listened to Elvis, Buddy Holly, Bobby Darin, Paul Anka, Frankie Avalon, and the Everly Brothers, among others, and were swept away by dance crazes such as the Twist, shown on *American Bandstand* and watched by teens all over the country. Other dance crazes included the Mashed Potato, the Swim, the Watusi, the Monkey and the Jerk.

In the mid sixties music changed radically, into many new genres. The Motown sound emerged, specializing in black rhythm and blues and featuring stars such as Gladys Knight and the Pips, the Supremes, Aretha Franklin, James Brown, the Temptations and Jimi Hendrix. Bob Dylan, Joan Baez, Peter Paul and Mary, Pete Seeger and others brought about a folk music revival, marrying it with "message" music protesting against war and social injustice, as in songs like *Blowin in the Wind* and *Where Have All the Flowers Gone.*

"Karen" remembered listening to Bob Dylan in the mid-sixties. "I was only fourteen," she shared, "and sheltered in middle class suburbia, so I was innocent about what was really going on in the world. But I had a friend with an older brother, who had a lot of Bob Dylan records, and when I was over at her house her brother would play his records for us and talk to us about war and racism and how god-awful the world really was. I loved to listen to him talk, and after a while I loved to listen to Bob Dylan too. When I first heard Dylan sing, I thought there must be something wrong with the record player. But then his voice, bad as it was, started to get to me. It was such a contrast to those mellow, smooth ballad singers my mother liked. Dylan's voice was raw and scratchy and just the right voice to sing about the truth — the real truth, not the prettified version served to children. And his scraggly, almost sleazy looks fit his voice perfectly. He looked like he slept in a bar after arguing politics all night and didn't bother to comb his hair because clean neat hair wasn't very important, really. I knew instinctively my mother would not invite him to dinner. So obviously he must be a prophet."

Popular music was influenced by the drug scene. Amplified improvisational acid rock psychedelic rock, were popular. The Beatles, the Doors, Jefferson Airplane, and The Grateful Dead were part of this counterculture. The decade finished with a bang at 1969's Woodstock Music Festival, attended by 400,000 people, most of them stoned and many of them naked.

The seventies saw the deaths of Elvis Presley, Jim Morrison, Janis Joplin, and Jimi Hendrix, along with the break up of the world's most famous band, The Beatles; suddenly silencing some major influences. Splinter fads and styles sprung up, such as soft-rock, hard rock, heavy metal, country rock, folk rock, punk rock, and shock rock. Reggae gained huge popularity in the US, thanks to Jamaican Bob Marley. And of course, the dance craze of the decade: disco. Disco music was the first genre that used electronic instruments for commercial music, and its fast hard driving beat changed dance music forever. Some of the most popular names in music during the seventies were Aerosmith, the Bee Gees, Jackson Browne, the Eagles, ELO, Fleetwood Mac, Billy Joel, Elton John, Led Zeppelin, Kiss, Pink Floyd, Bob Seger, Bruce Springsteen, Rod Stewart, Van Halen, and the Who.

MTV was a phenomenon of the eighties, with an enormous impact on the music industry and especially young people. Another revolutionary introduction was that of the compact disc. MTV popularized dances such as slam dancing, lombada and break dancing. Madonna and Michael Jackson were the indubitable superstars of this decade, proving themselves masters of the MTV medium. Pop, rock, punk and country were popular in the eighties, joined by new wave and rap or hip hop. Rap had actually started in the sixties, invented by black prison inmates who had no instruments except their voices and imaginations. Early rap groups included Milli Vanilli, M.C. Hammer, and Vanilla Ice.

Theatre

All three decades were great for musical theatre. Audiences saw premieres of *Camelot, Hello Dolly, Fiddler on the Roof, Oliver!,*

Man of La Mancha, Funny Girl, and *Hair* in the sixties, and *Grease, Tommy* by the Who, and *A Chorus Line* in the seventies. In the eighties the musicals included *La Cage aux Folles, Annie,* and Andrew Lloyd Weber's mega hits *Cats, Starlight Express, Les Miserables* and *The Phantom of the Opera,* as well as Broadway revivals of *West Side Story, The Music Man,* and *The King and I.* The sixties was also the start of off-off-Broadway, where many new playwrights got their start. Famous playwrights of these decades included Edward Albee, who wrote *Who's Afraid of Virginia Woolf,* and Neil Simon who penned comedies such as *The Goodbye Girl.*

> *"Julie" was bitten by the theatre bug early in life, and subsequently made it her longtime avocation, both acting and directing in local and community productions for over thirty years. "Peter Pan was the first play I went to," she wrote. "I was seven. The minute the curtain came up and the lights went down I was hooked into that magical world where children flew and crocodiles ticked like clocks. When Tinkerbell asked the children to clap if they believed in fairies, I clapped so hard my hands were sore for days afterward. When I went home I tried to put on a neighborhood production of Peter Pan, using clothesline and the dog's leash as my flying apparatus. My two-year-old brother had the starring role because he was the only one light enough to actually rise in the air. He was a lousy actor, though, being too young to remember his lines."*

Movies

Movies in the sixties included blockbuster musicals such as *The Sound of Music, My Fair Lady,* and Disney's *Mary Poppins.* Spectacles like *Cleopatra* and *Lawrence of Arabia* were honored in the early sixties, but later in the decade movies began to change. Earlier taboos about sex, violence and language were increasingly ignored, leading to the film rating system initiated in 1968. The anti-hero was prevalent in such films as *Cool Hand Luke*, *Butch Cassidy and the Sundance Kid*, and *Easy Rider*. Sex became explicit, even non-traditional, as in *Midnight Cowboy* or *The Graduate*. James Bond was brought to life by Sean Connery, and was enormously popular in movies such as *Goldfinger* and *To Russia with Love*.

New technologies such as Panavision and Dolby sound revolutionized the movies in the seventies. The spectacular success of *Star Wars* was due to its swashbuckling adventure story, spiritual message ("may the force be with you") and especially its special effects. Other movies owing some success to technology included *The Towering Inferno* and *Earthquake*. Stallone's *Rocky* proved the American formula of "little guy makes good" was still as potent as ever, and our fondness for the scamp and the underdog was fed by *One Flew Over the Cuckoo's Nest*. Great scary movies included Steven Spielberg's *Jaws* and William Friedkin's *The Exorcist*. Nostalgia for an earlier, simpler time was seen in movies like *American Graffiti* and *Grease*. Disco fever sweeping the nation was fueled by John Travolta in *Saturday Night Fever*. The trauma of Vietnam was examined in movies such as *The Deer Hunter* and *Apocalypse Now*. Francis Ford Coppola's *The Godfather* series is still considered by many to be among the best movies ever made, of any genre.

Throughout the eighties, one of the biggest changes in movies was in where we watched them. Increasingly that meant at home. Sales of VCRs rose nearly 75% from 1981 to 1982, and in 1985 Blockbuster Video opened in Texas and quickly spread all over the country. By 1989, almost sixty percent of American households had cable service with HBO or Showtime. Memorable movies of the eighties included *On Golden Pond*, *Tootsie*, *E.T. The Extra-Terrestrial*, *Flashdance*, *Amadeus*, *Back to the Future*, *Rain Man*, *Fatal Attraction*, and *Platoon*.

Television

Sit-coms were big in the sixties, and included *The Dick Van Dyke Show*, *The Beverly Hillbillies*, and *The Andy Griffith Show*. The interest in supernatural and science fiction was shown in the popularity of shows like *Bewitched, The Addams Family, Star Trek, the Outer Limits*, and *The Twilight Zone*. Spies were in vogue, in shows like *The Man from U.N.C.L.E, The Avengers, Mission Impossible* and *Get Smart*. Variety shows such as *Ed Sullivan* had high ratings in the early sixties, and took on a sometimes political edge later in the decade in such programs as *Laugh In, Sonny and Cher*, and particularly *The Smothers Brothers Comedy Hour*. And of course we mustn't forget *Batman*, a genre all to itself at the time.

Television grew up in the seventies, tackling subjects previously unknown over the airwaves, such as race relations, abortion, religion, sexuality and homosexuality. Social satire abounded. Leading this trend were programs such as *All in the Family* and *Saturday Night Live*. News programs brought the horror of Vietnam vividly to life, intensifying anti-war sentiment and contributing to the great success of *M*A*S*H*. The miniseries *Roots* gathered a record audience and spawned interest in genealogy and African-American history. Nostalgia was served by *Happy Days* (remember the Fonz?), and children's programming got a boost from the new PBS, which gave us *Sesame Street*.

In the eighties the American family was portrayed as less than perfect in hits like *Roseanne* and *Married with Children*, but more than perfect in *The Cosby Show*. Tabloid TV became popular and made stars of hosts Geraldo, Phil, Sally and Oprah. Info-tainment grew bigger with *Nightline* and *20/20*, joining the bigger-than-ever *60 Minutes*, which had begun in 1968.

Take a look at the following and see what *you* remember ...

1960-1989 Events Timeline
Arts & Entertainment

1960		Hit songs from 1960 include:
		Alley Oop by The Hollywood Argyles
		Are You Lonesome Tonight by Elvis Presley
		Cathy's Clown by the Everly Brothers
		Everybody's Somebody's Fool by Connie Francis
		Georgia on My Mind by Ray Charles
		I'm Sorry by Brenda Lee
		Itsy Bitsy Teeny Weeny Yellow Polka Dot Bikini by Brian Hyland
		I Want to Be Wanted by Brenda Lee
		Mr. Custer by Larry Verne
		My Heart Has a Mind of Its Own by Connie Francis
		Running Bear by Johnny Preston
		Save The Last Dance for Me by The Drifters
		Stuck on You by Elvis Presley
		Teen Angel by Mark Dinning
		Theme from A Summer Place by Percy Faith
		The Twist by Chubby Checker
		Wonderful World by Sam Cooke
1960		Oscar winners from 1960 include:
		The Apartment as Best Picture
		Burt Lancaster in *Elmer Gantry* as Best Actor
		Elizabeth Taylor in *Butterfield 8* as Best Actress
		Peter Ustinov in *Spartacus* as Best Supporting Actor
		Shirley Jones in *Elmer Gantry* as Best Supporting Actress
		Billy Wilder, *The Apartment*, as Best Director
1960		Tony award winners include: *The Miracle Worker, The Sound of Music, Fiorello!*
1960		Emmy winners from 1960 include: Robert Stack, *The Untouchables*, Rod Serling, *The Twilight Zone, The Huntley Brinkley Report*
1960		Nobel Prize for Literature awarded to Saint-John Perse
1960		Pulitzer for Poetry to W.D. Snodgrass for *Heart's Needle*
1960		Pulitzer for Drama to Weidman & Abbott for *Fiorello!*
1960		Pulitzer for Fiction to Allen Drury for *Advise and Consent*
1960		Pulitzer for Music to Elliott Carter for *Second String Quartet*
1960		National Book Award: Philip Roth for *Goodbye Columbus*
1960		Joy Adamson's book *Elsa the Lioness* is published
1960	Jan	Johnny Cash plays his first free prison concert
1960	Feb	Jack Paar walks off the *Tonight Show*
1960	Feb	*Toys in the Attic* by Lillian Hellman premieres

1960	Mar	Ninth Symphony by Darius Milhaud premieres
1960	May	The musical *Fantasticks* premieres in NY City
1960	May	Elvis Presley appears on a Frank Sinatra TV special
1960	Sep	First prime-time animated TV show, *The Flintstones*
1960	Oct	*Route 66* premieres on TV
1960	Dec	Lerner and Loewe's *Camelot* premieres in NY City
1961		Hit songs from 1961 include:
		Big Bad John by Jimmy Dean
		Calcutta by Lawrence Welk
		Hit The Road Jack by Ray Charles
		The Lion Sleeps Tonight by The Tokens
		Michael Row the Boat Ashore by The Highwaymen
		Moody River by Pat Boone
		Mother in Law by Ernie K Doe
		Please Mr. Postman by The Marvelettes
		Pony Time by Chubby Checker
		Quarter to Three by Gary U.S. Bonds
		Runaround Sue by Dion
		Runaway by Del Shannon
		Running Scared by Roy Orbison
		Surrender by Elvis Presley
		Take Good Care of My Baby by Bobby Vee
		Tossin and Turnin by Bobby Lewis
		Travelin' Man by Rick Nelson
1961		Oscar winners from 1961 include:
		West Side Story as Best Picture
		Maximillian Schell in *Judgment at Nuremberg* as Best Actor
		Sophia Loren in *Two Women* as Best Actress
		George Chakiris in *West Side Story* as Best Supporting Actor
		Rito Moreno in *West Side Story* as Best Supporting Actress
		Best Director: Jerome Robbins/Robert Wise, *West Side Story*
1961		Tony award winners include: *Beckett, Bye Bye Birdie*
1961		Emmy winners from 1961 include: Barbara Stanwyck, Don Knotts, *The Andy Griffith Show*, Raymond Burr, *Perry Mason*
1961		Ivo Andric wins Nobel Prize for Literature
1961		Pulitzer for Fiction: Harper Lee, *To Kill A Mockingbird*
1961		Pulitzer for Music to Walter Piston for *Symphony No 7*
1961		Pulitzer for Drama to Tad Mosel for *All The Way Home*
1961		Pulitzer Prize for Poetry awarded to Phyllis McGinley
1961		National Book Award: Conrad Richter, *The Waters of Kronos*
1961		*Catch-22* by Joseph Heller is published
1961	Jan	Premiere of Pablo Casals' oratorio *El Pesebrio*
1961	Jan	Motown Records sign The Supremes

1961	Jan	NBC TV premieres *Sing Along with Mitch* with Mitch Miller
1961	Mar	*Mary, Mary* by Jean Kerr premieres in NY City
1961	Mar	Pablo Picasso, 79, marries his 37 year old model
1961	Apr	Bob Dylan makes his first appearance, in Greenwich Village
1961	Apr	Ray Charles wins four Grammys
1961	May	Newton Minnow of FCC says TV is a "vast wasteland"
1961	Jun	Soviet ballet dancer Rudolf Nureyev defects to the West
1961	Jul	Ernest Hemingway commits suicide
1961	Sep	*Car 54 Where are You?* premieres on TV
1961	Oct	*Ben Casey* premieres on TV
1961	Oct	*The Dick Van Dyke Show* premieres on CBS TV
1961	Oct	*Mr Ed* premieres on TV
1961	Dec	*Night of the Iguana* by Tennessee Williams premieres
1961	Dec	Artist Grandma Moses dies at age of 101

1962   Hit songs from 1962 include:

Big Girls Don't Cry by The Four Seasons
Breaking Up Is Hard to Do by Neil Sedaka
Don't Break the Heart That Loves You by Connie Francis
Duke of Earl by Gene Chandler
He's a Rebel by The Crystals
Hey Baby by Bruce Channel
I Can't Stop Loving You by Ray Charles
Johnny Angel by Shelly Fabares
The Loco-Motion by Little Eva
Mashed Potato Time by Dee Dee Sharp
Monster Mash by Bobby Boris Pickett & The Crypt Kickers
Peppermint Twist by Joey Dee
Roses are Red by Bobby Vinton
Sheila by Tommy Roe
Sherry by The Four Seasons
Stranger on the Shore by Mr. Acker Bilk

1962   Oscar winners from 1962 include:

Lawrence of Arabia as Best Picture
Gregory Peck in *To Kill A Mockingbird* as Best Actor
Anne Bancroft in *The Miracle Worker* as Best Actress
Ed Begley in *Sweet Bird of Youth* as Best Supporting Actor
Patty Duke in *The Miracle Worker* as Best Supporting Actress
David Lean, *Lawrence of Arabia*, as Best Director

1962   Tony award winners include: *A Man for All Seasons, How to Succeed in Business Without Really Trying*

1962   Emmy winners from 1962 include: E.G. Marshall, *The Defenders*, Shirley Booth, *Hazel*, *Car 54 Where Are You*, Carol Burnett on *The Garry Moore Show*, *The Bob Newhart Show*

1962   John Steinbeck awarded Nobel Prize for Literature

1962		Pulitzer for Music to Robert Ward for his opera, *The Crucible*
1962		Pulitzer Prize for Poetry awarded to Alan Dugan
1962		Pulitzer for Drama awarded to Frank Loesser and Abe Burrows for *How To Succeed in Business Without Really Trying*
1962		Pulitzer for Fiction to Edwin O'Connor, *The Edge of Sadness*
1962		National Book Award: Walker Percy for *The Moviegoer*
1962		Artist Andy Warhol's first show in the Stable Gallery showcasing "Pop Art" which he originated
1962	Jan	Nightime version of *Password* with Allen Ludden premieres
1962	Jan	Bollingen prize for poetry awarded to John Hall Wheelock
1962	Feb	Beach Boys introduce a new musical style, "surfing music"
1962	Mar	Beatles have their TV debut on BBC
1962	Apr	Walter Cronkite begins anchoring *CBS Evening News*
1962	Aug	Ringo Starr replaces Pete Best as drummer for the Beatles
1962	Aug	Peter, Paul & Mary release their first hit *If I Had A Hammer*
1962	Aug	Marilyn Monroe dies at age of 36
1962	Sep	Beatles release *Love Me Do* and *PS I Love You*
1962	Sep	First color TV series debuts, *The Jetsons*
1962	Sep	Lincoln Center for the Performing Arts opens in NYC
1962	Sep	*The Beverly Hillbillies* premieres on CBS
1962	Oct	Johnny Carson hosts his first *Tonight Show*
1962	Oct	John Steinbeck is awarded the Nobel Prize in Literature
1962	Dec	Vaughn Meader's *The First Family* comedy album goes #1
1963		Hit songs of 1963 include:

Blue Velvet by Bobby Vinton

Deep Purple by Nino Tempo and April Stevens

Dominique by The Singing Nun

Fingertips by Little Stevie Wonder

Go Away Little Girl by Steve Lawrence

He's So Fine by The Chiffons

Hey Paula by Paul and Paula

It's My Party by Leslie Gore

I Will Follow Him by Little Peggy March

My Boyfriend's Back by The Angels

Our Day Will Come by Ruby & the Romantics

Puff the Magic Dragon by Peter, Paul & Mary

Sugar Shack by Jimmy Gilmer & The Fireballs

Sukiyaki by Kyu Sakamoto

Surf City by Jan and Dean

Walk Like a Man by The Four Seasons

Walk Right In by The Rooftop Singers

| 1963 | | Oscar winners from 1963 include: |

Tom Jones as Best Picture

Sidney Poitier in *Lilies of the Field* for Best Actor

Sharing My Stories—Elvis' Little Sister, That's Me

My father nicknamed everyone he loved. My nickname was "Little Sister" even though I was the oldest child in the family and thus nobody's little sister. Later I learned that he called me Little Sister because I reminded him of his youngest sister, my Aunt Miriam. This connection in his mind was so strong that he often mixed up my birthday with my aunt's, to the annoyance of us both. To this day he still calls her Kim sometimes.

Another of my father's endearing traits was to give presents for no reason. He liked to give them just because he was thinking of you. His presents for Christmas and birthdays often lacked imagination, but his "no reason" presents were always special. Such was the case in 1961, when I was 11 years old.

One day while in the city Dad passed by a music store, and in the window he noticed an advertisement for a 45 record called "Little Sister." Because it was his special name for me, he went in and bought it. It was typical of my father that he paid no attention to the recording artist listed on the label.

When he came home that night he gave it to me. I was thrilled – a 45 record of my own, just like teenagers had – and by Elvis Presley, no less! My father's face creased into a frown when I shrieked, "Elvis!" in jubilation, but that was nothing compared to his open-mouthed horror when I played the record and Elvis' sultry voice sang out, "Little Sister don't you do as your big sister does."

Except both my father and I heard the words as "*won't* you do as your big sister does." I took this as an invitation; Dad took it as a threat.

Perhaps that's why Dad took the present back, the only time he ever did so. I don't have any memory of its replacement, but I am completely sure that it didn't half measure up to Elvis.

		Patricia Neal in *Hud* for Best Actress
		Melvyn Douglas in *Hud* for Best Supporting Actor
		Best Supporting Actress: Margaret Rutherford, *The V.I.P.s*
		Tony Richardson, *Tom Jones*, as Best Director
1963		Tony award winners include: *Who's Afraid of Virginia Woolf?*, *A Funny Thing Happened on the Way to the Forum*
1963		Emmy winners from 1963 include: *Dick Van Dyke Show*, *Andy Williams Show*, EG Marshall, Shirley Booth
1963		Nobel Prize for Literature awarded to Giorgos Seferis
1963		Pulitzer for Music to Samuel Barber for *Piano Concerto No 1*
1963		Pulitzer for Fiction to William Faulkner for *The Reivers*
1963		Pulitzer for Poetry awarded to William Carlos Williams
1963		National Book Award won by J.F. Powers for *Morte d'Urban*
1963		Maurice Sendak's *Where the Wild Things Are* is published
1963		Motown releases Stevie Wonder's first record
1963		Roald Dahl publishes *Charlie and the Chocolate Factory*
1963		*The Bell Jar* by Sylvia Plath is published
1063		Shel Silverstein publishes *Lafcadio: the Lion Who Shot Back*
1963	Jan	*Mutual of Omaha's Wild Kingdom* with Marlin Perkins debuts
1963	Jan	*Oliver!* opens on Broadway
1963	Feb	Robert Frost wins the Bollingen Prize for poetry
1963	Feb	The *Mona Lisa* comes to the Metropolitan Museum of Art
1963	Mar	The first "Pop Art" exhibition held in New York
1963	May	Peter, Paul & Mary win a Grammy for *If I Had a Hammer*
1963	Aug	Allan Sherman releases *Hello Mudda, Hello Fadda*
1963	Aug	*Louie Louie* labeled obscene by some radio stations
1963	Sep	*The Fugitive* premieres on TV
1963	Dec	Beach Boys make their first TV appearance on *Shindig*
1963	Dec	*Let's Make a Deal* premieres on NBC-TV
1964		Hit songs from 1964 include:
		Baby Love by The Supremes
		Can't Buy Me Love by The Beatles
		Chapel of Love by The Dixie Cups
		Do Wah Diddy Diddy by Manfred Mann
		Everybody Loves Somebody by Dean Martin
		Hello Dolly! By Louis Armstrong
		The House of the Rising Sun by The Animals
		I Feel Fine by The Beatles
		I Get Around by The Beach Boys
		I Want to Hold Your Hand by The Beatles
		Leader of the Pack by The Shangri-Las
		Love Me Do by The Beatles
		My Guy by Mary Wells
		Pretty Woman by Roy Orbison

		Rag Doll by The Four Seasons
		She Loves You by The Beatles
		Where Did Our Love Go by The Supremes
1964		Oscar winners from 1964 include:
		My Fair Lady as Best Picture
		Rex Harrison in *My Fair Lady* for Best Actor
		Julie Andrews in *Mary Poppins* for Best Actress
		Peter Ustinov in *Topkapi* as Best Supporting Actor
		Lila Kedrova in *Zorba the Greek* for Best Supporting Actress
		George Cukor, *My Fair Lady*, as Best Director
1964		Tony award winners include: *Luther, Hello Dolly*
1964		Emmy winners from 1964 include: *Dick Van Dyke Show*, Mary Tyler Moore, Danny Kaye
1964		Jean-Paul Sartre wins Nobel Prize for Literature
1964		Pulitzer for Poetry awarded to Louis Simpson
1964		National Book Award won by John Updike for *The Centaur*
1964		Whiskey-A-Go-Go, first disco in America, opens
1964		Marc Chagall paints the ceiling of the Paris Opera House
1964	Jan	US Version of *"That Was the Week That Was"* premieres
1964	Jan	*Dr. Strangelove* premieres
1964	Feb	The Beatles land at JFK airport for their first US tour
1964	Feb	Beatles appear on *Ed Sullivan Show* to 74 million viewers
1964	Mar	Grammy award winners include *Days of Wine & Roses*, Barbra Streisand
1964	Apr	*In His Own Write* by John Lennon published in US
1964	Jul	Artist David Hockney's first American exhibition
1964	Sep	*Bewitched* premieres on ABC-TV
1964	Sep	*The Man from U.N.C.L.E* premieres on NBC-TV
1964	Dec	*The Pink Panther* cartoon series premiers
1965		Hit songs from 1965 include:
		Eight Days a Week by The Beatles
		Eve of Destruction by Barry McGuire
		Get Off of My Cloud by The Rolling Stones
		Hang on Sloopy by The McCoys
		Help! by The Beatles
		Help Me Rhonda by The Beach Boys
		I Got You Babe by Sonny & Cher
		I'm Henry VIII I Am by Herman's Hermits
		Mr. Tambourine Man by The Byrds
		My Girl by The Temptations
		Satisfaction by The Rolling Stones
		Stop in the Name of Love by The Supremes
		This Diamond Ring by Gary Lewis & The Playboys
		Ticket to Ride by The Beatles

		Turn Turn Turn by The Byrds
		Yesterday by The Beatles
		You've Lost That Lovin' Feelin' by The Righteous Brothers
1965		Oscar winners from 1965 include:
		The Sound of Music as Best Picture
		Lee Marvin in *Cat Ballou* as Best Actor
		Julie Christie in *Darling* as Best Actress
		Best Supporting Actor: Martin Balsam *A Thousand Clowns*
		Best Supporting Actress: Shelley Winters *A Patch of Blue*
		Robert Wise, *The Sound of Music*, as Best Director
1965		Tony winners include *The Subject Was Roses, Fiddler on the Roof*
1965		Emmy winners from 1965 include: *Bonanza, Dick Van Dyke Show, My Name is Barbra, The French Chef*
1965		Michail Sholokhov wins Nobel Prize for Literature
1965		Pulitzer for Fiction: Shirley Ann Grau, *The Keepers of The House*
1965		Pulitzer for Drama to Frank Gilroy for *The Subject was Roses*
1965		Pulitzer for Poetry to John Berryman for *77 Dream Songs*
1965		National Book Award won by Saul Bellow for *Herzog*
1965		Allen Ginsberg organizes the first "Be In" in San Francisco
1965		Folk-rock group The Warlocks forms, later called The Grateful Dead
1965	Jun	John Lennon's *A Spaniard in the Works* is published
1965	Jul	Rock group "Jefferson Airplane" forms
1965	Jul	Bob Dylan releases *Like a Rolling Stone*
1965	Jul	At Newport Festival, Dylan uses an electric guitar and "folk rock" is born
1965	Sep	*Get Smart* premieres on TV
1965	Dec	*Dr Zhivago* premieres
1966		Hit songs from 1966 include:
		Ballad of the Green Berets by Barry Sadler
		Cherish by The Association
		Good Vibrations by The Beach Boys
		Last Train to Clarksville by The Monkees
		Monday, Monday by The Mamas & The Papas
		My Love by Petula Clark
		96 Tears by The Mysterians
		Paperback Writer by The Beatles
		Reach Out I'll Be There by The Four Tops
		The Sounds of Silence by Simon and Garfunkel
		Strangers in the Night by Frank Sinatra
		Summer in the City by The Lovin Spoonful
		We Can Work It Out by The Beatles
		When A Man Loves a Woman by Percy Sledge

		Wild Thing by The Troggs
		Winchester Cathedral by The New Vaudeville Band
		You're My Soul and Inspiration by The Righteous Brothers
1966		Oscar winners for 1966 include:
		A Man for All Seasons for Best Picture
		Paul Scofield in *A Man For All Seasons* as Best Actor
		Best Actress:Elizabeth Taylor *Who's Afraid of Virginia Woolf?*
		Best Supporting Actor: Walter Matthau, *The Fortune Cookie*
		Sandy Dennis in *Who's Afraid of Virginia Woolf?* as Best Supporting Actress
		Fred Zinnemann, *A Man for All Seasons*, as Best Director
1966		Tony award winners include: *Marat/Sade, Man of LaMancha*
1966		Emmy award winners from 1966 include: Dick Van Dyke, Bill Cosby in *I Spy*, Mary Tyler Moore, *Bewitched, The Fugitive, The Andy Griffith Show*
1966		Nobel Prize for Literature: Samuel Agnon and Nelly Sachs
1966		Pulitzer for Fiction awarded to Katherine Anne Porter
1966		Pulitzer for Musi: Leslie Bassett for *Variations for Orchestra*
1966		Pulitzer Prize for Poetry awarded to Richard Eberhart
1966		National Book Award:Katherine Anne Porter
1966		Robert Indiana unveils his "Love" sculpture
1966	Jan	Dance Theatre of Harlem debuts
1966	Jan	Beatles' *Rubber Soul* album goes #1
1966	Jan	*Batman* with Adam West and Burt Ward premieres on TV
1966	Mar	James Goldman's *Lion in Winter* premieres in NY City
1966	Mar	Buffalo Springfield forms with Steven Stills and Neil Young
1966	Mar	8th Grammy award winners include Taste of Honey, Tom Jones, Frank Sinatra and Barbra Streisand
1966	Jun	Janis Joplin plays her first live concert in San Francisco
1966	Aug	Comedian Lenny Bruce dies of drug overdose
1966	Aug	Beatles release *Revolver* album in US
1966	Sep	*Star Trek* premieres
1966	Sep	*That Girl* with Marlo Thomas premieres
1967		Hit songs from 1967 include:
		All You Need is Love by The Beatles
		Baby I Love You by Aretha Franklin
		The Beat Goes On by Sonny & Cher
		Groovin by The Young Rascals
		The Happening by The Supremes
		Happy Together by The Turtles
		Hello Goodbye by The Beatles
		Incense and Peppermints by Strawberry Alarm Clock
		Kind of a Drag by The Buckinghams
		The Letter by The Box Tops

		Light My Fire by The Doors
		Ode to Billie Joe by Bobbie Gentry
		Penny Lane by The Beatles
		Respect by Aretha Franklin
		Ruby Tuesday by The Rolling Stones
		Somethin' Stupid by Frank and Nancy Sinatra
		Windy by The Association
1967		Oscar winners for 1967 include:
		In The Heat of the Night as Best Picture
		Rod Steiger in *In The Heat of the Night* as Best Actor
		Katharine Hepburn in *Guess Who's Coming to Dinner* as Best Actress
		Best Supporting Actor: George Kennedy, *Cool Hand Luke*
		Best Supporting Actress: Estelle Parsons in *Bonnie and Clyde*
		Mike Nichols, *The Graduate*, as Best Director
1967		Tony award winners include: *The Homecoming, Cabaret*
1967		Emmy winners for 1967 include: Don Adams in *Get Smart*, Bill Cosby in *I Spy*, Barbara Bain in *Mission Impossible*
1967		Nobel Prize for Literature to Miguel Angel Asturias
1967		Pulitzer for Music to Leon Kirchner for *Quartet No. 3*
1967		Pulitzer for Fiction to Bernard Malamud for *The Fixer*
1967		Pulitzer for Drama to Edward Albee for *A Delicate Balance*
1967		Pulitzer for Poetry awarded to Anne Sexton for *Live or Die*
1967		National Book award: Bernard Malamud for *The Fixer*
1967	Jan	PBS begins as a 70-station network
1967	Feb	Poet Langston Hughes dies on his 65th birthday
1967	Feb	*Purple Haze* recorded by Jimi Hendrix
1967	Feb	*The Smothers Brothers Comedy* Hour premieres on CBS
1967	Feb	Bollingen Prize for poetry awarded to Robert Penn Warren
1967	Mar	Grammy winners include *Strangers in the Night* and *Michele*
1967	Mar	Jimi Hendrix begins his tradition of burning his guitar
1967	Apr	Andrew Wyeth Retrospective at Art Institute of Chicago
1967	May	Film of Dylan's 1965 UK tour, *Don't Look Back*, is released
1967	May	*Mister Rogers' Neighborhood* debuts on PBS
1967	Jun	50,000 attend Monterey International Pop Festival
1967	Jul	Beatles' *Sgt. Pepper's Lonely Hearts Club Band* album goes #1
1967	Jul	15,000 attend Fantasy Faire and Magic Mtn Music Festival
1967	Oct	The musical *Hair* is first performed
1967	Oct	Walt Disney releases *The Jungle Book*
1967	Nov	BBC bans Beatles' *I Am the Walrus*
1967	Dec	Otis Redding dies in plane crash at age of 26
1967	Dec	Jim Morrison of The Doors arrested on stage
1967	Dec	Ian Anderson forms rock group Jethro Tull
1967	Dec	"The Trouble with Tribbles" episode of *Star Trek* airs

1968		Hit songs from 1968 include:
		All Along the Watchtower by The Jimi Hendrix Experience
		Angel of the Morning by Merilee Rush
		Born to Be Wild by Steppenwolf
		Classical Gas by Mason Williams
		Do You Know the Way to San Jose by Dionne Warwick
		Harper Valley PTA by Jeannie C. Riley
		Hello I Love You by The Doors
		Hey Jude by The Beatles
		Honey by Bobby Goldsboro
		I Heard It Through the Grapevine by Marvin Gaye
		Love Child by Diana Ross & The Supremes
		Love is Blue by Paul Mauriat & His Orchestra
		Mrs. Robinson by Simon and Garfunkel
		People Got to Be Free by The Rascals
		Dock of the Bay by Otis Redding
		This Guy's In Love with You by Herb Alpert
1968		Oscar winners from 1968 include:
		Oliver! as Best Picture
		Cliff Robertsons in *Charly* as Best Actor
		Barbra Streisand in *Funny Girl* as Best Actress
		Best Supporting Actor: Jack Albertson *The Subject was Roses*
		Ruth Gordon in *Rosemary's Baby* as Best Supporting Actress
		Sir Carol Reed, *Oliver!*, as Best Director
1968		Tony award winners include: *Rosencrantz and Guilderstern Are Dead, Hallelujah Baby*
1968		Emmy award winners include: *Get Smart, I Spy*, Lucille Ball, *Rowan & Martin's Laugh In*, Milburn Stone
1968		Nobel Prize for Literature awarded to Yasunari Kawabata
1968		Pulitzer for Music awarded to George Crumb
1968		Pulitzer for Fiction to William Styron for *The Confessions of Nat Turner*
1968		Pulitzer for Poetry to Anthony Hecht for *The Hard Hours*
1968		National Book Award: Thornton Wilder for *The Eighth Day*
1968		Placido Domingo debuts at the Metropolitan Opera in NY
1968	Jan	Jay Allen's *The Prime of Miss Jean Brodie* premieres
1968	Mar	NBC makes announcement that *Star Trek* will return
1968	Mar	Grammy winners include *Up, Up & Away, Sergeant Pepper*
1968	May	First performance of Roger Sessions' 8th Symphony
1968	Jul	John Lennon has first full art exhibition
1968	Jul	*Yellow Submarine* animated film premieres in London
1968	Jul	Iron Butterfly's *In-a-gadda-da-vida* becomes first heavy metal song to hit charts
1968	Aug	100,000 attend Newport Pop Festival in Costa Mesa, CA

1968	Sep	*60 Minutes* premieres on TV
1968	Oct	Motion Picture Association of America adopts the film rating system
1968	Nov	Beatles release their White Album, their only double album
1968	Dec	Author John Steinbeck dies at age of 66
1968	Dec	Led Zeppelin's concert debut as opener for Vanilla Fudge
1968	Dec	100,000 attend Miami Pop Festival
1969		Hit songs from 1969 include:

And When I Die by Blood, Sweat & Tears
Aquarius/Let the Sunshine In by The Fifth Dimension
Come Together by The Beatles
Crystal Blue Persuasion by Tommy James & The Shondells
Daddy Sang Bass by Johnny Cash
Dizzy by Tommy Roe
Get Back by The Beatles
Honky Tonk Women by The Rolling Stones
Hot Fun in the Summertime by Sly & The Family Stone
I Can't Get Next to You by The Temptations
In the Year 2525 by Zager & Evans
Leaving on a Jet Plane by Peter, Paul and Mary
Love Theme from Romeo & Juliet by Henry Mancini
Someday We'll Be Together by Diana Ross & The Supremes
Sugar, Sugar by The Archies
Suspicious Minds by Elvis Presley
Wedding Bell Blues by The Fifth Dimension

| 1969 | | Oscar winners from 1969 include: |

Midnight Cowboy as Best Picture
John Wayne in *True Grit* as Best Actor
Maggie Smith in *The Prime of Miss Jean Brodie* as Best Actress
Gig Young in *They Shoot Horses Don't They* as Best Supporting Actor
Goldie Hawn in *Cactus Flower* as Best Supporting Actress
John Schlesinger, *Midnight Cowboy*, as Best Director

1969		Tony award winners include: *The Great White Hope, 1776*
1969		Emmy award winners include: Werner Klemperer in *Hogan's Heroes*, Hope Lange in *The Ghost and Mrs. Muir*, Susan St. James in *The Name Of the Game*, *Smothers Brothers Comedy Hour*, Harvey Korman on *The Carol Burnett Show*
1969		Nobel Prize for Literature awarded to Samuel Beckett
1969		Pulitzer for Music awarded to Karel Husa
1969		Pulitzer for Fiction to Scott Momaday, *House Made of Dawn*
1969		Pulitzer for Drama to Howard Sackler, *The Great White Hope*
1969		Pulitzer for Poetry to George Oppen for *Of Being Numerous*
1969		National Book Award won by Jerzy Kosinski for *Steps*

1969		Mario Puzo publishes *The Godfather*
1969	Jan	Actress/Singer Judy Garland dies at age 48
1969	Jan	Lorraine Hansberry's *To Be Young, Gifted and Black* premieres
1969	Jan	Beatles perform their last gig together, a 40 minute free concert on the roof of Apple Records HQ
1969	Mar	Grammy award winners include *Mrs. Robinson, By the Time I Get to Phoenix*
1969	May	Monty Python comedy troupe forms
1969	May	The Who release the rock opera *Tommy*
1969	May	Movie *Midnight Cowboy* released with X rating
1969	May	John Lennon and Yoko Ono record *Give Peace a Chance*
1969	Jun	Bob Dylan and Johnny Cash combine on a Grand Ole Opry TV special
1969	Jun	50,000 attend Denver Pop Festival
1969	Jun	*Hee Haw* with Roy Clark and Buck Owens premieres
1969	Jun	150,000 attend Newport 69 Festival, Jimi Hendrix appears
1969	Jul	140,000 attend Atlanta Pop Festival featuring Led Zeppelin and Janis Joplin
1969	Jul	78,000 attend Newport Jazz Festival
1969	Jul	70,000 attend Seattle Pop Festival
1969	Aug	110,000 attend Atlantic City Pop Festival
1969	Aug	Woodstock Music and Art Fair Festival opens in upstate NY on Max Yasgur's Dairy Farm, over 400,000 attending
1969	Aug	25,000 attend New Orleans Music Festival
1969	Aug	120,000 attend Texas Pop Festival
1969	Aug	25,000 attend Sky River Rock Festival in Tenino, WA
1969	Nov	*Sesame Street* premieres on PBS
1969	Dec	Arlo Guthrie releases *Alice's Restaurant*
1969	Dec	Jackson Five makes their first TV appearance
1970		Hit songs from 1970 include:

Ain't No Mountain High Enough by Diana Ross
American Woman by The Guess Who
Bridge Over Troubled Water by Simon and Garfunkel
Close to You by The Carpenters
Cracklin Rosie by Neil Diamond
Everything is Beautiful by Ray Stevens
I'll Be There by The Jackson 5
Let It Be by The Beatles
The Long and Winding Road by The Beatles
The Love You Save by The Jackson 5
Mama Told Me Not to Come by Three Dog Night
My Sweet Lord by George Harrison
Raindrops Keep Falling on My Head by BJ Thomas
The Tears of a Clown by Smokey Robinson & The Miracles

		War by Edwin Starr
1970		Oscar winners from 1970 include:

Patton as Best Picture
George C. Scott in *Patton* as Best Actor
Glenda Jackson in *Women in Love* as Best Actress
John Mills in *Ryan's Daughter* as Best Supporting Actor
Helen Hayes in *Airport* as Best Supporting Actress
Franklin Schaffner, *Patton*, as Best Director

1970		Tony award winners include: *Borstal Boy, Applause*
1970		Emmy award winners include: *Sesame Street, My World and Welcome To It, Marcus Welby MD, Room 222, David Frost Show*
1970		Nobel Prize for Literature to Alexander Solzhenitsyn
1970		Pulitzer for Music to Charles Wuorinen for *Time's Encomium*
1970		Pulitzer Prize for Fiction to Jean Stafford for *Collected Stories*
1970		Pulitzer for Drama to Charles Gordone *No Place to Be Somebody*
1970		Pulitzer for Poetry to Richard Howard for *Untitled Subjects*
1970		National Book Award won by Joyce Carol Oates for *Them*
1970		Richard Bach publishes *Jonathon Livingston Seagull*
1970		Tom Wolfe publishes *Radical Chic & Mau-mauing the Flak Catchers*
1970	Jan	Movie rating system modifies "M" rating to "PG"
1970	Feb	Abstract Expressionist artist Mark Rothko commits suicide
1970	Mar	Grammy award winners include Aquarius, Crosby Still & Nash, Peggy Lee
1970	Jun	The Who's *Tommy* is performed at NY's Lincoln Center
1970	Jul	200,000 attend Atlanta Pop Festival
1970	Jul	30,000 attend Powder Ridge Rock Festival in Connecticut
1970	Sep	Jimi Hendrix dies of drug overdose at age of 27
1970	Sep	*Mary Tyler Moore Show* premieres
1970	Oct	Janis Joplin dies of drug overdose
1971		Hit songs from 1971 include:

Brown Sugar by The Rolling Stones
Family Affair by Sly & The Family Stone
Go Away Little Girl by Donny Osmond
Gypsies, Tramps & Thieves by Cher
How Can You Mend a Broken Heart by The Bee Gees
I Feel the Earth Move by Carole King
Imagine by John Lennon & The Plastic Ono Band
Indian Reservation by The Raiders
It's Too Late by Carole King
Joy to the World by Three Dog Night
Knock Three Times by Dawn
Maggie Mae by Rod Stewart

Me and Bobby McGee by Janis Joplin
Theme from Shaft by Isaac Hayes
Uncle Albert by Paul McCartney
Want Ads by Honey Cone
You've Got a Friend by James Taylor

1971   Oscar winners from 1971 include:
The French Connection as Best Picture
Gene Hackman in *The French Connection* as Best Actor
Jane Fonda in *Klute* as Best Actress
Best Supporting Actor: Ben Johnson, *The Last Picture Show*
Cloris Leachman in *The Last Picture Show* as Best Supporting
Actress
William Friedkin, *The French Connection*, as Best Director

1971   Tony award winners include: *Sleuth, Company*
1971   Emmy winners from 1971 include: *The Carol Burnett Show,*
The Undersea World of Jacques Cousteau, Wide World of Sports,
Jack Klugman in *The Odd Couple*, Jean Stapleton in *All in the*
Family, Edward Asner in *The Mary Tyler Moore Show*
1971   Nobel Prize for Literature awarded to Pablo Neruda
1971   Pulitzer Prize for Music awarded to Mario Davidovsky
1971   Pulitzer for Drama to Paul Zindel for *The Effect of Gamma*
Rays on Man in the Moon Marigolds
1971   Pulitzer for Poetry to William Merwin, *The Carrier of Ladders*
1971   National Book Award to Saul Bellow for *Mr. Sammler's Planet*
1971   *All in the Family* premieres
1971   George Harrison releases *My Sweet Lord*
1971   Grammy award winners include *Bridge over Troubled Waters*,
The Carpenters
1971   Andrew Wyeth paints his first Helga picture
1971   May   National Public Radio begins programming
1971   May   Benjamin Britten's opera *Owen Wingrave* premieres
1971   May   Stephen Schwartz' musical *Godspell* premieres off Broadway
1971   Jul   Jim Morrison of the Doors dies at 28, in Paris
1971   Jul   Louis Armstrong dies at age of 70
1971   Aug   Masterpiece Theatre presents *The Six Wives of Henry VIII*
1971   Aug   George Harrison's concert for Bangladesh takes place
1971   Aug   Paul McCartney announces the group Wings
1971   Sep   Artist Judy Chicago establishes Feminist Art Program
1971   Sep   Kennedy Center for the Performing Arts opens
1971   Dec   *Homecoming – A Christmas Story* introduces the Waltons
1971   Dec   X-rated *A Clockwork Orange* premieres
1972   Hit songs from 1972 include:
Alone Again Naturally by Gilbert O'Sullivan
American Pie by Don McLean

Baby Don't Get Hooked on Me by Mac Davis
Ben by Michael Jackson
Black and White by Three Dog Night
The Candy Man by Sammy Davis Jr.
The First Time Ever I Saw Your Face by Roberta Flack
Heart of Gold by Neil Young
Horse with No Name by America
I Am Woman by Helen Reddy
I Can See Clearly Now by Johnny Nash
Lean on Me by Bill Withers
Mr. and Mrs. Jones by Billy Paul
My Ding-a-Ling by Chuck Berry
Papa Was a Rolling Stone by The Temptations
Song Song Blue by Neil Diamond
Without You by Nilsson

1972		Oscar winners from 1972 include:
		The Godfather as Best Picture
		Marlon Brando in *The Godfather* as Best Actor
		Liza Minnelli in *Cabaret* as Best Actress
		Joel Gray in *Cabaret* as Best Supporting Actor
		Best Supporting Actress: Eileen Heckart in *Butterflies are Free*
		Bob Fosse, *Cabaret*, as Best Director
1972		Tony award winners include: *Sticks and Bones, Two Gentlemen of Verona*
1972		Emmy winners from 1972 include: Glenda Jackson in *Elizabeth R*, Carroll O'Connor, Peter Falk in *Columbo*, *Sonny & Cher Comedy Hour*, Mary Tyler Moore, Carol Burnett
1972		Nobel Prize for Literature awarded to Heinrich Boll
1972		Pulitzer for Music awarded to Jacob Druckman for *Windows*
1972		Pulitzer for Fiction to Wallace Stegner for *Angle of Repose*
1972		Pulitzer Prize for Poetry awarded to James Wright
1972		National Book award: Flannery O'Connor, *Complete Stories*
1972		Home Box Office debuts
1972		Richard Bach's *Jonathan Livingston Seagull* is published
1972	Feb	BBC bans *Give Ireland Back to the Irish* by Wings
1972	Feb	*Grease* opens on Broadway
1972	Jun	Dion & The Belmonts hold reunion concert at Madison Square Garden
1972	Jul	200,000 attend Mt. Pocono rock festival in Pennsylvania
1972	Sep	*M*A*S*H* premieres on TV
1972	Dec	Neil Simon's *The Sunshine Boys* premieres
1973		Hit songs from 1973 include:

Bad Bad LeRoy Brown by Jim Croce
Crocodile Rock by Elton John

Delta Dawn by Helen Reddy
Half-Breed by Cher
Killing Me Softly by Roberta Flack
Let's Get It On by Marvin Gaye
Midnight Train to Georgia by Gladys Knight & The Pips
My Love by Paul McCartney & Wings
The Night The Lights Went Out in Georgia by Vicki Lawrence
Nights in White Satin by The Moody Blues
Superstition by Stevie Wonder
Tie A Yellow Ribbon by Tony Orlando & Dawn
Time in a Bottle by Jim Croce
Touch Me in the Morning by Diana Ross
We're an American Band by Grand Funk Railroad
You Are the Sunshine of My Life by Stevie Wonder
You're So Vain by Carly Simon

1973		Oscar winners from 1973 include:
		The Sting as Best Picture
		Jack Lemmon in *Save the Tiger* as Best Actor
		Glenda Jackson in *A Touch of Class* as Best Actress
		John Houseman in *The Paper Chase* as Best Supporting Actor
		Tatum O'Neal in *Paper Moon* as Best Supporting Actress
		George Roy Hill, *The Sting*, as Best Director
1973		Tony award winners include: *That Championship Season, A Little Night Music*
1973		Emmy winners from 1973 include: *All in the Family*, Jack Klugman, Richard Thomas in *The Waltons*, Mary Tyler Moore, Michael Learned, *Kung Fu*
1973		Nobel Prize for Literature awarded to Patrick White
1973		Pulitzer for Music to Elliott Carter for *String Quartet No. 3*
1973		Pulitzer for Fiction to Eudora Welty, *The Optimists Daughter*
1973		Pulitzer for Drama to Jason Miller, *That Championship Season*
1973		Pulitzer Prize for Poetry to Maxine Kumin for *Up Country*
1973		National Book Awards won by John Barth for *Chimera* and Ursula K. LeGuin for *The Farthest Shore*
1973	Jan	Poet James Merrill wins Bollingen Prize
1973	Mar	Robert Joffrey Dance Company opens
1973	Mar	Grammy award winners include America, Roberta Flack
1973	Sep	Singer/Songwriter Jim Croce dies in plane crash at 30
1973	Nov	*Good Morning America* premieres on ABC
1973	Dec	Singer Bobby Darin dies at age of 37
1973	Dec	*The Young and the Restless* soap opera premieres
1973	Dec	*The Exorcist* premieres, rated X
1973	Dec	Alexander Solzhenitsyn publishes *Gulag Archipelago*
1974		Hit songs from 1974 include:

Annie's Song by John Denver
Band on the Run by Paul McCartney & Wings
Bennie and the Jets by Elton John
Cat's in the Cradle by Harry Chapin
I Shot the Sheriff by Eric Clapton
The Joker by The Steve Miller Band
The LocoMotion by Grand Funk
Rock Me Gently by Andy Kim
Seasons in the Sun by Terry Jacks
The Streak by Ray Stevens
Sundown by Gordon Lightfoot
Sunshine on My Shoulders by John Denver
Whatever Gets You Through the Night by John Lennon
You Ain't Seen Nothing Yet by Bachman Turner Overdrive
You Haven't Done Nothin by Stevie Wonder
You're Having My Baby by Paul Anka
You're Sixteen by Ringo Starr

1974		Oscar winners from 1974 include:
		The Godfather Part II as Best Picture
		Art Carney in *Harry and Tonto* as Best Actor
		Best Actress: Ellen Burstyn, *Alice Doesn't Live Here Anymore*
		Best Supporting Actor: Robert DeNiro, *The Godfather Part II*
		Ingrid Bergman in *Murder on the Orient Express* as Best Supporting Actress
		Francis Ford Coppola, *The Godfather Part II*, as Best Director
1974		Tony award winners include: *The River Niger, Raisin*
1974		Emmy winners from 1974 include: Alan Alda in *MASH*, Mary Tyler Moore, Cicely Tyson in *The Autobiography of Miss Jane Pittman*, Telly Savalas in *Kojak*, Rob Reiner, Marlo Thomas for *Free To Be You and Me*, Lily Tomlin, *Upstairs, Downstairs* on *Masterpiece Theatre*
1974		Pulitzer for Music awarded to Donald Martino for *Notturno*
1974		Pulitzer Prize for Poetry to Robert Lowell for *The Dolphin*
1974		National Book Award: Isaac Bashevis Singer, *A Crown of Feathers*
1974		Stephen King publishes his first novel, *Carrie*
1974		Shel Silverstein publishes *Where The Sidewalk Ends*
1974		Judy Chicago creates *The Dinner Party*, feminist art exhibition
1974	Jan	*Happy Days* begins its 11 year run on ABC TV
1974	Jan	*Jaws* by Peter Benchley is published
1974	Feb	Mel Brooks' *Blazing Saddles* opens in theatres
1974	Mar	Grammy award winners include Roberta Flack and Bette Midler
1974	Mar	Streaker runs behind presenter David Niven at the Oscars

		on live TV
1974	Jun	Ballet dancer Mikhail Baryshnikov defects to the west
1974	Dec	Lindsay Buckingham and Stevie Nicks join Fleetwood Mac
1975		Hit songs from 1975 include:

Best of My Love by The Eagles
Black Water by The Doobie Brothers
Fallin in Love by Hamilton Joe Frank & Reynolds
Fame by David Bowie
Get Down Tonight by KC & The Sunshine Band
Hey Won't You Play by B.J. Thomas
I'm Sorry by John Denver
Island Girl by Elton John
Jive Talkin by The Bee Gees
Love Will Keep Us Together by The Captain & Tenille
One of these Nights by The Eagles
Philadelphia Freedom by Elton John
Rhinestone Cowboy by Glen Campbell
Sister Golden Hair by America
Thank God I'm a Country Boy by John Denver
That's the Way I Like It by KC & The Sunshine Band
You're No Good by Linda Ronstadt

1975	Oscar winners from 1975 include:

One Flew Over the Cuckoos Nest as Best Picture
Best Actor: Jack Nicholson in *One Flew Over the Cuckoos Nest*
Best Actress: Louise Fletcher, *One Flew Over the Cuckoos Nest*
George Burns in *The Sunshine Boys* as Best Supporting Actor
Lee Grant in *Shampoo* as Best Supporting Actress
Milos Forman, *One Flew Over the Cuckoos Nest*, Best Director

1975	Tony award winners include: *Equus, The Wiz*
1975	Emmy winners in 1975 include: *Mary Tyler Moore Show, Carol Burnett Show,* Cher, *MASH,* Laurence Olivier and Katharine Hepburn for *Love Among the Ruins,* Tony Randall in *The Odd Couple,* Robert Blake in *Baretta,* Peter Falk in *Columbo,* Valerie Harper in *Rhoda*
1975	Nobel Prize for Literature awarded to Eugenio Montale
1975	Pulitzer for Fiction to Michael Shaara for *The Killer Angels*
1975	Pulitzer Prize for Drama to Edward Albee for *Seascape*
1975	Pulitzer Prize for Poetry to Gary Snyder for *Turtle Island*
1975	Grammy award winners include: *I Honestly Love You,* Marvin Hamlisch
1975	National Book Award won by Robert Stone for *Dog Soldiers*
1975	Ansel Adams founds Center for Creative Photography
1975	*Jaws* is released
1975	*Shogun* by James Clavell is published

1975		Stephen King publishes *Salem's Lot*
1975		*Danny The Champion of the World* is published by Roald Dahl
1975	Mar	*Rocky Horror Picture Show* opens in NY City
1975	Jun	Janis Ian releases *At 17*
1975	Oct	*Saturday Night Live* premieres with host George Carlin
1975	Nov	First appearance of The Sex Pistols
1976		Hit songs from 1976 include

Afternoon Delight by The Starland Vocal Band
Disco Duck by Rick Dees & His Cast of Idiots
Disco Lady by Johnnie Taylor
Don't Go Breaking My Heart by Elton John & Kiki Dee
Fifty Ways to Leave Your Lover by Paul Simon
If You Leave Me Now by Chicago
I Write the Songs by Barry Manilow
Let Your Love Flow by Bellamy Brothers
Love Hangover by Diana Ross
Oh What a Night by The Four Seasons
Play That Funky Music by Wild Cherry
Rock 'n Me by The Steve Miller Band
Saturday Night by The Bay City Rollers
Shake Your Booty by KC & The Sunshine Band
Silly Love Songs by Paul McCartney & Wings
Tonight's the Night by Rod Stewart
You Should be Dancing by The Bee Gees

1976   Oscar winners from 1976 include:
Rocky as Best Picture
Peter Finch in *Network* as Best Actor
Faye Dunaway in *Network* as Best Actress
Best Supporting Actor: Jason Robards, *All The President's Men*
Beatrice Straight in *Network* as Best Supporting Actress
John G. Avildsen, *Rocky*, as Best Director

1976   Tony award winners include: *Travesties, A Chorus Line*
1976   Emmy winners from 1976 include: Lorne Michaels for
Saturday Night, Rich Man Poor Man, Eleanor & Franklin, Jack
Albertson in *Chico & The Man*
1976   Nobel Prize for Literature awarded to Saul Bellow
1976   Pulitzer Prize for Music to Ned Rorem for *Air Music*
1976   Pulitzer Prize for Fiction to Saul Bellow for *Humboldt's Gift*
1976   Pulitzer Prize for Drama to Michael Bennett & James
Kirkwood for *A Chorus Line*
1976   Pulitzer for Poetry to John Ashbery for *Self-Portrait in a Convex Mirror*
1976   National Book Award won by William Gaddis for *Jr.*
1976   Leon Uris' *Trinity* is published

1976		*Roots* by Alex Haley is published
1976		CB Radio craze is launched by CW McCall's *Convoy*
1976		The VCR debuts
1976	Jan	Writer Agatha Christie dies at age 85
1976	Jan	*MacNeil Lehrer Report* premieres on PBS
1976	Feb	Grammy award winners include Natalie Cole, *Love Will Keep Us Together*
1976	Jun	*The Gong Show* premieres on TV
1977		Hit songs from 1977 include:

Blinded by the Light by Manfred Mann
Da Doo Ron Ron by Shaun Cassidy
Dancing Queen by Abba
Dreams by Fleetwood Mac
Gonna Fly Now (Theme from Rocky) by Bill Conti
Got to Give It Up by Marvin Gaye
Hotel California by The Eagles
I'm Your Boogie Man by KC & The Sunshine Band
I Wish by Stevie Wonder
Looks Like We Made It by Barry Manilow
Evergreen by Barbra Streisand
New Kid in Town by The Eagles
Rich Girl by Daryl Hall & John Oates
Sir Duke by Stevie Wonder
Southern Nights by Glen Campbell
You Light Up My Life by Debby Boone
You Make Me Feel Like Dancing by Leo Sayer

| 1977 | | Oscar winners from 1977 include: |

Annie Hall as Best Picture
Richard Dreyfuss in *The Goodbye Girl* as Best Actor
Diane Keaton in *Annie Hall* as Best Actress
Jason Robards in *Julia* as Best Supporting Actor
Vanessa Redgrave in *Julia* as Best Supporting Actress
Woody Allen, *Annie Hall*, as Best Director

1977		Tony award winners include: *The Shadow Box, Annie*
1977		Emmy winners from 1977 include: *The Muppet Show, MASH, Mary Tyler Moore Show*, Mary Kay Place for *Mary Hartman, Mary Hartman*, James Garner in *The Rockford Files*, Bea Arthur in *Maude, Roots*
1977		Nobel Prize for Literature awarded to Vicente Aleixandre
1977		Pulitzer prize for Music awarded to Richard Wernick
1977		Pulitzer for Drama to Michael Cristofer for *The Shadow Box*
1977		Pulitzer prize for Poetry to James Merrill for *Divine Comedies*
1977		National Book Award: Wallace Stegner for *The Spectator Bird*
1977		*The Rocky Horror Picture Show* becomes a cult classic

1977		*Song of Solomon* by Toni Morrison is published
1977	Jan	Coneheads debut on *Saturday Night Live*
1977	Jan	The mini-series *Roots* holds America spellbound
1977	Mar	Jay Leno debuts on the *Tonight Show* with Johnny Carson
1977	Mar	Elvis Costello releases his first album
1977	May	Howard Stern begins broadcasting at WRNW
1977	May	*Star Wars* debuts
1977	Aug	Elvis Presley dies at age of 42
1977	Aug	Groucho Marx dies at age of 86
1977	Sep	First TV "viewer discretion" warning – for *Soap*
1977	Dec	*Saturday Night Fever* with John Travolta premieres
1978		Hit songs of 1978 include:

Boogie Oogie Oogie by A Taste of Honey
Double Vision by Foreigner
Grease by Frankie Valli
Hot Child in the City by Nick Gilder
Kiss You All Over by Exile
Le Freak by Chic
MacArthur Park by Donna Summer
Miss You by The Rolling Stones
Night Fever by The Bee Gees
Shadow Dancing by Andy Gibb
Stayin Alive by The Bee Gees
Thicker Than Water by Andy Gibb
Three Times a Lady by The Commodores
With A Little Luck by Paul McCartney & Wings
You Don't Bring Me Flowers, Barbra Streisand/Neil Diamond
You're the One That I Want by Olivia Newton John

1978   Oscar winners from 1978 include:
The Deer Hunter as Best Picture
Jon Voight in *Coming Home* as Best Actor
Jane Fonda in *Coming Home* as Best Actress
Best Supporting Actor: Christopher Walken, *The Deer Hunter*
Maggie Smith in *California Suite* as Best Supporting Actress
Michael Cimino, *The Deer Hunter*, for Best Director

1978   Tony award winners include: *Da, Ain't Misbehavin*
1978   Emmy winners from 1978 include: *All in the Family, The*
        Muppet Show, The Rockford Files, Meryl Streep in *Holocaust*,
        Gilda Radner, Edward Asner
1978   Nobel Prize in Literature awarded to Isaac Bashevis Singer
1978   Pulitzer Prize in Music to Michael Colgrass for *Déjà vu*
1978   Pulitzer for Fiction: James Alan McPherson for *Elbow Room*
1978   Pulitzer for Drama to Donald Coburn for *The Gin Game*
1978   Pulitzer Prize for Poetry awarded to Howard Nemerov

1978		American Music Awards include Stevie Wonder, Fleetwood Mac and Conway Twitty
1978		National Book Award won by Mary Lee Settle for *Blood Ties*
1978		John Belushi stars in *Animal House*
1978		Christopher Reeve stars in *Superman*
1978	Feb	*Jesus Christ Superstar* closes in NY City
1978	Feb	Grammy award winners include *Hotel California*, Fleetwood Mac, Debby Boone
1978	Mar	First episode of *Dallas* airs on CBS
1979		Hit songs from 1979 include:

Babe by Styx
Bad Girls by Donna Summer
Do Ya Think I'm Sexy by Rod Stewart
Don't Stop Til You Get Enough by Michael Jackson
The Pina Colada Song by Rupert Holmes
Heartache Tonight by The Eagles
Hot Stuff by Donna Summer
I Will Survive by Gloria Gaynor
Knock on Wood by Amii Stewart
Love You Inside Out by The Bee Gees
My Sharona by The Knack
Reunited by Peaches & Herb
Ring My Bell by Anita Ward
Sad Eyes by Robert John
Tragedy by The Bee Gees
What a Fool Believes by The Doobie Brothers

1979		Oscar winners from 1979 include:

Kramer vs. Kramer as Best Picture
Dustin Hoffman in *Kramer vs. Kramer* for Best Actor
Sally Field in *Norma Rae* as Best Actress
Melvyn Douglas in *Being There* for Best Supporting Actor
Best Supporting Actress: Meryl Streep, *Kramer vs. Kramer*
Robert Benton, *Kramer vs. Kramer*, as Best Director

1979		Tony award winners include: *The Elephant Man, Sweeney Todd*
1979		Emmy winners for 1979 include: *Friendly Fire, The Lion, The Witch & the Wardrobe, Little House on the Prairie, Taxi, Barney Miller, Lou Grant, Scared Straight*, Robert Guillaume in *Soap, MASH, Roots: The Next Generation*
1979		Nobel Prize in Literature awarded to Odysseus Elytis
1979		Pulitzer in Music to Joseph Schwantner
1979		Pulitzer in Fiction to John Cheever
1979		Pulitzer Prize in Drama to Sam Shepard for *Buried Child*
1979		Pulitzer in Poetry to Robert Penn Warren for *Now and Then*
1979		National Book Award: Tim O'Brian for *Going After Cacciato*

1979		Artist Judy Chicago finishes multimedia project *The Dinner Party*, premieres at San Francisco Museum of Modern Art
1979		Performance Art becomes a new art form
1979		Grammy award winners include *Just The Way You Are* by Billy Joel
1979	Jan	Golden Globe winners include *Midnight Express*
1979	Feb	Pink Floyd premieres live version of *The Wall*
1979	Apr	*Real People* premieres on NBC TV, first "reality TV"
1979	May	Country Music awards include Kenny Rodgers and Barbara Mandrell
1979	May	*Dancin Fool* by Frank Zappa is a hit
1979	Jun	John Wayne dies
1979	Aug	*Gilda Radner: Live from New York* opens on Broadway
1980		Hit songs from 1980 include:

Against the Wind by Bob Seger & The Silver Bullet Band
Another Brick in the Wall by Pink Floyd
Another One Bites the Dust by Queen
Call Me by Blondie
Crazy Little Thing Called Love by Queen
Do That to Me One More Time by The Captain and Tennille
Fame by Irene Cara
Funkytown by Lipps, Inc.
He Stopped Loving Her Today by George Jones
Hungry Heart by Bruce Springsteen
It's Still Rock and Roll to Me by Billy Joel
Starting Over by John Lennon
Lady by Kenny Rogers
Please Don't Go by KC & the Sunshine Band
Rock with You by Michael Jackson
Sailing by Christopher Cross
A Woman in Love by Barbra Streisand

1980		Oscar winners from 1980 include:

Ordinary People as Best Picture
Robert DeNiro in *Raging Bull* as Best Actor
Sissy Spacek in *Coal Miner's Daughter* as Best Actress
Timothy Hutton in *Ordinary People* as Best Supporting Actor
Mary Steenburgen in *Melvin and Howard* as Best Supporting Actress
Robert Redford, *Ordinary People*, as Best Director

1980		Tony award winners include: *Children of a Lesser God, Evita*
1980		Emmy winners from 1980 include: *Taxi, Lou Grant*, Richard Mulligan on *Soap,* Barbara Bel Geddes on *Dallas*, Harry Morgan on *MASH*
1980		Nobel Prize for Literature awarded to Czeslaw Milosz

1980		Pulitzer for Music to David Del Tredici
1980		Pulitzer for Fiction to Norman Mailer for *The Executioner's Song*
1980		Pulitzer for Drama to Landord Wilson for *Talley's Folly*
1980		Pulitzer Prize for Poetry awarded to Donald Justice
1980		National Book Award: John Irving, *The World According to Garp*
1980		Ansel Adams awarded the Presidential Medal of Freedom
1980		1000 Picasso paintings shown at Museum of Modern Art
1980	Jan	*The Blues Brothers* with Dan Ackroyd and John Belushi opens
1980	Feb	Grammy award winners include Streisand-Diamond duet
1980	May	Country Music Award winners include Barbara Mandrell
1980	May	American Book Award winners include William Styron for *Sophie's Choice* and Thomas Wolfe for *The Right Stuff*
1980	May	*The Empire Strikes Back* (*Star Wars* 2) premieres
1980	Nov	*Dallas* episode which reveals "Who Shot JR?" gets huge ratings
1980	Dec	John Lennon murdered by crazed fan
1980	Dec	Bravo network premieres on cable TV
1980	Dec	Bruce Springsteen gives concert at Madison Square Garden
1981		Hit songs of 1981 include:

Best That You Can Do by Christopher Cross

Bette Davis Eyes by Kim Carnes

Celebration by Kool & The Gang

Endless Love by Diana Ross and Lionel Richie

Every Little Thing She Does is Magic by The Police

I Love A Rainy Night by Eddie Rabbitt

Jessie's Girl by Rick Springfield

Keep On Loving You by REO Speedwagon

Kiss on My List by Daryl Hall and John Oates

Morning Train by Sheena Easton

9 to 5 by Dolly Parton

The One that You Love by Air Supply

Physical by Olivia Newton John

Private Eyes by Daryl Hall and John Oates

Slow Hand by The Pointer Sisters

The Tide is High by Blondie

| 1981 | | Oscar winners from 1981 include: |

Chariots of Fire as Best Picutre

Henry Fonda in *On Golden Pond* for Best Actor

Katharine Hepburn in *On Golden Pond* for Best Actress

John Gielgud in *Arthur* for Best Supporting Actor

Maureen Stapleton in *Reds* for Best Supporting Actress

Warren Beatty, *Reds*, for Best Director

1981		Tony award winners include: *Amadeus, 42nd Street*
1981		Emmy winners for 1981 include: *Hill Street Blues, Shogun, Cosmos,* Steve Allen's *Meeting of Minds, WKRP in Cincinnati*
1981		Nobel Prize for Literature won by Elias Canetti
1981		Pulitzer Prize for Music to John Kennedy Toole for *A Confederacy of Dunces*
1981		Pulitzer for Drama to Beth Henley for *Crimes of the Heart*
1981		Pulitzer for Poetry to James Schuyler,*The Morning of the Poem*
1981		National Book Award won by Wright Morris for *Plains Song,* Beverly Cleary for *Ramona and her Mother*
1981		Steven Spielberg releases *Raiders of the Lost Ark,* introducing Indiana Jones
1981	Jan	Spinoff from *Dallas, Dynasty* starring Joan Collins premieres
1981	Jan	Bollingen Prize for poetry awarded to May Swenson and Howard Nemerov
1981	Feb	Grammy award winners include Christopher Cross and Billy Joel
1981	Mar	Dan Rather becomes primary anchor of CBS-TV News
1981	Aug	MTV premiers
1981	Sep	Judge Wapner and *The Peoples Court* premier
1981	Sep	*Entertainment Tonight* premieres
1981	Sep	Simon & Garfunkel reunite for NYC Central Park concert
1981	Oct	Unknown Prince opens for Rolling Stones concert in LA
1981	Dec	*CNN Headline News* debuts
1982		Hit songs from 1982 include:
		Abracadabra by The Steve Miller Band
		Centerfold by The J Geils Band
		Don't Talk to Strangers by Rick Springfield
		Ebony and Ivory by Paul McCartney and Stevie Wonder
		Eye in the Sky by Alan Parsons Project
		Eye of the Tiger by Survivor
		Freeze Frame by J. Geils Band
		Hard to Say I'm Sorry by Chicago
		Hurts So Good by John Cougar Mellencamp
		I Can't Go for That by Daryl Hall and John Oates
		I Love Rock n Roll by John Cougar
		Maneater by Daryl Hall and John Oates
		Open Arms by Journey
		Truly by Lionel Richie
		Up Where We Belong by Joe Cocker and Jennifer Warnes
		Who Can It Be Now by Men at Work
1982		Oscar winners from 1982 include:
		Gandhi as Best Picture
		Ben Kingsley in *Gandhi* as Best Actor

		Meryl Streep in *Sophie's Choice* as Best Actress
		Louis Gosset Jr in *An Officer and a Gentleman* as Best Supporting Actor
		Jessica Lange in *Tootsie* as Best Supporting Actress
		Richard Attenborough, *Gandhi*, as Best Director
1982		Tony award winners include: *The Life and Adventures of Nicholas Nickleby*, *Nine*
1982		Emmy winners from 1982 include: *Barney Miller*, *One Day at a Time*, *Hill Street Blues*, Alan Alda, Carol Kane, Ingrid Bergman in *A Woman Called Golda*
1982		Nobel Prize for Literature to Gabriel Garcia Marquez
1982		Pulitzer for Music to Roger Sessions for *Concerto for Orchestra*
1982		Pulitzer Prize for Fiction to John Updike for *Rabbit is Rich*
1982		Pulitzer for Drama to Charles Fuller for *A Soldier's Play*
1982		Pulitzer Prize for Poetry awarded to Sylvia Plath
1982		National Book Awards include John Updike for *Rabbit is Rich* and MauriceSendak for *Outside Over There*
1982	Jan	Bryant Gumbel becomes co-host of NBC's *Today Show*
1982	Jan	American Music Awards include Kenny Rogers
1982	Feb	*Late Night with David Letterman* premieres
1982	Feb	Grammy winners include *Double Fantasy*, *Bette Davis Eyes*
1982	Jun	Movie *ET the Extra Terrestrial* released
1982	Dec	*Thriller* is released by Michael Jackson
1983		Hit songs from 1983 include:
		Africa by Toto
		All Night Long by Lionel Richie
		Beat It by Michael Jackson
		Billie Jean by Michael Jackson
		Delirious by Prince
		Down Under by Men at Work
		Electric Avenue by Eddy Grant
		Every Breath You Take by The Police
		Flashdance by Irene Cara
		Girls Just Wanna Have Fun by Cyndi Lauper
		Islands in the Stream by Kenny Rogers and Dolly Parton
		Joanna by Kool and the Gang
		Let's Dance by David Bowie
		Maniac by Michael Sembello
		Say Say Say by Paul McCartney and Michael Jackson
		Sweet Dreams by The Eurythmics
		Tell Her About It by Billy Joel
1983		Oscar winners from 1983 include:
		Terms of Endearment as Best Picture
		Robert Duvall in *Tender Mercies* as Best Actor

Shirley MacLaine in *Terms of Endearment* as Best Actress
Best Supporting Actor: Jack Nicholson, *Terms of Endearment*
Linda Hunt in *The Year of Living Dangerously* as Best
Supporting Actress
James L. Brooks, *Terms of Endearment*, as Best Director

1983   Tony award winners include: *Torch Song Trilogy, Cats*
1983   Emmy winners for 1983 include: *Cheers, Hill Street Blues, The*
                Thorn Birds, Ed Flanders in *St. Elsewhere*, Shelly Long in
                Cheers, Tyne Daley in *Cagney & Lacy*
1983   Nobel Prize for Literature awarded to William Golding
1983   Pulitzer Prize for Music to Ellen Taaffe Zwilich
1983   Pulitzer for Fiction to Alice Walker for *The Color Purple*
1983   Pulitzer for Drama to Marsha Normal for *Night Mother*
1983   Pulitzer Prize for Poetry awarded to Galway Kinnell
1983   National Book Award: Alice Walker for *The Color Purple*
1983   Bollingen Prize for poetry awarded to Anthony Hecht
1983   The compact disc introduced
1983   Jasper Johns paints autobiographical picture, *Racing Thoughts*
1983   Jan   Golden Globe winners include *ET* and *Tootsie*
1983   Feb   Grammy winners include Rosanna, Toto, Men at Work
1983   Feb   Michael Jackson's *Thriller* album goes #1 for 37 weeks
1983   Feb   Final episode of *MASH* gathers record audience
1983   May   Country Music winners include Alabama and Willie Nelson
1983   May   *Return of the Jedi (Star Wars 3)* released
1984   Hit songs of 1984 include:
                Against All Odds by Phil Collins
                Caribbean Queen by Billy Ocean
                Footloose by Kenny Loggins
                Hello by Lionel Richie
                I Just Called to Say I Love You by Stevie Wonder
                Jump by Van Halen
                Let's Go Crazy by Prince & The Revolution
                Let's Hear it For the Boy by Deniece Williams
                Like a Virgin by Madonna
                Missing You by John Waite
                Out of Touch by Daryl Hall and John Oates
                Owner of a Lonely Heart by Yes
                Purple Rain by Prince & The Revolution
                The Reflex by Duran Duran
                Time After Time by Cyndi Lauper
                What's Love Got to Do With It by Tina Turner
                When Doves Cry by Prince and the Revolution
1984   Oscar winners from 1984 include:
                Amadeus as Best Picture

F. Murray Abraham in *Amadeus* as Best Actor
Sally Field in *Places in The Heart* as Best Actress
Haing S. Ngor in *The Killing Fields* as Best Supporting Actor
Best Supporting Actress: Peggy Ashcroft, *A Passage to India*
Milos Forman, *Amadeus*, as Best Director

1984		Tony winners include: *The Real Thing, La Cage aux Folies*
1984		Emmy winners include *Cheers, The Dollmaker, Kate & Allie*, Tom Selleck in *Magnum PI*, John Ritter in *Three's Company*, Tyne Daly in *Cagney & Lacey*
1984		Nobel Prize for Literature awarded to Jaroslav Seifert
1984		Pulitzer Prize for Music to Bernard Rands for *Canti del Sole*
1984		Pulitzer Prize for Fiction to William Kennedy for *Ironweed*
1984		Pulitzer for Drama to David Mamet for *Glengarry Glen Ross*
1984		Pulitzer for Poetry to Mary Oliver for *American Primitive*
1984		PG-13 movie rating adopted
1984		Arnold Schwarzenegger stars in *The Terminator*
1984	Feb	American Music award won by Michael Jackson
1984	Feb	Robert Penn Warren is named first US Poet Laureate
1984	Feb	Michael Jackson wins 8 Grammy awards
1984	Mar	People's Choice Award winners include Brooke Shields
1984	Apr	Ansel Adams dies
1985		Hit songs from 1985 include:

Born in the USA by Bruce Springsteen
Can't Fight This Feeling by REO Speedwagon
Crazy for You by Madonna
Everything She Wants by Wham
Everytime You Go Away by Paul Young
Heaven by Bryan Adams
I Want to Know What Love Is by Foreigner
Money for Nothing by Dire Straits
One More Night by Phil Collins
One Night in Bangkok by Murray Head
The Power of Love by Huey Lewis & The News
Saving All My Love For You by Whitney Houston
Say You Say Me by Lionel Richie
Separate Lives by Phil Collins & Marilyn Martin
Shout by Tears for Fears
A View to a Kill by Duran Duran
We Built This City by Starship

1985		Oscar winners from 1985 include:

Out of Africa as Best Picture
William Hurt in *Kiss of the Spider Woman* as Best Actor
Geraldine Page in *The Trip to Bountiful* as Best Actress
Don Ameche in *Cocoon* as Best Supporting Actor

		Anjelica Huston in *Prizzi's Honor* as Best Supporting Actress
		Sydney Pollack, *Out of Africa*, as Best Director
1985		Tony award winners include *Biloxi Blues, Big River*
1985		Emmy winners from 1985 include: *Miami Vice, The Cosby Show, Cagney & Lacy, The Jewel in the Crown*
1985		Nobel Prize for Literature awarded to Claude Simon
1985		Pulitzer Prize for Music won by Stephen Albert
1985		Pulitzer Prize for Fiction to Alison Lurie for *Foreign Affairs*
1985		Pulitzer for Drama to Stephen Sondheim
1985		Pulitzer Prize for Poetry awarded to Carolyn Kizer for *Yin*
1985		National Book Awards: Don DeLillo for *White Noise*
1985		Georgia O'Keefe presented the National Medal of Arts
1985		*Lake Woebegon Days* by Garrison Keillor published
1985	Jan	*Amadeus* wins at Golden Globes awards
1985	Feb	Grammy award winners include Cyndi Lauper, *What's Love Got to Do With It*
1985	Mar	People's Choice Awards include Bill Cosby with 4 awards
1985	May	Country Music Awards include Alabama and The Judds
1985	Aug	Michael Jackson buys ATV Music and all Beatles songs
1986		Hit songs from 1986 include:
		Addicted to Love by Robert Palmer
		Glory of Love by Peter Cetera
		Higher Love by Steve Winwood
		Holding Back the Years by Simply Red
		How Will I Know by Whitney Houston
		Kiss by Prince & The Revolution
		Live to Tell by Madonna
		Papa Don't Preach by Madonna
		Sara by Starship
		Sledgehammer by Peter Gabriel
		Stuck with You by Huey Lewis & The News
		These Dreams by Heart
		They'll Be Sad Songs by Billy Ocean
		True Colors by Cyndi Lauper
		Walk Like an Egyptian by The Bangles
		When I Think of You by Janet Jackson
		You Give Love a Bad Name by Bon Jovi
1986		Oscar winners from 1986 include:
		Platoon as Best Picture
		Paul Newman in *The Color of Money* as Best Actor
		Marlee Matlin in *Children of a Lesser God* as Best Actress
		Best Supporting Actor: Michael Caine, *Hannah and her Sisters*
		Dianne Wiest in *Hannah and her Sisters* as Best Supporting Actress

		Oliver Stone, *Platoon*, as Best Director
1986		Tony award winners include: *I'm Not Rappaport*, *The Mystery of Edwin Drood*
1986		Emmy winners include *Murder She Wrote*, *Moonlighting*, Michael J. Fox in *Family Ties*, Betty White in *The Golden Girls*, Dustin Hoffman in *Death of a Salesman*
1986		Nobel Prize in Literature awarded to Wole Soyinka
1986		Pulitzer Prize in Music to George Perle for *Wind Quintet IV*
1986		Pulitzer in Fiction to Larry McMurtry for *Lonesome Dove*
1986		Pulitzer in Poetry to Henry Taylor for *The Flying Change*
1986		National Book Award: E.L. Doctorow for *World's Fair*
1986	Jan	Rock N Roll Hall of Fame inducts Chuck Berry, James Brown, Ray Charles, Fats Domino, Everley Brothers, Jerry Lee Lewis and Elvis Presley
1986	Jan	Golden Globe Award winners include Whoopi Goldberg, *The Color Purple*
1986	Feb	Grammy Award winners include Sade and Phil Collins
1986	Mar	Artist Georgia O'Keefe dies at the age of 98
1986	May	*Top Gun* premieres
1987		Hit songs from 1987 include:

Alone by Heart
Bad by Michael Jackson
Didn't We Almost Have It All by Whitney Houston
Faith by George Michael
Here I Go Again by Whitesnake
I Knew You Were Waiting by Aretha Franklin / George Michael
I Still Haven't Found What I'm Looking For by U2
I Wanna Dance with Somebody by Whitney Houston
Jacob's Ladder by Huey Lewis & The News
La Bamba by Los Lobos
Lean on Me by Club Nouveau
Livin on a Prayer by Bon Jovi
Mony Mony Live by Billy Idol
Nothing's Gonna Stop Us Now by Starship
Open Your Heart by Madonna
Shakedown by Bob Seger
You Keep Me Hangin On by Kim Wilde

1987   Oscar winners from 1987 include:

The Last Emperor as Best Picture
Michael Douglas in *Wall Street* as Best Actor
Cher in *Moonstruck* as Best Actress
Sean Connery in *The Untouchables* as Best Supporting Actor
Olympia Dukakis in *Moonstruck* as Best Suporting Actress
Bernardo Bertolucci, *The Last Emperor*, as Best Director

1987		Tony award winners include: *Fences, Les Miserables*
1987		Emmy award winners include: *The Golden Girls, LA Law, Carol, Carl, Whoopi & Robin,* Bruce Willis in *Moonlighting, Max Headroom*
1987		Nobel Prize for Literature awarded to Joseph Brodsky
1987		Pulitzer for Music to John Harbison for *The Flight into Egypt*
1987		Pulitzer for Fiction to Peter Taylor, *A Summons to Memphis*
1987		Pulitzer Prize for Drama to August Wilson for *Fences*
1987		Pulitzer Prize for Poetry to Rita Dove for *Thomas and Beulah*
1987		National Book Award: Larry Heinemann for *Paco's Story*
1987		Rock N Roll Hall of Fame inducts Aretha Franklin
1987		Joel and Ethan Coen release *Raising Arizona*
1987		Glenn Close and Michael Douglas star in *Fatal Attraction*
1987		National Museum of Women in the Arts opens
1987		National Gallery of Art exhibits Andrew Wyeth's Helga paintings, its first exhibition of works by a living artist
1987	Mar	Vincent Van Gogh's *Sunflowers* sells for record $40 million
1987	Apr	Fox TV premieres with first shows *Married With Children* and Tracy Ullman
1987	Nov	Van Gogh's *Irises* sells for over $50 million at auction
1988		Hit songs from 1988 include:

Anything for You by Gloria Estefan
Bad Medicine by Bon Jovi
Father Figure by George Michael
The Flame by Cheap Trick
Get Outta My Dreams, Get into My Car by Billy Ocean
Got My Mind Set on You by George Harrison
A Groovy Kind of Love by Phil Collins
Look Away by Chicago
Love Bites by Def Leppard
Man in the Mirror by Michael Jackson
Monkey by Goerge Michael
Need You Tonight by Inxs
Roll With It by Steve Winwood
Seasons Change by Expose
So Emotional by Whitney Houston
Sweet Child O'Mine by Guns N Roses
The Way You Make Me Feel by Michael Jackson

| 1988 | | Oscar winners from 1988 include: |

Rain Man as Best Picture
Dustin Hoffman in *Rain Man* as Best Actor
Jodie Foster in *The Accused* as Best Actress
Best Supporting Actor: Kevin Kline, *A Fish Called Wanda*
Best Supporting Actress: Geena Davis, *An Accidental Tourist*

		Barry Levinson, *Rain Man*, as Best Director
1988		Tony award winners include: *M.Butterfly*, *The Phantom of the Opera*
1988		Emmy award winners include *The Wonder Years*, *thirty something*, *Star Trek: The Next Generation*, Bea Arthur in *Golden Girls*
1988		Nobel Prize for Literature awarded to Naguib Mahfouz
1988		Pulitzer for Music to William Bolcom
1988		Pulitzer Prize for Fiction to Toni Morrison for *Beloved*
1988		Pulitzer for Drama to Alfred Uhry for *Driving Miss Daisy*
1988		Pulitzer for Poetry to William Meredith for *Partial Accounts*
1988		National Book Award includes Pete Dexter for *Paris Trout*
1988	Jan	Golden Globes include Sally Kirkland and Michael Douglas
1988	Jan	American Music Award winners include Anita Baker, Paul Simon and Whitney Houston
1988	Mar	Grammy Award winners include Paul Simon, Joshua Tree and Jody Watley
1988	Mar	People's Choice Awards: *Fatal Attraction* and Bill Cosby
1988	May	Jackson Pollock's *Search* sells for nearly $5 million
1988	May	Edgar Degas' *Dansereje* of 14 sells for over $10 million
1988	Aug	Writer's Guild ends 6 month strike
1988	Sep	Bronx Museum for the Arts opens
1988	Nov	Picasso's *Acrobat & Harlequin* sells for over $38 million
1989		Hit songs from 1989 include:

Another Day in Paradise by Phil Collins
Baby Don't Forget My Number by Milli Vanilli
Batdance by Prince
Cold Hearted by Paula Abdul
Don't Wanna Lose You by Gloria Estefan
Good Thing by Fine Young Cannibals
Hangin Tough by New Kids on the Block
I'll Be Lovin You by New Kids on the Block
I'll Be There For You by Bon Jovi
I'm Gonna Miss You by Milli Vanilli
Like a Prayer by Madonna
Miss You Much by Janet Jackson
Satisfied by Richard Marx
Straight Up by Paula Abdul
Toy Soldiers by Martika
We Didn't Start the Fire by Billy Joel
Wind Beneath My Wings by Bette Midler

1989	Oscar winners from 1989 include:

Driving Miss Daisy as Best Picture
Daniel Day-Lewis in *My Left Foot* as Best Actor

		Jessica Tandy in *Driving Miss Daisy* as Best Actress
		Denzel Washington in *Glory* as Best Supporting Actor
		Brenda Fricker in *My Left Foot* as Best Supporting Actress
		Oliver Stone, *Born on the Fourth of July*, as Best Director
1989		Tony award winners include: *The Heidi Chronicles, Jerome Robbins' Broadway*
1989		Emmy award winners include: *Lonesome Dove, Cheers, LA Law*, Candice Bergen in *Murphy Brown*
1989		Nobel Prize for Literature awarded to Camilo Jose Cela
1989		Pulitzer for Music to Roger Reynolds, *Whispers Out of Time*
1989		Pulitzer Prize for Fiction to Anne Tyler for *Breathing Lessons*
1989		Pulitzer for Drama to Wendy Wasserstein, *The Heidi Chronicles*
1989		Pulitzer Prize for Poetry awarded to Richard Wilbur
1989		Disney releases *The Little Mermaid*
1989		I.M. Pei's sculpture unveiled at the entrance to the Louvre
1989		Amy Tan publishes *The Joy Luck Club*
1989	Jan	Rock N Roll Hall of Fame inductees include Otis Redding, Rolling Stones, Temptations, Stevie Wonder
1989	Jan	Golden Globe winners include *Rain Man, Working Girl*
1989	Feb	Grammy award winners include Tracy Chapman, Faith, *Don't Worry Be Happy*
1989	Apr	Film critics Siskel & Ebert film their 500th show
1989	May	Gilda Radner dies at age of 42
1989	May	Van Gogh's *Portrait of Dr. Gachet* auctioned for $825 million
1989	May	*Indiana Jones & The Last Crusade* premieres
1989	Jun	The movie *Batman* premieres

Writing Topic Suggestions
Arts and Entertainment

Pick one of the topics below and write for fifteen to twenty minutes. Remember the rules:

- Don't stop writing until the limit is up.
- Use "trigger sentences" if you get stuck.
- Don't be polite.
- Be specific and remember you have at least five senses.
- You don't have to be right, rational or logical.
- Forget about the rules of grammar or spelling.
- Trust yourself.

Remember, you are creating a *primary source*. Write about what you *did*, what you *saw*, what you *thought*, what you *felt*.

1. Scan the timelines. Does a movie, TV show, book, song, performer, artist or event, strike a reminiscent chord? What memories does it bring back? Write about those memories.

2. Write about a book that influenced you, such as *Catcher in the Rye*, *For Whom the Bell Tolls*, *Gone With the Wind*, *The Grapes of Wrath*, *To Kill A Mockingbird*, *Catch-22*, *The Color Purple*. Did it change your opinions or beliefs? What did it teach you? Did it motivate you to action? Did it challenge you, or did it affirm and resonate with your own experiences? Did you recommend this book to others, or discuss it with others? Was this book recommended to you? Or was it a "forbidden" book?

3. Were you a writer, or did you want to be a writer? Did you envy the writer's life? Did you have writer heroes, such as Ernest

Hemingway, Margaret Mitchell, Pearl Buck, John Updike, Toni Morrison? What did you write? Do you still write? What do you think the role of writers in the world is, or should be?

4. Were you a painter or sculptor, or did you want to be one? Were you "good at drawing?" Which painters did you admire – Diego Rivera, Jackson Pollock, Andrew Wyeth, Andy Warhol, Georgia O'Keefe? Did you enjoy going to art museums? What is it about the visual arts that moves you? Did you ever have a big reaction to a painting or sculpture? Which one, and why?

5. Music and memories are closely linked. What kind of music do you think of as "your" generation's music? Swing? Rock n' Roll? Read the timeline of hit songs. Do you remember any of them? Which ones, and why? Where were you when you first heard it? Was it a song you shared with someone special? Did you dance to it? Where? What memories do these hit songs bring back to you?

6. Did you play an instrument, or sing, or dance? How did music affect your life? Did you take music lessons? What instrument? What kinds of music did you sing or play? Did you sing in the choir at church, or were you a member of the band at school? Did your family teach you to love music? Who were your musical heroes – popular artists such Bing Crosby, Glenn Miller, Frank Sinatra, Rosemary Clooney, Patsy Cline, Elvis Presley, the Beatles, Elton John, Whitney Houston, or classical artists such as Bach and Beethoven? Why those particular artists? Did you have aspirations of becoming a musician, and did you have any success?

7. Music and musicians became an important political and social force during the 60s and 70s. "Message" songs were everywhere – anti-war, anti-racism, pro-drugs. Concerts and Music festivals like Woodstock came into fashion and were attended by huge crowds. Were you, or your children, among them? Musicians were seen as leaders-teachers-gurus of lifestyles and life choices. Were you, or your children, influenced by the messages found in popular music?

How did it motivate you or them? Was this a good thing or a bad thing?

8. Did you go to the theatre? Did your parents take you as a child or teenager, or did you learn about theatre on your own? Did you act in school plays? Did you want to be an actor? Tell about your first theatre experience. Did you like light-hearted theatre such as Neil Simon plays or musicals such as *My Fair Lady* and *South Pacific*, serious theatre like Arthur Miller and Tennessee Williams, or classical theatre like Shakespeare? What about the theatre fascinated you? Did you work in the theatre in any capacity, such as stage hand, costumes, choreographer?

9. Were movies important to you, and why? Read the timeline regarding movies. Do you remember going to see any of these movies? Who were you with? What was the theater like? Did this movie move you to tears or laughter? Which actors or actresses inspired you? Why did you like that particular actor or actress? Did you want to go to Hollywood to work in the movies? Did any of the movies you remember change you in any way; inspire you or anger you? What is the first movie you saw that moved you in any way? Did you like comedy, action, or romance movies better? Did you work in the movie industry in any capacity?

10. Did you listen to the radio? Which radio programs or stations were your favorites? How often did you listen to the radio? Did your family listen to the radio together during the thirties and forties, before the advent of TV – to FDR's fireside chats, or *Fibber McGee & Molly*, or *Burns and Allen*, or *The Shadow*? What kind of a radio did you have? Did it have a special place in the living room? Did you listen to the radio in the sixties, seventies and eighties? What kind of radio -- hard rock, easy listening, oldies, or talk radio? What station was your favorite? Did you have a favorite DJ? Did you make your living in a radio related industry?

11. How often did you watch TV? Did you watch with your family? Were you a "tv junkie"? What kinds of shows did you like the best – Westerns, Private Eyes, variety, news, sports, sit-coms, cartoons? Look over the timeline – do you remember any of the shows listed? Do you remember any specific episode well, such as Lucy Having Her Baby, Elvis or the Beatles on *The Ed Sullivan Show*, The "tribble episode" on *Star Trek*, the last episode of *MASH*, the "Went With the Wind" skit on *The Carol Burnett Show*? Were your opinions and beliefs changed by what you saw on TV, for example did *Free To Be You and Me* or *Roots* affect you in any way? Did you encourage your children to watch TV? Did you sometimes use TV as a babysitter? What were your kids' favorite shows? Did the TV have a prominent place in the living room? Did you make your living in a television related industry?

Chapter Sixteen
Lifestyle Activities
Moving Around — Advertising, Media & Consumerism — Food — Fashion — Toys & Games — Sports

In this chapter we explore subjects that give texture, color and flavor to our lives. We examine how we moved from place to place and what we saw when we got there; where, why and how we bought things; what we wore; what we ate; and what games we played.

1930 through 1959

Moving Around

These decades saw an explosion of personal travel and movement. In 1930 Congress approved the building of the transcontinental highway system, and America's love affair with the automobile took a giant leap forward. In 1932 Route 66 between Chicago and LA opened, in 1940 the first California freeway, the Arroyo Seco, debuted, and in 1951 the New Jersey turnpike came into being, to name only a few. Bridges and tunnels were built, connecting cities and improving access to previously remote areas, such as the George Washington Bridge connecting New York and New Jersey in 1931, the Golden Gate Bridge in San Francisco in 1933, and New York's Lincoln Tunnel in 1937. Travel along these roads was made easier with such innovations as traffic lights, the first being installed in New York City. The cars themselves changed too. The V-8 engine was patented by Ford in 1932, the first Volkswagens rolled onto the production line in 1936, power steering was introduced in 1951, and radial tires in 1953. The first RV was introduced, complete with a swimming pool. Fashion in cars included not only the basic black sedan, but station wagons, hot rods, sedans with huge fins, the minimalist Volkswagen Beetle, and in 1953 one of the coolest cars ever made was introduced, the Corvette. Many class participants have written about their first car — like your first love, it is rarely forgotten.

Besides car travel, air travel grew by leaps and bounds. Transcontinental service began in the thirties, and airlines put great effort into making air travel more comfortable. The first "air hostess" started work in 1936. Women were recruited for this position on the theory that they would add hominess and a sense of safety. Pressurized cabins were introduced in 1938, and tourist class in 1952. In New York City, two huge airports opened, LaGuardia in 1939, and Idlewild in 1948.

"Maria" worked for airlines and airports for over forty years, beginning in 1942 as a cleaning woman. "It was my job to clean out the planes after everyone got off," she remembered. "And boy, you wouldn't believe what people would stuff down behind their seats, drop under their seats, or even stick on the ceiling. The most innocent was chewed gum. You had to have a strong stomach for the work." Later she was transferred to the cleaning crew at the San Francisco airport terminal, and rose to the rank of supervisor. "Supervisor didn't mean much," she shared. "I still cleaned toilets. Once I was cleaning the men's bathroom and a man rushed in, obviously in need of the toilet. When he saw me, he stopped short and jabbered at me furiously as he jumped up and down holding his crotch. I couldn't understand him because he wasn't speaking English. Suddenly he grabbed my mop and poked me with it, trying to make me leave the bathroom. That made me mad. So I just took him by the arm and pushed him out the door and told him to wait. When I came out a few minutes later, he was still waiting outside the door, and as soon as he saw me he made a mad dash into the bathroom. Later on I was told

that the man I'd thrown out of the bathroom was the the King of Malaysia!"

So where was everyone going? Lots of us were going on vacation, or to new attractions such as fairs and amusement parks. Despite the Depression, the thirties saw a number of parks and attractions begun, such as Old Ironsides dedicated as a national shrine in 1930, Mt. Rushmore in 1933, Glacier National Park in 1932, Great Smokey National Park in 1934, the Los Angeles Planetarium in 1935 (the first in the U.S.) and the first US Aquarium, Marineland in Florida in 1938. The Century of Progress Exposition opened in Chicago in 1934, the New York World's Fair in 1939, and The San Francisco Exposition in 1939. With the baby boom after the war, it was perhaps inevitable that the next Big Thing was the opening of Disneyland in 1955, where every child in America dreamed of going, and millions did.

Advertising, Media & Consumerism

Magazines during these decades enjoyed great popularity, and new magazines sprouted. Henry Luce started *Fortune Magazine* in the 1930s, catering to businessmen. Also debuting in the thirties were *Newsweek, Esquire, Life, Look, Women's Day* and *Glamour*. These new magazines had a slicker, glossier look than the more scholarly appearing magazines of earlier decades, such as *The New Yorker* or *Atlantic Monthly*. The forties saw the introduction of *Parade* and *Gourmet* Magazines, and in the fifties *Jet, Mad Magazine, Sports Illustrated* and *TV Guide* all began, catering to sharply defined audiences.

"I remember when Fortune Magazine began its Fortune 500 in the mid-fifties," shared "Hal." "I worked for one of the companies named to the list, and boy, were we proud. The management was so puffed up you'd have thought we invented penicillin or something, instead of just making a lot of money. But making money is how you define achievement in

*the business world, and to be recognized by Forbes made each
of us feel like a success."*

Influential columnists included Herb Caen in the San Francisco
Examiner, Eleanor Roosevelt's column "My Day," and Dear Abby,
syndicated in 1956.

*"Terry" wrote to Dear Abby in 1958, when she was
16. "I had just discovered – through a gossipy aunt — that
I was born only six months after my parents were married,"
she remembered, "and I was confused because my mother was
extremely modest and shy, especially about sex. I was stunned
when I found out she had 'gone all the way' before she was
married. I wanted to ask her about it but I didn't know
how. I thought Abby might tell me what to say, so I wrote
to her at the Chicago newspaper. But she never answered me.
Then I was angry with my mother and Abby both. It seemed
to me that all grown-ups were hypocrites, even the famous
ones in the newspaper."*

Advertising drove the media, both in print and over the airwaves. Jingles become a part of the American mainstream via radio
during the thirties and forties, and in the fifties through television
as well. Jingle tunes and advertising slogans that you haven't heard
for over fifty years return easily to your mind, with the simplest
nudge. Who could forget the thirties introductions of the "pause
that refreshes" (Coca Cola), "mm-mm good Campbell's soups, Elsie
the Borden's Cow, or Betty Crocker as a symbol for General Foods?
From the forties came these familiar phrases: "snap crackle pop"
Rice Krispies, "which twin has the Toni (Toni Home Permanents);
"you can trust your car to the man who wears the star (Texaco),
and Brylcream's "a little dab'll do ya." In the fifties slogans, jingles,
mascots and spokescreatures multiplied. Alka Seltzer introduced

Speedy; Anacin claimed "fast fast relief"; Peter Paul claimed "sometimes you feel like a nut, sometimes you don't;" Winstons "taste good like a cigarette should;" M&M's "melt in your mouth, not in your hand;" Chevrolet asked you to "see the USA in your Chevrolet;" Timex claimed their watches "take a licking and keep on ticking;" Pepsodent toothpaste asked "do you wonder where the yellow went?"; Clairol questioned "does she or doesn't she?"; and one of the most popular icons of all time was introduced, the Marlboro Man.

> *As a teenager in the late fifties, "Howie" tacked up a full page advertisement of the Marlboro Man on his bedroom wall. "He was so cool," he shared. "I wanted to be just like him. Some of my buddies wanted to be like James Dean or Marlon Brando, and wear leather jackets and ride motorcycles. But that wasn't my style, and besides, I didn't think my mother would let me ride a motorcycle. But the Marlboro Man – he was somebody everyone thought was cool, even your mother. Nobody would cross him. When my friends and I started to smoke, we all smoked Marlboros. Nobody even considered smoking anything else."*

The products being advertised multiplied with dizzying speed with the advancement of technology. Labor saving appliances such as the washing machine, vacuum cleaner, electric range, blender, dishwasher, microwave oven and electric can opener were all introduced, making the housewife's job much different than her mother's had been. Other new products designed to ease a woman's life included Tampax, Tupperware, granulated Tide laundry soap, aluminum foil, disposable diapers, and saran wrap. Not only what, but how she bought was different too. The first shopping mall in America opened in 1954, and in 1958 Bank of America introduced the credit card. The consumer age was born.

Food

Despite hard economic times in the thirties, most people were not starving — but they were economizing. Magazines and radio shows ran features on how to cook on a budget. Dishes such as casseroles, soups and "creamed" anything over biscuits, were popular because they could be stretched to feed more people. Entertaining often took the form of ladies' luncheons or teas, where refreshments rather than full course dinners were served.

Laborsaving foods were introduced by the food industry, such as frozen foods, canned soup, pre-sliced bread, canned baby food, Jell-O, Bisquik, Macaroni and cheese packaged mix, canned tuna fish, and ready-made desserts such as Twinkies. Many candy bars made their debuts in the thirties.

Prohibition was repealed in 1933, giving the bar-restaurant a comeback. The Rainbow Room in New York City and the Pump Room in Chicago served a steak dinner for under a dollar and a scotch-and-soda for a quarter.

Rationing and shortages were the food facts most people remember about the war years of the early to mid forties. Sugar, coffee, canned goods, meat, butter and cheese were limited according to a complicated points system. Families were encouraged to grow "victory gardens" for their own fresh produce, even if they lived in the city. Home cooks were told it was their patriotic duty to "make do." Honey, corn syrup and molasses were used in place of sugar. Margarine was substituted for butter.

"Jeannie" has vivid memories of margarine. "Margarine was white and looked like a lump of lard," she shared. "It came with a yellow color capsule that you broke into it, to make it look like butter. It was one of my jobs to stir the yellow into the margarine. I hated this job because my older brother told me an elaborate and dirty story about that yellow capsule. He said that the margarine factories paid their workers to go to the bathroom in special jars, which they

filled the capsules from. It saved money, he said, and it was their patriotic duty to go to the bathroom to make margarine capsules. I was only seven, and my brother was ten, so I actually believed this ridiculous story. I believed it even when my mother told me he was lying. (He got in a lot of trouble for telling it, too.) Every time I had to stir in the color I felt sick to my stomach, and I certainly never ate any margarine. In fact, even today it makes me a little queasy."

After the war and throughout the fifties, people were tired of "making do." Interest in foreign and gourmet foods increased, with recipes for beef stroganoff, bouillabaisse, and crepes suzette becoming popular. Convenience foods were also popular in suburbia, along with television and modern appliances. In fact, the fifties is often called the "casserole decade" because so many recipes called for dishes made with canned soup. Outdoors in suburbia, the backyard barbecue became popular, as husbands donned big aprons and grilled hamburgers. Sales of outdoor cooking equipment skyrocketed to $30 million a year by the mid fifties.

Convenience foods included what we now call "fast foods." McDonalds, Burger King, Dairy Queen, and Shakey's Pizza all started their franchising in the fifties, eventually revolutionizing the way Americans eat.

Fashion

The Depression turned the fashion industry upside down, necessitating cutbacks in the way clothes were cut and purchased. Most families tried to economize and make clothes last longer. Dresses were short and hung straight, not full, which saved on material.

"Mae," who grew up in Iowa in the thirties, remembered the flour-sack dresses that she and her sisters wore. "I wasn't

ashamed of them," she wrote. "All the kids at my school were farm kids, and the girls all wore dresses made of flour sacks, gunny sacks, old curtains, you name it — whatever could be salvaged. Besides, my mother was a whiz with her beat-up old sewing machine. The clothes she made almost looked like they came from the store. I remember showing off her new creations and thinking I looked pretty darn good."

Style was important despite hard times. Men's suits sported padded shoulders and peaked lapels, creating an image of strength with broad shoulders and a wide chest. In women's clothes the popular look was genteel and ladylike, with sleek, tailored suits along with veiled hats and gloves. Two women designers in the thirties became famous for perfumes and other accoutrements as well as dress. Elsa Schiaparelli and Coco Chanel were fierce competitors. Schiaparelli designed the wide-shouldered suit look for Marlene Dietrich, copied all over Hollywood, and one of her practical ideas was the pioneering use of the zipper in women's dresses.

Uniforms and the patriotic look dominated fashion for both men and women during the war years of the early and mid forties. A high percentage of men were in the service, and there was less demand for men's clothing. Even civilian men wore clothes that mimicked the uniform look. One exception was the zoot suit which became popular in the early forties, although it had originated in the twenties and thirties with black and Hispanic youth.

For women too, simple economical styles were preferred, and looked upon as patriotic. Glitz and glamour were frowned upon as non-essential. Clothes had to be practical and give free movement, especially since many women were working in factories. Women's pants came into vogue. Hair was often hidden under turbans or scarves, originally to keep the hair out of the machinery, but which became a fashion statement of the time.

It wasn't just patriotism that called for simple, practical styles; it was a necessity because of rationing and shortages. Many fabrics were difficult, if not impossible, to get. Clothing coupons did not stretch far, and everyone was encouraged to "mend and make do." Darning was an essential home-making skill.

After the war, people were tired of austerity, hard times and restricted clothing. Good times were on their way back. In 1947 Christian Dior introduced his "New Look" clothing line, which featured longer, fuller skirts that used lavish amounts of fabric. This look became popular almost overnight, and dominated fashion throughout most of the fifties.

"Annie" remembered the New Look very well. "It seemed like hemlines dropped six inches overnight," she shared. "And because the new fashion was for longer and fuller, there was no way to alter the clothes you already had. You had to buy new ones. I remember a fur coat that my husband bought for me in 1942, just before he was shipped overseas. I made a vow I wouldn't wear it until he came home — it was like a good luck charm. After the war he was still stationed in post-war Europe, working with refugees, so he didn't come home until sometime in 1947. But by then my fur coat was totally out of style. It was so short it looked ridiculous with my new dresses, so I never got to wear it."

After the New Look, other fashions introduced in the late fifties included the Sack dress, which looked just like it sounds, and the Trapeze dress, a triangular concoction later shortened into the "baby doll" dress of the early sixties. Accessories of the fifties included stiletto heels, sometimes up to as much as 5 inches high; glittery spectacles with exaggerated corner wings, frosted lipsticks, pancake make-up, and bouffant hairdos.

Also in the fifties, a new fashion market emerged: teenagers. They were split into two basic groups, the greasers and the preppies. Greasers were influenced by film and rock stars such as James Dean, Marlon Brando and Elvis Presley, making denim jeans, black leather jackets, T-shirts as outerwear, and slicked-back hair fashionable for boys. The preppie style was neat and tidy: girls wore full circular skirts with appliqué (like poodles) over petticoats, knotted scarves around their necks, bobby sox and pony tails.

Another fashion sub-group of the fifties were the beatniks, precursors of the sixties' hippies, who favored long oversized cowl neck or turtle necked sweaters worn over close fitting slacks. All in black, of course.

Toys & Games

One of the most popular games of all time was about the world of big business, and introduced during the heart of the Depression: Monopoly. Other classic games introduced during these decades include Bingo in 1935, Scrabble in 1948, and Clue in 1949. Inspired by the post-war baby boom (all these kids have got to do something!) the fifties market was crammed with new toys, many of which are still selling well today: Silly Putty from 1949, Mr. Potato Head from 1952, Play Doh from 1955, the Frisbee and the Hula Hoop from 1958, and of course the most popular doll in history: Barbie, introduced by Mattel in 1959.

Sports

Baseball was *the* sport in America. These decades featured many of the greatest baseballers of all time, including Lou Gehrig, Casey Stengel, Joe DiMaggio, Ted Williams, Satchel Paige, Dizzy Dean, Stan Musial, Jackie Robinson, Leo Durocher, Mickey Mantle, Hank Aaron, Willie Mays, Sandy Koufax, and of course Babe Ruth.

"Al" still remembers his meeting with Babe Ruth,
although it was nearly seventy years ago. "I was only 8 years

*old, but I knew who Babe Ruth was," he shared. "He was
my father's hero, and Dad knew everything there was to
know about him. Instead of bedtime stories, my father would
tell me sagas of the Babe's best games and famous home runs.
So when we heard that Babe Ruth was visiting Honolulu,
where we lived, we were very excited. Of course we didn't
think we would actually see him, but it was an honor just to
have him visit our city. That day my dad went off to work,
and I had just left our house on my way to school, when a
car came down the street – and in the car was* Babe Ruth! *I
was so surprised my mouth fell open and I stopped dead,
almost in the middle of the street. The car had to slow down
to go around me, and Babe Ruth looked right at me. He
touched his forehead in a casual salute and said, "Hiya
kid," as they passed. It still ranks as one of the most
magical moments of my life."*

Other popular sports had their great stars. In basketball, Wilt
Chamberlain began his career in 1956, and the Boston Celtics, sporting
such stars as Bob Cousy, began their amazing dominance. In
football, the first bowl games began in 1935. In boxing, such names
as Primo Carnera, Max Baer, Max Schmelling, Jersey Joe Walcott,
Sugar Ray Robinson, Jake LaMotta, Rocky Marciano, Floyd
Patterson, Ingemar Johanson, and of course the great Joe Louis,
were known by all, even those who didn't follow the sport. Sonje
Henie and Dick Button popularized ice skating. Elizabeth Ryan,
Helen Wills Moody, and Althea Gibson put women's tennis in the
limelight. In track, Roger Bannister was the first to break the four-
minute mile, and Jesse Owens made all America proud in the 1936
Berlin Olympics on the eve of World War II. Some of the greatest
golfers of all time were at the height or beginnings of their careers,
such as Bobby Jones, Sam Snead, Ben Hogan, Babe Didrikson, and
Arnold Palmer. And in horseracing, famous names like Eddie Arcaro,
Whirlaway, Willie Shoemaker, and Seabiscuit were in the news.

"Stan" remembers the great race between Seabiscuit and War Admiral in November 1938. "I was working as a busboy in a busy Los Angeles restaurant," wrote Stan. "The owner, my boss, was a horse-racing fanatic — in fact he spent a lot more time at the track than he did at the restaurant. He was also a superstitious man who believed that cheering fans, even if they were only listening on the radio, could influence the way the race turned out. On the day of Seabiscuit's big race at Pimlico the boss closed the restaurant for the day and gave us all the day off — with the condition that we had to listen to the race and root for Seabiscuit. He had a lot of money riding on the race. The next day when we went back to work the boss was so happy (and rich) that he gave us all a $5 bonus!"

Take a look at the following and see what *you* remember …

1930-1959 Events Timeline
Lifestyle Activities

1930	Feb	First red & green traffic lights installed (in NY City)
1930	Mar	Congress appropriates $50,000 for Inter-American highway
1930	Mar	USS Constitution (Old Ironsides) becomes a national shrine
1930	Mar	Babe Ruth signs 2-year contract with Yankees for $160,000
1930	May	Babe Ruth hits 3 consecutive home runs
1930	Sep	Bobby Jones completes the Grand Slam of Golf
1930	Sep	Lou Gehrig ends errorless streak at 885 consecutive games
1930	Oct	First scheduled transcontinental air service begins
1930	Oct	Philadelphia A's beat St. Louis Cardinals in 27th World Series
1930	Dec	Tommy Armour wins 13th PGA Championship
1930		Coca Cola's slogan is "The pause that refreshes"
1930		Bird's Eye Frosted Foods introduced
1930		Bisquick introduced by General Mills
1930		The Good Humor bar comes out
1930		Jiffy Biscuit Mix is introduced
1930		Lime Jell-o introduced
1930		Snickers Bars go on the market
1930		Toll House cookies invented by Ruth Wakefield
1930		Twinkies go on sale
1930		Sliced Wonder Bread goes on the market
1930		The Good Humor Bar invented
1930		The Flashbulb introduced
1930		The first electric range offered for sale
1930		3M introduces Scotch Tape
1930		Phrase "Triple Crown" coined for the Kentucky Derby, the Preakness Stakes and the Belmont Stakes
1931	Feb	Maribel Vinson wins US Ladies Skating Championship
1931	Apr	Jackie Mitchell becomes first female in pro baseball
1931	Oct	George Washington Bridge connecting NY to NJ opens
1931		Alka-Seltzer goes on the market
1931		Beech-Nut introduces their baby food
1931		Cryst-O-Mint life savers go on the market
1931		Deyhdrated onion flakes offered for sale
1931		*The Joy of Cooking* published
1931		The Tootsie Pop introduced
1932	Jan	Eddie Arcaro wins his first race
1932	Feb	Sonja Henie wins 6th World Women's Figure Skating title
1932	Feb	Third Winter Olympics open in Lake Placid, New York
1932	Mar	Ford unveils the V-8 engine
1932	Jul	10th Summer Olympics opens in Los Angeles

1932	Jul	First class postage goes up to 3 cents
1932	Sep	NY Yankees win their 7th pennant
1932	Oct	Washington Redskins (Boston Braves) play first NFL game
1932		Hallmark Cards says "When you care enough to send the very best"
1932		3 Musketeers Bar introduced
1932		Jell-O Chocolate Pudding introduced
1932		Skippy Peanut Butter goes on the market
1932		Fritos go on the market
1932		US Route 66 opens from Chicago to Los Angeles
1932		Zippo Lighter introduced
1932		Glacier National Park established in Montana
1932		First exposure meter for cameras goes on the market
1932		College men wear wide legged pants called "Oxford Bags"
1932		Kellogg's ads say Rice Krispies go "Snap! Crackle! Pop!"
1933	Feb	First issue of Newsweek magazine published
1933	Mar	Mt. Rushmore dedicated
1933	May	Century of Progress Exposition opens in Chicago; fan dancer Sally Rand becomes national celebrity
1933	Apr	University Bridge in Seattle opens
1933	Apr	First airplane flight over Mt. Everest
1933	Jul	Works begins on the Oakland Bay Bridge
1933	Oct	NY Giants beat Washington Senators in 30th World Series
1933	Oct	Coit Tower dedicated in San Francisco
1933		Prohibition repealed, a scotch & soda mixed drink costs about 25 cents
1933		Elsa Schiaperelli puts zippers in women's dresses
1933		Ernesto & Julio Gallo Winery founded in Modesto, CA
1933		Ritz crackers introduced
1933		7-Up goes on the market
1933		Miracle Whip introduced
1933		Sloppy Joes invented
1933		V-8 juice introduced
1933		Waldorf Salad invented
1933		Esquire Magazine begins publication
1933		Claire Booth Luce becomes managing editor of Vanity Fair
1933		Racetrack betting becomes legal in California
1934	Jan	Babe Ruth signs 1934 contract for $35,000, a $17,000 cut
1934	Jan	Kennesaw Mountain Landis denies Joe Jackson's appeal for reinstatement
1934	Jan	First ski rope tow in US begins operation in Vermont
1934	Feb	Casey Stengel becomes manager of the Brooklyn Dodgers
1934	Mar	Primo Carnera wins heavyweight boxing title
1934	Mar	First Golf Masters Championship, won by Horton Smith

1934	May	TWA begins commercial service
1934	Jun	Great Smokey Mountains National Park is dedicated
1934	Jun	US Highway planning surveys are authorized
1934	Jun	Max Baer KO's Primo Carnera
1934	Sep	Babe Ruth's farewell Yankee appearance at Yankee Stadium
1934	Sep	Lou Gehrig plays in his 1500th consecutive game
1934	Sep	US Rainbow beats England's Endeavor in America's Cup
1934	Dec	NY Giants defeat Chicago Bears for NFL Championship
1934	Dec	First youth hostel in US opens, in Massachusetts
1934		The first Girl Scout cookie sale takes place
1935	Jan	First Sugar Bowl and Orange Bowl
1935	Feb	Monopoly goes on sale
1935	Apr	Gene Sarazen wins his 2nd Masters Tournament
1935	May	Griffith Planetarium in Los Angeles opens
1935	May	NFL adopts the annual college draft
1935	May	Babe Ruth hits his last 3 home runs
1935	May	Jesse Owens equals or breaks 6 world records in one hour
1935	Jun	Joe Louis defeats Primo Carnera at Yankee Stadium
1935	Jul	Helen Wills Moody wins her 7th Wimbledon championship
1935	Jul	Parking meter invented, and first installed in Oklahoma City
1935	Aug	Babe Ruth's final game at Fenway Park
1935	Sep	US wins Davis Cup for 7th straight year
1935		First Howard Johnsons opens, in Boston
1935		Wheaties become the "Breakfast of Champions"
1935		Bingo becomes popular
1935		Beer in cans go on sale
1935		Campbell's Soup introduces Chicken Noodle and Cream of Mushroom; their ads say they are "Mmm mmm good"
1935		Passing beam in devised for auto headlights
1936	Jan	First photo-finish camera installed, at Hialeah Race track
1936	Jan	First players elected to the Baseball Hall of Fame; Ty Cobb, Babe Ruth, Honus Wagner, Christy Mathews
1936	Feb	4th Winter Olympics open in Germany; Sonie Henie wins 3rd consecutive gold medals
1936	Feb	Volkswagens go into production
1936	May	First Air Hostess begins work
1936	May	RMS Queen Mary leaves Southampton for New York on maiden voyage
1936	May	Joe DiMaggio makes his major league debut
1936	Jul	Triborough Bridge opens in New York City
1936	Aug	Hitler opens the Berlin Olympic Games; Jesse Owens wins 4 gold medals
1936	Oct	NY Yankees beat NY Giants in 33rd World Series
1936	Nov	First issue of Life Magazine

1936	Dec	Su-Lin, imported giant panda from China, arrives in US
1936		Betty Crocker is advertising symbol for General Foods
1936		Dom Perignon champagne introduced
1936		The Mars Bar introduced
1936		The Waring Blender introduced
1936		The Dagwood Sandwich invented
1936		Tampax introduced
1936		Consumer Reports Magazine debuts
1936		Oakland Bay Bridge completed
1936		Fluorescent lighting introduced
1936		Eleanor Roosevelt begins writing column, "My Day"
1937	Mar	First permanent automobile license plates issued
1937	Jun	War Admiral wins Triple Crown
1937	Oct	NY Yankees win 34th World Series
1937	Dec	Lincoln Tunnel in NY City opens to traffic
1937	Dec	19 year old Ted Williams joins the Red Sox
1937		Look Magazine debuts
1937		Spam introduced
1937		Kraft Macaroni & Cheese introduced
1937		The A&P Supermarket chain begins
1937		The Good & Plenty Bar appears
1937		The Kit Kat Bar appears
1937		Kix cereal introduced
1937		Ragu Spaghetti Sauce introduced
1937		First issue of Women's Day appears
1937		First supermarket cart introduced, in Oklahoma City
1938	Jun	Marineland opens in Florida, nation's first aquarium
1938	Jun	Joe Louis KOs Max Schmelling in Yankee Stadium
1938	Jul	Herb Caen pens first column for San Francisco Chronicle
1938	Sep	Ocean liner Queen Elizabeth launched
1938	Oct	NY Yankees beat the Cubs in the 35th World Series
1938	Nov	40 million listeners hear Seabiscuit beat War Admiral
1938		Ladislaw and Georg Biro invent the ballpoint pen
1938		Nylon is patented. First product is the toothbrush
1938		Nestle introduces instant coffee
1938		Bumble Bee Tuna introduced
1938		Copper-bottomed Revere Ware introduced
1938		Cabins become pressurized in passenger airplanes
1938		Fiberglass developed
1939	Feb	Golden Gate Exposition opens in San Francisco
1939	Feb	Miler Glenn Cunningham says 4-minute mile impossible
1939	Mar	Glamour Magazine begins publication
1939	Mar	First NCAA Basketball Championship
1939	Apr	Boston Bruins beat Toronto Maple Leafs for Stanley Cup

1939	Apr	New York World's Fair opens
1939	Apr	Whitestone bridge connecting Bronx & Queens opens
1939	Jun	Baseball Hall of Fame opens in Cooperstown New York
1939	Oct	NY Yankees sweep the 36th World Series
1939	Oct	LaGuardia Airport opens in NY City
1939		Elsie, Borden's Cow, makes her debut
1939		Nestle creates the first chocolate chips
1940	May	Joe Louis KOs Johnny Paycheck and retains boxing title
1940	May	1940 Olympics cancelled because of war
1940	Oct	Pennsylvania Turnpike, first toll throughway, opens
1940	Dec	California's first freeway opens (Arroyo Seco Parkway)
1940		Power brakes become available for trucks
1940		A&P Supermarkets sell first cellophane-wrapped meat cuts
1940		The first Dairy Queen opens
1940		The first McDonalds opens, before Ray Kroc
1940		James Beard publishes his first cookbook
1941	May	First issue of Parade magazine goes on sale
1941	Jan	Joe Louis KOs Red Burman and retains title
1941	Feb	Joe Louis KOs Gus Dorazio and retains title
1941	Mar	First baseball player is drafted into the service
1941	June	Eddie Arcaro riding Whirlaway wins Triple Crown
1941	Jul	Joe DiMaggio's 56-game hitting streak finally ends
1941	Oct	NY Yankees win 38th World Series
1941		The first aerosol can is patented (it contains bug spray)
1941		Gourmet magazine premieres
1941		M&Ms introduced
1941		Cheerios introduced (called Cheerioats until 1946)
1941		General Electric puts the garbage Disposall on the market
1942	Jan	Joe Louis KOs Buddy Baer again and retains title
1942	Jan	FDR asks commissioner to continue baseball during WWII
1942	Feb	NY Yankees announce 5,000 uniformed soldiers will be admitted free at each upcoming game
1942	May	Sam Snead wins 25th PGA Championship
1942	Oct	Alaska Highway completed
1942	Dec	Massachusetts issues first US vehicle license plate tabs
1942		Magnetic recording tape is developed
1942		Dannon Yogurt offered for sale
1942		Kelloggs puts Raisin Bran on the market
1942		Corn dogs make their debut
1942		Rationing begins of sugar, coffee, canned goods, meat, fish, butter, cheese, shoes – on a complicated points system
1942		Millions of people plant Victory Gardens
1942		Polyester clothing introduced
1942		Metropolitan Life issues the first "ideal" weight tables

1943	Oct	New Chicago subway system opens
1943		First telephone answering machine is used, in Switzerland
1943		Zoot suits with pleats are fashionable
1943		The All American Girls Baseball League is founded
1944	Oct	St. Louis Browns win World Series
1944	Dec	Green Bay Packers win NFL championship
1944		First hi-fidelity recordings are released
1944		Chiquita Bananas release their memorable jingle
1945	Oct	Detroit Tigers win 42nd World Series
1945		Dr. Claus Maertens invents Doc Marten shoes
1945		First microwave oven patented in US
1945		Constant Comment tea first appears
1945		Junior Mints introduced
1945		Bumperstickers first appear
1945		Hairstyles such as the Tony Curtis, the Boston Box, and the flattop appear on teenage boys
1945		Frozen orange juice is offered
1946	Jun	Assault wins the Triple Crown
1946	Jun	First TV sports spectacular: Joe Louis vs. Billy Conn
1946	Aug	Ben Hogan wins PGA Championship
1946	Aug	St. Louis Cardinals win 43rd World Series
1946	Nov	First drive-up bank window established (in Chicago)
1946	Dec	US wins first Davis Cup since 1938
1946		First car with electric windows debuts
1946		Ektachrome color film introduced by Eastman Kodak
1946		Tide laundry soap introduced by Proctor & Gamble
1946		Tupperware introduced
1946		Mrs. Paul's frozen foods introduced
1946		Pepsi Cola's ads say "Pepsi Cola hits the spot"
1946		Toni Permanent ads ask "which twin has the Toni?"
1946		Pedal pushers and bobby sox are "in" with teenage girls
1947	Apr	Jimmy Demaret wins his 2nd Masters tournament
1947	May	Philadelphia wins the first NBA Championship
1947	Oct	NY Yankees win 44th World Series
1947	Nov	Man O'War dies
1947	Dec	Joe Louis beats Jersey Joe Walcott to retain title
1947		Christian Dior premieres his "New Look" – no wartime austerity, instead full skirts with lots of material
1947		Aluminum foil introduced by Reynolds
1947		The food processor introduced
1947		Kraft introduces cheese "singles"
1947		Polaroid camera introduced
1947		Epoxy glue is developed
1947		The tubeless tire is developed by Goodyear

1947		Almond Joy introduced by Peter Paul
1947		Everglades National Park in Florida is established
1947		Texaco ads proclaim "You can trust your car to the men who wear the star"
1948	Jan	Winter Olympic games open in St. Moritz, Switzerland; Dick Button becomes 1st world skating champion from US
1948	May	Baltimore wins NBA championship
1948	Jun	Eddie Arcaro becomes first jockey to win triple crown twice
1948	Jul	Satchel Page debuts in majors at age of 42
1948	Jul	Olympic games open in London; Fanny Blankers-Koen from Netherlands is first woman to win 3 gold medals
1948	Jul	Truman dedicates Idlewild Field (now Kennedy airport)
1948		Baskin-Robbins starts selling ice cream
1948		Long playing (LP) vinyl record is invented
1948		Scrabble is introduced
1948		DeBeers ads say "a diamond is forever"
1948		Panty-girdles become popular for women
1949	Feb	Joe DiMaggio is first baseball player to earn $100K a year
1949	Apr	Sam Snead wins Masters Golf tournament
1949	May	Minneapolis wins NBA championship
1949		Silly Putty, invented by accident, goes on sale
1949		RCA introduces the 45 rpm record
1949		The board game Clue debuts
1949		Sara Lee Cheesecake introduced
1949		The first Pillsbury Baking Contest takes place
1949		KitchenAid introduces the electric dishwasher
1949		Maidenform ads say "I dreamed I went shopping in my Maidenform bra"
1949		Hawaiian shirts and western wear become popular men's casual wear
1949		Brylcreem's ad say "a little dab'll do ya"
1950	Jan	Jackie Robinson signs highest contract in Dodger history
1959	Mar	Babe Didrikson-Zaharias wins 5th US Women's Open
1950	Jun	Minneapolis wins NBA championship
1950	Aug	Althea Gibson becomes first black competitor in tennis
1950	Aug	Sugar Ray Robinson KOs Jose Basora
1950	Oct	NY Yankees win 47th World Series
1950		Minute Rice introduced
1950		Betty Crocker's Picture Cook Book is a best seller
1950		Dunkin' Donuts opens
1950		Green Giant canned foods go on sale
1951	Feb	Sugar Ray Robinsons defeats Jake LaMotta
1951	Apr	Ben Hogan wins Masters golf tournament
1951	Apr	Boston Marathon won by survivor of Hiroshima

1951	May	Maritime Museum in San Francisco opens
1951	May	Mickey Mantle hits his first homerun
1951	Jul	Citation becomes first horse to win a million dollars in races
1951	Oct	Yankees beat Giants in World Series, and Joe DiMaggio plays his final game
1951	Oct	Rocky Marciano defeats Joe Louis
1951	Dec	Joe DiMaggio announces his retirement
1951		Chrysler Corporation introduces power steering
1951		Jet Magazine debuts
1951		Super Glue introduced
1951		Ore-Ida Foods begins
1951		Alka Seltzer introduces its spokesman, Speedy
1952	Apr	Sam Snead wins his 2nd Masters tournament
1952	May	Mad Magazine debuts
1952	May	TWA introduces tourist class
1952	May	Mr. Potato Head introduced
1952	Jun	Minneapolis wins NBA championship
1952	Jul	Olympic games opens in Helsinki, Finland
1952		No-cal Ginger Ale is first sugar-free soft drink
1952		The first Holiday Inn opens, in Tennessee
1952		Saran Wrap introduced
1952		Lipton introduces its onion soup mix
1952		Fish sticks go on sale
1952		Pez is first sold in the US
1952		Anacin claims "Fast, fast, fast relief"
1952		RV "Flagship" introduced, featuring onboard swimming pool and sundeck
1952		Tony the Tiger introduced for Sugar Frosted Flakes
1953	Apr	TV Guide publishes first issue
1953	May	Minneapolis wins NBA championship
1953	Aug	First sales tax appears (in California)
1953	Sep	Swanson sells its first "TV dinner" (for 98 cents)
1953	Jul	NY City transit begins using subway tokens
1953	Oct	NY Yankees win 50th World Series
1953	Dec	Willie Shoemaker wins 485 times in one year
1953		White Rose Redi-Tea is first instant ice tea mix
1953		Spike heels (stilettos) become popular
1953		Chevrolet introduces the Corvette
1953		Radial tires introduced
1953		Cheez Whiz offered for sale
1953		Jello Instant Pudding goes on sale
1953		Irish Coffee invented in San Francisco
1953		Peter Paul proclaims "sometimes you feel like a nut, sometimes you don't"

1953		The DA is popular hairstyle for teenage boys
1954	Apr	Hammerin' Hank Aaron hits the first of his 755 home runs
1954	May	Roger Bannister of Britain breaks the 4 minute mile
1954	May	Minneapolis wins NBA championship
1954	Aug	Sports Illustrated publishes its first issue
1954	Sep	Willie Mays makes his famous over-the-shoulder catch
1954	Nov	Iwo Jimo Memorial of servicemen raising US flag is dedicated in Arlington
1954		Fuel injected engines introduced by Mercedes Benz
1954		The first Burger King opens; burgers & milkshakes cost 18 cents each
1954		GE offers the first colored appliance
1954		Shakey's Pizza opens
1954		Ads claim M&Ms "melt in your mouth, not in your hands"
1954		Ads claim "Winston tastes good like a cigarette should"
1954		Hamms beer says it's from "the land of sky blue waters"
1955	Jan	Board game Scrabble debuts
1955	Jan	Sony makes the first transistor radio
1955	Apr	Ray Kroc starts McDonalds and hands out its first franchise
1955	Apr	Detroit Red Wings win Stanley Cup
1955	May	Rocky Marciano KOs Don Cockell
1955	May	Bob Sweikert wins Indy 500
1955	Jun	Mickey Mantle hits his 100th home run
1955	Jun	First automobile seat belt legislation enacted (in Illinois)
1955	Jun	Syracuse wins NBA championship
1955	Jul	Disneyland opens in rural Orange County, California
1955		A-line skirts introduced by Christian Dior
1955		Bermuda shorts introduced
1955		Kentucky Fried Chicken says it is "finger lickin good"
1955		Kenner Toys introduces Play-Doh
1955		First microwave oven marketed for home use
1955		The Marlboro Man makes his appearance
1955		Chevrolet sings "See the USA in your Chevrolet"
1955		A Timex watch "takes a licking and keeps on ticking"
1955		The ponytail is a popular hairdo for teenage girls
1956	Jan	"Dear Abby" column first appears in newspapers
1956	Jan	Olympic Winter games open in Cortino d'Ampezzo, Italy
1956	Jun	Philadelphia wins NBA championship
1956	Jul	Last Ringling Brothers Circus under a canvas tent
1956	Oct	Brooklyn ends its streetcar service
1956	Dec	Wilt Chamberlain plays first college game, scores 52 points
1956		Pampers disposable diapers introduced
1956		Comet Cleanser makes its debut
1956		Chex Mix invented

1956		Crest, first fluoride toothpaste, introduced
1956		Teflon Company introduces first non-stick cookware
1956		Sales of outdoor cooking equipment hit $30 million a year as barbequing becomes popular
1956		Pepsodent says "you'll wonder where the yellow went, when you brush your teeth with Pepsodent"
1956		Allstate Insurance says "you're in good hands with Allstate"
1956		Lever Brothers introduces Wisk, the first liquid detergent
1957	Jan	Wham-O produces the first Frisbee
1957	Apr	Jamestown Virginia celebrates its 350th anniversary
1957	Jun	Boston Celtics win NBA championship
1957	Jul	Mickey Mantle hits his 200th home run
1957	Sep	Ford Motor Co introduces the Edsel
1957	Oct	NY Yankees appear in their 26th World Series
1957		Portable electric typewriters introduced by Smith-Corona
1957		The Sack Dress becomes fashionable
1957		First sushi bar opens in America
1957		Pam vegetable cooking spray patented
1957		Margarine outsells butter for the first time
1957		Clairol first asks "does she or doesn't she?"
1957		Greyhound says "Take the bus and leave the driving to us"
1958	Feb	Jockey Eddie Arcaro rides his 4,000th winner
1958	Apr	Arnold Palmer wins his first major golf tournament
1958	May	St. Louis wins NBA championship
1958	Aug	First class postage goes to 4 cents (was 3 cents for 26 years)
1958		Yves St. Laurent comes out with his first fashion line
1958		BankAmericard& American Express issue first credit cards
1958		Wham-O introduces the Hula Hoop and sells 20 million in the first 6 months
1958		Sweet 'n' Low debuts
1958		Cocoa Puffs introduced by General Mills
1958		International House of Pancakes opens
1958		Rice a Roni introduced
1958		Crest ads say "Look Ma! No cavities!"
1959	Feb	Boston Celtic Bob Cousy sets NBA record with 28 assists
1959	Mar	San Francisco Giants rename stadium Candlestick Park
1959	Mar	Barbie goes on sale for first time
1959	Apr	Boston Celtics win 8th consecutive NBA championship
1959	May	Floyd Patterson KOs Brian London for heavyweight title
1959	Jun	Ingemar Johansson of Sweden defeats Floyd Patterson
1959		Haagen Dazs ice cream introduced
1959		Maxwell House says its coffee is "good to the last drop"
1959		Xerox introduces the plain paper copier

Sharing My Stories—Peas & Carrots

Peas and carrots! To this day, the thought of peas and carrots makes my blood pressure soar. Peas and carrots were a battleground in the war between my mother's taste and my own.

To my mother, raised poor during the Depression, buying canned vegetables was a mark of luxury. She could open a can, pour into a pan and just heat on the stove. What a miracle! No picking, washing, shelling, peeling, chopping, boiling, bottling or capping. No sweating in a hot kitchen on a summer afternoon. Just poof and abracadabra, your children are served a nourishing vegetable in a mere five minutes.

In 1959 no one cared about preservatives packed into those cans. No one cared, either, how awful they tasted. At least not my mother, because no matter how much my brother and I complained, canned vegetables appeared on the dinner table every night. Canned green beans that tasted like tin, canned corn that tasted like grit, canned beets that stained your teeth, canned spinach with the texture of slime, and my least favorite of all, canned peas and carrots.

The mushy, pillowy peas were bad enough, but the carrots – no words can describe their awful texture and worse taste. Even their shape was bad – uniform cubes that never came from a real carrot.

I hid peas and carrots underneath my mashed potatoes or inside. my napkin. I fed them to the dog (who refused to eat them.) I transferred them to my brother's plate and threatened him with torture if he complained. And finally, when she just would not stop serving those cubes and pillows of hell, I graduated to outright rebellion. I simply refused to eat them, no matter what. I made a principle out of canned peas and carrots, a principle I defended with 10-year-old fervor.

I even wrote a story about a girl who died rather than betray her right to her own taste. It was an affecting story; heavy on funeral details. The poor child lay nestled in a small pink coffin, surrounded by pink rosebuds. Beside the coffin sat her mother, weeping over her dead child, so sorry now that she had ruined her daughter's short life by making her eat canned peas and carrots.

1960 through 1989

Moving Around

"Baseball, hot dogs, apple pie and Chevrolet" ran one of television's hottest ads in the seventies. It points out a truism: the car is a symbol of American life. One of the most popular cars ever was introduced in the sixties: the Ford Mustang. Also increasingly popular in the sixties were foreign cars, such as the Volkswagen Beetle and the Volkswagen bus, which, with tie-dye curtains in the windows and psychedelic paint along the sides, became a symbol for the hippies of that era.

> *"The first car my husband and I bought after we were married in 1969 was an old VW bus," remembered "Gretchen." "We called it 'the Slug' because it couldn't go much faster than 20 if you went up a hill, even a mild incline, and on the freeway if you pushed it past 50 it started making this wierd gutteral whine. But it was great for camping and weekend jaunts. I made tie-dye curtains for the windows and a matching bedspread for the lumpy mattress. Once we even let a friend stay in our bus for a month, and he got along just fine, except after he left we found dozens of beer bottles and hundreds of roaches stashed under the seats.*
>
> *We drove the Slug for five years, all over the country, until one day it finally just up and died. The day before we sold it to the junk yard we gave a "Slug Wake" for all our friends to pay their last respects, which turned out to be one of the best parties I ever gave."*

The energy crisis of the seventies changed the way we drove: the speed limit on freeways was cut back to 55 to save gas, and gas rationing curtailed some activities. The energy crisis also increased interest in alternate modes of transportation, such as rapid transit and electric and solar powered vehicles. Amtrak began operation in 1971, and rapid transit systems began, such as San Francisco's BART in 1972. Honda began manufacturing cars in Ohio during the seventies, and they along with other Japanese manufacturers made vast inroads into the American market, causing headaches for American auto manufacturers. Lee Iacocca became one of the few businessman-superstars when he resurrected Chrysler from almost-certain bankruptcy in the late seventies. In the eighties cars sported mandatory seat belts, a new law in 1985, and some had car phones, symbolic of that image-conscious decade.

Air travel became easier and faster. The prototype of the Concorde was unveiled in 1967. In 1963 Boeing's 727 made its first flight, and in 1968 the 747 rolled off the production line. In response to terrorist hijackings, the seventies saw new laws such as mandatory luggage inspection. American Airlines introduced the first frequent flyer program in 1981.

New and popular vacation spots or attractions during the sixties included the Halakaila National Park in Hawaii, the Seattle Worlds Fair with its symbol the Space Needle, in 1962, Gateway Arch in St. Louis built in 1968, and the San Antonio Hemisfair in 1968. In 1964, ground was broken for the World Trade Center in New York, which opened to the public in 1974. Walt Disney world and EPCOT Center were announced in 1975. In the eighties, Tokyo Disney and Paris Disney opened. The Vietnam War Memorial in Washington DC was finished in 1984, which has proven to be one of that city's most powerful attractions. Finally, during these decades the word "RV" became a verb as well as a noun, as in "let's go rv-ing."

Advertising, Media & Consumerism

The consumer was a focus of these decades. The way we bought things changed by our increasing use of credit cards. BankAmericard was introduced in 1960 (it was changed to VISA in 1977), and Mastercharge in 1966. Consumer debt started to grow. Consumers were offered new places to buy things, such as K-Mart and Wal-

Mart, both of which opened their first stores in 1962. Bank ATMS were introduced in 1969, making it easier to get cash to buy things. Some consumer products introduced in the sixties were Nike sneakers, touch tone phones, cassette tapes, and waterbeds. The Truth in Packaging Law went into effect in 1966, intended to educate and protect consumers. Cigarette packages had to carry health warnings on their labels. Some famous slogans and jingles that you might remember from the sixties include "let Hertz put you in the driver's seat," matched by Avis' "we try harder"; "Please don't squeeze the Charmin"; and the Yellow Pages' "let your fingers do the walking."

The most important product introduced during the seventies was undoubtedly the personal computer. The Apple II was introduced in 1977, as was Radio Shack's TRS-80. Other new products included the VCR in 1976 and the Sony Walkman in 1979, and the country went through a CB radio craze, sparked by a country music hit. Famous companies formed included Fed X, which began in 1973, Blockbuster Video in 1976, and Home Depot in 1979. Changes in how we bought things included the introduction of child safety caps in 1970, and the use of barcodes in the supermarket, beginning in 1974. Cigarette advertising was banned from television beginning in 1971. Other advertising highlights included Coke's "it's the real thing" and 7-Up's "uncola"; McDonald's "You deserve a break today" and Burger King's "have it your way"; and Alka Seltzer's famous duo, "I can't believe I ate the whole thing" and "Plop plop fizz fizz oh what a relief it is."

IBM joined the computer frenzy in 1980, with its introduction of the IBM PC; by 1988 over three million had been sold. Other product introductions of the eighties include 3M's Post-it notes in 1980, the compact disk in 1983, color computers in 1983 (remember green on black?), the computer mouse in 1983, car phones in 1983 (the first cell phone prototype had been unveiled by Motorola in 1973), the Macintosh PC in 1984, and in 1985 Coca-Cola jettisoned its tried and true formula and introduced the New Coke. It was such a spectacular flop that only two months later they had to reintroduce Classic Coke. The Home Shopping Network debuted on cable TV in 1985, launching a whole new way to buy things. In

1987, the first anti-smoking ads appeared on TV, along with condom commercials specifically targeted at slowing the AIDS epidemic. Two advertising icons appeared, Spuds MacKenzie for Bud Light Beer in 1987 and the Energizer Bunny in 1989. Popular ad slogans and jingles included the US Army's "be all that you can be"; Wendy's "Where's the beef?"; and Nike's "just do it."

Food

French food was all the rage in the early 1960s, due to the French chef hired by Jackie Kennedy for the White House, and the popularity of Julia Child's cookbook and television show. Other foreign foods also became popular when they were introduced at Worlds Fairs in Seattle and New York, among others. Americans tasted Indian, Korean, Japanese, and African foods, and they not only ate them, they learned to make them. Other food trends in the sixties were the continuing popularity of fast and convenience foods. MacDonalds introduced its Big Mac in 1968, and Taco Bell opened its first franchise in the sixties. Perhaps coincidentally with America's increasing dependance on fast foods, we became more and more concerned with our weight. Fashion models like Twiggy made skinny fashionable, and products and programs were introduced to get us there. Jean Nideitch founded Weight Watchers in 1963. Diet colas such as Tab were introduced in the early sixties, and Nutra Sweet in 1965. In 1967 Irwin Stillman published his *Quick Weight Loss Diet*, combining both obsessions: weight loss and speed. The sixties also saw the beginning of the Health food movement, with its emphasis on natural foods, brown rice and other whole grains, vegetarianism, and yogurt.

This interest in natural foods continued in the seventies. One introduction during this decade was granola; it became possibly the most widely accepted health food. Another notable introduction in the seventies was the salad bar, also seen as a healthy alternative to heavy french food and greasy drive-in foods. Robert Atkins published his *Dr. Atkins Diet Revolution* in 1972. In 1971 Starbucks opened its doors in Seattle, Washington and lauched the coffee bar craze.

Probably the most popular food fad of the decade was quiche, and yes, even real men ate it.

"Trendy" was the word for food during the eighties. Trendy restaurants with celebrity chefs and food such as Wolfgang Puck's "designer pizza" were on offer. Exotic ingredients like sun-dried tomatoes, goat cheese, balsamic vinegar, carmelized onions, and roasted garlic were the rave. Regional cooking became popular, such as Paul Prudhomme's Cajun style "blackened" fish and meats. Image was important even for what went in your mouth.

Fashion

In the early sixties youth was in. Even the First Lady was young (such a contrast to Mamie Eisenhower!) and her fashion choices set styles — remember the pillbox hat? Women's fashion was characterized by pale lipstick, bouffant or beehive hairdos, and heavy eye makeup. In the mid sixties the youth theme was even more accented, symbolized by the popularity of model Twiggy, with her little-girl, almost androgenous figure, and mini-skirted baby doll dresses. Mini skirts were a popular fashion statement, with hemlines about six to seven inches above the knee. They were only made possible by the introduction of pantyhose, which heralded the death of stockings, garter belts and girdles. For men in the sixties, suits were tight fitting with narrow pants and a more "feminine" look. Men wore paisley shirts in bright colors, bell bottoms (sometimes velvet bell bottoms), and even puffy sleeves.

Hair was the most prominent statement of the hippie look which came in the late sixties. Long hair for men horrified people when it first became fashionable with the young, popularized by musicians such as the Beatles, even though when the Beatles first came to America their hair barely covered their ears. By the end of the decade, young men's hair often flowed down their backs, and they also sported beards and sideburns. The length of a man's hair often was a political or social statement, and certainly a symbol of rebellion. Hippie girls wore their hair long and straight (often ironed) and parted in the middle, and young African Americans of both sexes wore Afros, in which they flaunted with pride the curly hair their parents had tried to straighten. Other hippie fashion statements included denim jeans (torn), peasant skirts, beads, and tie-dye t-shirts. It was a very colorful decade.

Hot pants and go-go boots were the height of sexiness for women in the seventies, complementing the men's disco look popularized by John Travolta in *Saturday Night Fever* – polyester bell bottom pants, bright floral shirts with wide collars, and platform shoes. Long hair on men was more respectable, as were sideburns, and worn by many, not just hippies. Polyester leisure suits were another fashion statement for men of any age. For women, freedom had arrived in the form of de-regulated skirt lengths – they could choose mini, midi or maxi, and still be right in style. The unisex fashion appeared during this decade, as in women wearing men's suits like Diane Keaton in *Annie Hall*. Ethnic clothing and accessories such as macrame bags, Afghan fur coats, Chinese quilted jackets, caftans, kimonos, djellabas, muumuus – all were fashionable during this time. Jogging suits and sneakers for both sexes reflected the burgeoning interest in health and athleticism. The womens' hair statement of the decade was set by Farrah Fawcett from *Charlie's Angels*: a tousled, rough cut look which was touted as natural, but actually demanded a lot of work with tongs or rollers to get it to look right.

In the eighties, image was the thing. Designer logos sprouted everywhere, and wearing advertising on your lapels was chic. It proved you knew what the best brands were. Fashion setters for women included Madonna on one end of the spectrum and Princess Diana on the other, and for men the *Miami Vice* look of Don Johnson was super hot. The "power suit" was born during this decade, focused on the yuppies. *Dress for Success* by John Molloy was a best seller, and heeded by both men and women. The "new Romantic" look of the eighties both contrasted and complemented the sober business attire of power dressing by suggesting a woman could be both glamourous and powerful. Glitz and glamour in fabrics and jewelry, modeled after the popular TV show *Dynasty*, projected an image of affluence. At the other end of the fashion spectrum, teenagers were increasingly favoring the more punk look of body piercings and tattoos.

Toys & Games

Popular toys for children in the sixties included Barbie, introduced in 1959, and GI Joe, a doll for boys, introduced in 1964. The popularity of California surfing led to the introduction of the skateboard, launching a craze which still continues. Other popular toys were troll dolls, Nerf balls, and talking dolls such as "Chatty Cathy."

In the seventies and eighties toys can be defined as "crazes" which swept through the buying public, including Cabbage Patch dolls, My Little Pony, Hot Wheels, pet rocks, Muppets dolls from Sesame Street, Fisher Price toys, and legos. Board games introduced in the eighties were Trivial Pursuits and Pictionary. Atari released Pong in 1973, and the video game industry took off. The popularity of electronic games continued and increased in the eighties with offerings such as Pac Man and Nintendo games.

"When I asked my 9-year-old grandson what he wanted for his birthday in 1988, he gave me a list of Nintendo games," remembered "Thelma." "I didn't even know what a Nintendo was, so I asked him to tell me about it. When he got through explaining all the rules and characters — those Super Mario Brothers and Super Mushrooms and I don't know what all — I still didn't know what a Nintendo was. That was the first year I sent him a check instead."

Sports

Some of the greatest athletes of all time played their respective sports during these decades. Baseball was still the all-American game, and included such stars as Mickey Mantle, Roger Maris, Hank Aaron whose 715th home run broke Babe Ruth's record in 1974, Pete Rose, Sandy Koufax, Catfish Hunter, Reggie Jackson, Dave Concepcion,

Nolan Ryan, and many more. But baseball was not the only sport to capture public awareness. Football and basketball especially were hot. The first Super Bowl was held in 1967 between Green Bay and Kansas City. Famous football players included Joe Namath, Roger Staubach, Lynn Swan, and OJ Simpson, among others. In basketball, the 1960s were dominated by the Boston Celtics, who won eight consecutive NBA Championships. Great basketball players included Bill Russell, Elgin Baylor, Wilt Chamberlain, Rick Barry, Kareem Abdul-Jabbar, Julius Erving, Bill Walton, Larry Bird, Magic Johnson and Michael Jordan. In tennis, Billie Jean King, Chris Evert, Martina Navratilova, Arthur Ashe, Bjorn Borg and Jimmy Connors were some of the heroes of the game. In golf, Jack Nicklaus gained enormous popularity. Mark Spitz, Peggy Fleming, Dorothy Hamill, Scott Hamilton and Eric Heiden won Olympic medals and lasting fame. In sports that were just gaining some popularity in America, greats such as Pele in soccer and Wayne Gretzky and Gordie Howe in hockey were recognized names. Interest in hockey got a boost in 1980 when the US Olympic team beat the "unconquerable" Russians. Finally, one of the most celebrated athletes of all sport, Muhammad Ali, floated like a butterfly and stung like a bee, and entered world consciousness as an American icon. Known for not only his amazing athletic prowess, but also his flamboyant personality and controversial political stands, he remained a fixture in the public eye for all three decades.

One of the biggest changes in sports during these decades was the emphasis placed on competitive sports for women and girls. Girls could play softball, soccer or basketball in community leagues or on school teams. It wasn't just the traditional tomboys who turned out for these teams, either. Girls were not only accepted in competitive sports, but by the mid seventies, in some cases they were *expected* to choose a sport to compete in.

"Julia" shared her daughter's softball experience in the early 1980s. "My daughter played softball for nearly ten

years, from the age of six to sixteen," she remembered. "For the first three years she was a mediocre player whose favorite part of the game was sitting on the bench, gossiping and giggling with her friends. When she did play she played right field, where no one ever hit the ball. Going to her games was so boring I had to bring a book to read with me. At nine she wanted to quit and take dance lessons instead, but then she got put on a team with a great coach who saw something in her. Somehow he got her to believe that she could hit the ball, and of course when she believed it, she started to hit the ball. She hit it hard and straight and seldom struck out. Soon she was the best hitter on the team, and all the players on the other teams, especially the pitchers, were afraid of her. The next year the coach told her she could pitch, and of course she believed him. She became an awesome pitcher, with a mean fastball. By the time she was twelve everyone in the league knew her name. When I went to her games I usually came home hoarse from cheering so much. And it all came of just one person believing in her so she could believe in herself. What a lesson for both of us. That's what sports gives us, and I am so thankful that my daughter as well as my son could have the opportunity to learn it."

Take a look at the following and see what *you* remember ...

1960-1989 Events Timeline
Lifestyle Activities

1960	Jan	Pete Rozelle elected NFL commissioner
1960	Feb	Demolition begins on Brooklyn's Ebbets Field
1960	Feb	Winter Olympics open in Squaw Valley, California
1960	Apr	Arnold Palmer wins his 2nd Masters tournament
1960	May	Pancho Gonzalez retires from tennis
1960	Jun	Boston Celtics win NBA championship
1960	Aug	Summer Olympics open in Rome
1960	Sep	Cassius Clay wins Olympic Gold Medal
1960	Oct	Cassius Clay's first professional fight (he wins)
1960	Nov	Elgin Baylor of LA Lakers scores 71 points in one game
1960	Nov	Wilt Chamberlain gets 55 rebounds in a game, a new record
1960		Felt tipped pens go on the market
1960		Drinks first packaged in aluminum cans
1960		Crew cuts are popular haircut for men and boys
1960		Bouffant hairdos are popular hairdos for women
1960		Dominos Pizza opens in Detroit
1960		Sprite makes its debut
1961	Jan	Houston voters approve bond to build domed stadium
1961	Mar	Floyd Patterson KOs Ingemar Johansson
1961	Mar	Poppin Fresh Pillsbury Dough Boy introduced
1961	Apr	Gary Player is first non-American golfer to win the Masters
1961	Apr	ABC debuts *Wide World of Sports*
1961	May	Boston Celtics win NBA championship
1961	Jul	Haleakala National Park established in Hawaii
1961	Jul	First in-flight movie shown
1961	Sep	Mickey Mantle hits home run #400
1961	Oct	Roger Maris sets record of 61 home runs
1961	Dec	AP names Wilma Rudolph female athlete of the year
1961		Herman Taller publishes *Calories Don't Count*
1961		Charlie the Tuna becomes the spokesfish for Starkist Tuna
1961		*Mastering the Art of French Cooking* by Julia Child is published
1961		First electric toothbrush goes on the market
1961		IBM introduces the Selectric typewriter
1961		Coffee-mate non-dairy creamer introduced
1961		Green Giant introduces line of frozen vegetables
1961		Mrs. Butterworth syrup offered for sale
1961		Hertz ads say "Let Hertz put you in the driver's seat"
1962	Mar	K-Mart opens its doors
1962	Mar	Wilt Chamberlain scores 100 points in one game
1962	Apr	Seattle's Century 21 Exposition opens with Space Needle

1962	May	Boston Celtics win NBA championship
1962	Jul	Hank Aaron hits homerun #500
1962	Sep	Sonny Liston KOs Floyd Patterson for heavyweight title
1962		Kiwi fruit first imported to America
1962		Wal-Mart opens
1962		Dulles Airport, first airport designed for jets, opens
1962		Diet Rite Cola introduced
1962		Taco Bell opens
1962		Volkswagen ads say "think small"
1963	Jan	First discotheque opens, the Whiskey-a-go-go in LA
1963	Jan	First class postage goes to 5 cents
1963	Feb	First flight of a Boeing 727 jet
1963	Mar	Pete Rose debuts at his first spring training
1963	Apr	Jack Nicklaus wins his first Masters tournament
1963	Jun	Boston Celtics win NBA championship
1963	Jul	US Post Office institutes zip codes
1963	Aug	Evergreen Point Floating Bridge connecting Seattle and Bellevue, WA, opens
1963	Oct	LA Dodgers win 60th World Series
1963		Jean Nidetch starts Weight Watchers
1963		Julia Child makes her TV debut on *The French Chef*
1963		Touch tone telephones introduced
1963		Metal tennis rackets patented
1963		Cassette tapes introduced
1963		Chiquita first puts the blue sticker on bananas
1963		Kellogg's Pop Tarts introduced
1963		Fruit Loops go on sale
1963		The self-cleaning oven introduced
1963		Avis says "we try harder"
1964	Jan	Winter Olympics open in Innsbruck, Austria
1964	Feb	GI Joe debuts
1964	Feb	Baskin-Robbins introduces Beatle Nut ice cream
1964	Feb	Cassius Clay, who says he "floats like a butterfly, stings like a bee" TKOs Sonny Liston and wins heavyweight title
1964	Feb	Cassius Clay changes his name to Muhammad Ali
1964	Mar	First Ford Mustang is produced (base price of $2368)
1964	Apr	World's Fair in Flushing Meadow, NY, opens
1964	May	Boston Celtics win NBA championship
1964	Oct	Olympics open in Tokyo
1964		Tang is introduced to public as what the astronauts drink
1964		Topless bikini, or "monokini" introduced
1964		Charmin says "please don't squeeze the Charmin"
1964		Esso gasoline says it "puts a tiger in your tank"
1964		Yellow Pages ads say "let your fingers do the walking"

1964		Pepsi Cola ads talk about "the Pepsi Generation"
1964		Nike begins selling sneakers
1965	Jan	Quarterback Joe Namath signs with the New York jets
1965	Mar	TGI Fridays first restaurant opens, in New York City
1965	May	Spaghetti-Os first sold
1965	May	Boston Celtics win NBA championship
1965	Oct	LA Dodgers with Sandy Koufax win 62nd World Series
1965	Dec	Houston Astrodome opens
1965		Gatorade introduced
1965		Cool Whip introduced
1965		Mini skirts, go-go boots, and the "Mod" look fashionable
1965		Skateboards introduced
1965		Nutra-sweet introduced
1965		Men's hair starts getting longer in youthful circles
1966	Jan	All US cigarette packages must carry health caution warning
1966	Mar	Scott Paper begins selling paper dresses for $1
1966	Apr	Pan Am buys 25 Boeing 747s for $525,000,000
1966	May	Boston Celtics win 8th consecutive NBA championship
1966	Jul	Billie Jean King wins her first Wimbledon singles title
1966		Robert Mondavi Winery is founded
1966		Bill Russell becomes first black coach in NBA
1966		MasterCharge debuts
1966		Congress passes "truth in packaging" law requiring manufacturer to list ingredients on the package
1967	Jan	First Super Bowl held; Green Bay wins over Kansas City
1967	Apr	First Boeing 737 rolls out
1967	Apr	Muhammad Ali refuses induction into army & is stripped of boxing title
1967	May	Philadelphia wins NBA championship
1967	Dec	SST prototype "Concorde" first shown in France
1967		Irwin Stillman publishes his *Quick Weight Loss Diet*
1967		*Rolling Stone* magazine begins, first specialty magazines
1967		*New York Magazine* debuts, herald of new popularity of regional magazines
1967		English model Twiggy shows the emaciated look
1967		Day-glo paint debuts
1967		Long hair for men is a political statement as well as fashion
1967		Women's hair is fashionable worn long and straight
1967		Baked beans ads say "Beanz means Heinz"
1967		L'Oreal ads say "Because I'm worth it"
1968	Feb	Winter Olympics open in Grenoble, France; Peggy Fleming wins figure skating gold medal
1968	Feb	First 911 Phone system goes into service (Alabama)
1968	Apr	HemisFair 1968 opens in San Antonio, Texas

1968	May	Boston Celtics win NBA Championship
1968	May	Jim Catfish Hunter pitches perfect game
1968	May	Gateway Arch in St. Louis is dedicated
1968	Sep	First US Tennis Open; Arthur Ashe wins
1968	Sep	First Boeing 747 rolls out
1968	Oct	Olympic games in Mexico City, Tommie Smith & John Carlos give "black power" salute during US anthem
1968		Waterbeds introduced
1968		Jacuzzis introduced
1968		Nehru jackets are in style
1968		MacDonald introduces the Big Mac
1968		Beards and mustaches join long hair as fashionable for young men
1968		The Afro is popular hairdo for blacks of both sexes
1968		Wisk detergent ads talk about "ring around the collar"
1969	Jan	Concorde jetliner makes first test flight
1969	Feb	Last issue of *Saturday Evening Post* published
1969	Feb	World's largest airplane, Boeing 747, makes first flight
1969	May	Ocean liner Queen Elizabeth II maiden voyage
1969	May	Boston Celtics win NBA championship
1969	Oct	Government bans use of cyclamates artificial sweeteners
1969	Oct	Ralph Nader sets up consumer organization known as Nader's Raiders
1969	Nov	Pele scores his 1000th soccer goal
1969		Dave Thomas opens first Wendy's (in Ohio)
1969		Pringles Potato chips introduced, first to come out of a can
1969		Sugarless gum is introduced
1969		Whirlpool introduces the trash compactor
1969		Penthouse Magazine begins publication
1969		First ATM machines introduced (Chemical Bank in NY)
1969		The Gap opens in San Francisco
1970	Mar	USSR wins 8th straight world hockey championship
1970	May	New York wins NBA championship
1970	Sep	IBM announces System 370 computer
1970		Hamburger Helper introduced
1970		Orville Redenbacher introduces Gourmet Popping Corn
1970		NY City holds its first marathon
1970		Midi length coats, dresses and skirts come into fashion
1970		Medicine bottles adopt child-safety caps
1970		Coca Cola says "it's the real thing"
1970		FDA recalls canned tuna because of possible mercury
1970		IBM introduces the floppy disk
1971	Jan	Cigarette ads are banned from TV
1971	Mar	Joe Frazier beats Muhammad Ali for boxing title

1971	May	Amtrak begins operation
1971	May	Milwaukee wins NBA championship
1971	Oct	Walt Disney World in Orlando Florida opens
1971	Oct	Billie Jean King is first female athlete to win $100,000
1971		*How to Keep Slim, Healthy & Young by Juice Fasting* published
1971		*How to Be Your Own Best Friend* published
1971		The first Starbucks opens in Seattle, Washington
1971		*Look* Magazine folds after 34 years
1971		Bounty paper towels are "the quicker picker upper"
1971		McDonalds says "you deserve a break today"
1972	Jan	LA Lakers win 33rd consecutive game (NBA record)
1972	Jan	Dallas Cowboys with Roger Staubach win Super Bowl VI
1972	Feb	Olympic Winter games open in Sapporo, Japan
1972	Feb	Airlines begin inspection of passengers and baggage
1972	Mar	Kareem Abdul Jabbar named MVP of NBA
1972	Mar	Wilt Chamberlain plays his last pro basketball game
1972	May	LA Lakers win NBA championship
1972	Jul	*Ms Magazine* begins
1972	Jul	Billie Jean King beats Evonne Goolagong at Wimbledon
1972	Aug	Summer Olympics open in Munich, West Germany
1972	Sep	Mark Spitz is first athlete to win seven Olympic gold medals
1972	Sep	BART begins service from Oakland to Fremont, CA
1972	Sep	Bobby Fisher defeats Boris Spassky for world chess title
1972	Oct	Guided tours of Alcatraz by US Park Service begin
1972	Nov	Construction begins on the Kingdome in Seattle
1972	Dec	*Life Magazine* ceases publication
1972	Dec	Roberto Clemente dies in plane crash at age of 38
1972		*Dr. Atkins Diet Revolution* by Robert Atkins is published
1972		Snapple is introduced
1972		Jogging and warm-up suits become popular
1972		McDonalds premieres the Egg McMuffin
1972		Top Ramen introduced
1972		Life Cereal ads say "Hey Mikey!"
1973	Jan	Miami Dolphins win Super Bowl VII
1973	Feb	Triple crown winner Secretariat bought for $5.7 million
1973	Mar	Ken Norton defeats Muhammad Ali
1973	May	New York wins NBA championship
1973	Jun	Little League's "no girls" rule challenged in lawsuit
1973	Jul	Billie Jean King beats Chris Evert at Wimbledon
1973	Sep	Billie Jean King beats Bobby Riggs in battle-of-the-sexes
1973	Sep	Concorde flies WA DC to Paris in 3 hours 33 minutes
1973	Dec	Pirates of the Caribbean ride opens at Disneyland
1973	Dec	OJ Simpson becomes first to rush 2000 yards in a season
1973		Borden retires Elsie the Cow

Sharing my Stories—The Politics of Fashion

In 1968 I was 19 and attending the University of Washington, a West Coast hotbed of politics, drugs and long-haired hippies. I fit in. I wore my hair long, straight and parted in the middle. Sometimes I wore it in braids, adding a headband with a feather hanging down over my ear. I wore long silver dangling earrings and no make-up.

In rebellion against my mother's ideals of being a "lady," I threw away all my dresses and skirts, except for one long peasant skirt that went well with my peasant sandals. The rest of my wardrobe consisted of jeans, a leather jacket, a cable knit sweater that I fondly believed made me look like an Irish rebel, and a severe black turtleneck which I thought made me look serious – there was a war on, you know. To pamper my femininity I had several low-cut tank tops that I wore without a bra.

My mother viewed my appearance with characteristic worry. If I wore my black turtleneck, she worried that I looked "unfeminine" and hoped I wasn't one of those opinionated girls who never got a boyfriend. When I wore a tank top with my breasts popping out, she said I looked "too feminine" – which meant she thought I looked like a slut.

My father didn't seem to care what I wore, only what my grades were. But I wasn't aware that the tempestuous sixties, with their excess and noise, politics and drugs, scared the pants off any parent who had a child in college. I didn't understand my father's unease with my lifestyle until I completed my fashion statement by throwing away my contact lenses and buying a pair of John Lennon-type wire-rimmed glasses.

I wore them home one Sunday and my father erupted. "You are wearing a symbol of the element that is destroying the only country I know and love!" he yelled at the top of his voice. "I! Will! Not! Have! It!" He stormed out of the house, slamming the door behind him. We heard his car door bang and the roar of the engine. He called about an hour later with an ultimatum: I could only come home if I wore a dress and "normal" glasses or contacts. Otherwise he was cutting me off.

What could I do? He paid my tuition and my living expenses. I went on a tight-lipped shopping expedition and bought the ugliest dress I could find, dark blue with yellow dots, and a pair of brown horn-rimmed glasses.

I kept this outfit — with a bra — in a box in a dark corner of my closet. I only wore it when I went home, and for the next year my family never saw me wearing anything else. I referred to it as "Dad's Revenge."

1973		Stove Top Stuffing introduced
1973		Cuisinart food processor introduced
1973		Universal Product Codes first appear on grocery products
1973		Supermarket bar codes introduced
1973		Univ. of Miami first to offer athletic scholarships to women
1973		Burger King says you can "have it your way"
1973		Merrill Lynch says it is "bullish on America"
1973		7-Up says it is the "uncola"
1973		Federal Express begins
1973		Motorola introduces the prototype for first cellular phone
1974	Jan	Maximum speed limit lowered to 55 MPH to conserve gas
1974	Jan	Miami wins Super Bowl VIII
1974	Feb	*People Magazine* begins
1974	Mar	First class postage raised from 8 cents to 10 cents
1974	Apr	World's then-tallest building, World Trade Center, opens
1974	Apr	Hank Aaron hits 715th home run, breaks Babe Ruth's record
1974	May	Boston Celtics win NBA championship
1974	Jun	NFL grants franchise to Seattle Seahawks
1974		Miller introduces the first light beer and says it "tastes great, less filling"
1974		Calculators become affordable
1974		Pop-top clothing debuts
1974		"Streaking" or going nude in public, becomes a craze
1974		The first retail barcode scanner goes into operation
1975	Jan	Chrysler Corporation offers first car rebates
1975	Jan	Pittsburgh Steelers win Super Bowl IX
1975	Jan	Space Mountain ride opens in Disneyland
1975	May	Golden State Warriors win NBA championship
1975	Jul	Arthur Ashe wins men's single championship at Wimbledon
1975	Jul	Plans announced for EPCOT Center in Florida
1975		David Reuben publishes the *Save Your Life Diet*
1975		Catalytic converters installed into cars
1975		American Express says "don't leave home without it"
1975		The BMW says it is "the ultimate driving machine"
1975		Jell-O ads feature Bill Cosby and kids
1975		The leisure suit makes its fashion debut
1976	Jan	Dorothy Hamill wins 3rd ntl figure skating championship
1976	Jan	Pittsburgh Steelers win Super Bowl X
1976	Feb	Winter Olympics opens in Innsbruck, Austria
1976	May	Boston Celtics win NBA championship
1976	Nov	Rick Barry ends his then-longest free-throw streak of 60
1976	Nov	Free agent Reggie Jackson signs contract with NY Yankees
1976		Dorothy Hamill's "wedge" and Farrah Fawcett's "wings" are popular hairdos for women

1976		CB Radio craze launched by CW McCall's hit single *Convoy*
1976		Call waiting becomes available
1976		The VCR debuts on the market
1976		Alka Seltzer ads sing "plop plop fizz fizz oh what a relief it is" and say "I can't believe I ate the whole thing"
1977	Jan	Oakland Raiders win Super Bowl XI
1977	Feb	Sugar Ray Leonard wins his first professional fight
1977	Mar	Bank of America adopts name VISA for their credit cards
1977	Apr	NY's famed disco Studio 54 opens
1977	May	Janet Guthrie becomes first woman to drive in Indy 500
1977	May	Muhammad Ali beats Alfredo Evangelista for boxing title
1977	Jun	The first personal computer, the Apple II, goes on sale
1977	Jun	Portland Trailblazers win NBA championship
1977	Jun	The Main Street Electrical Parade premieres at Disneyland
1977	Jun	Seattle Slew wins the Triple Crown
1977	Jul	Bjorn Borg wins Wimbledon singles championship
1977	Aug	Radio Shack introduces the TRS-80 computer
1977	Oct	Brazilian soccer star Pele retires
1977		Blush wines are introduced
1977		The first Mrs. Fields cookie shop opens, in California
1977		Clogs are popular shoewear for men and women
1977		Movie *Annie Hall* makes menswear popular for women
1977		Generic products offered, cheaper than brand names
1977		Yoplait Yogurt introduced
1978	Jan	Dallas Cowboys win Super Box XII
1978	Feb	Leon Spinks beats Muhammad Ali for heavyweight title
1978	Jun	Washington Bullets win NBA championship
1978	Jul	Lee Iacocca fired as president of Ford Motor Co.
1978	Dec	Pres. Carter more than doubles national park system size
1978	Dec	Susan B Anthony dollar is issued
1978		Ben & Jerry's begins, in Vermont
1978		Herman Tarnower publishes *The Scarsdale Medical Diet*
1978		The jogging craze begins
1979	Jan	Pittsburgh Steelers win Super Bowl XIII
1979	Jun	Seattle Sonics win NBA championship
1979		Paul Prudhomme opens K-Pauls restaurant in New Orleans
1979		Nathan Pritikin publishes the *Pritikin Program*
1979		Sony introduces the walkman
1979		Trivial Pursuits debuts on the market
1979		AT&T says "reach out and touch someone"
1979		The first Home Depot opens, in Atlanta Georgia
1980	Jan	Pittsburgh Steelers win Super Bowl XIV
1980	Jan	PGA begins its Seniors Tour
1980	Feb	Joanne Carner wins LPGA Gold Championship

1980	Feb	Gordie Howe becomes first player to score 800 career goals
1980	Feb	Olympics Winter games opens in Lake Placid, NY; USA beats USSR for gold medal in hockey; Eric Heiden wins all 5 speed skating gold medals
1980	Apr	Wayne Gretzky breaks Bobby Orr's assist record
1980	Apr	Seve Ballesteros becomes youngest winner of the Masters
1980	May	LA Lakers win NBA championship
1980	May	Larry Bird is NBA Rookie of the Year, over Magic Johnson
1980	Jun	Ted Turner's Cable News Network begins broadcasting
1980	Jun	ESPN begins televising college world series games
1980	Jun	Bjorn Borg beats John McEnroe at Wimbledon
1980	Jun	John McEnroe beats Bjorn Borg at US Open
1980	Jul	Johnny Bench hits 314th home run
1980	Aug	Jack Nicklaus wins PGA championship for 5th time
1980	Oct	Larry Holmes beats Muhammad Ali to retain title
1980	Oct	First consumer use of home banking by computer
1980	Nov	Calvin Klein's jeans ad featuring Brooke Shields banned
1980		3M introduces the Post-it note
1980		Rollerblades introduced
1980		Preppy clothing comes into fashion
1981	Jan	Richard Nixon Museum at San Clemente, CA opens
1981	Jan	Oakland Raiders win Super Box XV
1981	Mar	Torvill & Dean win World Ice Dance championship
1981	May	Boston Celtics win NBA Championship
1981	May	Bobby Unser wins then loses then wins Indy 500
1981	Jun	John McEnroe misbehaves at Wimbledon
1981	Jul	Major league baseball strike ends after 42 days
1981	Aug	Pete Rose tops Stan Musial's record of 3,630 hits
1981	Aug	IBM introduces the PC
1981	Nov	Anatoly Karpov retains World Chess championship
1981	Dec	Muhammad Ali's last fight
1981		Pac Man video game is introduced
1981		Aspartame approved by FDA
1981		Stouffer's Lean Cuisine introduced
1981		Lays Potato Chips challenges "betcha can't eat just one"
1981		The US Army says "be all that you can be"
1981		American Airlines introduces first frequent flyer program
1982	Jan	Hank Aaron elected to Hall of Fame
1982	Jan	San Francisco 49ers win Super Bowl VXI
1982	Feb	Joanne Carner wins LPGA Elizabeth Arden Golf Classic
1982	Apr	Alberto Salazar wins Boston Marathon
1982	May	LA Lakers win NBA championship
1982	May	Worlds Fair in Knoxville, TN opens
1982	Jul	Martino Navratilova wins at Wimbledon

1982	Aug	Greg Louganis becomes first diver to score 700 in 11 dives
1982	Oct	EPCOT Center opens in Orlando, Florida
1982	Nov	Vietnam War Memorial dedicated in Washington DC
1982		*USA Today* begins publication
1982		Honda begins making cars in Ohio
1982		Diet Coke introduced
1982		Wolfgang Puck opens Spago, introduces "designer pizza"
1982		Paul Newman founds Newman's Own
1983	Jan	Washington Redskins win Super Bowl XVII
1983	Mar	Compact Disc recordings introduced by Phillips & Sony
1983	Apr	Nolan Ryan strikes out his 3,500th batter
1983	May	Philadelphia 76ers sweep NBA championship
1983	Aug	Edwin Moses sets 400m hurdle record
1983		Cabbage Patch dolls are hot
1983		Apple Computer introduces the mouse
1983		Movie *Flashdance* makes cutoff sweatshirts fashionable
1983		Cellular phones for cars go on the market; they sell for $3,000 plus $150 a month service fee
1983		Nutrasweet introduced
1984	Jan	Clara Peller for Wendy's asks "Where's the beef?"
1984	Jan	US Figure Skating championships won by Rosalynn Summers and Scott Hamilton
1984	Jan	LA Raiders win Super Bowl XVIII
1984	Jan	Apple Computer introduces the Macintosh PC
1984	Feb	Olympics Winter games open in Sarajevo, Yugoslavia
1984	Feb	Bill Johnson first American to win downhill skiing gold
1984	Mar	Part of Central Park is named Strawberry Fields in honor of John Lennon
1984	May	World of Rivers Exposition opens in New Orleans
1984	Jun	Boston Celtics win NBA championship
1984	Jul	John McEnroe beats Jimmy Conners at Wimbledon
1984	Aug	Olympic Summer games opens in Los Angeles; Carl Lewis wins 4 gold medals, Japan wins gold medal in basketball
1984	Aug	Lee Trevino wins PGA tournament
1984		Stonewashed jeans are popular
1984		Don Johnson and Philip Michael Thomas of *Miami Vice* make fashion statements for men
1984		Leg warmers become popular women's athletic wear
1984		Frozen tofu, "tofutti" becomes a food fad
1984		Madonna makes underwear, outerwear
1984		Hidden Valley introduces ranch dressing
1985	Jan	First mandatory seat belt law goes into effect
1985	Jan	VH-1 makes broadcasting debut
1985	Jan	San Francisco 49ers win Super Bowl XIX

1985	Feb	Brian Boitano wins US male Figure Skating championship
1985	Mar	Mike Tyson KOs Hector Mercedes in his first pro fight
1985	Apr	New Coke debuts
1985	May	Michael Jordan named NBA Rookie of the Year
1985	Jun	LA Lakers win NBA championship
1985	Jun	Coca Cola announces they will bring back their old formula
1985	Sep	200-millionth guest comes to Walt Disney World
1985	Nov	Gary Kasparov wins World Chess Championship
1985		Home Shopping Network debuts on TV
1985		Nintendo video games debut
1985		Bomber jackets are popular men's attire
1986	Jan	Chicago Bears win Super Bowl XX
1986	May	Reggie Jackson hits 537th home run, passing Mickey Mantle
1986	May	Boston Celtics win NBA championship
1986	Aug	Jackie Joyner-Kersee sets record for heptathlon
1986	Oct	IOC decides to stagger Winter & Summer Olympics
1986		Singer Company stops making sewing machines
1986		The punk rock look of chains and safety pins are popular with teenagers
1987	Jan	Jack Sikma begins NBA free throw streak of 51 games
1987	Jan	New York Giants win Super Bowl XXI
1987	Feb	Anti-smoking ad airs for first time on TV
1987	Apr	Julius Erving is third NBA player to score 30,000 points
1987	Jun	LA Lakers win NBA championship
1987	Sep	Walter Payton scores NFL record 107th rushing touchdown
1987	Dec	Steve Largent sets record, catches 752nd pass
1987		Condom commercials are allowed on TV
1987		Soy milk introduced
1987		Spuds MacKenzie, spokesdog for Bud Light Beer, debuts
1988	Feb	Olympics Winter games opens in Calgary, Canada; Brian Boitano wins gold for figure skating, Bonnie Blair wins gold in speed skating, Alberto Tomba wins golds for downhill
1988	May	LA Lakers win NBA championsip
1988	Jul	Steffi Graf beats Martina Navratilova at Wimbledon
1988	Aug	Jose Canseco is 11th to hit 30 home runs and steal 30 bases
1988	Sep	IBM announces shipment of 3-millionth PS/2 PC
1988		Nike says "just do it"
1989	Jan	San Francisco 49ers win Super Bowl XXIII
1989	Jan	Michael Jordan scores his 10,000th NBA point
1989	May	Detroit wins NBA championship
1989	Nov	SAS bans smoking on many flights
1989		Los Angeles Herald Examiner folds after 86 years
1989		The Energizer Bunny makes his debut

Writing Topic Suggestions
Lifestyle Activities

Pick one of the topics below and write for fifteen to twenty minutes. Remember the rules:

- Don't stop writing until the limit is up.
- Use "trigger sentences" if you get stuck.
- Don't be polite.
- Be specific and remember you have at least five senses.
- You don't have to be right, rational or logical.
- Forget about the rules of grammar or spelling.
- Trust yourself.

Remember, you are creating a *primary source*. Write about what you *did,* what you *saw,* what you *thought,* what you *felt.*

1. Scan the events timelines. Is there something that sparks a memory and makes you think, "oh yeah, I remember that!" If so, write about it. What did this event mean to you? Did it change your life in some way? Did you participate or contribute to this theme/event? How?

2. Describe your first car. What make was it? What color, what year? Where did you buy it? How much did it cost? How did you learn to drive? How long did you have this car? What places did you drive to? Across country? To work and back? To pick up your girlfriend(s)? Drive-in movies, or fast-food joints? How did you feel about your car? Were you proud or ashamed of it? Did your car help your self image?

3. Did you work in the automobile or a related industry? If so, what was your job? How did your work affect or enhance cars? Are

or were you a car fanatic, or someone fascinated by the mystique of cars? Or were you related to a car fanatic? Why do cars interest you? What is the best car you ever owned? What made it special?

4. Pick a city you lived in. What changes to the transportation system, such as bridges, tunnels, roads, dams, freeways, transit systems, parking lots, etc., were built during the time you lived there? How did the city change? Did it grow or shrink? How did the traffic patterns change? Did you contribute to the construction or building of new roads, bridges or tunnels? Did you work in construction or a related field, did you vote on levies or bond issues, did you sell land to the city? Describe how new transportation systems changed your life or the lives of others in the city.

5. Where did you go on vacations? Who did you go with — your parents, your children? Did you have special "adult" vacations, or were vacations a family thing? How did you get there – drive, fly, by train or bus? Did you go on Sunday drives, and if so, where did you drive to? Who drove? Did you play car games, and if so, which ones? Did you go camping, or participate in the RV craze? What was the best camping trip you ever went on, and what made it special? Did you go to State Fairs, International Expos, Arts Festivals? Did you go to Disneyland? Zoos? Did you visit national shrines such as Mt. Rushmore, Old Ironsides, the Alamo, the Vietnam War Memorial? Did you go to museums or science exhibitions such as planetariums and aquariums? What did visiting these places mean to you, or your parents, or your children? Did they inspire you to greater learning or new careers? Did they give you a sense of history or patriotism, or a feeling of family togetherness?

6. Describe a favorite dress or outfit you wore as a child, teenager or adult. What color was it, what material? Why was it your favorite? Where did you wear this outfit? Did you wear it all the time, or on special occasions only? What adjectives describe you when you wore this outfit – cool, elegant, sexy, tough? Or write about a hairstyle you remember. Did you wear a beehive? An Afro? If you are

a woman, did you wear your hair like Shirley Temple, Bette Davis, Farrah Fawcett, Princess Di, Dorothy Hamill? If you are a man, did you wear your hair long in the 60s and 70s? Was hair a big deal? Did you wear a beard or mustache? Or write about fad fashions, such as the poodle skirt, bobby sox, bell bottoms, tie dye t-shirts, designer logos – what was "cool" for your circle? Who were your fashion heroes? Movie stars, popular kids in school, people famous for their fashion flair, such as Jackie Kennedy or Princess Diana? Did you, or your mother, make your clothes, or were they store bought? What brands of clothing were popular when you were a teenager? Did you work in a fashion related industry, as a seamstress, tailor, model, designer, or salesperson? How did you affect fashion?

7. What were your favorite toys when you were a child? Did you play with dolls? What kind – Barbie? Cabbage Patch? GI Joe? Did you play cowboys and Indians, or detective, or nurse? Did you play games such as Monopoly or card games in your family? Who did you play with? What was the toy everybody had to have when you were a child? Or did you play outdoors and make your own toys? If you are a parent, what toys did you buy your children? What were their favorites? Did they play video games such as Pong or Nintendo? How had toys changed from your childhood to theirs? Were you indulgent with your children regarding toys? What effects do you think the toys you played with had on you, or your children?

8. What is your favorite sport? Did you play this sport as a child, teenager or adult? Did you play sports for your high school or college? Are or were you a good athlete? How important was athletics to you, or your family? Did you coach a team, and if so, what team? Were you a cheerleader? Did you or any member of your family make your living in the sports world? If so, what did you do, and how did you affect sports? Did you have sports heroes? Who were they? What was special about them? Did you aspire to compete in the Olympics? Did Olympic athletes inspire you? If so, which ones? Did you attend spectator sports, read the sports news? Do you have memories of a special game you saw, or a special person

you saw play, such as Babe Ruth, Joe DiMaggio, Wilt Chamberlain, Arnold Palmer, OJ Simpson, Pete Rose, Joe Namath, Muhammad Ali? Did you attend a World Series game, an NBA Championship game, a Super Bowl, or the Olympic Games? Write about the best sporting event you ever attended.

9. If you cooked for your family, which recipes were your favorites? Did you appreciate and use new "labor saving" gadgets and appliances, such as dishwashers or microwave ovens? How did they change your cooking habits? How is your cooking style similar to your mother's? How is it different? Were you a fancy cook or a "meat and potatoes" cook? Did you like to barbeque or picnic? In the thirties, how did the Depression and its shortages affect how you cooked? In the forties how did your cooking change because of rationing? In the fifties did you use canned soups and frozen foods in your cooking? In the sixties did you watch Julia Child on television, or read her cookbooks? What was your favorite cookbook? Betty Crocker? The Joy of Cooking? In the seventies did you become aware of the health food craze? Did you learn to make your own granola, or yogurt, or bread? In the eighties, did you embrace the "designer food" craze? If you were not the cook in your family, apply these questions to your mother, wife, or whoever did the cooking. Or, did you make your living in the food industry? Were you a chef or a waitperson? If so, write about your job and what kinds of food you worked with, and how they were created. How did you see food change over the years?

10. What were your favorite foods as a child or teenager? Did you hail "fast foods" with delight or disgust? Do you remember the first McDonalds or other fast food joint you went to? What did you have to eat? What did it cost? Did you have a favorite candy bar? If so, which one? What did your mother cook that you liked especially? What did you hate?

12. What magazines and/or newspapers did you read? Were there columnists that you read regularly, such as Eleanor Roosevelt's "My

Day," Herb Caen, Jack Anderson, Erma Bombeck, or Dear Abby? Did you read only the sports page, or the comics, or the arts section, or the "women's" section? Or did you read the paper cover-to-cover? Did you sell newspapers or magazines, or write for newspapers or magazines, or work in a publishing related field? Did you ever write a "Letter to the Editor" or write for advice from Abby or Ann Landers? If so, describe your letter. How did the magazines and/or newspapers you read affect your opinions? What did you learn from them?

13. Did any of the newly introduced products such as Twinkies, Wonder Bread, Fritos, 7-Up, Scotch tape, ballpoint pens, Tupperware, Tide, Crest toothpaste, cassette tapes, VCRs, CDs, walkmans, or others, become staples in your home? How did you hear about them – did you see ads in magazines, newspapers or billboards? Did you hear jingles on the radio or TV? Did the advertising for these products affect your shopping habits? What did you buy because you saw or heard it on an ad? Did the use of advertising icons such as the Marlboro Man encourage you to buy those products? Did you work in an advertising related field? What kind of advertising did you create or sell?

14. Consumer spending skyrocketed during the years after World War II, and the way we purchased products changed radically. When and where was the first shopping mall you visited? What stores were in the mall? How big was it? How did shopping in a mall compare to your previous shopping habits? Was it easier and more efficient, or did the proximity of shops encourage you to spend more? When did you get your first credit card? What kind of credit card was it? Did you use it sparingly, or with abandon? Were you suspicious of credit card buying, or did you embrace it enthusiastically? Did credit cards bring you financial freedom or plunge you into debt? How did credit cards change your spending habits?

Or anything else you want to write about ...

Chapter Seventeen
The Weird, Trivial, & Hard-to-Classify
Scandals & Gossip — Paranormal & Unexplained Phenomena — Comics & Cartoons — New Words & Slang — Animals & Pets

In this oddly assorted chapter we examine those subjects that don't fall neatly into other categories. We tell stories that are serious or funny, tragic or infuriating, thought-provoking or little more than mind candy. Or all of these at once.

1930 through 1959

Scandals & Gossip

Possibly the biggest scandal followed by Americans in the thirties wasn't even American: the abdication of Britain's King Edward VIII in order to marry an American divorcee, Wallis Warfield Simpson. The American fascination with royalty was also tweaked by Queen Elizabeth II's marriage to Philip Mountbatten in 1947 and Grace Kelly's marriage to Prince Rainier of Monaco in 1956.

Hollywood gossip was stoked by a new profession: gossip columnist, such as Louella Parsons and Hedda Hopper. There was an immense scandal in 1949 when Ingrid Bergman ran away with director Roberto Rossellini, tarnishing (at least for a time) her studio image. In the fifties the love affairs, marriages and divorces of Liz Taylor and Marilyn Monroe were always sure to make headlines.

> *"Fred" remembered his mixed emotions when Joe DiMaggio married Marilyn Monroe. "Part of me was disappointed," he wrote. "Joe DiMaggio was my hero, and I felt it was a comedown for him to fall for a film star. But the other part of me — well, it was just pure envy at his incredible luck."*

Comics & Cartoons

The thirties saw a host of comic characters born who are still going strong today, including Dick Tracy, Blondie, Betty Boop, Lil' Abner, Flash Gordon, Bugs Bunny, and of course the Disney characters – Goofy, Donald Duck and Mickey Mouse. Great cartoonists such as Peter Arno and Charles Addams began their careers in the thirties, and continued throughout these decades. In 1934 Dell introduced the modern comic book, which was a great success. In the late thirties, the Superhero was born with Superman in 1938 and Batman in 1939, giving Depression era folks some hope, even if it was on the pages of a comic book.

The duo of Hanna and Barbara entered the comic world with the debut of Tom and Jerry in 1940. Archie and Jughead were born in 1942, Brenda Starr in 1940, and Sylvester and Tweety in 1945.

In the fifties, Charlie Brown and Snoopy premiered in Charles Schultz's *Peanuts*. Dennis the Menace too was born during this decade, personifying the baby boomers. In 1954, reflecting the political temper of the times, the Comic Book Code Authority was formed to prevent the spread of violence, homosexuality, and other "wrong ideas" in American youth.

Paranormal, Mysteries & Unexplained Phenomena

Many of us often hold ambivalent and highly divergent opinions about paranormal or mysterious phenomena such as ghosts, fantastic creatures, flying saucers, or ESP. On the one hand, we suspect anything outside proven science as being superstition, yet we are fascinated by stories that seem to be outside the normal experience, and in many of us our "scientific bent" is only a veneer.

In 1933 the first photographic "evidence" of the Loch Ness Monster was presented to a disbelieving yet intrigued public. In 1934 the Great Stone Balls of Costa Rica were discovered, and to this day have not been completely explained to everyone's satisfaction. In 1945 the Lost Squadron crashed east of Florida and launched the enduring mystery of the Bermuda Triangle.

Probably because of the great advancements in aviation and astronomy during these decades, there was much attention and focus on space and the beings that might or might not live there. In 1938 Orson Welles' *War of the Worlds* brought panic because people believed it to be real, not fiction, proving that the belief in UFOs was widespread and didn't lie too far under the surface. In 1947 flying saucers were observed flying over Mount Rainier in Washington. Also in 1947, UFOs were reported to crash in Roswell, New Mexico, which the US Army denied then and has been denying since, since the controversy over this incident is still being hotly debated. In 1954 California was host to the first gathering of the UFO "Contactee" movement, a group who claimed to have met aliens personally.

A respected scientist, JB Rhine of Duke University, began his celebrated ESP experiments in 1930, lending his scientific authority to experiences that had previously belonged only to mystics. Many class participants have written about their experiences with the unexplained.

"Joan's" mother not only believed in psychic divination, she practiced it. "She read tea leaves," Joan shared. "And she was very good at it, especially in matters of birth and death. All the pregnant women in the neighborhood would consult with her to see if their babies would be healthy, and what the sex would be. I guess you could believe she was only guessing, but she must have been an awfully good guesser – I never knew her to be wrong.

During World War II, women with sons in the service often came to tea with Mom, so she could read their leaves and tell them if their sons were okay. Strangely, even the women who didn't believe in "those things" came to tea.

Although she said she knew when people were dying, Mom would never tell them so. She was afraid she might

*cause more suffering, and besides she was always aware that
she might be wrong. When she got older, she stopped reading
tea leaves altogether, because the older she got, the more people
she knew who were dying soon, and it made her unhappy.
She switched to tea bags instead."*

Animals & Pets

Pets have always held a vital place in the American heart. There
were some changes in the care of domestic animals during these
decades. The first Animal Shelter opened in 1935. The ASPCA directed animal rescue efforts during natural disasters, issued instructions for care of animals during wartime air raids, and in 1952 began the first investigation into the care and conditions of laboratory research animals. The use of "seeing eye" dogs was introduced
in 1938. In 1944 the first obedience training class for dogs and their
owners opened. The Humane Society was founded in 1954 specifically for the protection and humane treatment of animals.

Famous animals during these decades included Fala, FDR's Scot-
tie who can be seen in many presidential photographs; General
Patton's bulldog Willie (short for William the Conqueror); and
Eisenhower's Scottie Telek, who was present at the surrender of
Germany.

Heroic animals included the dogs and chimps who became the
first live creatures in outer space, some of whom gave their lives for
this privilege.

Hollywood animals with huge followings included the horses
Pie from *National Velvet*, Flicka from *My Friend Flicka*, Roy Rogers'
Trigger, and faithful dogs Lassie and Rin Tin Tin.

New words & Slang

One thing that defines a generation is their way of speaking,
especially the slang developed in their teens and twenties. These
words often reflect the political changes and social preoccupations

of the time. At the end of each decade in the event timelines you will find newly coined words and slang expressions.

In the thirties, many of these words are taken from the world of jazz musicians, such as groovy, jam and schmaltz, which swept into our language due to the powerful new medium of radio.

Along with sarcastic slang for bureaucratic doubletalk such as "gibberish" and "doubletalk" itself, much of the slang of the forties has to do with body parts, such as "meathooks" for hands, "breadbasket" for stomach, "drumsticks" for legs, and "biscuit" for head.

"Pete" shared his opinion that he and his fellow soldiers used the humorous body slang because it acted as a barrier between them and the bloody reality of war. "Lost both his drumsticks" was somehow less horrifying than "lost both his legs."

In the fifties the popular vernacular veered back to the world of music, intermixed with political jargon such as "Big Brother" and "brainwashing," reflecting some of the paranoia of that decade.

Take a look at the following and see what *you* remember ...

1930-1959 Events Timeline
The Weird, Trivial & Hard-to-Classify

1930	Jan	Mickey Mouse first appears, in a comic strip
1930	Aug	Betty Boop debuts in *Dizzy Dishes*
1930	Sep	First appearance of the comic strip *Blondie*
1931	Oct	*Dick Tracy* comic strip debuts
1930		J.B. Rhine conducts experiments in ESP at Duke University
1931		The Professional Dog Handlers' Association is formed
1932	May	Goofy, then as Dippy Dawg, first appears in *Mickey's Revue*
1933		Purina sends dog food to the South Pole with Admiral Byrd
1934	Jan	*Flash Gordon* comic strip debuts
1934	May	Dell introduces the comic book with *Famous Funnies*
1934	Jun	First Donald Duck cartoon released, *The Wise Little Hen*
1934		*Lil Abner* comic strip debuts
1934		The mysterious Great Stone Balls of Costa Rica discovered
1934		*Mandrake the Magician* makes his first appearance
1935		Chain letter craze sweeps the country
1935		Charles Addams submits his first cartoon to the *New Yorker*
1935		First Animal Shelter opens in Cape Cod.
1936	Dec	Su-Lin, first giant panda to come to US, arrives
1937		SPCA directs Mississippi flood animal-rescue efforts.
1938	Apr	First use of a seeing eye dog
1938	Jun	Action Comics introduces Superman
1938	Nov	Al Capp, author of *Lil Abner*, creates Sadie Hawkins Day
1938		Bugs Bunny makes screen debut
1938		Chinese archeologists discover strange discs covered with unreadable writings, and skeletons of delicate, large-headed human-like beings in Tibetan caves
1938		*The Lone Ranger* becomes a comic strip
1938		Mussolini bans publication of American comic strips – with the exception of Mickey Mouse
1938		*The Shadow* first appears as a comic strip
1939	Feb	Haunted mansion Borley Rectory destroyed in a fire
1939	May	Batman makes his first comic book appearance
1939	Jun	First King and Queen of England to visit the US, George VI and Elizabeth eat hot dogs at FDR party
1939	Dec	Montgomery Ward introduces Rudolph the 9th reindeer
1930s		New words, phrases, idioms and slang of the 30s include:

alligator, a fan of swing music

Aryan – a race declared by Hitler

babysitter – someone to care for your children

biggie – something really big

bra – woman's undergarment, replacing bustier or brassiere

canary – a woman who sings with a band, or someone who sings to the cops

cat – a person, as in "cool cat"

cool – from Black English, meaning good or stylish

crooner – a singer with a mellow sound, such as Bing Crosby

eye shadow – make up for eyelids

fake – to play music by ear

fan dancer – a partially nude dancer

fifth columnist – applied to Rebels during Spanish Civil War

flake out – fall asleep

groovy – Black English for stylish, cool

hep cat – someone who knows what's what

Hooverville – tent camp filled with the dispossessed

Hot jazz – swing jazz, as opposed to sweet jazz

jam – to play music without an arrangement

jingle – catchy tune that promotes products on the radio

jitterbug – dance craze

juke box – machine to play hit songs

negligee – a slinky nightgown

nylon – not only the material but the stockings made of it

schmaltz – overly sentimental

send – as in "you send me"

senior citizen – someone over retirement age

skins, skin ticklers – drums and drummers

soap opera – entertainment genre popularized on radio

stateless person – someone without a homeland

strip tease – dance while slowing taking off one's clothes

supermarket – all food items in one store

tin ear – someone who does not like music schmaltz

underpants – new term for drawers

whodunit – a murder mystery genre

1940	Feb	Joe Barbera and William Hanna give birth to Tom and Jerry
1940	Jun	*Brenda Starr*, irst comic strip written by a woman, appears
1940		Angell Memorial Animal Hospital launched the first veterinary intern training program in the US
1940		Fala, FDR's Scottie dog, is adopted by the President
1941	Nov	Wonder Woman makes her debut
1942	Feb	*Archie* comic book debuts
1942		ASPCA conducts courses on the care of animals in the event of air raids
1942		Guide Dogs for the Blind is incorporated.
1943	Aug	Stones from the sky pelt woman's house in Oakland, CA
1943		Walt Kelly's *Pogo* makes first appearance

1944	Feb	*Batman & Robin* comic strip premieres in newspapers
1944	Mar	General Patton acquires his famous bull terrier, who he named Willie, short for William the Conqueror
1944		ASPCA introduces obedience training classes for dogs
1945	Jan	Pepe LePew debuts in cartoon *Odor-able Kitty*
1945	May	General Eisenhower brings his Scottie, Telek, with him to accept Germany's surrender
1945	Dec	"Lost Squadron" crashes near Florida and starts stories of the Bermuda Triangle
1945		Warner Brothers' *Sylvester the Cat* premiered
1947	Jun	Nine flying saucers sighted over Mt. Rainier in Washington
1947	Jul	UFOs crash in Roswell, New Mexico, and investigated by the US Army, who says they are weather balloons
1947	Aug	Balsa raft Kon Tiki crashes into a Polynesian reef
1947	Nov	Princess Elizabeth of England marries Philip Mountbatten
1947		Bubblegum blowing contests become popular
1948		Air Force establishes project SIGN to study UFOs, as well as project GRUDGE explaining away all sightings to public
1949	Sep	Loony Tunes introduces the *Roadrunner* cartoons
1949		Ingrid Bergman leaves husband for Roberto Rosellini
1940s		New words, phrases, idioms and slang used in 40s include:

ack ack – anti-aircraft guns

antibiotic – used to kill microorganisms in human body

baby boom – describing the escalating birth rate

banzai – a cheer or war cry, from the Japanese

bebop – jazz term derived from syllables of scat singing

bikini – scanty 2 piece bathing suit named for atoll where atomic testing done

biscuit – your head

blackout – extinguishing lights visible to enemy aircraft

blinkers – your eyes

blitz, blitzkrieg – war terms to mean all out attack

bobby soxer – an adolescent girl

bone box – your mouth

bonkers - crazy

boogie – to dance

boondocks – used by US soldiers to mean remote area

bread basket – your stomach

brush – your mustache

chewers – your teeth

choppers – your teeth

chops – your jaws

clocker – your heart

dome – your head

doubletalk – language hard to understand, meant to confuse

drumsticks – your legs

dukes – your fists

face lace – your whiskers

fallout – radioactive refuse of nuclear bomb, coming to mean any after-effect

feelers – your fingers

flak – bursting shells fired from anti-aircraft guns

flippers – your ears

floppers – your arms

flying saucer – disc shaped flying objects, later called UFOs

frame – a girl's overall figure

gams – your legs

genocide – deliberate destruction of an entire people

gibberish – language hard to understand, meant to confuse

gobbledygook - language hard to understand, meant to confuse

grabbers – your hands

grey market – a market employing irregular but not necessarily illegal methods

Ground Zero – origin of violent change, or the beginning

gungho – enthusiastic, from Chinese gonghe, meaning work together

hinges – your elbows

Holocaust –results of the Nazi program of extermination

honcho – boss or leader, from Japanese hancho,squad leader

hot rod – souped-up car

idea pot – your head

iron curtain – the division between east and west

jeep – small 4-wheel drive vehicle used by US army

kamikaze – suicidal attack, literally means divine wind

lamps – your eyes

lugs – large ears

meat hooks – your hands

moss – your whiskers

mumbo jumbo – hard to understand, meant to confuse

napalm – developed in 1942 and used in incendiary bombs

noggin – your head

paws – your hands

phiz – your face

pickers – your fingers

prayer dukes – your knees

psycho – deranged person

pump – your heart

puss – your face

sails – your ears
schnozz – your nose
shutters – your eyelids
snafu – army acronym for "situation normal all fouled up"
sneezer – your nose
sonar – means of locating objects in water by sound waves
stems – your legs
stretcher – your neck
think box – your head
ticker – your heart
wigglers – your fingers

1950	Oct	*Peanuts* comic strip premieres
1950		A kitten follows climbers to the top of the Matterhorn
1950		*Beetle Bailey* comic strip appears
1951	Jan	Liz Taylor's first divorce, from Conrad Hilton Jr.
1951		*Dennis the Menace* premieres
1952	Jul	UFO sightings in Washington DC area, plus radar reports of UFOs, culminate in Pentagon press conference
1952	Sep	Group of people in West Virginia sight a supposed meteor fall from the sky, then find a throbbing globe and an animal with a "blood red face" in a tree
1952		Air Force Director of Intelligence orders a new UFO study
1952		The ASPCA begins inspection of New York laboratories that use animals for research, the first of its kind in the US
1953	Mar	American B-47 accidentally drops a nuclear bomb on South Carolina, which doesn't go off
1954	Jan	Marilyn Monroe marries Joe DiMaggio
1954	Mar	People claiming contact with beings from other planets attend the Contactee Convention in California
1954	Oct	Comics Code Authority formed to regulate comic violence
1954		The Humane Society founded
1955	Dec	Dr. Joyce Brothers wins $64,000 Question
1955		Mad Comics becomes *Mad Magazine*
1956	Apr	Grace Kelly marries Prince Rainier III of Monaco
1956	Oct	Monkey falls out of sky and crashes into a clothesline post in California
1956		*The Search for Bridie Murphy* published, about reincarnation
1957	Oct	Jerry Lee Lewis bigamously marries his 13-year-old cousin
1957	Nov	The oldest recorded cat, a female tabby named Ma, dies at the age of 34
1958	Aug	California man finds huge footprints by his truck; the Humboldt Times coins the word "BigFoot"
1959	May	Eddie Fisher and Debbie Reynolds divorce so he can marry Liz Taylor

Sharing My Stories—The Planet Myron

During the summer nights of the late fifties, my brother Mike and I often camped outside in our backyard. With the hulk of our house nearby, warm in our sleeping bags, we lay on our backs with our eyes on the zillions of stars above. Soothed by the songs of frogs and the warm drowsy chuckles of the hens that were our father's current project, we contemplated the vast summer sky and wondered about things.

We talked about ordinary stuff like what kind of bike was the best, and going fishing with Dad, and how to get out of eating the disgusting vegetables that Mom put on the dinner table. But our best conversations centered on the stars glittering above us. Who was up there, really? Did they look like us, or like the goggle-eyed monsters on TV? If they came to earth, could we talk to them? Could we travel that far and meet them?

Mike loved me to tell stories about these faraway planets. He admired my storytelling abilities, and his appreciation inspired me to flights of imagination that wandered from the sublime to the ridiculous. One of his favorite sagas was the series of stories I told him the year our grandfather died. The story had a startling beginning. "Grandpa's not really dead," I said. "Nobody really dies. They just go live on a different planet."

Grandpa's planet was right at the far tip of the Big Dipper. Grandpa chose that planet, because it was in trouble and needed help. It was overrun by creatures from the planet Wayne. (Wayne was the name of the neighborhood bully, a boy Mike hated.) The Waynians were blue-skinned and had only one eye, which they could hold in their hands like a marble. They used this eye as a spy device to see into people's minds, and a weapon that shot a gluey substance that clogged up your nose and ears and mouth.

Grandpa had many adventures fighting against the Waynians, until he finally sent the Waynians packing by pouring warm fish guts into their eyes. The fish guts dissolved the glue and rendered the Waynians helpless.

The native inhabitants of the planet were so grateful that they named the planet after Grandpa, whose name was Myron. So now this planet at the far tip of the Big Dipper is known as the planet Myron.

I can still feel my brother shaking with chuckles as Grandpa saved the planet Myron from the Waynians. By the light of the remembered moon I see Mike's eyes shining with mischief and grace, a combination uniquely his own which even today peeks from his middle-aged eyes.

1959	Sep	Nikita Khruschev denied entry into Disneyland
1959	Nov	Rocky the flying squirrel and Bullwinkle the Moose born
1959		The first veterinary intensive-care unit built
1950s		New words, phrases, idioms and slang used in 50s include:

beatnik — person who rejects traditional mores of society

Big Brother — the government or just the big "Them"

brainwashing —systematic indoctrination into set of beliefs

cat – a beat person, as in cool cat

coffee bar – where the beatniks hung out

Cold War – Western capitalism vs Eastern Communism

cube – someone old

dosh – money

fast food – term originating from drive-in restaurants

gas – a good time, as in "it's a gas"

high rise – tall office and apartment buildings

hip – knowledgeable about what's cool, as in "I'm hip"

hit parade – list of popular songs

jet set – wealthy travelers

jive, jive talk – Black English from Harlem; conversation

mushroom cloud – describing visible result of The Bomb

nerd – socially unattractive person

nukes – pet name for nuclear weapons

overkill – from effect of The Bomb; too much power

paper tiger – a braggart with no substance

ponytail – a girl's hairdo

real time – a computer term

rock – short for rock and roll, and a euphemism for sex

rock n' roll –music genre encompassing rhythm and blues, jazz, folk, and other music forms

scene – what's happening, as in "make the scene"

see you later alligator – goodbye

skam – what's happening

skull – your mind, as in "you're outta your skull"

sleaze – shoddy, inferior

smog – dirty air

split – leave, as in "split the scene"

square – a cool person

swinging – with it, musically

teenager – an adolescent

the most – the best

think tank – referring to a group of intellectuals

third world – underdeveloped nations

ville – used as a suffix to many words, as in "wierdsville"

with it – in style

1960 through 1989

Scandals & Gossip

Liz Taylor's changing marital status continued to make Hollywood gossip in the sixties, reaching a fever pitch on the set of *Cleopatra* when she left Eddie Fisher (the focus of an earlier scandal) for Richard Burton. Marilyn Monroe's death in 1963 of course made headlines, and is still the subject of debate today. As it always does, the hot combination of politics and sex made big news in the sixties, as in the 1963 scandal involving British cabinet minister John Profumo and Christine Keeler, a showgirl with supposed ties to the Soviet embassy.

America's fascination with the Kennedy family began in the sixties, starting with the heyday of Camelot and its handsome king and glamorous queen, and continuing after JFK's death. Paparazzi followed Jackie Kennedy's every move, and the attention was especially frenzied over her romance and marriage with Aristotle Onassis. The sad tale of Ted Kennedy and his plunge off the Chappaquiddick bridge mesmerized the public.

The excesses of the sixties and seventies were symbolized by another group: rock stars. Drugs busts, lewd behavior and shocking language became commonplace. Much media attention in this group went to The Beatles, both before and after they broke up. Paul McCartney was rumored to be dead even when he denied it, secret meanings were said to be found by playing Beatles' songs backwards, and simply anything that John Lennon did or said was avidly reported in the press, especially after he married Yoko Ono.

In the seventies the huge political scandal of Watergate dwarfed any others, making household names of two reporters, Woodward and Bernstein, and bringing down a presidency. Other celebrity gossip of this decade included Clifford Irving's hoax "autobiography" of Howard Hughes, the palimony suit against Lee Marvin, Jean Harris' murder of "diet doc" Herman Tarnower, and Christina Crawford's expose of her mother's child rearing methods, *Mommie Dearest*.

In the eighties Americans were again spellbound by the spectacle of royalty and wealth; the media stars being Britain's Prince Charles and Princess Diana. From their marriage in 1981, Diana replaced Jackie Onassis as the media's first darling. Prince Andrew and his bride Sarah Ferguson, or "Fergie," collected their share of media attention too.

"I was born the same year as Princess Di," shared "Kathleen." "I too got married in 1981, just two months before she did, to a man much older than I. He was on the fast track in his career, but I was still in college when we got married. I remember going to company functions with him and meeting all those high powered executives and their spouses, all of them at least 10 to 15 years older (and wiser) than me. It was a terrifying experience. One of the ways I got through it was to pretend that I was Princess Di. It always helped. After all, if she could meet heads of state, Hollywood celebrities, and big shot billionaires without losing her cool, then I could hold my own with a few snooty middle managers!"

Comics and Cartoons

The baby boom generation was the first raised on Saturday morning cartoons, and the sixties delivered a tremendous wallop of classic cartoons to feed their hungry appetites. Rocky and Bullwinkle, along with their friends Boris and Natasha, were introduced in late 1959 and developed a following that lasts until today. The team of Hanna Barbera gave us *The Flintstones, Yogi Bear*, and *The Jetsons* during this decade. "Yabba dabba doo" and "smarter than the average bear" became part of our language. In comic books, the superhero Spiderman was born in 1962.

In the seventies *Scooby Doo* was a big hit, and for the young adult baby boomers the comic strip with an attitude, *Doonesbury*, premiered in 1970. Garfield the Cat was born in 1978, and comic books saw the introduction of *Conan the Barbarian.*

Hugely popular with children in the eighties were the Care Bears, who debuted in 1983, and the Smurfs, who emigrated from Europe to the US in 1981. 1984 saw the birth of the Teenage Mutant Ninja Turtles, a marketing phenomenon. In comic books dark fantasy and horror were popular genres.

Paranormal, Mysteries & Unexplained Phenomena

The abiding interest in UFOs, alien visits, and alien abductions continued. The popularity of movies such as Kubrick's *2001: A Space Odyssey* and Speilberg's *Close Encounters of the Third Kind,* and television shows such as *Star Trek,* contributed to the widespread belief that Earth was not the only inhabited planet in the universe. The phenomenon of crop circles, which came to public attention in the seventies and eighties, were also sometimes theorized to be alien artifacts, although there were other theories to their origin as well.

There were reports of strange things falling from the sky, such as golf balls, fish and rocks. Sightings of weird creatures, such as huge bat-like creatures flying through the sky, prehistoric birds, and enormous cat-like monsters, were reported by average folks. Even photographs (highly controversial) were taken, such as the 1967 photograph of Big Foot in Northern California, and another Loch Ness Monster photo in 1974.

There was a high degree of interest and speculation about devils, ghosts and hauntings. Stephen King's best-selling novels dealt with the occult and the bizarre. Three of the most popular movies of these decades were *Rosemary's Baby, The Exorcist,* and *The Amityville Horror,* supposedly based on a true story. Another reported true story was about the ghosts of Flight 401 in 1972.

Famous psychics, mystics and paranormal researchers of these decades included Uri Geller, who bent spoons and performed other "impossible" acts with the power of his mind alone; Padre Pio, whose piety enabled him to perform miracles such as displaying the stigmata and performing bilocation; and Raymond Moody, who in his 1975 bestselling book *Life After Life* explored the concepts of life after death and reincarnation, and coined the phrase "near-death experience."

Animals & Pets

A revolution in caring for pets and wildlife took place during these decades. Increasing strides were made in protecting endangered wildlife and their habitats, especially in the area of public awareness. The Humane Society, ASPCA, and other organizations such as PAWS and PETA worked tirelessly to reduce the swelling pet population by the establishment of spay and neuter clinics and humane shelters, plus campaigning against cruel practices used on animals in laboratory testing. Greenpeace and other organizations helped publicize the plight of hunted animals such as the slaughter of baby harp seals, which caused a public outcry in the seventies and eighties.

New and creative uses for animal "labor" were developed. Dogs were trained to sniff out drugs and explosives, dolphins were used for Navy exercises, and the role of animals in therapeutic roles expanded considerably.

"Maryanne" remembered her elderly mother's experience in a nursing home in the late seventies. "When she first moved there, she was very depressed," shared Maryanne. "She wouldn't even get dressed, but just sat on her bed staring out the window, all day long. But then the nursing home started an animal visitor program. All her life my mother had loved Pekinese dogs — she must have owned and trained at least twenty throughout her life. And one morning she was sitting on her bed staring out the window when her door opened and in trots this little honey-colored Pekinese with a blue bow in her hair. My mother just opened her arms and that little dog

jumped right in them, as if she had known Mom all her life. When she left, Mom was smiling, and the next morning she got dressed."

Maryanne was so impressed by the benefits the animal visits brought her mother that she volunteered her own dog Choo-Choo to be a visitor dog. "Choo-Choo just loved visiting the nursing home," she shared. "He knew everyone and everyone knew him. Thursday was our day to visit, and the nurses told me many residents saved sausage or bacon from their Thursday breakfasts so they could give treats to Choo-Choo. One woman even made him a coat with his name embroidered on the back."

Famous animals of these decades included presidential pets such as LBJ's Him and Her and First Lady Barbara Bush's springer spaniel Millie; Hollywood animals like Mr. Ed, Flipper and the *Born Free* lioness Elsa; and advertising icons such as Morris the Cat and Spuds McKenzie, who debuted in the 1987 Super Bowl.

New words & Slang

The radical flavor of the sixties showed up noticeably in the slang of the baby boom generation. The sixties were all about shocking the establishment, and the slang certainly tried for shock value, especially in the use of four-letter words in "polite" company. The "s-word" and "f-word" were the most popular expletives, and they were used everywhere, in every form – nouns, verbs, adjectives, adverbs, compound words – used for disapproval, approval, excitement, anger, you name it. Slang also borrowed terms from the jazz musicians of the thirties and African-American slang, such as groovy, cool, far-out, and the ubiquitous "man" tacked on to everything. There were many new words used for drugs and drug paraphernalia.

In the seventies the revolution in sexual roles was reflected in new phrases such as male chauvinist, gender gap, palimony, sex object, significant other, the word "person" used in place of "man" in words such as "chairman," and the title Ms. for a woman regardless of her marital state. The word "gay" underwent a change in meaning, from lighthearted to homosexual (although the word gay has had homosexual connotations since the 1920s, especially within the gay community.) The seventies saw the birth of compound words ending in the suffix "gate" to mean corrupt or scandalous, from of course, the scandal of the time, Watergate. And finally, the slang of this decade included dozens of terms for vomit or the act of vomiting. (I don't know why.)

The eighties brought Valley Girl speak into the national consciousness, patterned after the way adolescent girls spoke in a small upscale area of Los Angeles. The world of high-tech (itself a new phrase) and economics also contributed slang.

Take a look at the following and see what *you* remember ...

1960-1989 Events Timeline
The Weird, Trivial & Hard-to-Classify

1960	Aug	UFO is sighted by 3 California patrolmen
1960		Hanna-Barbera introduces *The Flintstones*
1961		Fossil encrusted geode is found in Coso Mountains of California; it has an artificially made "spark plug like" object inside the 500,000 year old geode
1961		Veterinarians first perform open-heart surgery on a dog
1961		Yogi Bear and Boo Boo introduced by Hanna-Barbera
1961		Comic strip *Apartment 3-G* debuts
1962		*The Jetsons* premieres
1962		Spiderman is born
1963	Mar	British Minister of War John Profumo denies having sex with Christine Keeler
1963		Dr. Tsum Um Nui publishes his findings on the "Grooved Script of Spaceships that landed on earth 12,000 years ago"
1964	Mar	Elizabeth Taylor divorces Eddie Fisher and marries Richard Burton
1964	Apr	Policeman sees landing of egg-shaped craft with blue and orange exhaust and emergence of two humanoids
1964		Operation Gwamba in Surinam is launched, saving nearly 10,000 animals from hydroelectric dam flooding
1965	Jan	Porcupine in Washington DC zoo dies at 27, the oldest known rodent
1965	Feb	105 USAF cadets resign after found cheating on exams
1965	Mar	Rolling Stones fined 5 pounds each for public urination
1965		Ted Serios uses a Polaroid Camera to take pictures of his face; the resulting photos show his thoughts
1965		"All You Add is Love" ads launched for Purina Dog Food
1965		Roy Rogers' horse Trigger dies, and is stuffed for display
1966	Mar	John Lennon says of the Beatles, "We are more popular than Jesus."
1966	May	Tortoise given to Tonga's King by Captain Cook in 1773, finally dies
1966	Jul	In Alabama Beatles products burned due to John Lennon's "Jesus" remark
1966	Nov	7-foot bat-like creature seen flying through the sky by 9 people in West Virginia; the creature abducts a dog
1966		Frank Sinatra, 50, marries 21-year-old Mia Farrow
1966		US Air Force sponsors another UFO investigation, studying 59 cases, of which 23 remained unexplained when Air Force abruptly halted the project

1966		ASPCA celebrates its 100th anniversary
1966		First museum devoted to comic art opens in Japan
1967	May	Elvis Presley marries Priscilla Beaulieu
1967	Dec	LBJ's daughter Lynda marries in the White House
1967	May	Evel Knievel and his motorcycle jump over 16 automobiles
1967	Oct	Film of creature claimed to be Bigfoot shot in No. Calif.
1967		PAWS, an organization for homeless pets, founded
1968	Jan	Evel Knieval fails to jump Caesar's Palace Fountain
1968	Oct	Jacqueline Kennedy marries Aristotle Onassis
1968	Nov	John Lennon & Yoko Ono appear nude on cover of album
1968	Nov	Padre Pio's stigmata disappear from his hands, three days before his death
1968	Dec	Julie Nixon marries David Eisenhower
1969	Mar	John Lennon and Yoko Ono marry and stage their first bed-in for peace at the Amsterdam Hilton
1969	Jul	Mary Jo Kopechne and Ted Kennedy plunge off Chappaquiddick bridge
1969	Sep	Northern Star starts a rumor that Paul McCartney is dead, which is denied by Paul McCartney
1969	Sep	Hundreds of golf balls suddenly fall from the sky in Punta Gorda, Florida
1969	Sep	*Scooby Doo* premieres on television
1969	Nov	John Lennon returns his MBE
1969	Dec	50 million TV viewers watch Tiny Tim marry Miss Vicky on the *Tonight Show*
1969		Uri Geller begins his amazing career
1969		Morris the Cat becomes spokescat for Purina' catfood
1960s		New words, phrases, idioms and slang used in the 1960s include:

acid – LSD, a psychedelic drug

aerobics – cardiovascular exercise

Age of Aquarius – the 1960s youth generation

badass – a mean guy

bag – to steal

ball, balling – sexual intercourse

be-in – organized event where people "hang out"

biodegradable – product which naturally rots

biorhythm – inherent biological rhythm

bitchin – really good

black hole – celestial object with strong gravitational pull, comes to mean continually draining a resource, as in "financial black hole"

body count – first used in Vietnam for enemy dead

boss – stylish, cool

bread – money

bummer – a drag

byte – a computer term meaning 8 binary digits

chick – a girl

clod – someone stupid

condo – short for condominium

crash – stay somewhere, as "crash at my pad, man"

dig – to understand, as in "can you dig it?"

dip – an idiot

ditch – to walk away from someone or something

don't have a cow – don't get upset

doobie – marijuana cigarette

doofus – an idiot

dope – marijuana, sometimes other drugs

douche bag – ugly woman

endangered species – species on the verge of extinction

fab – term of commendation, excellent, as in "the fab four"

far out – renew of 1930s term to mean excellent

flower child – a hippie

four letter words – the "f" and the "s" words attached to
sentences, used as nouns, verbs, adverbs, adjectives, as well
as names and pejoratives

fuzz – policemen

gear – excellent, cool

glitch – an error or flaw

go ape – go crazy

gofer – a person who runs errands

grass – marijuana

groady, groaty, grotty – slovenly or unkempt

groovy – renewal of 1930s term to mean very cool, excellent

gross, gross out – nasty, or to react to something nasty

grubby – deliberately unkempt

grungy – dirty or messy

heavy – meaningful, important, as in "that's heavy, man"

hell no we won't go – slogan for draft & anti-war protestors

high – intoxicated on drugs

high five – a hand slap in the air

hippie – member of youth counter culture, distinguished by
clothes and hair

hit – a drag from a marijuana cigarette

homeboy – member of a youth gang

humongous – really big

hype – oversell

jazzed – excited

joint – marijuana cigarette
knockout – excellent, beautiful
laid back - relaxed
light my fire – excite me
live long and prosper – a greeting made popular by *Star Trek*
loaded – intoxicated on drugs
love-in – gathering for the purpose of expressing love
macho – aggressively masculine
make love not war – anti-war slogan
make out – heavy petting
make the scene – attend a party or gathering
man – attached as a tag end to sentences, as in "hey, man"
mellow out – relax, come down
miniskirt – extremely short skirt fashionable in mid sixties
mother-f**er – pejorative, often shortened to "mother"
out of sight – renewal of 1930s term to mean very cool
out to lunch – ignorant
pad – place to live
panty waist – weak, ineffectual
pantyhose – pull on one-piece stockings
paparazzi – intrusive photographers
pigs – policemen
pot – marijuana
psychedelic – name given to a class of hallucinogenic drugs
pulsar – celestial source of electromagnetic radiation
put down – squelch, humiliate
quark – elementary particle
quasar - powerful and extremely distant celestial objects
rank – humiliate, put down
raunchy –disgusting
right on – absolutely correct
scuzzy – very dirty
serial killer – a person who kills over and over again
sexism – judgments based solely on gender
sit-in – organized non-violent protest
skinny dip – swim naked
sock it to me – tell me about it, from *Laugh In*
speed – amphetamines
square – someone out of touch
square one – the very beginning
stacked – term for a busty woman
stoned – intoxicated on drugs
teach-in – gathering to raise political awareness
teenybopper – teenage girl

Sharing My Stories—Far Out and Totally Rad, Man

When I left home for college in the autumn of 1967, my idea of swearing was damn and hell. I had never heard the "s-word" or the "f-word" while attending my suburban high school.

I made up for lost time in college. Now they are commonplace, but in the sixties the "s-word" and "f-word" still held the power to shock, and the sixties college scene was all about shocking the establishment. These supremely flexible words could be used as nouns, verbs, adjectives and adverbs. You could even stick them inside words and create new words, as in "ab-so-f'in-lutely." You could use them to bolster phrases of disbelief or amazement, as in "no s**t!" or "far-f'in-out."

Besides the four letter words, my slang included other hippieisms such as "far out" and "right on," although by 1968 "groovy" was passé. So was "fuzz" – by the time I arrived the police were pigs. Even "hippie" was on its way out – now we were "freaks", as opposed to the "straights" who didn't smoke dope. Straight had nothing to do with sexuality then.

The slang of your youth stays with you, unfortunately. In the eighties my comments such as "cool, man" or "right on!" sent my teenage children into fits of laughter or bouts of eye-rolling. They showed how rad, phat, tubular they were by using – guess! – those same four-letter words I tried to erase from my vocabulary. One Christmas morning my 11-year-old daughter announced, "It be Christmas and s**t!" She soon graduated upward to the f-word, too. It was impossible to legislate against this language without sounding like a total hypocrite.

If their use of four letter words was familiar, the rest of their eighties vocabulary was a mystery to me. In the sixties we may have had some new words, but at least we used them in sentences. The eighties way was to abbreviate everything to its shortest and most impenetrable code. One day my 15-year-old daughter and her friend were talking.

Friend: "Happenin'"

Daughter: "Later!"

Friend: "Burnt."

Daughter: "Mega."

They laughed as if they had just communicated. Oh well, I guess it meant something to their generation. Like I say: far-f'in-out and right on.

thongs – things to wear on your feet

tie dye – hippie way to decorate one's clothes

together —a commendation, as "that's really together, man"

toke – drag from a marijuana cigarette

tokenism – making only a symbolic effort to combat racism or other social ills

totally – as in "totally far out, man"

tune in – know what's going on

turn on – get high

trip, bad trip, trippy – the experience of being on LSD

unisex – clothing or hairstyles worn by both genders

unleaded – gasoline made without lead

uptight – stressed out

weed – marijuana

wimp – weak or passive person

winner – paradoxical use meaning loser, as in "he's a real winner, man"

would you believe — from *Get Smart*

yabba dabba doo — hooray, from *The Flintstones*

yesterday – out of style, as in "that's so yesterday"

1970	Oct	*Doonesbury* comic strip debuts in 28 newspapers
1970	Oct	*Conan the Barbarian* introduced
1971	Mar	Mick Jagger marries Bianca Perez Morena de Macias
1971	Jun	Tricia Nixon and Edward Cox marry at the White House
1971	Aug	Sad faces appear on the floor tiles of a house in Spain; workmen remove them, uncover a medieval cemetery
1971		Smilies or the yellow happy face becomes popular
1971		Tender Vittles catfood is introduced
1971		Hoover the famous talking seal featured on *Good Morning America* and NPR
1972	Jan	Howard Hughes comes out of seclusion and declares Clifford Irving's "autobiography" a fake
1972	Mar	Evel Knievel breaks 93 bones after clearing 35 cars
1972	Aug	First sighting of crop circle being made, in England
1972	Dec	Eastern Airlines Flight 401 crashes, killing 99 passengers and crew; later many witnesses claim to have seen the ghosts of the pilot and flight engineer
1972		James Herriott's *All Creatures Great and Small* published, about the adventures of a Yorkshire veterinarian
1973		ASPCA Adoptions Department begins compulsory spay/neuter of animals
1973		Two fishermen harassed by storms of falling pebbles
1974		Charles Berlitz publishes a best seller on the mystery of the Bermuda Triangle

1974	Jan	The Loch Ness Monster is allegedly photographed
1974	Mar	Cher files for separation from Sonny Bono
1974	Jun	Elizabeth Taylor divorces Richard Burton
1974	Aug	Philippe Petit walks tightrope strung between towers of World Trade Center
1974		Streaking becomes a craze
1975	Jun	Cher marries Gregg Allman
1975	Oct	NY Daily News runs headline "Ford to City: Drop Dead"
1975		Raymond Moody coins the phrase "near death experience" in his book, *Life After Life*
1976	Feb	People in Texas report seeing a giant bird identified as a Pterosaur, flying through the sky
1976	Mar	Greenpeace leads first intervention against harp seal hunt
1976	Apr	Howard Hughes, reclusive billionaire, dies and has to be identified by his fingerprints
1976	Sep	Representative Wayne Hays resigns because of scandal about Elizabeth Ray
1976	Sep	Playboy releases an interview with Jimmy Carter in which he says he has "lusted in his heart"
1977	Apr	Two separate groups of teenagers in Massachusetts claim to see a 4-foot big-headed creature with round orange eyes, later dubbed the "Dover Demon"
1977	Jul	NY City experiences a 25 hour blackout
1977		Brigitte Bardot helps publicize the plight of baby harp seals
1978	Mar	Charlie Chaplin's coffin stolen from a Swiss cemetery
1978		*Garfield the Cat* comic strip premieres
1978		Christina Crawford publishes her expose *Mommie Dearest*
1979		Lee Marvin faces the first palimony suit, brought by his longtime girlfriend
1979		First annual Mutts n Stuff amateur dog show event
1970s		New words, phrases, idioms and slang used in the 1970s include:

acid rain – polluted rain

ageism – judgments based solely on age

bag lady – homeless woman carrying her possessions in shopping bags

barf – vomit

bean counter – someone concerned with financial matters

bliss out – very relaxed or high

blow – cocaine

blow chunks – vomit

buyout – one corporation buying another

catch 22 – from Joseph Heller's book, a paradoxical rule or impossible situation *chip* – made from silicon, not potatoes

clone – exact duplicate

coke – cocaine, not the coke you drink

couch potato – a lazy person

decorate your shoes – vomit

disco, disco fever, discotheque – style of music and dancing

downsize – eliminate employees

ecology – environmental science

floppy disk – computer peripheral

full frontal – total nudity

futon – Japanese sofa bed

gas guzzler – car that gets poor gas mileage

gate – a suffix added to any word to make it scandalous or corrupt

gay – homosexual

gay-bashing – prejudice against homosexuals

gender gap – lack of understanding between men and women

global warming – the process of the earth heating up

golden handshake – good compensation from a big corporation

gridlock – traffic jam

heavy metal – music genre

hip hop – music genre

hurl – vomit

I'm Chevy Chase and you're not – from *Saturday Night Live*

junk food – food low in nutritional value but often popular

landfill – buried garbage

leisure suit – informal jacket and pants, made of polyester

make an offer you can't refuse – from *The Godfather*

male chauvinism – preferential treatment for men over women

marginalize – relegate to a marginal position in society

may the force be with you – good luck, from *Star Wars*

miniseries – short dramatic series on TV

Ms. – title for a woman, regardless of marital status

nanu nanu – popular phrase from TV show *Mork and Mindy*

palimony – alimony for non-married partners

person – substitution for "man" in words like "chairperson"

petrodollars – money made from oil

photo op – short for photographic opportunity

politically correct – reflects the current social mores

pooper scooper – implement used to clean up after your pet

porcelain bus – toilet, as in "drive the porcelain bus"

porcelain god – toilet, as in "worship the porcelain god"

ralph – vomit

real men don't eat quiche – reflecting gender confusion

s/he – an attempt to be gender inclusive

sex object – viewing a woman merely for sexual gratification

shades – sunglasses

significant other – unmarried sexual partner

slam dunk – a basketball term meaning a sure thing

snow - cocaine

soundbite – brief recorded public statement

speed bump – bumps on roads that make motorists reduce their speed

straight – heterosexual

surrogate mother – mother of a "test tube" baby

thongs – skimpy swimwear or underwear

scarf – eat fast

threads - clothing

toss your cookies – vomit

unbundling – price separately

up ya nose with a rubber hose – to hell with you

user friendly – originally a computer term, easy to use

virus – computer malady, not the kind that attacks humans

wedgie – a prank played with underwear

where's the beef? – from Wendy's TV commercial

whistle blower – employee who reports on corruption of his/her employer

wicked – a term of admiration, as in "that's a wicked dress"

wild and crazy guy – from Steve Martin and Dan Ackroyd on *Saturday Night Live*

yak - vomit

1980	Jan	Studio 54 owners Steve Rubell and Ian Schrager fined and sentenced to prison for tax evasion
1980	May	Marlo Thomas and Phil Donahue marry
1980		Crop circles attract media attention
1980		Cartoon *Heathcliff the Cat* debuts
1980	Nov	NY City Mayor Ed Koch admits to trying marijuana
1980		PETA (People for the Ethical Treatment of Animals) is founded, dedicated to education about animal abuse
1981	Feb	Prince Charles announces engagement to Diana Spencer
1981	Apr	Washington Post's Janet Cooke wins Pulitzer Prize, and later admits her story on a heroin addict was a hoax
1981	Jul	Prince Charles marries Princess Diana
1981		Carol Burnett wins $1.6 million libel suit against the National Enquirer
1981		Silver Springs monkey case results in first arrest and conviction of animal experimenters in the US on charges

		of cruelty to animals
1981		The cartoon Smurfs emigate to the US from Europe
1982	Jun	Prince William born to Prince Charles and Princess Diana
1982	Sep	Princess Grace of Monaco killed in a car accident
1982	Sep	The Dog Museum of America opens
1982	Dec	Senator Ted and Joan Kennedy get a divorce
1982		Little Green Holm Island off Scotland made a Grey Seal Sanctuary
1983	Mar	Time Magazine cover has a typo (contol instead of control), the only time it has happened; all magazines recalled
1983	Apr	Hundreds of sheep in England are slain by a huge cat-like creature dubbed "The Beast of Exmoor"
1983	May	60 volume set of Hitler's diaries are proved to be a hoax
1983	Sep	Texas resident spies a huge bird-like creature flying through the sky
1983		Survey finds link between child abuse and animal abuse
1984	Jan	Ball lightning enters a Russian airplane, flies above passengers' heads, divides into two crescents and exits the plane, leaving two holes behind
1984	Jul	Vanessa Williams, first black Miss America, resigns due to scandal over her nude photos
1984	Nov	The AKC celebrates its 100th anniversary
1984		Uri Geller erases computer tapes with the power of his mind alone
1984		Mirage Comics introduces *Teenage Mutant Ninja Turtles*
1985	May	34 fish fall out of a cloud in the sky and into a Fort Worth, Texas yard
1985		A Government Affairs office opened in Washington DC to monitor and lobby for legislation to protect animals.
1985		Eleven year old girl is saved from a blizzard by a pet Newfoundland dog
1985		Comic strip *Calvin & Hobbes* goes into syndication
1986	May	7 million people hold hands in "Hands Across America"
1986	Jul	Britain's Prince Andrew marries Sarah Ferguson, dubbed "Fergie"
1986		Spay/Neuter Assistance Program established to battle pet overpopulation
1987	Mar	PTL Leader Jim Bakker resigns amid sex scandal with Jessica Hahn
1987	Aug	Astrological Harmonic Convergence hailed as Dawn of a New Age
1987		First annual Humane Awards salutes heroic animals
1988	Feb	Televangelist Jimmy Swaggart confesses his sins
1988	Apr	Burt Reynolds and Loni Anderson marry

1988	May	New Jersey Devils' coach Jim Schoenfeld tells referee to "eat another doughnut, you fat pig!" and is suspended; press dubs the incident "Doughnutgate"
1988	Jun	Wade Boggs faces a palimony suit
1988	Jun	Mike Tyson faces reports that he allegedly beat his wife, Robin Givens
1988	Sep	Lab tests reportedly show Shroud of Turin is not Christ's burial cloth
1988	Oct	Potbellied pygmy pigs are popular as pets
1988	Oct	US and USSR combine to free 2 grey whales from the frozen Arctic
1988	Nov	Geraldo Rivera's nose broken in a brawl between Roy Innis and skinheads at TV taping
1988		Rocky and Barco, two drug-sniffing dogs, seized $182 million worth of drugs along the Texas border
1988		Architect takes detailed photos of UFOs at Gulf Breeze
1989	Aug	The "Swastika" crop circle formation discovered
1989	Oct	Post Office issues a stamp which labels an Apatosaurus incorrectly as a Brontosaurus
1989		Pete Rose banned from baseball for life for gambling
1989		PETA launches a campaign exposing horrific killing methods in fur farms
1989		Walk for the Animals begins
1989		First public blood drive for pets is held
1980s		New words, phrases, idioms and slang used in the 1980s include:

AIDS – acronym for the disease of acquired immuno deficiency syndrome

awesome – 80s way of saying great, wonderful

beemer – BMW car

bimbettes – young bimboes

biodiversity – biological diversity in an environment

bogus – old word for sham, resurrected

bonking – sexual intercourse

boom box – portable radio and cassette player

brat pack – group of young actors, after the 1960s rat pack

break dancing – acrobatic dancing

cellphone – portable phone connected via radio waves instead of land lines

chill out – calm down, relax

crack – smokeable highly purified cocaine

cyberspace – the online world of computer networks

deregulation – removing restrictions on trade

designer drugs – popular drugs with yuppies

dirty dancing – dancing with a sexual component
don't worry be happy – from a popular song of the same name
dosh – money
dude – a masculine person
eco-friendly – good for the environment
empty nester – parent of grown children
excellent – from 1989's *Bill and Ted's Excellent Adventure*
gag me with a spoon, or gag me – ick
ghetto blaster – portable radio and cassette player
goth – short for gothic; style of dress consisting of black
grody – Valley Girl speak, renewal of 1960s groatty
help line – telephone information service
I want my MTV – slogan from MTV
information superhighway – the internet
Internet – communications network connecting computers
around the world
like, oh my god – Valley girl speak
mad cow disease – bovine encephalitis
massive – word of approval, like cool
mega – word of approval, like great
mosh, mosh pit – frenzied collision at a rock concert
phat – excellent, originally a rap term
PIN – personal identification number
power suit, power dressing – business wear designed to impress
and/or intimidate
rad, radical – cool; word of approval
reaganomics – coined to describe Reagan's economic policy
safe sex – using a condom
shock jock – radio dj whose patter shocks listeners
slam dancing – dance craze
sooo gnarly – really icky
spin doctor – a person who manipulates public viewpoint
stressed out – uptight
techno, techno pop – electronic dance music with fast beat and
synthesized sound
thirty-something – upwardly mobile baby-boomers
toggle – switch back and forth
totally, totally rad – really good
toy boy – good looking masculine escort
tubular – word of approval
valley girl – teenage girl from Los Angeles
voodoo economics – economic theory difficult to understand
walkman – Sony's small portable radio/cassette player
yuppie – from young urban professional

Writing Topic Suggestions
The Wierd, Trivial and Difficult to Classify

Pick one of the topics below and write for fifteen to twenty minutes. Remember the rules:

- Don't stop writing until the limit is up.
- Use "trigger sentences" if you get stuck.
- Don't be polite.
- Be specific and remember you have at least five senses.
- You don't have to be right, rational or logical.
- Forget about the rules of grammar or spelling.
- Trust yourself.

Remember, you are creating a *primary source*. Write about what you *did*, what you *saw*, what you *thought*, what you *felt*.

1. Scan the events timelines. Is there something that sparks a memory and makes you think, "Oh yeah, I remember that!" If so, write about it. What did this event mean to you? Did it change your life in some way? Did you participate or contribute to this theme or event? How?

2. When you were a teenager or young adult, what slang did you use? What words meant "great" or wonderful?" What words meant "not so great" or "unfashionable?" In the thirties did you use jazz terms such as alligator or skins? In the forties did you refer to your teeth as "choppers" or your hands as "meathooks?" In the fifties did you use beat terms such as "wierdsville" or "cool cat?" In the sixties did you liberally sprinkle your speech with four letter words? In the seventies did you talk about vomiting in colorful terms? In the eighties did you borrow from Valley Girl speak? How did your slang express your sense of belonging to your particular genera-

tion? How did it differentiate you from your parents' generation? Or write about your children's slang and how it affected you. Were you shocked, angered, or amused?

3. Did you pay attention to public scandals and gossip? Did you follow the romantic careers of movie stars like Liz Taylor or Marilyn Monroe? Did you read movie magazines? Did you approve or disapprove of their doings? Were you fascinated by the lives of the famous such as Charles and Diana, Jackie Onassis, or the Beatles? Were you a member of a fan club? Did you write letters to famous people? Did you feel betrayed by stars who behaved counter to social mores or laws, such as Ingrid Bergman in the 1950s, rock stars in the 1960s and 1970s arrested for drug use, or the eighties' activities of Jim and Tammy Faye Bakker or Jimmy Swaggart? Do you remember public scandals such as Ted Kennedy at Chappaquidick, Clifford Irving's hoax biography of Howard Hughes, Lee Marvin and the palimony suit? What is the public scandal you remember the best? Why do you remember that one? Did the "fallout" from any of these scandals affect your life? Were you fascinated by fame? Did you want to be famous? Were you ever famous, even in a small way? What was that like?

4. Do you remember the first Disney comic short you saw? Was it Mickey Mouse, Donald Duck, Dumbo? Did you enjoy the comic reels shown before the movie feature? Who were your favorites? Bugs Bunny? Betty Boop? Pepe Le Pew? Which animated television programs did you enjoy? Rocky & Bullwinkle? The Flintstones or The Jetsons? Roadrunner? Porky Pig? Scooby Doo? Why did you like those cartoons the best? Did you watch cartoons on Saturday morning? Or did your children watch cartoons? What social or moral values did you or your children learn from watching cartoons?

5. Did you read comic books, or follow the comics in the newspaper? Which were your favorites? Superheroes like Batman, Superman or Flash Gordon, or teenage stories like Archie & Jughead? Did you like Dick Tracy, Lil Abner, Brenda Starr, Peanuts,

Doonesbury, Garfield the Cat? Why did you like or dislike those particular comics? Did you want to be a cartoonist? Did you admire particular cartoonists, such as Charles Addams, Peter Arno, Al Capp, Gary Trudeau? Did you create cartoons of your own?

6.   Do you keep an open mind on subjects such as UFOs, alien abductions, Sasquatch or Bigfoot, the Loch Ness Monster, the Bermuda Triangle, Bridie Murphy, crop circles? Or do you think it is all hooey? Were you interested in the experiments of JB Rhine and Russian scientists on ESP, telepathy and clairvoyance? Did you follow the careers of people like Uri Geller or Padre Pio? Did you participate in any studies of paranormal phenomena? Did you or anyone you know have any experience with something you cannot rationally explain? Tell about this experience. Or did you or anyone you know ever fall for a hoax?

7.   Did you have pets when you were growing up? Did you allow your children to have pets? What kinds of pet did you have – dogs, cats, turtles, parakeets, horses, snakes, monkeys? What were their names? Describe their personalities. What made them special? Did they do tricks? How did they show they loved you? Did your work take you around animals; for instance, were you a veterinarian, or work for the Humane Society, or work on a farm with animals? Did you work to prevent animal cruelty? What did you learn from your pets or the animals in your life?

Or anything else you'd like to write about ...

.

Conclusion

The Really Big Stuff

"Everthing's got a moral,
if only you can find it."

Lewis Carroll

Chapter Eighteen
The Meaning of Life

If you've read this far, you know the point of this book is that your life matters. What you say, think, feel and do has consequences. You affect not only those close to you, but the whole of history. Your life has meaning.

But just what is that meaning? Why are you here upon this earth, at this time? What is your purpose, and are you fulfilling it?

Here's your chance to wax philosophical, and answer the really big questions, the ones that never go away, no matter how cynical you get or how practical you are; the ones with answers that keep changing over time, and the ones that every individual answers through their actions, even if they don't know they do.

Here is a last set of suggested writing topics. Pick one, or two, or all of them, and write down what you think and feel and remember. And remember the unrules:

- Don't stop writing until the limit is up.
- Use "trigger sentences" if you get stuck.
- Don't be polite.
- Be specific and remember you have at least five senses.
- You don't have to be right, rational or logical.
- Forget about the rules of grammar or spelling.
- Trust yourself.

Remember, you are creating a *primary source*. Write about what you *did*, what you *saw*, what you *thought*, what you *felt*.

1. What will you tell your grandchildren about the decade of the (pick one) thirties, forties, fifties, sixties, seventies or eighties? What

does that decade have to teach those who did not live though it? What moral standards were present during that decade? How have these standards changed over your lifetime? How do you feel about those standards today? What did you learn during that decade? Was it a good decade for you, and if so, why? Or was it difficult and challenging? How did you deal with the difficulties and challenges? Now pick another decade and answer the same questions.

2. What were, or are, your passions? When were you most happy, most excited, most proud? For how long have you had this passion? Where in your body does this passion reside? Do you feel it in your gut? Does your desire to do this thing feel like fire in your veins? If you followed your passion, did your life get easier, or harder? Did you feel that it was something you were put on earth to do?

3. What were your favorite games, toys and plays as a child? Did you prefer to play alone, with a group of friends. or with just one special friend? What did you want to be when you grew up? Did you follow this dream? If not, why not? How does your childhood dream relate to your actions as an adult? How did your dreams change over time? What thing did you "grow out of" that you wish you hadn't?

4. Did you consciously develop goals for your life? If so, what were your goals at age 10, or 20, 30, 40, 50 or 60? Did your goals change over time? How? Which goals have you accomplished, and was it worth whatever it cost? What goals did you not accomplish, and why not?

5.   Who did and do you love? Why do you love that person(s)? What qualities do they have that call forth your love? How have you shown your love to that person or persons? Who loves and loved you? How did you know you were loved? What did your loved one teach you? What did you teach them?

6. Who was, or is, your champion, the one who always thought well of you, encouraged you, was a positive force in your life? Your grandmother, your second grade teacher, your baseball coach, your Aunt Rosie? Or an imaginary champion, like Superman? Your dog, your teddy bear? Hear their voice speaking to you or about you. What things are they saying? How do they praise you? Try writing about yourself in the voice of this person.

7. What are the secrets of your life? Which secrets were you never allowed to share with anyone? What is something that people don't know about you? Should those secrets be kept, or should they be told? Why or why not?

8. What are the failures in your life? Write about a time you failed, or someone failed you. Tell the story – what happened, who said or did what? What did you learn from this failure? Did you do better the next time, or was there a next time? Is failure always bad?

9. What are your regrets? If you could do something over, what would it be? How would you do it differently? What are the things you didn't do, but wish you had? How would your life be different if you had made other choices?

10. Who is the kindest person you ever met? How did s/he show kindness? Who is the cruelest person you've ever met? How was s/he cruel? What lessons did the kindness or cruelty of others teach you? How have you been kind, or cruel, in your life? How did this affect others?

11. What makes you so angry you nearly foam at the mouth? What injustices do you want to right? When were you the angriest? Who or what were you angry with? How did your anger manifest? Did you yell or scream? Did you hit things or other people? Did you get

sarcastic? Did you pursue revenge? Did your anger accomplish anything? If so, what? If not, why not?

12. Write about what scares you. When were you the most frightened? Describe what happened: who was there with you; what were the sounds and smells of the experience; did it happen outside or inside, was it hot or cold? How did you show you were scared? Did you cry and shake and scream, run away, fight, whimper and curl into a fetal position, act mean and cruel? How did you get over your fear? What did this fear teach you?

13. What are your beliefs about death? Which of your loved ones have died during your lifetime? How did you handle their death(s)? What did their death(s) teach you? How do you want people to react to your death? When you die, who will grieve? What will be said at your eulogy, and who will say it? What do you want written on your grave marker?

14. How has the history of the world changed because you were here? How did events or trends change because of what you did, said, thought or felt? Who and what was affected by your life?

Or anything else you want to write about ...

Sharing My Stories
Why I Write

When I think about my life purpose, I always come back to writing. My first published book was *Eating Mythos Soup: poemstories for Laura.* It was not autobiographical, but it contains the best piece of writing I have ever done about why I do what I do. I would like to share it here:

I write because when I do I am alive. I write because without writing I live in the half-light of a dull November day when everyone else is at a birthday party. I write because then I am at the party too. I play with balloons and wear colored streamers in my hair.

I write because the world smells good and the light is so bright and beauty sits like a beating pulsing bursting heart underneath my skin, and if I don't put it down on paper I bleed from every pore.

I write because my life is important and I want everyone to know that my life began and ended and in between love flowed through me and my spirit danced with God.

I write because every signpost I come to points me back to the writer's path, even from the depths of the electronic jungle. I write because when I do I feel the soothing aahh begin in my own throat, and I hear it echoed from the throats of my loved ones as they see me finally coming home.

I write because if I don't my life is ashes and lice, and a gluey film of dust lies thick over my skin. I write because it is my protection from the vast and awful fear of nothingness; because it is the narrow plank I have laid across the chasm of the Great Void.

I write because God lives in my pen and my keyboard and my hands. Over my left shoulder I see the air currents swirling around Her. Her immense presence settles around me like a thick warm quilt, and we are wrapped together snug on a snowy winter day while we watch my genius burn. I feel the warmth on my back growing yellow, and my skin turning peach brown with the soft smell of joy.

I write because God *says.*

Excerpt from Eating Mythos Soup: poemstories for Laura, ©2000 by Kim Pearson.

Sources and Suggested Reading

Websites: Most of the timeline data in *Making History* is from Internet sources. There are thousands of websites with information on the subjects covered in this book. A partial list of these web resources is below. Keep in mind that URLs change often, so some of the websites listed may have changed or no longer exist.

80s Children   www.80schildren.com/
Century of Well Kept Secrets   www.becker.k12.mn.us/ourtown/1930%27s/timeline.html
Comparative Chronology of Money   www.ex.ac.uk/%7ERDavies/arian/amser/chrono.html
Chronology of Japanese American History   www.janet.org/janet_history/niiya_chron.html
Academy of Achievement   www.achievement.org
Academy of Television Arts & Sciences   www.emmys.com
Ad Age, Crain Communications   www.adage.com/century
Advertising Slogan Hall of Fame   www.adslogans.co.uk/hof/hofindx2.html
American Experience on PBS   www.pbs.org/wgbh/amex
American Food Century   www.geocities.com/foodedge/index.com
Annals of Improbable Research   www.improbable.com/
Anomalies & Enigmas   www.enigmas.org
Any Year in History   www.scopysys.com/anyday
Ask Oxford World of Words   www. askoxford.com/worldofwords/history
Baseball Hall of Fame   www. baseballhalloffame.org/history
Biography   www.biography.com
BOOMER-ING!   www.alexiebooks.com/boomering.ivnu
Center for Cooperative Research   www.cooperativeresearch.org/timelines.jsp
Chronology of Space Exploration   www.solarviews.com/eng/craft1.htm
Comic Page, The   www.dereksantos.com/comicpage
Crime Library   www.crimelibrary.coAm
Crop Circle Research   www.cropcircleresearch.com
Dates in History   www.datesinhistory.com
Encyberpedia   www.encyberpedia.com/ency.htm
Fact Index   www. fact-index.com
Factofile   www.swishweb.com
Family Pets, History of Pets & Animals   www.familypets.net/historyofpet&animals.htm
Fascinating Mysteries Area 51   www.geocities.com/hngibson/paranews.htm
Fashion Era   www.fashion-era.com
Food Reference   www.foodreference.com
Greatest Films   www.filmsite.org/
History of Toys & Games   www.onenorthpole.com/toyshop/toystory
Idioms Site   www.idiomsite.com/
Internet Modern History Sourcebook   www.fordham.edu/halsall/mod/modsbook.html
Kingwood College Library   www.kclibrary.nhmccd.ed/1980.htm
Morris County Library's Food Timeline   www.gti.net/mocolib1/kid/food
Mysterious Reality   www.mysteriousreality.com
NASA, Human Space Flight   www.spaceflight.nasa.gov/history/index.html
NBA History   www.nba.com/history/
NFL History   www.nflhistoryguide.com
Nobel Prize Internet Archive   www.almaz.com/nobel

Occultopedia	www.occultopedia.com/index1.htm
Olden Times	theoldentimes.com/
Olympics History	www.olympic.org
Paranormal Phenomena	www.paranormal.about.com
Pulitzer Prizes	www.pulitzer.org
Rusty Zipper Vintage Clothing	www.rustyzipper.com
Sea Shepherd Conservation Society	www.sealhunt.seashepherd.org
Slanguage	www.slanguage.com/timetunnel
Space Place, The	www.thespaceplace.com/history
Super 70s	www.super70s.com
Timelines of History	http://timelines.ws/
Tony Awards	www.tonyawards.com
Top 40 Hits of 1930-1998	www.ntl.matrix.com.br/pfilho/html/top40/index.html
Twentieth Century Edibles & Quaffables	www.geocities.com/foodedge/timel;ine.htm
Where Were You	www.wherewereyou.com/
Widipedia	www.wikipedia.org
Writers Free Reference	www.writers-free-reference.com

Printed sources:

Louise Bernikow, *The American Women's Almanac: an inspiring and irreverent Women's History*, Berkley Books, 1997

Harold Evans, *The American Century*, Alfred A. Knopf, 1998

Peter Jennings & Todd Brewster, *The Century*, Doubleday, 1998

National Geographic, *Eyewitness to the 20th Century*, National Geographic Society, 1998, 1999, 2001

David Wallechinsky, *The People's Almanac Presents the Twentieth Century: history with the boring parts left out*, The Overlook Press, 1999

Recommended books on writing and creativity:

Julia Cameron, *The Artist's Way*, G.P. Putnam's Sons, 1992

Natalie Goldberg, *Writing Down the Bones*, Shambhala Publications, 1986

Natalie Goldberg, *Wild Mind: Living the Writer's Life*, Bantam Books, 1990

About Kim Pearson and Primary Sources

Kim Pearson is an author, ghostwriter, teacher and the owner of Primary Sources, a writing service that helps others communicate their stories, histories and ideas.

In addition to *Making History: how to remember, record, interpret and share the events of your life*, she has authored three books of fiction, two books of poetry, and a non-fiction work titled *You Can Be An Author, Even If You're Not a Writer.*

Kim has ghostwritten more than thirty non-fiction books and memoirs, telling the stories of a wide variety of people and covering a broad range of topics. She elicits color, drama, depth and detail that make these stories come alive on the page.

Kim teaches workshops and teleclasses on writing and history, helping people find their authentic voices, realize their inner wisdom, and discover compelling topics that wow their readers. A new teleclass based on *Making History* will be introduced in 2008.

Kim provides a conduit for storytelling in many forms. She believes that telling your stories can free you, heal you, and inspire others. It is her goal to assist in this process.

More about the services of Primary Sources and Kim Pearson can be found on www.primary-sources.com. To contact Kim Pearson, email kim@primary-sources.com.

How to Order
Making History

Order online
www.primary-sources.com
www.amazon.com

Making History makes an excellent premium or incentive for your organization. Cost-effective customized versions can be made available; add your organization's name and/or logo to the cover or title page. Ideal for customer or employee gifts, trade shows, sales incentives, and more. Please contact Primary Sources to learn more.

Primary Sources
www.primary-sources.com
425-865-0409
info@primary-sources.com

Printed in the United States
200820BV00003B/1-21/A